LEGAL RESEARCH HANDBOOK

Fourth Edition

LEGAL RESEARCH HANDBOOK

Fourth Edition

Douglass T. MacEllven, B.A., J.D., M.L.L.
past Director of Legal Research & Libraries
Law Society of Saskatchewan

Michael J. McGuire, B.A., LL.B., M.L.S.
past Director of Legal Research & Libraries
Law Society of Saskatchewan

with special assistance by
Denis LeMay, B.A., LL.B., LL.M., M.L.S.
Law Librarian, Université Laval

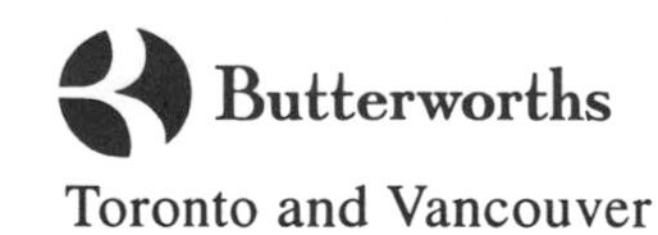

Toronto and Vancouver

Legal Research Handbook
© 1998 Butterworths Canada Ltd.
March 1998

The Butterworth Group of Companies

Canada:
75 Clegg Road, MARKHAM, Ontario L6G 1A1
and
1721-808 Nelson St., Box 12148, VANCOUVER, B.C. V6Z 2H2
Australia:
Butterworths Pty Ltd., SYDNEY
Ireland:
Butterworth (Ireland) Ltd., DUBLIN
Malaysia:
Malayan Law Journal Sdn Bhd, KUALA LUMPUR
New Zealand:
Butterworths of New Zealand Ltd., WELLINGTON
Singapore:
Butterworths Asia, SINGAPORE
South Africa:
Butterworth Publishers (Pty.) Ltd., DURBAN
United Kingdom:
Butterworth & Co. (Publishers) Ltd., LONDON
United States:
Michie, CHARLOTTESVILLE, Virginia

Canadian Cataloguing in Publication Data

MacEllven, Douglass T.
Legal research handbook

4th ed.
Includes index.
ISBN 0-433-40944-4 (bound) ISBN 0-433-40945-2 (pbk.)

1. Legal research – Canada – Handbooks, manuals, etc. I. McGuire, M. (Michael).
II. Title

KE250.M33 1998 340'.07'2071 C97-932647-8
KF240.M33 1998

Printed and bound in Canada.

Dedicated to our spouses,
Kathryn MacEllven and Shirley McGuire,
to our families and to our staffs over the years
at the Law Society of Saskatchewan

Preface

This fourth edition represents modification to about one-third of the prior edition since so much has changed with the advance of electronic formats in law publishing. I thank Mike McGuire for the completely revised Chapter 10, "Computer-Assisted Legal Research" and for his review of the entire book, his portion of the updating work, and suggestions regarding the integration of electronic sources into the whole text. We thank Denis LeMay for continuing his explanation of Quebec legal materials in his Chapter 12, "Researching Quebec Law.

The explanation of basic Canadian materials in Chapters 2 through 12 has changed due to the appearance of new publications and due to expansion of electronic format availability (online services, CD-ROM format, and the Internet). The expansion of electronic sources is highlighted by changes to Chapter 11, "Research Checklists", and the new Appendix B which gathers electronic sources cited in various chapters. Canadian availability of electronic sources for foreign material is cited throughout Chapters 13 through 15.

I express my appreciation to my spouse, Kathi, who has worked with me in my updating work on this fourth edition and who continues to work with me in indexing legislation. I also acknowledge the assistance of the Butterworths' staff in preparing this edition. Butterworths' editors who guided preparation of this edition through its stages include Janine Denney-Lightfoot (product development editor), Lisa Krueger (Managing Editor), Sherri Jackson (Editor) and Jane Austin (Coordinator).

As Mike McGuire departs the Law Society of Saskatchewan to become a legal information consultant and antiquarian bookstore owner in Victoria, we represent directing 21 of the 22 years of the Saskatchewan Courthouse library system's existence. This textbook had its origins in the early days of the system when Saskatchewan had no private firm librarians. In the early 1980's, the Saskatchewan Law Foundation and Benchers supported my efforts to visit every city and town where a lawyer practised to explain the coming wonders of the computer age. Without in-province law firm librarians and having been able to spend only a few hours in some centres, I wrote this textbook to aid rural Saskatchewan law firms. Some staff members from the early days continue with the system. Peta Bates, Saskatoon Courthouse Librarian, has been assisted for many years by Pat Kelly and Leila Olfert. In Regina, Maxine Seeley worked with both Mike and myself, and other Regina staff continuing are Christine Godlien, Sheila Balkwill, and Joanne Zapshala. Shirley Hurnard, from the early Regina days, became and remains the Court of Appeal's first librarian.

Preface

Acknowledgements

Authors and/or publishers have been most generous in giving permission for the reproduction of work already in print. It is convenient for us to list below, for the assistance of the reader, those for whose courtesy we are most grateful.

Every effort has been made to obtain permissions. The following is organized by publisher in alphabetical order:

Barron's Educational Series, Inc.	— Yogis, Canadian Law Dictionary, p. 214
British Columbia Superior Court Website	— Introductory page of British Columbia Superior Courts website
Canada Law Book Inc.	— British Columbia Statute Citator (R.S.B.C. 1979 ed.), pp. 91-1 and 91-2 — Dominion Law Reports (4th), Index for Volumes 40 to 79, pp. ix, A-5
Carolina Academic Press	— Wydick, Plain English for Lawyers (1985) (basic concepts and points)
Carswell, a division of Thomson Canada Limited	— 5 Alberta Law Reports (2d) 391 — Alberta Law Reports (2d) Cumulative Index for Vols. 1-11, pp. 63, 92 — Canadian Abridgment (2nd), Vol. R14B, p. 95, case digest # 545 — Family Law Partner on CD-Rom, Query Templates — Statutes of British Columbia Judicially Considered, May 1980-1982, pp. 146 and 147
Centre de recherche en droit public	— Supreme Court of Canada search screens
Law Society of Saskatchewan Libraries	— Index to the Statutes of Saskatchewan (to Nov. 1, 1990), pp. 26, 170

Marianne Scott	— Index to Canadian Legal Periodical Literature, 1978, p. A-41
Maritime Law Book Ltd.	— Alberta Reports Digest and Index, Vols. 1 to 10, pp. 170, 181,199, 216, and 541 — National Reporter Digest and Indexes, Vols. 11 to 20, p. 500
Osgoode Hall Law School	— Screens illustrating location of legal materials
Supply and Services Canada	— Canada Gazette Part III, Oct. 2, 1992, p. 11 — Consolidated Regulations of Canada, 1978, Vol. 1. p. 7 — Canada Gazette Part II, Consolidated Index of Statutory Instruments, Jan. 1, 1955 to June 30, 1992, p. 78 Reproduced by permission of the Minister of Supply and Services Canada.
West Publishing Co.	— Weihofen, Legal Writing Style (St. Paul, Minn., 1961), p. 129
Western Legal Publications	— Civil Cases Index to [1992] Alberta Decisions — [1992] Alberta Decisions, p. 1534-02
Yahoo!	— Screens illustrating location of Canadian legal materials

Table of Contents

List of Illustrations

List of Illustrations

Chapter 1

Legal Research Concepts

This chapter provides a brief explanation of the nature and purpose of primary authority legal material, which consists of statutes, subordinate legislation such as regulations, and case law. Secondary legal literature, such as legal encyclopedias, is discussed as a means of finding primary authority legal material. An approach to analyzing legal problems is given so that a researcher may commence a search either with printed legal materials, or on computer.

A. FINDING RELEVANT LAW POSSESSING PRIMARY AUTHORITY

1. Relevant law: jurisdiction, fact, and legal concept

When a legal researcher is presented with a problem, the objective is to find existing law relevant in terms of jurisdiction, fact, and legal concept. The stated law applicable to the researcher's problem may be in the form of legislation or judicial opinion. The legislation may be a federal statute enacted by Parliament, while a judicial opinion may be a judge's written opinion in a case arising in a federal or provincial court. Legislation and judicial opinion are written legal materials that are said to possess primary legal authority. Primary authority material is the law itself. The primary authority law that the researcher hopes to find should be relevant to the researcher's problem in the following respects:

(a) Relevant jurisdiction

The researcher hopes to find law from the jurisdiction in which the legal problem arose. In this sense, "jurisdiction" means the geographical area having law relevant to the problem. The jurisdiction may be the country as a whole (federal law), a province, a territory, or a municipality (a city bylaw). The researcher must be aware as to whether the problem involves federal or provincial law, since a legal problem arising in a particular province may be governed by federal law. Generally speaking, a researcher would hope to find Ontario law relevant to a problem arising in Ontario unless it was a matter governed by federal law.

(b) Relevant facts

The researcher hopes to find law that has facts similar to the researcher's current problem. The problem may involve factual subject matter such as a motor vehicle, and the researcher must distinguish between essential and non-essential aspects of the subject matter.

If the problem specifically deals with a collision at an intersection, judicial opinions about other collisions may be relevant if the opinions discuss any type of motor vehicle (weight and type of vehicle may be irrelevant). "Motor vehicle" would be an essential fact without regard to such non-essentials as the vehicle being a truck, van, station wagon, *etc.*, of a particular weight. Other essential facts might be the inattention of the driver, or brake failure.

If the problem specifically involves proper licensing of a vehicle, the weight and type of vehicle may be essential facts. The researcher may be looking for judicial opinions discussing the licensing of a particular weight and type of vehicle, therefore, facts about the driver or mechanical condition would not be essential (*i.e.*, not relevant).

(c) Relevant legal concepts

Many statements of primary authority law contain legal concepts such as negligence, divorce, *etc*. The legal researcher may find statements of the law that discuss relevant subject matter, but that apply different legal concepts from those involved in the researcher's current problem. The researcher may find a judicial opinion involving the same motor vehicle type contained in the researcher's problem, but the legal concept analyzed by the judicial opinion may be the negligent manufacture of the vehicle, rather than the negligent operation of the vehicle, which is the researcher's problem.

2. Primary authority: legislation and case law

Primary authority legal material is the law itself, rather than writings about the law (such as textbooks). Primary authority material consists of legislation and judicial opinions known as "case law".

"Legislation" refers to statutes passed by the federal Parliament or provincial legislatures, and to subordinate legislation passed by administrative bodies pursuant to enabling statutes. Statutes are individual Acts creating laws to govern societal activity such as criminal conduct, marriage, divorce, education, income tax, *etc*. Statutes are often broad in scope, while the expertise for supplying detail lies in administrative bodies other than Parliament or legislatures. Statutory instruments include rules, orders, regulations, and ordinances issued or made pursuant to power granted by a statute to a body subordinate to Parliament or to legislature. A statute may have dozens of regulations made pursuant to it, or it may have none.

Judicial opinions, which are collectively known as case law, are the writings of judges who in each case have related the relevant legal concepts to the essential facts of the dispute, to yield a written decision that supplies reasons for the decision rendered. Some legal problems, such as motor vehicle licensing requirements, are susceptive to resolution by statute or regulation. Other legal problems may involve diverse fact situations, which defy detailed treatment by legislation or subordinate legislation. Problems such as deciding the liability of drivers involved in a collision at an intersection require detailed analysis of the individual situations, and are more susceptive to individual judicial opinions. If the meaning of a licensing statute is in doubt, case law may be searched for a judicial interpretation of the statute.

3. Stability, change, and stare decisis

When searching for relevant primary authority law, one of the most significant facets of the law is the interplay between stability and change. As society changes, the law changes, but there should be an element of stability in the law so that members of the society can foresee the legal consequences of their conduct. Legislatures may sense that society wants new statutes enacted and existing statutes repealed. Statutes can be partially amended or repealed by their enacting bodies. Examples of recent statutory change are the many changes in family law statutes. While all statutes could be changed in a given legislative session, repeated wholesale change in statutory language would mean that society would be largely unaware of many statutorily imposed duties.

The interplay between stability and change in case law must be considered with the concept of *stare decisis*. *Stare decisis*, a Latin term, means that a problem that is similar to an earlier problem should be settled in the same manner as the earlier problem. This approach provides the stability of defining expected behaviour for society through the ability to predict judges' future decisions on particular types of problems. *Stare decisis* also promotes the concept that all persons should be treated alike in the same circumstances. In deciding whether past cases and the current problem are very similar, the researcher must compare the essential facts and legal concepts involved in the problem.

The concept of *stare decisis* began in English law almost 1,000 years ago, when people were able to bring disputes to travelling judges. The judges began to record their decisions, which became guides for later cases with similar facts and legal concepts. This body of law became common to all of England, and became the "common law" which forms the legal basis of our provinces and territories (except Québec), England, other Commonwealth countries, and the United States. The term "common law" may refer to all of the tradition of English law, including the case law and statutes that formed the initial basis of the legal systems in much of Canada. The common law may also refer to the body of case law developed in England and other countries, in contrast to law as stated in statutes.

Québec law traces its origin to the civil law system of continental Europe which is based upon Roman law. The civil law system stresses the importance of legislation and de-emphasizes the precedential value of case law and *stare decisis*. In this context, "civil" refers to an entire legal system rather than the distinction between civil law and criminal law. The federal law pertains to Québec, but other aspects of the Québec legal system are rooted in the civil law tradition. For a more complete explanation of the Québec legal system, see Chapter 12.

While *stare decisis* denotes stability, it is a general rule, and societal change may yield exceptions in the form of changing case law. In some subject areas such as family law, much of the changing case law results from judicial opinions interpreting new or amended statutes. Statute law may be enacted which changes the effect of prior existing case law, but case law may only interpret and not change statute law.

B. MANDATORY OR PERSUASIVE PRIMARY AUTHORITY LAW AND SECONDARY AUTHORITY LEGAL LITERATURE

1. Mandatory or persuasive authority: statutes, case law, and jurisdiction

When the researcher locates relevant primary authority law, the law's value to the court will depend upon whether its authority is described as mandatory or persuasive. Mandatory authority usually indicates that the court considering the current problem will make a decision consistent with the mandatory law, but law which is of persuasive authority may or may not be adopted by the court. Whether primary authority law is mandatory or persuasive depends upon jurisdiction and court level. Case law may be mandatory or persuasive, while statute law is either of mandatory authority or no authority.

Statutes are enacted to pertain to a particular group of persons; for example, an Ontario statute governing the activity of persons or organizations having a connection with Ontario. A differently phrased statute dealing with the same subject matter may pertain to and affect British Columbia residents in a different manner. Statutes possess mandatory authority in their jurisdictions, dictating that Ontario judges must be cognizant of Ontario statutes. Statutes possess no authority outside their own jurisdictions; therefore, Ontario judges do not usually have to be cognizant of British Columbia statutes.

Statutes are relevant to individual jurisdictions, while case law may be applicable across many jurisdictions. The basic considerations when deciding liability in a collision at an intersection may be similar in many provinces and even countries (case law), while a motor vehicle licensing statute in British Columbia has no relevance in Ontario, which has a differently worded statute. Case law from the present court's own jurisdiction may be considered mandatory authority, but cases from other jurisdictions possess only persuasive authority. Persuasive authority indicates that the court is not bound to adopt the law as its own; however, the researcher hopes that the court will be persuaded to accept the logic contained in the other jurisdiction's case law. The legal researcher involved in case law study must be concerned not only with *stare decisis* and the societal change factor of in-jurisdiction case law, but also with the precedential value of case law from different jurisdictions.

Several million cases have been generated in common law countries over the centuries, so that the task of researching each problem can be an awesome, time consuming task. In researching a particular narrow point of law, the researcher may find a recent British case and a recent American case holding one side of the issue, and a recent Australian case taking the opposite view. The researcher may find that there are no Canadian cases or only an older Canadian case siding with the Australian view. A researcher involved with a problem arising in Saskatchewan would hope to find Saskatchewan case law, which would be of mandatory authority. Failing this, case law from other provinces and even other common law countries could be considered to be persuasive authority.

Statutes relevant to the jurisdiction do have mandatory authority, and therefore, in a New Brunswick problem, the researcher is most concerned with New Brunswick statutes and regulations, federal statutes and regulations, and New Brunswick and federal case law, all of which are primary, mandatory authority material. Hence, the researcher initially would consider only a relatively few statutes and regulations from among the thousands existing in Canada, and only a very small percentage of the several million cases generated by courts throughout the common law world.

2. Mandatory authority case law: court level

Mandatory authority involves not only geographical areas but also levels of courts. If the dispute is to be settled in the courts by a judge and jury, the jury will decide whether to accept the witnesses' account of the facts. Upon considering similar problems, one jury might believe the facts are as stated by the plaintiff, while in another case the jury might accept the defendant's statement. The judge will decide the proper statement of the law to be applied to the facts. Some cases are appealed to higher courts; generally, the appeal is based upon questioning the statement of the law rather than questioning the veracity of the facts. Once a point of law has been appealed to and decided by higher courts, lower court judges will consider the higher court decisions to be mandatory, because the higher court will reach the same conclusion each time the point is appealed.

The structures of provincial court systems vary from province to province, but generally follow an arrangement consisting of:

(a) The lowest tier of criminal courts (Provincial Court or Magistrates Court) and civil courts (Small Claims Court, Family Court, Juvenile Court, *etc.*).

(b) A middle tier or tiers having both civil and criminal jurisdiction, designated as County Court, District Court, and/or Queen's Bench Court.

(c) The highest provincial court is usually designated as the Court of Appeal or the Supreme Court.

The highest federal court is the Supreme Court of Canada, while the lower courts are the Federal Court of Appeal and the Federal Court, Trial Division.

A judge in a Manitoba Queen's Bench Court facing a problem very similar to one recently decided in the Court of Appeal will consider the Court of Appeal decision to be mandatory authority. However, the effects of time and change upon stability is evidenced by mandatory authority's impact being lessened by societal change generated over a period of years. A Queen's Bench judge might or might not adopt the law as stated in a 1935 Court of Appeal case. Even a recent change in the membership of the court's judges can be a factor. The judicial philosophy of several new appointees to the Court of Appeal may yield a different statement of the law from that expressed by the justices composing the court several years before.

If a particular type of legal problem has not reached the highest court level, judges of a lower court may adopt different views. The decision of one Queen's Bench justice in Manitoba is not binding on another, since the appeal from both justices' opinions would be to the Court of Appeal. True mandatory authority case law relevant to the problem before the Queen's Bench judge in Manitoba would be earlier cases decided by higher courts (Manitoba Court of Appeal and Supreme Court of Canada), when the judicial philosophy of the judges rendering those higher court decisions is the same as the judicial philosophy of the present higher court justices.

3. Persuasive rather than mandatory primary authority law

Failing to locate mandatory primary authority law, the researcher should investigate primary authority law possessing persuasive authority. Persuasive authority does not have to be followed by the court considering the problem, but the researcher hopes that the logic contained in the persuasive authority law is of sufficient logic to result in that law being adopted by the present court. The search for persuasive authority law is often imprecise, and the more jurisdictions that have taken a similar view on an issue, the more likely it is that the present court will follow the prevailing view.

Statutes from other jurisdictions have no authority outside their own boundaries; however, case law that interprets the wording of statutes can be of persuasive authority. If a researcher can find no cases considering the wording of a particular section of a Nova Scotia statute, there may be a case interpreting the wording of an identically or very similarly worded Ontario statute. The researcher would hope that a Nova Scotia court would adopt the reasoning of the Ontario court when it interpreted the Ontario statute.

4. Secondary authority legal literature

While primary authority law exists in the form of statutes, subordinate legislation, and cases, there are other forms of legal writing that possess secondary authority. Secondary authority legal literature (texts, journals, encyclopedias, *etc.*) is narrative comment upon the law as it exists or as the author views it should be. Indexes and finding aids to the law (periodical indexes, case law abstracts, or digests) are also in this category. Since secondary authority legal literature has not been generated by legislatively authorized bodies such as a legislature or administrative agency, and since it has not been formulated by a court, it cannot be considered mandatory authority.

The feature which distinguishes secondary authority legal materials from non-legal textbooks, encyclopedias, and journals is the high number of footnotes since one of the key purposes of secondary legal literature is to summarize the law while citing many specific statutes, regulations, and cases. A work of secondary legal authority usually contains tables of statutes and cases cited. Even though this type of literature cites primary authority law and the narrative portions of this literature are never of mandatory authority, secondary authority literature can be used in court.

Secondary authority literature can be persuasive, since many legal scholars' narrative comments contain valuable logic for resolving particular disputes. The narrative comment in an encyclopedia may be cited by a court as a valid summation of the law in a particular area. Similarly, a textbook or journal author's view on how a particular area of law should be changed may be adopted.

Periodical indexes and other such finding aids merely provide access to the law, so the question of authority is not relevant. While narrative summaries of the law in a particular area may be cited from works such as an encyclopedia, the citation of a summary in a case digest should be avoided. An editor's digest of a judge's written opinion is not an exact statement of the judge, and therefore cannot be considered mandatory. While the digest might be persuasive, a better authority is a quotation from the judge's written opinion, which is primary authority.

C. FRAMING THE LEGAL ISSUE WITH KEY WORDS AND CONDUCTING THE SEARCH

1. Using fact and legal concept words to frame the legal issue

The researcher's quest for primary or secondary authority legal material may be simplified by already knowing about a relevant statute or leading case relating to the problem at hand. The researcher may examine the table of statutes or table of cases in legal textbooks, encyclopedias, and journals to locate discussion of the statute or case. The statute or case will be discussed in the context of related statutes and cases which will add support to the researcher's thesis. If such material is not initially known, the researcher must delve into the indexes to statutes and case law reports, secondary legal literature sources, and computer databases. The initial steps to legal research involve framing the legal issue and identifying key words.

An issue is a statement of the problem that must be resolved. It is composed of fact key words and legal concept key words. An issue might be stated narrowly through the use of more specific fact words or legal concept words. A narrow issue might be: "is a grocery store owner negligent, and therefore liable for damages resulting from a personal injury suffered by a customer who slipped on spilled produce in the store aisle, after the owner had received notification of the hazardous situation, but did not clean up the spill?" An issue might be stated more generally by using fewer key words. A more general issue could be stated as: "is a store owner liable for customer accidents resulting from hazardous in-store conditions?"

Whether the researcher initially states the issue in broad terms or narrow terms, he or she must insure that all essential elements of the issue are present and then must think of possible synonyms or alternatives for the key words used. Once key words and alternatives have been determined, research can commence, either in printed indexes or on computer.

The five steps to formulating the issue and alternative key words are:

STEP 1: Identify the subject matter of your problem by deciding whether essential fact words might be found in the Persons, Action, Place, or Objects involved in your problem. Examples are:

(a) Persons involved in your problem: a special class of persons such as infants, a particular occupation such as doctors, or a particular relationship such as solicitor/client.
(b) The action or activity that has created the problem: a sports activity, driving a vehicle, or walking on ice.
(c) The place in which the problem has occurred: at a playground, in a mine, or at an office.
(d) An inanimate object involved in the problem: a motor vehicle, a television set, or a washing machine.

STEP 2: The legal concept key words can be determined by thinking of the problem in terms of the cause of action involved, the defence raised, or the relief sought. Examples are:

(a) Cause of action: liability based upon negligence, when personal injury is involved.
(b) Defence raised: assumption of the risk.
(c) Relief sought: damages.

STEP 3: The legal concept key words and fact key words are integrated to formulate the statement of the problem, which is called the issue. For example, is a grocery store owner negligent, and therefore liable for damages resulting from a personal injury suffered by a customer who slipped on spilled produce in the store aisle?

STEP 4: The number of fact key words can be expanded by thinking of alternative key words, which might provide the basis for commencing legal research. The problem might involve a van, but other essential words that might yield relevant cases might be cases with fact words such as automobile, motor vehicle, truck, etc.

STEP 5: Legal concept key words can be expanded by considering alternative names for the terminology that was initially used. If the issue is libel or slander, the researcher may want to also use the more general term, defamation.

2. General approaches to conducting the search: key word and legal topic

Once the researcher has framed the issue and devised a list of alternative key words, a general strategy of research should be employed. The two general approaches to legal research are the key word search approach and the legal topic approach. The objective of research is to find relevant primary legal authority; this is accomplished largely through a search of secondary legal literature by using either of the two approaches. Because the law is constantly changing, it is essential that a check be made to ensure that the law found is current. The researcher must be sure that a statute has not been repealed or amended, and that later cases do not change the law as stated in earlier cases that the researcher initially finds.

The key word search approach involves three aspects:

(a) Search of the indexes of primary authority legal material to see if the fact key words and legal concept key words from the issue are contained in the statute or law report indexes.

(b) Search of indexes in secondary legal literature such as encyclopedias, textbooks, separately published digests, *etc.*, to see if the fact or legal concept key words are contained in those indexes. Those indexes lead to digests or narrative discussions that cite cases or statutes.

(c) A "words and phrases" search may be made if the issue involves an attempt to legally define a particular word or phrase. There are separate "words and phrases" publications or sections of publications which present digests of cases or listings of cases that have attempted to legally define terms. Legal definitions may be different from the more general definitions contained in standard dictionaries.

The legal topic approach may be employed by more experienced researchers who are familiar with the legal topic arrangement of most legal publications. Legal encyclopedias, texts, and digests usually have contents arranged in a flow to give discussion of topics and subtopics of a legal nature. If the problem involves injury to a spectator at a sporting event, the researcher may know that part of the issue involved is the legal concept of assumption of risk. If the legal topic approach is employed, the researcher would turn to the table of contents of the book to find the section dealing with assumption of the risk, and bypass the index to the work. If the legal concept is not known, the researcher probably would start research by searching indexes for such fact words as sporting events, or the particular type of sport involved. The key word would lead from the index of a publication to the chapter discussing assumption of the risk.

3. The requirement of updating the search

Once cases or statutes have been found through either the key word search of indexes approach or the legal topic search in tables of contents approach, the researcher may concentrate on researching a particular case or statute, which includes updating. The researcher may search for comments on a particular case in such publications as legal periodicals under the "case comment" sections, or in text-books by examining the table of cases. Update the search by looking in the "cases judicially considered" sections to see if later cases have commented upon the case initially found. The researcher may search statute citators for cases commenting upon a statute. Update the statute search to see whether the statute has been amended, and to be certain that the statute is still in force. A check should be made for regulations which might deal with specifics not explicitly set forth in the statute.

The researcher using secondary authority materials must also be aware of how the publication is supplemented and what updating is necessary. There is a growing trend to use the looseleaf binder format for Canadian legal textbooks and encyclopedias, but the date of the latest insert releases should be checked to determine the timeliness of the publication's updating. A hard-bound textbook may be supplemented by a "pocket part" which slips into a pocket inside the book's cover, or it may be updated by an annual or irregularly published paperbound cumulative supplement.

4. New research sources and the computer

Having framed legal issues, derived alternative key words, and decided which general research approach to employ, the researcher must choose whether to begin research in printed book indexes or by computer (online databases or CD-ROM products). A number of secondary literature sources have been in use for many decades, but the 1980s and 1990s have seen the appearance of a high number of new Canadian legal research sources. No single research tool provides access to all of Canadian primary law, and the researcher must understand the value of each source in order to decide which sources to use or not use in researching a particular problem. Computerized searches may be used at the start of research, and the researcher must decide whether the computer will be used in place of manual research, or as a complement to it. Some types of legal research can only be performed by computer search because the lack of commercially-produced print form sources makes some types of manual search impractical. The *British Columbia Decisions* series (B.C.D.) includes digests of many unreported cases which consider earlier cases, but there is no printed table of these earlier cases. The only way to access cases considered in B.C.D. is by searching for a particular case in the CD-ROM or online database versions of B.C.D. The *Dominion Report Service* existed as a standard print form looseleaf publication from 1968 to 1991, but now it is continued only in computer database form.

Chapter 2

Law Reports

Law reports publish primary authority case law, which consists of judges' written opinions and tribunal board decisions. Canada has several law report publishers; this raises issues of the duplication of cases among report series and comparative time lag in publishing cases. The number of report series of potential use to the researcher requires an awareness of the common features and specific titles of law report series, and familiarity with their indexes and digests.

This chapter covers law reports, while the next chapter covers indexes and digests of case law, and a research approach to reports, indexes, and digests.

A. ANALYZING LAW REPORTS

1. Duplication and timeliness

Collectively, the many law reports publish all written judgments of appellate level courts and selected trial court judgments. Law reports may cover judgments from a particular court level (*e.g.*, *Canada Supreme Court Reports*), a geographical region (*Atlantic Provinces Reports*), a province (*Alberta Law Reports*), or cases on a subject area (*Canadian Criminal Cases*).

Some publishers report cases the editors deem significant, while other publishers print more cases, giving the lawyer the opportunity to decide which cases are significant. Because there are a number of Canadian publishers producing law reports, different publishers' reports covering the same subject matter may contain different cases, and one case may be reported in several law report series. The same case may be retrieved by computer search of several different databases. Another concern is the timeliness of cases appearing in law report publications.

The time lag for publishing cases in law report series may vary within publications and between publications. The latest loose part may have cases ranging from three or four months old to those almost one year old. There are rapid digesting services, which provide brief abstracts of all cases from the various jurisdictions, and research can be updated in these digests from the approximate cutoff date of coverage by the law reports. For example, cases in the *Dominion Law Reports* may be several months old, but an advance service to this report in digest form is the *All-Canada Weekly Summaries*, which digests very recent cases.

2. Elements of a reported case

In every case report, there are preliminary elements appearing before the judge's opinion, which serve to immediately distinguish the case from others.

(a) The *style of cause* is the names of the party or parties involved. Examples include:
Smith v. Jones: a civil dispute in which a plaintiff, Smith, is versus (*v.*) a defendant, Jones.
R. v. Jones: the Crown's action against a party, Jones, in a criminal matter. Crown prosecutors represent society in taking action against the accused.
For more detailed treatment, see Chapter 17: "Legal Citation".

(b) The *court name* and *judge's name.*

(c) *Date of the case*: this may include both a hearing date and judgment date. If only one date is given, it is usually the date of judgment.

(d) The *headnote or summary of the case*, prepared by the publishing company. The judge's opinion may be many pages long, but the publishers provide a key worded digest in the form of the headnote so that these digests may later be separately arranged by subject, in order to provide manual access to cases or provide for a computer database search. Cases are generally printed in chronological order, without regard to subject matter, necessitating separately published digests in subject arrangement.

(e) *Names of counsel* appearing in the case.

(f) *Docket number* assigned to each case by the court.

(g) *Citation of the case*. Each volume of law report series is individually numbered. The citation or abbreviation for an individual case consists of the volume number, abbreviation of the law report series, and the page number at which the case report begins. An example is *Smith v. Jones* (1981), 118 D.L.R. (3d) 609. For more detailed treatment, see Chapter 17: "Legal Citation," and Appendix A: "Table of Report and Digest Abbreviations."

(h) *Other Preliminary Elements*. The preliminary elements may also include lists of statutes and cases considered in the judgment, words and phrases defined in the case, and publications cited in the judgment. Some law reports contain annotations or articles written by legal scholars to explain the significance of the case.

ILLUSTRATION 1
5 Alberta Law Reports (2d) 391

Adams et al. v. McLeod et al. Spence J. 391[a]

SUPREME COURT OF CANADA[b]

Martland, Ritchie, Spence, Dickson and Beetz JJ.[c]

Adams et al. v. McLeod and Ramstead[d]

Infants — Custody — Guardianship of baby granted to niece and nephew of infant's father — Order reversed on appeal — Further appeal allowed — Infant's interest considered foremost — No mistakes of law by trial judge awarding guardianship — His decision affirmed.

The grandmother and aunt of the infant made a joint application for guardianship, which was disallowed ... An appeal was made to the Supreme Court of Canada.

Held, the appeal was allowed. The original grant of guardianship by the trial Judge was restored. The cardinal issue in custody matters is the best interest of the child, and the trial Judge is the best equipped to decide that matter ... The religious issue was not such as to be a deciding factor in the dispute.[e]

Bickley v. Bickley, [1957] S.C.R. 329, 7 D.L.R. (2d) 465 (sub nom. *Re Bickley; Bickley v. Blatchley*); *Retzer v. Retzer*, [1975] 2 S.C.R. 881, 19 R.F.L. 365, 52 D.L.R. (3d) 159, 4 N.R. 159; *MacDonald v. MacDonald*, [1976] 2 S.C.R. 259, 21 R.F.L. 42, 62 D.L.R. (3d) 301; *Talsky v. Talsky*, [1976] 2 S.C.R. 292, 21 R.F.L. 27, 62 D.L.R. (3d) 267, 7 N.R. 246 referred to.

McKee v. McKee, [1951] A.C. 352, 2 W.W.R. (N.S.) 181, [1951] 1 All E.R. 942, [1951] 2 D.L.R. 657 followed.[f]

[Note up with 13 C.E.D. (West. 2nd) *Infants*, s. 49.][g]

A. Germain, for appellants.
J. Coutu, for respondents.[h]

21st March 1978.[i] The judgment of the court was delivered by

SPENCE J.[j]:—This is an appeal from the judgment of the Appelate [*sic*] Division of the Supreme Court of Alberta pronounced on 11th May 1977 ....

---

[a] Page number for citation of case.
[b] The court.
[c] The judges' names.
[d] The style of cause.
[e] The headnote.
[f] The cases considered.
[g] Cross references to other sources.
[h] Counsel.
[i] Date of case.
[j] The judge's name and written decision.

Following the above mentioned preliminary elements is the judge's written opinion which relates relevant points of law to the facts of the case to arrive at a decision. Other elements of the litigation such as counsel's facta and courtroom transcripts are not reproduced in the law reports.

Almost all law reports first appear in paperbound loose part form. Such a paperback part may appear on a weekly basis. After several numbered paper parts appear for a volume, the cases are cumulated and published in a single numbered bound volume.

B. SPECIFIC LAW REPORT TITLES

With a number of publishers producing law report series, and with coverage varying according to court, geographical area, jurisdiction, or subject area, it is useful to enumerate the current law report series.

Research access to the reports is provided by indexes or index-digests within the report series, by separately published digests, or by searching the reports in their electronic versions. The indexes and index-digests to specific law report titles are discussed in conjunction with the separately published digests in Chapter 3. Discussed along with the digests are the various research features of law report series, such as cases judicially considered, statutes judicially considered, *etc*. The following list is an overview of the diversity of law report titles. If the reports are available in electronic versions, such availability is noted in an "electronic sources" note at the beginning of the subsections below.

1. Federal case reporting

Electronic sources for federal case reporting:

Internet:

- Supreme Court of Canada judgments from 1989, *Bulletin of Proceedings*, press releases, and recent rulings (www.droit.umontreal.ca).
- *Federal Court Reports* judgments from 1993 (www.fja.cmf.gc.ca).
- *National Reporter* (www.mlb.ca).

Online database sources:

- Supreme Court of Canada judgments are available from LEXIS-NEXIS and from QL Systems Ltd. within a very short time of release by the court.
- Federal Court decisions are available from LEXIS-NEXIS and from QL.
- The *National Reporter* is available from LEXIS-NEXIS.

CD-ROM:

- The *National Reporter* is available from Maritime Law Book Ltd.
- Carswell Publishing's "The Canada Reporter National Courts" CD-ROM contains decisions from the Supreme Court, Federal Court, Exchequer Court, and the Privy Council.

Federal court decisions are published in both official government and unofficial commercial reports. The wording of an opinion should not vary from one report to another. Separately published digests discussed in Chapter 3 also cover federal case reporting.

(a) Canada Supreme Court Reports / Recueil des arrêts de la Cour suprême du Canada (1876-)

This series reports decisions of the Supreme Court of Canada on cases usually appealed from lower federal courts and provincial courts. In earlier years, not all Supreme Court cases appeared in this series. From 1923 to 1969, the title was *Canada Law Reports, Supreme Court of Canada*. Each case appears in both English and French versions.

(b) Canada Federal Court Reports / Recueil des arrêts de la Cour fédérale du Canada (1971-)

The *Federal Court Act*, S.C. 1970-71-72, c. 1, created this court with an Appeal Division and a Trial Division. A selection of the judgments handed down by the two Divisions is reported and all judgments of both Divisions not selected for full-text reporting are digested and published. The court's jurisdiction includes matters formerly handled by the Exchequer Court as well as some additional areas, including appeals from decisions of federal administrative bodies. All cases are published in both languages.

(c) Exchequer Court Reports (1875-1969)

These reports have had several title variations, including *Canada Law Reports, Exchequer Court* (1923-1970). The subject matter jurisdiction included patents, copyright, expropriation, income tax appeals, admiralty, citizenship appeals, and cases where relief was claimed against the government. The cases were reported only in the language of the court's written decision.

(d) National Reporter (1974-)

This unofficial series reports all Supreme Court and Federal Court Appeal Division cases. Also included are Court Martial Appeal Court judgments, and, from 1985, selected judgments from the British House of Lords and the Judicial Committee of the Privy Council. The series publishes cases several months in advance of the official reports noted above.

(e) Federal Trial Reports (1986-)

This unofficial series reports Federal Court Trial Division cases and is published by the company which produces the *National Reporter.*

(f) Other sources of federal decisions

Slip decisions are available from both federal courts immediately upon the court's rendering of judgments. Federal decisions are also published in some unofficial multi-jurisdiction reports (*e.g., Dominion Law Reports*), and in single-jurisdiction reports that contain cases appealed from provincial courts to the Supreme Court of Canada. Rapidly produced digests discussed in Chapter 3 give quick access to the Supreme Court of Canada judgments.

2. Multi-provincial reports

Electronic sources for multi-provincial reports:
Internet:

- *Dominion Law Reports* (D.L.R.) free update service (www.canadalawbook.ca).
- *Western Appeal Cases* (W.A.C.) and *Atlantic Provinces Reports* (A.P.R.) (www.mlb.nb.ca).

Online database sources:

- D.L.R. and A.P.R. are available on LEXIS-NEXIS.
  D.L.R., W.A.C., and W.W.R. are available on QL.

CD-ROM:

- D.L.R. from Canada Law Book.
- W.A.C. and A.P.R. from Maritime Law Book.
- W.W.R. from Carswell Publishing.

There are a number of past and current reports publishing decisions from all the common law provinces or from either the western or eastern regions of Canada. Separately published digests discussed in Chapter 3 also provide national or individual provincial coverage.

(a) Dominion Law Reports (1912-)

This is the only report series that contains cases from the higher courts of all provinces as well as selected Supreme Court and Federal Court cases. Each weekly advance part and later bound volume has a subject index. The cumulative index volumes contain the index classification scheme, the subject index, annotations (case citator), and table of cases.

(b) Western Weekly Reports (1911-)

This series contains selected cases from British Columbia, Alberta, Saskatchewan, Manitoba, the Yukon Territory, and the Northwest Territories, as well as cases appealed to the Supreme Court of Canada and the Federal Court. The series superseded the *Western Law Reporter* (1905-1916).

(c) Western Appeal Cases (1992-)

This title reports cases from the Courts of Appeal for British Columbia, Alberta, Saskatchewan, and Manitoba. An index of unreported cases lists judgments which did not merit reporting at time of receipt by the publisher.

(d) Atlantic Provinces Reports (1975-)

This series appears in bound volume form only and reproduces cases published in report series for the individual Maritime Provinces. Earlier reports for the region were the *Maritime Provinces Reports* (1929-1968) and the *Eastern Law Reporter* (1906-1914).

3. Subject reports

Electronic sources for subject reports:

Internet:

- *Native Law Cases* new cases monthly (http://portal.mbnet.mb.ca/firstper/index.html).
- All raw tax court judgments are on Carswell's Taxnet. (Address unavailable at time of writing).
- Alberta Labour Relations Board recent decisions (www.gov.ab.ca.~alrb/Decisions/DecisionsOpening.html).

Online database sources:

- Many subject reports are available online as noted under the law reports titles below. For example, "(QL 1984-)" would indicate coverage on QL starting with 1984 material.

CD-ROM:

- *Canadian Criminal Cases* on Canada Law Book's "Canadian Criminal Law Library" CD-ROM, which includes *Martin's Criminal Code* (see Chapter 6, section C).
- *Criminal Reports* on Carswell's "Criminal Law Partner" CD-ROM, which includes case digests (see Chapter 3), legislation, and contents from *Crankshaw's Criminal Code* (see Chapter 6, section C).

- *Reports of Family Law* on Carswell's "Family Law Partner" CD-ROM, which includes cases pre-dating R.F.L., case digests (see Chapter 3), legislation, and textbook commentary.

While reports publishing cases concerned with topics under federal jurisdiction (such as criminal law, bankruptcy, and patents) have existed for many years, a number of subject reports have commenced publication in recent decades. Listed below are current law report series and looseleaf reporters which provide transfer binders for the past year's decisions. The annotations include specific subject content as indicated by the frequent occurrence of the listed key words from the indexes of recent issues. To facilitate review, the reports are listed under the following very broad subject groupings: Business/Commerce, Criminal Law, Environmental Law/Natural Resources, Family Law/Estates, Human Rights, Labour/Employment, Property/Municipal, Tax, and Miscellaneous. The contents of any particular publication may actually fall under several of the broad categories. Separately published digests discussed in Chapter 3 also cover the various subject areas. The title of the current series is given, but the starting date is that of the title's first series.

(a) Business/Commerce

(1) Business Law Reports (Second Series) (1976-)
Carswell (QL Systems Ltd. 1984-)

Banking and Banks
Bills of Exchange
Competition Act
Contracts
Corporations
Creditors
Debentures
Debtors
Fiduciary Duty
Foreign Investment Review
Guarantees
Master and Servant
Partnerships
Products Liability
Promissory Notes
Receivers
Receivers and Managers
Sale of Business
Sale of Goods
Securities
Shareholders' Rights
Wrongful Dismissal

(2) Canadian Bankruptcy Reports (Third Series) (1920-)
Carswell (QL 1983-)

Acts of Bankruptcy
Avoidance of Transactions
  Prior to Bankruptcy
Banking and Banks
Bankruptcy
Bankruptcy Offences and Penalties
Bankruptcy Petition for
  Receiving Orders
Fraudulent Conveyances
Mechanics Liens
  (Construction Liens/Builders Liens)
Personal Property
Preferred Creditors
Proceedings after Bankruptcy
Property of the Bankrupt
Proposals

Corporations
Discharge of Bankruptcy
Discharge of Debtor
Receivers
Secured Creditors

(3) Canadian Cases on the Law of Insurance (Second Series) (1983-)
Carswell (QL 1984-)

Québec decisions in French with English summaries.

Accident and Sickness Insurance
Automobile Insurance
Disclosure
Fire Insurance
Indemnity
Insurable Interest
Insurance Contracts
Insurance Risk
Liability Insurance
Liability of Agents
Life Insurance
Marine Insurance
Subrogation
Trials

(4) Canadian Cases on the Law of Securities (1992-)
Carswell (QL 1992-)

This law report series gives decisions of provincial securities commissions and court decisions including appeals from the commissions.

(5) Canadian Insurance Law Reporter (1934-)
CCH Canadian Ltd. (QL 1985-)

This law report series gives insurance law topic coverage on life, health, accident, fire, casualty, and automobile insurance. Full text of decisions on insurance contracts are given, but only digests of tort decisions are included.

(6) Construction Law Reports (1983-)
Carswell (QL 1984-)

Agency
Architects
Bonding
Building Contracts
Contracts
Engineers
Mechanics Liens (Construction Liens/Builders Liens)
Negligence
Real Property
Sale of Land
Limitation of Actions

(7) Trade and Tariff Reports (1990-)
Butterworths (LEXIS-NEXIS)

This successor to *Canadian Customs and Excise Reports* (1980-1990) forms a part of Butterworths' looseleaf service titled *National Trade and Tariff Service*. The reported cases are from courts (federal and provincial) and panels (*e.g.*, Canadian International Trade Tribunal and Canada-United States Binational Dispute Resolutions Panel). An entry in the "Topical Index" is "Words and Phrases".

The service's monthly newsletter is *Tradewinds*. The relevant statutes are covered by full texts of the statutes plus case annotations in the legislation binder and by a "Table of Statutes Judicially Considered" in the case law binder. The statutes reproduced and considered are:

Canada-U.S. Free Trade Agreement Implementation Act
Canadian International Trade and Tribunal Act
Customs Act
Customs Tariff Act
Customs and Excise Offshore Application Act
Export and Import Permits Act
Special Import Measures Act

(b) Criminal Law

(1) Canadian Criminal Cases (Third Series) (1898-)
Canada Law Book Ltd (QL: digests 1971-1986; full text 1987-)
(LEXIS-NEXIS)

This series (C.C.C., C.C.C. (2d), C.C.C. (3d)) reports criminal and quasi-criminal cases from federal and provincial courts. Each volume has a subject index. The Cumulative Index, Annotations, and Table of Cases volume has the same features as the D.L.R. Index volume. Earlier indexing is provided by *Chitty's Abridgment of Canadian Criminal Case Law.* Case coverage dates back to 1892, the year the *Criminal Code* was enacted. *Canadian Criminal Cases* beginning from 1898 and *Martin's Criminal Code* (see Chapter 6, section C) comprise Canada Law Book's CD-ROM title "Canadian Criminal Law Library". There is some duplication in reporting with C.R.'s .

(2) Criminal Reports (Fourth Series) (1946-)
Carswell (QL 1984-)

This series (C.R., C.R.N.S., C.R. (3d), and C.R. (4th)) covers criminal cases from federal and provincial jurisdictions, and has some duplication in reporting with the C.C.C.'s. The report volumes have annotations in the format of journal articles. These annotations are indexed in the *Index to Canadian Legal Periodical Literature* and the *Index to Canadian Legal Literature.* The consolidated index covers cases appearing in this title while the *Criminal Law Digest* (extracts from the *Canadian Abridgment* (2nd)) digests cases from all reported criminal cases (*e.g.,* C.R.'s, C.C.C's, *etc.*). *Criminal Reports* is on Carswell's "Criminal Law Partner" CD-ROM, which includes case digests (see Chapter 3), legislation, and contents from *Crankshaw's Criminal Code* (see Chapter 6, section C).

(3) Motor Vehicle Reports (Second Series) (1979-)
Carswell (QL 1984-)

Admissibility of Certificate Analysis
Breathalyzers
Care or Control
Charter of Rights
Dangerous Driving
Failure to Remain
Highway Traffic
Licensing
Motor Vehicles
Presumption of Alcohol Content
Refusal of Breathalyzer Samples
Registration
Sentencing

(c) Environmental Law/Natural Resources

(1) Canadian Environmental Law Reports (New Series) (1972-)
(QL 1986-)

Originally published by the Canadian Environmental Law Research Foundation, the new series is published by Carswell.

Aboriginal Rights
Administrative Law
Constitutional Law
Costs
Criminal Code
Crown Liability
Due Diligence
Environmental Protection Act
Fisheries Act
Hazardous Products Act
Limitation Periods
Nuisance
Occupational Health and Safety
Ontario Water Resources Act
Pollution Control
Public Health
Public Inquiries Act
Radioactive Waste
Sentencing
Statutory Interpretation
Waste Management
Water Course

(d) Family Law/Estates

(1) Reports of Family Law (Third Series) (1970-)
Carswell (QL 1994-)

The consolidated index covers cases appearing in this title, while Carswell's *Family Law Digests* are extracts from *Canadian Abridgment* (2nd) which covers reported cases from all sources. Now in the Third Series, this publication began in 1970.

Reports of Family Law (Reprint Series) contains five volumes of pre-1970 cases of continuing authority at the time of publication. The series is modelled after the *All England Law Reports Reprint Series*. It has a distinctive characteristic in that each volume is devoted to a different area of family law: torts, contracts, infants, matrimonial property, and marriage.

Reports of Family Law, pre-1970 cases, case digests, legislation, rules of practice, and textbook commentary are included in Carswell's CD-ROM, "Family Law Partner".

(2) Estates and Trusts Reports (1977-)
Carswell (QL 1984-)

A specialized full text law report series giving court and tax board decisions from all the jurisdictions.

Charities
Costs
Dependent's Relief
Devolution of Estates
Executors and Administrators
Gifts
Income Tax
Real Property
Trusts and Trustees
Wills

(e) Human Rights

(1) Canadian Human Rights Reporter (1980-)

This independently published reporter consists of a binder containing federal and provincial human rights legislation and regulations, plus binders for each year to 1992 (hardbound 1993-), containing decisions and comments. The decisions are primarily from the Canadian Human Rights Commission and provincial Human Rights Commissions. The decisions binder has an index. Québec decisions are in French. Some federal decisions are in both official languages.

Accommodation
Age Discrimination
Complaints
Damages
Disability
Employment
Native Peoples
Race, Colour, and Ethnic Origin
Reasonable Cause
Sex Discrimination and Harassment

(2) Canadian Native Law Reporter (1979-)/Canadian Native Law Cases (1763-1978)
(QL full text 1979-)

These are published by the University of Saskatchewan Native Law Centre. *Canadian Native Law Reporter* is a combination of journal articles and full text case reports. Its predecessor during 1977-78 was entitled *Canadian Native Law Bulletin.*

Canadian Native Law Cases is a collection of reported and previously unreported cases dealing "with the affairs of Canada's original peoples: Indians, Inuit, and Métis". New cases appear monthly at the Internet address (http://portal.mbnet.mb.ca/firstper/index.html).

Aboriginal Rights
Constitutional Acts
Criminal Law
Family Law
Hunting and Fishing Rights
Indian Acts
Reserves
Traffic Laws
Treaties

(3) Canadian Rights Reporter (Second Series) (1982-)
(LEXIS-NEXIS)

Butterworths' specialized law report series giving the full text of *Charter of Rights* decisions.

Appeal
Arbitrary Detention or Imprisonment
Bail
Burden of Proof
Compellability
Counsel
Court of Competent Jurisdiction
Cruel or Unusual Treatment or Punishment
Delay in Informing Accused of Offence Charged
Double Jeopardy
Exclusion of Evidence
Fair and Public Hearing
Interpretation
Liberty, Fundamental Justice
Presumption of Innocence
Reasonable Limits
Remedies
Retroactivity and Retrospectivity
Search or Seizure
Self Incrimination
Trial Within Reasonable Time

(4) Immigration Law Reporter (Second Series) (1987-)
(QL 1987-)

Immigration Law Reporter (1985-1987)
Immigration Appeal Cases — CLIC Digest (1977-1985)
Immigration Appeal Cases/Affaires d'Immigration en Appel (1972-1977)

Immigration Appeal Cases was published in 11 volumes before the project was terminated. The set produced full texts of Immigration Appeal Board decisions. The full text judgments, headnotes, and indexing was presented in both English and French. Coverage of Immigration Appeal Board cases was continued in digest form only in CLIC's *Notes of Recent Decisions Rendered by the Immigration Appeal Board. Immigration Law Reporter* was privately published in two volumes before Carswell began the Second Series in 1987. This series reports court decisions and decisions of the Immigration Appeals Board. Carswell also published *Index to the Decisions Rendered by the Immigration Appeal Board* (1976-1987).

(f) Labour/Employment

(1) Canadian Cases on Employment Law (1983-)
Carswell (QL 1984-)

Constructive Dismissal
Damages
Demotion
Dismissal for Cause
Employment Contracts
Employment Standards
Mandatory Retirement
Master and Servant
Pensions
Profit Sharing
Wages
Wrongful Dismissal

(2) Canadian Cases on Pensions & Benefits (1994-)
Carswell (QL 1993-)

A full text law report series with cases from provincial and federal courts and tribunals.

Employee Share Ownership Plans
Group Benefit Plans
Group RRSPs
Phantom Stock Plans
Profit Sharing Plans
Registered & Unregistered Pension Plans

(3) Canadian Labour Law Cases (1944-1987)

This full text law report series gives national labour law coverage of decisions from federal and provincial courts, labour relations boards and human rights commissions. It continued after 1987 as the looseleaf service titled *Canadian Labour Law Reporter* by CCH Canadian.

(4) Canada Labour Relations Board Decisions, Conseil canadien des relations du travail decision/information (di) (1973-)
(QL 1973-)

A series giving the full text of reasons for decisions as well as summaries of applications and complaints. Provides statistics on C.L.R.B. activity.

(5) Canadian Labour Relations Boards Reports (Second Series) (1974-)
Butterworths (LEXIS-NEXIS)

A full text law report series giving federal and provincial labour relations board decisions.

(6) Canadian Occupational Health and Safety Cases (1988-1995)
Carswell (QL 1988-1995)

A law report full text series which drew from administrative tribunals and all levels of courts.

Due Diligence Defence
Inspectors
Reprisal Complaints
WHMIS Compliance
Work Refusals

(7) Employment and Immigration Canada, Decisions of the Umpire/ Emploi et Immigration Canada, Decision de L'arbitre (1943-)

A looseleaf service giving full text decisions of the Umpire concerning the *Unemployment Insurance Act* and regulations.

(8) Labour Arbitration Cases (Fourth Series) (1948-)
Canada Law Book (QL 1987-) (LEXIS-NEXIS)

A specialized full text law report series covering the full text of labour arbitration decisions. Now in its Fourth Series, this reporter has cross references from the cases reported to the looseleaf text by Brown and Beatty, *Canadian Labour Arbitration*, 3rd ed. (Canada Law Book).

Arbitrability
Bargaining Unit
Classification
Collective Agreement
Damages
Disciplinary Penalties
Discipline and Discharge Estoppel
Grievance Procedure
Health and Safety
Holidays
Illness and Disability
Interpretation
Lay-Off
Leave of Absence
Management Rights
Overtime
Probationary Employee
Remedies
Seniority
Skill and Ability
Transfer
Wages

(9) Ontario Labour Relations Board Reports (1944-)

A series covering selected decisions of the board in full text.

(g) Property/Municipal

(1) Land Compensation Reports (1971–)

Canada Law Book's specialized full text law report series giving court and board decisions on land compensation.

Abandonment
Appeal
Arbitral Tribunal
Costs
Disturbance Damages
Evidence
Injurious Affection
Interest
Market Value
Partial Taking
Procedure
Statutes

(2) Municipal and Planning Law Reports (Second Series) (1976-)

A specialized full text law report series of court and planning tribunal decisions on municipal law.

Assessment
By-Laws
Conflict of Interest
Development Control
Judicial Review
Municipal and School Taxes
Municipal Corporations
Negligence
Public Officers
Subdivision Control
Trade Regulation

(3) Ontario Municipal Board Reports (1973-)

Canada Law Book's specialized law report series covering Ontario Municipal Board decisions, cabinet decisions and court judgments.

(4) Personal Property Security Act Cases (1977-)

A specialized law report series covering full text of court decisions on personal property security matters considering personal property security legislation from British Columbia, Alberta, Saskatchewan, Manitoba, and Ontario. Rather than appearing in loose parts, the newly published cases appear as releases to be inserted into a binder of the looseleaf text by McLaren, *Secured Transactions in Personal Property in Canada*, 2nd ed. (Carswell). Hardbound volumes are issued later. Case coverage is from 1977.

Attachment
Conflict of Laws
Perfection
Priorities
Registration
Remedies
Sale of Goods
Scope
Security Agreement
Security Interest
Transition Provisions

(5) Real Property Reports (Second Series) (1977-)
Carswell (QL 1978-)

Agency
Agreement for Purchase and Sale
Barrister and Solicitor
Condominiums
Contracts
Damages
Easements
Expropriation
Fixtures
Immovable by Nature
Landlord and Tenant
Limitation of Actions
Mortgages
Municipal and School Taxes
Restrictive Covenants
Sale of Land
Vendor and Purchaser

(h) Tax

(1) Canada Tax Cases (1917-)
Carswell ("Canadian Tax Online" databases)

A specialized full text law report series giving tax decisions from courts, the Tax Review Board and now the Tax Court of Canada. The looseleaf *Canada Tax Cases Index and Citator* is updated irregularly with a consolidated topical index and case and statute citations since 1972.

Index terms: Coverage indicated by Acts listed:

Bankruptcy Act
Canada Evidence Act
Charter of Rights
Federal Court Act and Rules
Income Tax Act and Regulations
Income Tax Agreements and Conventions

(2) Dominion Tax Cases (1920-)
CCH Canadian Ltd. (QL 1920-)

A specialized looseleaf full text law report series giving tax decisions from courts, the Tax Review Board and now the Tax Court of Canada.

Index Terms: Coverage indicated by Acts listed in the citator section:

Charter of Rights
Excise Tax Act
Income Tax Act and Regulations
Tax Agreements

(3) Canadian GST & Commodity Tax Cases (1993-)

This CCH publication consists of a looseleaf current binder and annual hard-bound volumes. In full text, it reports the written reasons for judgment of all GST and commodity tax cases released by the Tax Court of Canada, the Canadian International Trade Tribunal, the higher courts of the provinces, and the Supreme and Federal Courts of Canada.

New cases are reported as they are released by the courts. A report letter includes case summaries. Case comments appear under a separate tab section. Subject index and statute citator are included.

(i) Miscellaneous

(1) Administrative Law Reports (Second Series) (1983-)
Carswell (QL 1983-)

A law report full text series covering administrative law from courts and boards.

Administrative Law
Applications for Judicial Review
Canadian Charter of Rights and Freedoms
Estoppel
Injunction
Judges and Courts
Judicial Review
Municipal Corporations
Prerogative Remedies

(2) Canadian Cases on the Law of Torts (Second Series) (1976-)
Carswell (QL 1983-)

Québec cases in French with English summaries.

Conspiracy
Contributory Negligence

Damages (principles of assessment more than quantum)
Defamation
Economic Torts
Exemption or Exclusion Clauses
Medical Negligence
Medicine and Surgery

Negligence
Nuisance
Products Liability
Professional Negligence

(3) Canadian Intellectual Property Reports (1984-1990)
Carswell (QL 1984-1989)

Conspiracy
Contracts
Copyright
Discovery
Industrial Design
Judges and Courts
Judgments and Orders
Patents of Invention
Pleadings
Practice

(4) Canadian Patent Reporter (Third Series) (1942-)
Canada Law Book (QL 1977-) (LEXIS-NEXIS)

A specialized full text law report series of court and board decisions giving coverage relating to patents, industrial and intellectual property.

(5) Carswell's Practice Cases (Third Series) (1976-)
Carswell (QL 1976-)

A specialized law report series giving court judgments relating to practice. Legal research in this index complements research in Power's *Western Practice Digest* (now out of print) and *Weekly Digest of Civil Procedure.*

Administrative Law
Appeals
Bankruptcy
Barristers and Solicitors
Costs
Creditors & Debtors
Discovery
Evidence
Injunction
Institution of Proceedings
Judges and Courts
Judgments and Orders
Limitation of Actions
Matrimonial Causes
Parties
Pleadings
Prerogative Remedies
Service
Third Party Proceedings

(6) Copyright Board Reports (1990-1994)
Copyright Appeal Board Reports (1936-1989)
Carswell

A specialized full text report series of board decisions relating to such topics as retransmission of distant radio and television signals, public performance of musical works, and copyright owners who cannot be located.

(7) Court Martial Appeal Reports/Rapports du Tribunal d'Appel des Cours Martiales (1957-)
(QL 1978-)

Covers the full text of decisions of the Court Martial Appeal Court. Volumes 1-3 are English only; Volume 4 is bilingual. The current volume is looseleaf with some decisions in French.

4. Individual provincial and territorial reports (common law jurisdictions)

There are now reports published for each of the provinces, but only Ontario and Québec have had continuous reporting throughout the years. Most other provinces had report series starting in the earlier part of the century followed by a gap until recent decades. The current series of provincial reports are listed below with beginning publication dates for each title.

The reports listed below, which are published by Maritime Law Book Ltd., utilize Maritime's Topical Index system. Each report includes all cases from the highest provincial court, other selected provincial decisions, and selected cases appealed to the federal courts. Separate cumulative *Digest* and *Indexes* volumes appear after every ten volumes in each report series. Separate *Index to Cases* volumes provide a comprehensive Table of Cases to each series. The reports have loose parts and bound volumes. The cases from the Maritime Provinces also appear in the *Atlantic Provinces Reports*. Cases from Courts of Appeal in the West also appear in *Western Appeal Cases*. All of Maritime Law Book Ltd.'s reports now appear on diskette in addition to the other formats.

The series which are published by Carswell contain selected significant cases from provincial courts as well as some appeals to the federal courts. Separate consolidated indexes are published for each series. The reports have loose parts and bound volumes. While there is a certain amount of duplication with the W.W.R.'s, many of the cases are considered to have significance primarily for each province's practitioners.

Electronic sources for common law provincial and territorial reports are:
Internet:

- All reports published by Maritime Law Book Ltd. (www.mlb.nb.ca).

- British Columbia Supreme Court and Court of Appeal since 1996 (www.courts.gov.bc.ca/SC/Sc-main.htm); (www.courts.gov.bc.ca/CA/Ca-main.htm).

Online databases:
See Appendix B for a listing of databases on LEXIS-NEXIS and QL Systems Ltd.

- All of the reports are available online. (check QL's dates of coverage, which start with digests for initial years of coverage and then changes to full text).

CD-ROM:

- All reports published by Maritime Law Book Ltd.
- All reports published by Carswell.
- *Alberta Law Reports (Third Series)* (1977-) (Carswell).
- *Alberta Reports* (1976-) (Maritime).
- *British Columbia Appeal Cases* (1991-) (Maritime).
- *British Columbia Trial Cases* (1997-) (Maritime).

  Note: B.C.T.C. is only available in electronic format.
- *British Columbia Law Reports (Second Series)* (1976-) (Carswell).
- *Manitoba Reports (Second Series)* (1979-) (Maritime).
- *New Brunswick Reports (Second Series)/Recueil des arrêts du Nouveau-Brunswick* (1968-) (Maritime); *New Brunswick Reports (2nd series) Supplement* (1997-) (Maritime).

  Note: N.B.R. (2nd Supp.) is only available electronically and includes untranslated decisions not published in N.B.R. (2d).
- *Newfoundland and Prince Edward Island Reports* (1970-) (Maritime).
- *Northwest Territories Reports* (1983-) (Carswell).
- *Nova Scotia Reports (Second Series)* (1969-) (Maritime).
- *Ontario Appeal Cases* (1984-) (Maritime).
- *Ontario Reports (Third Series)* (1882-) (Butterworths).

  This series has had sundry title variations and is the successor to several older Ontario reports published prior to, and simultaneously with, the Ontario Reports.
- *Ontario Trial Cases* (1994-) (Maritime).
- *Saskatchewan Reports* (1979-) (Maritime).
- *Yukon Reports* (1987-1989) (Maritime).

5. Québec law reports

Below are listed Québec law reports with brief annotations. Many titles are available electronically, but dates of coverage may vary from the print version. Research methods for Québec materials are discussed in Chapter 12, Researching Québec Law.

(a) Judicial reports: general series

- *Recueil de jurisprudence du Québec* (R.J.Q.)

  The main series of law reports in Québec under that title since 1986. The R.J.Q.'s are a merger of former separate series for the Court of Appeal (C.A.), the Superior Court (C.S.), and the Court of Québec, and includes the Québec Human Rights Tribunal.

  Electronic sources: summaries since 1976 in EXPRESS online database. Full text of Court of Appeal judgments since 1987.

- *Revue de droit judicaire* (*R.D.J.*) (1983-)

  The main topic of coverage is procedure. This series continues the *Québec Practice Reports* which began in 1898.

- *La revue* légale (*R.L.*) (1869-)

  This long-established series is a general law report series with cases from many diverse areas such as family law, labour law, municipal law, environmental law, real property, and wills.

- QL System Ltd.'s online database "Québec Judgments" with an access code of QJ, 1987-.

- *Québec Appeal Cases* (Q.A.C.) (1986-1995)

  Maritime Law Book Ltd. (QL 1986-1995)

(b) Judicial reports: by topic

- Insurance and Liability

  Recueil en responsibility et assurance (1986-) (R.R.A.).
  Electronic sources: Part of EXPRESS database.

- Family Law

  Recueil de droit de la famille (1986-) (R.D.F.).
  Electronic sources: Part of EXPRESS database.

- Taxation

  Recueil de droit fiscal québecois (1987-) (R.D.F.Q.).
  Electronic sources: Part of EXPRESS database.

- Real Estate

  Recueil de droit immobilier (1986-) (R.D.I.).
  Electronic sources: Part of EXPRESS database.

Chapter 3

Digests and Indexes for Law Reports

A. ANALYZING DIGESTS AND INDEXES

1. Traditional digests and new digests

Law report publications (*e.g.*, *Ontario Reports*) publish cases in chronological order rather than by subject matter; therefore, the only practical research access to such cases is through the reports' own indexes or through case digests arranged in subject order (*e.g.*, Butterworths' *Lawyers Weekly Consolidated Digest*). Many cases are never published, and access to some of these unreported cases is through digest publications (*e.g.*, *Nova Scotia Law News*).

This chapter covers trends, problems, and approaches to working with law reports indexes and digests published in provinces other than Québec. Some Québec cases are covered by indexes and digests in this chapter because Québec cases are appealed to the Supreme Court of Canada and because federal statutes and regulations are applied and interpreted in the courts of Québec. For example, a researcher would expect to find a number of Québec cases in *Canadian Criminal Cases* or *Criminal Reports* which largely report cases applying the federal *Criminal Code*. Chart M presents a listing of Québec digests with brief annotations, but a full discussion of research methods for Québec law is the subject of Chapter 12, Researching Québec Law.

Searching many indexes to law report publications involves a two-step process. The researcher surveys alphabetical listings of key words (fact words such as "highway", or legal concepts such as "negligence" in *Motor Vehicle Reports Cumulative Index*) and if key words in the index indicate relevance, the researcher can turn to the cited case for full reading. Searching many digest publications involves a three-step process, starting with the publication's index of key words, leading to a review of the individual case digests, and on to a study of the cited case if review of the case digest indicates relevance (*e.g.*, Can. Abr. Rev. (2nd) General Index to Vol. R25 "Motor Vehicles" to a case in O.R. (2d)). The process is considered two-step for some rapid digesting services (*e.g.*, *Saskatchewan Decisions*) which cannot cite law reports yet to print the cases.

For many years, digests such as the *Canadian Abridgment* have served researchers as excellent digest access to Canadian case law. However, choosing an index or digest now has become a more complicated decision with the recent appearance of many new reports with key word indexes and new digest publications. More than half the indexes and digests cited in this chapter have appeared since 1970. Not every high quality publication survives, and two of the more respected printed digests have ceased in recent years (*Dominion Report Service*, 1968-1991, and Butterworths' *Ontario Digest*, 1901-1989). D.R.S. does continue on computer only.

Even if a search can be narrowed to a particular digest or to an index for a particular law report (*e.g.*, W.W.R. or A.P.R.), the researcher should also consider researching in one of the newer digests containing unreported decisions. Such digests (*e.g.*, *Manitoba Decisions* or *All-Canada Weekly Summaries*) may yield cases that have not yet or never will be published in the law reports. The indexes providing access to these new digests are not as detailed as the "reported" cases' digests; however, computerized search of the full text of the digests of unreported cases can make research easier.

The topic of duplication between case law reports and lag in reporting time relate to choice of research in traditional and new digests. These topics were examined in "The Canadian Case Law Reporting Studies" prepared by Shirley Lounder in the late 1970s and printed in *Case Law Reporting in Canada* (1982), Canadian Law Information Council (CLIC) Occasional Paper #4, edited by Lorna Rees-Potter.

The average length of time it took for cases to appear in the rapid digesting services was slightly less than two months, while the average length of time it took for a case to appear in report series offering full texts of judgments was approximately seven-and-a-half months. A 1985 study, *A Guide to Purchasing Law Reports* prepared by MacEllven, Tanguay, and Rees-Potter (Canadian Law Information Council, 1985), indicates that the time lag for some law reports had improved. While the problem of time lag for reported cases may continue to some extent, the appearance of some judgments in online databases or on the Internet has reduced this problem to nil for these judgments.

In the 1982 study, the problem of duplication and incomplete coverage was discussed by identifying three types of publications that could supply access to a case: rapid digesting services, which contain digests of many cases that are never fully reported; general law reports series covering regions, courts, and provinces; and finally, the subject specialty law report series. The study did not consider the appearance of a case befitting a subject specialty report in all three types of publications to be "true" duplication; rather, true duplication was defined as cases being published in several titles within the same type of category (*e.g.*, appearance of the same case in the C.C.C.'s and C.R.'s). It is not surprising, given the number of publishers producing digests and law reports, that true duplication was found for half of all cases (*e.g.*, more than half of the cases in the *Criminal Reports* appear in the *Canadian Criminal Cases*; the same is true of the *Alberta Law Reports (Second Series)* and the *Alberta Reports*).

The related problem of dispersion concerns a researcher's ability to find all cases dealing with a particular jurisdiction in one publication. At the time of the studies, Alberta was served by one rapid digesting service (now three), two full provincial reports, and two general reports (now three). It was necessary to refer to all five sources in order to gain access to all Alberta written decisions. It is generally thought that a rapid digesting service digests all written decisions, but the study found that only slightly more than 90 per cent of all written decisions from across the country were covered by one or more rapid digesting services. The coverage by any single rapid digesting service may only contain coverage of 80 to 90 per cent of the cases that the researcher would expect to find. Some reports that include more than one jurisdiction were found to be stronger than others in the percentage of cases reported from one region or jurisdiction. For these reasons, researchers do not have the luxury of turning to one particular publication in order to conduct thorough research. Researchers must be aware of all potential sources, in order either to investigate them or to make an informed decision not to investigate. The above-mentioned studies are examples of CLIC's focus on improving access to the law. Unfortunately, CLIC has ceased operation due to funding tightness in the 1990s. In the years immediately preceding its demise, the Canadian Law Information Council (CLIC) was renamed Canadian Legal Information Centre.

This chapter paints a broad picture of many digests, and it may seem to be an onerous task to make a thorough search through so many publications. Chapter 10 discusses computerized legal research and the computer's impact on sorting through so many years of so many digests. The computer is so established now that some titles are only available on computer. The long respected *Dominion Report Service* (1968-1991 as a print form digest) survives as a QUICKLAW database. However, before you can fully grasp the importance of the computer, you must first understand the relationship of the many case law digests to each other.

2. Factors to consider when choosing a digest or index

When choosing an index or digest, the researcher must be familiar with its essential characteristics, and must be aware of how a computerized search might complement manual search. The essential characteristics to be considered are:

(a) Material digested

(i) As stressed above, ask whether the publication digests only reported cases, or does it include unreported cases as well?

(A) Reported case digests: law report series generally publish cases that the publisher views as significant. The selection and publishing process can take several months or more; hence, the latest release of some digest publications contains digests of cases that range from several months to a year old. Many of these services include some rapid digesting of cases such as Supreme Court of Canada judgments.

(B) Unreported case digests (rapid services): some publishers attempt to rapidly digest all cases from a jurisdiction. This rapid process is in advance of cases being selected and published in law reports, so when the cases appear in these rapidly produced digests, they all may be termed "unreported". Some of the cases become "reported" after inclusion in law reports (*e.g.*, some A.C.W.S. summaries are selected for full reporting in D.L.R.).

(C) Unreported case digests (looseleaf services): The purpose of looseleaf reporter services (discussed in Chapter 9, B) is to provide frequent updates in specific subject areas through commentary, legislative and regulatory change notification, and sometimes through case law digests or full text reports. Because of the time necessary to prepare the editorial commentary, these services are not as quick as the rapid digesting services, but because they cover some subject specialties not usually covered by law reports series, many of the looseleaf services' case reports and digests will remain unreported. Some law reviews and journals also selectively digest or fully report cases.

(ii) Does it cover a court (*e.g.*, *Supreme Court of Canada Reports Service*), the nation (*e.g.*, Can. Abr. Rev. (2nd)), a region (*e.g.*, W.W.R. Index), or a province (*e.g.*, Sask. R. Digest and Index volume)?

(iii) Does it cover civil cases, criminal cases, both, or a subject (family law, real property, bankruptcy, *etc.*)?

(b) Indexing scheme used

The researcher must understand how the publisher chooses and arranges key words and key legal concepts to construct the digest.

(c) Starting date and cumulations

What is the starting date of coverage, *i.e.*, earliest case digested or indexed? How often are cumulations made, and how frequently are loose parts or releases issued? Some print-form cumulations are further cumulated into online database or CD-ROM format. How is research updated when using the publication? Note that frequency, cumulations, and updating relate to publishing schedules rather than to average time lag from date of judgment until the case appears in the publication.

(d) Research features

(i) Table of cases: an alphabetical list of cases digested by name of plaintiff or by plaintiff and defendant. For law reports indexes, the cases listed also are reported in full within the publication.

(ii) Cases judicially considered: a listing of all prior cases cited by cases digested in the publication. For law reports indexes, many of the prior cases would have been originally reported in other law reports, while the citing cases all appear in full text within this publication.

(iii) Statutes judicially considered: a listing of all statutes, regulations, and court rules cited by cases digested in the publication.

(iv) Words and phrases considered: a listing of all words and phrases defined by cases digested in the publication.
(v) Secondary authority literature cited: a listing of textbooks, journal articles, encyclopedia articles, *etc.*, cited by cases digested in the publication.

(e) Relation to other indexes/digests

Having searched in a particular index/digest, should search be made in another publication for cases not included in the index/digest reviewed? How does this index/digest tie into other indexes and digests produced by the same publisher?

(f) Computer search

As more cases become retrievable from online databases or from CD-ROM products, decide whether research will include a computer search. If present online databases or CD-ROMs contain law report series or unreported cases that might be relevant, the computer query may be made before or after manual search. Computerized search after manual research can sometimes yield cases not readily retrievable by printed indexes/digests, which key only on selected words from case headnotes/cases, while the computer scans all words in a headnote/case. Hence, if manual search yields no relevant cases, the computerized search may retrieve a case or confirm the lack of on-point authority.

B. SELECTION OF SPECIFIC DIGESTS AND INDEXES: APPLYING THE FACTORS TO BE CONSIDERED

The prior section discussed factors to consider when choosing a digest or index, but these factors can only be applied when the researcher is aware of growing numbers of Canadian digests and indexes. This chapter section presents chart form listings of Canadian digests and indexes with their research features plus a chart listing law reports and digests covering boards and tribunals.

The factors mentioned in subsection A.2 are related to specific titles below except for the factors of: "(b) Indexing scheme used" and "(e) Relation to other indexes/digests ... produced by the same publisher" (discussed below in C. SPECIFIC DIGESTS AND INDEXES: INSTRUCTIONS ON USE AND ILLUSTRATIONS). Another exception is "(d)(i) Table of Cases" which almost every legal index, digest, or looseleaf service contains. The concept of "(e) Relation to other indexes/digests ... [to] search ... for cases not included in the index/digest [being used]", can be ascertained by examining the groupings in the charts below. After review in the "reported" case digests and indexes, the researcher may transfer to the "unreported" case sources.

This chapter deals with indexes and digests, but a variety of publication types contain case law indexes and digests. Most law reports series have their own cumulative indexes, and there are many separately published digest titles which digest reported and/or unreported cases. A few journals covering narrow subject areas contain a case law section which is noted in the journal's index.

The statute citators arrange case digests under alphabetically listed statute names, but statute citators are usually thought of as a different type of publication than either a case law digest or index. The obvious exception is a *Criminal Code* citator which arranges case digests in a scheme similar to a criminal law digest — *i.e.*, by *Criminal Code* section, and in recognition of the exception, the author has listed the most current and comprehensive citator, *Crankshaw's Criminal Code* in nine looseleaf volumes (for other *Criminal Code* citators see Chapter 6).

Annotated legislation services are in the nature of statute citators and are found in Chapter 6 rather than the tables below.

The charts below group titles by material digested (federal, national, regional, provincial, or subject which has the breakdown: Business/Commerce, Criminal Law, Environmental Law/Natural Resources, Family Law/Estates, Human Rights, Labour/Employment, Property/Municipal, Tax, and Miscellaneous). The provincial chart lists older, non-current law report or digest series since 1900 in addition to the current publications.

Most charts list commercial services covering board decisions as well as court decisions. Chart M expands the board and tribunal listing to include board/tribunal services published by government agencies and to include decisions only available through electronic sources.

Research features are noted in charts as indicated by the following legend explanation for the chart's column headings:

TITLE (type) year: The title of the publication is given with the code for the publication type and the starting date of coverage (not the starting date of publication which is often later). "Current" indicates a primary purpose of stating the current status of the law. Type codes:

LR = law report
D = digest
CIT = statute citator
LLF = looseleaf reporter service
JNL = journal

CUM INDEX: "X" indicates that there is a cumulative index covering at least one year or more. "—" indicates that there is not such a cumulative index. Some law reports only index individual volumes. Some digests arrange summaries within the detailed Table of Contents scheme and do not have an index.

ELECTRONIC SOURCES: Commercial online databases are indicated by "QL" for QL Systems Ltd., "Lx" for LEXIS-NEXIS offered by Butterworths, or "online" for other databases. "CD" indicates availability in CD-ROM. "IN" indicates available through the Internet.

REPT-UNRP: "R" indicates that the publication prints cases in full text (therefore contains "reported" cases) or that the digest service primarily summarizes cases which have already been reported. "U" indicates that the publication is a rapid digesting service with many of the cases never later being fully reported or a looseleaf service digesting cases, many of which have not nor will be reported. Some services which formerly only digested reported cases, now rapidly digest cases not yet reported. These services are included in the "U" category.

STAT-CASE: "S" indicates a "table of statutes judicially considered". "Citator" indicates that the tables are found in a companion citator publication. "C" indicates a "table of cases judicially considered" by cases reported or digested in the publication. "S+C" indicates both tables. "—" indicates that neither table appears, but if the publication is available in electronic form, cases considered may be retrieved by computer search.

WORD + PH: "X" indicates tables of words and phrases considered by the publication's cases or digests. "—" indicates lack of such tables.

2nd LIT: "X" indicates tables of secondary authority literature (legal texts, dictionaries, encyclopedias, periodical articles, *etc.*) considered by the publication's cases or digests. "—" indicates lack of such tables.

ANNO + ART: "X" indicates that the publication (law report, journal, or looseleaf service) usually contains annotations, articles, case comments, *etc.* in addition to the case reports or digests. "—" indicates that the publication does not have or rarely contains articles.

HOW USE: indicates the example number in the next section (C. SPECIFIC DIGESTS AND INDEXES: INSTRUCTIONS ON USE AND ILLUSTRATIONS) which illustrates how to most efficiently use the research features of the publication. Examples in Section C are given to show how to use a grouping of publications (*e.g.,* published by the same company and using the same indexing scheme). Some individual publications not belonging to a logical grouping are not illustrated in Section C, and therefore, no example number is listed below for the publication.

PUB: publisher. Abbreviations are given for:
BTR = Butterworths
CAR = Carswell
CCH = CCH Canadian
CLB = Canada Law Book
MAR= Maritime
WLP = Western Legal Publications

Note that some looseleaf binder publications, with Carswell updating insert pages, may still be housed in DeBoo Publishing binders manufactured before DeBoo merged with Carswell. The book titles did not change with the merger of the companies.

Note that Maritime Law Book Ltd. markets "headnotes only" on CD-ROM or disc as a digest subscription separate from each of its law reports series.

Numbered items are:

1 = Canada Labour Relations Board
2 = Ontario Labour Relations Board
3 = Continuing Education Society of B.C.
4 = Supply and Services Canada
5 = Jonah Publishing
6 = Law Society of Saskatchewan Libraries
7 = Nova Scotia Barristers' Society
8 = Canadian Human Rights Reporter Ltd.
9 = Native Law Centre, University of Saskatchewan
10 = Workers' Compensation Appeal Tribunal of Ontario
11 = Gowling & Henderson Law Offices, Ottawa
12 = Supreme Court of Canada
13 = Lancaster House
14 = University of Alberta

1. Chart A: Federal — National — Regional

TITLE (TYPE) YEAR-	CUM INDEX	ELECTRONIC SOURCES	REPT UNRP	STAT CASE	WORD + PH	2nd LIT	ANNO + ART	HOW USE	PUB
FEDERAL									
Canada Supreme Court Reports (LR) 1876–	—	CD QL IN	R	S+C	—	—	—	—	4
Supreme Court of Canada Bulletin (D)	—	IN	U	—	—	—	—	—	10
Supreme Court of Canada Decisions (D) 1978–	X	CD QL	U	—	—	—	—	D	WLP
Supreme Court of Canada Reports Services 2nd (LLF) (pre-1970–)	X	—	U	S	—	—	—	K	BTR
Supreme Court of Canada Summaries (D) 1985–	—	—	U	—	—	—	—	—	9
National Reporter (LR) 1974–	X	CD LX IN	R	S+C	X	X	X	A	MAR
Canada Federal Court Reports (LR) 1975–	X	CD QL IN	R	S+C	—	—	—	—	4
Federal Court of Appeal Decisions (D) 1981–	—	CD QL IN	U	—	—	—	—	D	WLP
Federal Court of Canada Service (LLF) (pre–1970–)	X	—	U	—	—	—	—	—	BTR
Federal Trial Reports (LR) 1986–	X	CD LX IN	R	S+C	X	X	X	A	MAR
NATIONAL									
All Canada Weekly Summaries 3rd (D) 1977–	X	QL LX	U	—	X	—	—	J	CLB
Canadian Abridgment Revised 2nd Edition (D) 1809–	X	CD QL	R	S+C	X	X	—	G	CAR
Canadian Current Law (D) (current)	—	CD	R	S+C	X	X	—	H	CAR
Canadian Weeky Law Sheet (D) 1959–	X	—	R	—	—	—	—	E	BTR
Dominion Law Reports 4th (LR) 1912–	X	CD QL LX	R	C	—	—	—	I	CLB
Dominion Report Service (D) 1968-	X	QL	U	S	—	—	—		QL
The Lawyers Weekly (D) 1983–	X	CD QL	U	—	—	—	—	F	BTR
REGIONAL									
Atlantic Provinces Reports (LR) 1970–	X	CD LX IN	R	S+C	X	X	—	A	MAR
Western Appeal Cases (LR) 1992–	X	CD LX IN	R	S+C	X	X	X	A	MAR
Western Weekly Reports (LR) 1911–	X	CD QL	R	S+C	X	X	—	B	CAR

2. Chart B: Provincial/Territorial

TITLE (TYPE) YEAR-	CUM INDEX	ELECTRONIC SOURCES	REPT UNRP	STAT CASE	WORD + PH	2nd LIT	ANNO + ART	HOW USE	PUB
ALBERTA									
Superseded law reports and digests:									
Alberta Law Reports									
Territories Law Reports									
Unreported Decisions of Alberta									
Western Law Reporter									
Western Weekly Digests									
Current publications:									
Alberta Case Locator (D)	—	QL	—	—	—	—	—	—	15
Alberta Corporations Law Guide (current)	See Business								
Alberta Decisions (& Citator) (D) 1975–	X	CD QL	U	Citator	—	—	—	D	WLP
Alberta Law Reports (3d) (LR) 1976–	X	—	R	S+C	X	X	—	B	CAR
Alberta, Northwest Territories & Yukon Tax Reporter (current)	See Tax								
Alberta Reports (LR) 1976–	X	CD LX IN	R	S+C	X	X	X	A	MAR
Alberta Weekly Law Digest (D) 1983–	X	QL	U	—	—	—	—	C	CAR
Canada Energy Law Service — Alberta (D)	X	—	U	—	—	—	X	—	CAR
Personal Injury Damage Assessment in Alberta (D)	X	—	U	—	—	—	—	—	BTR
BRITISH COLUMBIA									
Superseded law reports and digests:									
British Columbia Reports									
British Columbia Unreported Decisions									
Solicitors Liability Index									

2. Chart B: Provincial/Territorial — *Continued*

TITLE (TYPE) YEAR-	CUM INDEX	ELECTRONIC SOURCES	REPT UNRP	STAT CASE	WORD + PH	2nd LIT	ANNO + ART	HOW USE	PUB
Western Law Reporter									
Western Weekly Digests									
Current publications:									
Apportionment of Liablity in B.C.	X	—	U	—	—	—	—	—	BTR
B.C. Appeal Cases (LR) 1991–	X	CD LX IN	R	S+C	X	X	X	A	MAR
B.C. Corporations Law Guide (current)	See Business								
**B.C. Decisions Civil Cases & Citator* (D) 1972–	X	CD QL	U	Citator	—	—	—	D	WLP
B.C. Law Reports (2d) (LR) 1976–	X	CD QL	R	S+C	X	X	—	B	CAR
**B.C. Decisions Criminal Cases 1972–*	See Criminal								
**B.C. Decisions Labour Arbitration 1972–*	See Labour								
**B.C. Labour Relations Board Decisions 1980–*	See Labour								
B.C. Real Estate Law Guide (current)	See Property								
B.C. Tax Reporter (current)	See Tax								
B.C. Trial Cases (LR) 1997–	—	CD LX IN	U	—	—	—	—	A	MAR
B.C. Weekly Law Digest (D) 1982–	X	QL	U	—	—	—	—	C	CAR
Personal Injury Damage Assessments in B.C. (D)	X	—	U	—	—	—	—	—	BTR

*Note: The above titles marked with an asterisk (*) are the basic rapid digesting services offered by Western Legal Publications (WLP). As separate "special series" subscriptions, WLP sells the following extracts from British Columbia Decisions: Family Law Cases, Insurance Law Cases, Municipal Law Cases, Personal Injury Damage Cases, Accounting Profession, Banking & Insolvency, Corporations, Contracts, Labour Relations, Mortgages & Foreclosure, Personal Property Transactions, Practice, Real Estate Agents, Securities, Taxation, Wills-Trusts-Estates. You may design your own "special series" subscription.

2. Chart B: Provincial/Territorial — *Continued*

TITLE (TYPE) YEAR-	CUM INDEX	ELECTRONIC SOURCES	REPT UNRP	STAT CASE	WORD + PH	2nd LIT	ANNO + ART	HOW USE	PUB
MANITOBA									
Superseded law reports and digests:									
Manitoba Reports									
Territories Law Reports									
Western Law Reporter									
Western Weekly Digest									
Current publications:									
Manitoba Decisions + Citator (D) 1975–	X	CD QL	U	Citator	—	—	—	D	WLP
Manitoba Reports (2d) (LR) 1979–	X	CD LX IN	R	S+C	X	X	X	A	MAR
Manitoba & Saskatchewan Tax Reporter (current)	See Tax								
NEW BRUNSWICK									
Superseded law reports and digests:									
Eastern Law Reporter									
Maritime Provinces Reports									
New Brunswick Law News									
New Brunswick Reports									
Current publications:									
New Brunswick Reports (2d) (LR) 1968–	X	CD LX IN	R	S+C	X	X	X	A	MAR
New Brunswick Reports, 2nd Supp.	—	CD LX IN	—	—	—	—	—	A	MAR
NEWFOUNDLAND									
Superseded law reports and digests:									
Eastern Law Reporter									

2. Chart B: Provincial/Territorial — *Continued*

TITLE (TYPE) YEAR-	CUM INDEX	ELECTRONIC SOURCES	REPT UNRP	STAT CASE	WORD + PH	2nd LIT	ANNO + ART	HOW USE	PUB
Maritime Provinces Reports									
Newfoundland Supreme Court Reports									
Current publication:									
Newfoundland & P.E.I. Reports (LR) 1970–	X	CD LX IN	R	S+C	—	—	—	A	MAR
NORTHWEST TERRITORIES									
Northwest Territories Reports (LR) 1983–	X	CD QL	R	S+C	X	X	—	B	CAR
Alberta, Northwest Territories, and Yukon Tax Reporter	See Tax								
NOVA SCOTIA									
Superseded law reports and digests:									
Eastern Law Reporter									
Maritime Provinces Reports									
Nova Scotia Reports									
Current publications:									
Nova Scotia Law News (D) 1974–	X	QL	U	S	—	—	X	—	6
Nova Scotia Reports (2d) (LR) 1969–	X	CD LX IN	R	S+C	X	X	X	A	MAR
ONTARIO									
Superseded law reports and digests:									
All-Canada Weekly Summaries Ontario Edition (1981–1986)									
Butterworths' Ontario Digest									
Family Law Reform Act Cases									

2. Chart B: Provincial/Territorial — *Continued*

TITLE (TYPE) YEAR-	CUM INDEX	ELECTRONIC SOURCES	REPT UNRP	STAT CASE	WORD + PH	2nd LIT	ANNO + ART	HOW USE	PUB
Family Law Reform Reporter									
Ontario Court of Appeal Summaries of Reasons for Judgment (Blue Pages)									
Ontario Law Reports									
Ontario Lawyers Weekly (1983–1987 when name changed to *The Lawyers Weekly*)									
Ontario Reports									
Ontario Weekly Reporter									
Ontario Weekly Notes									
Current publications:									
Ontario Accident Benefit Case Summaries	See Miscellaneous								
Ontario Appeal Cases (LR) 1983–	X	CD LX IN	R	S+C	X	X	X	A	MAR
Ontario Corporations Law Guide (current)	See Tax								
Ontario Decisions 1980–	See Criminal								
Ontario Labour Relations Board Reports 1944–	See Labour								
Ontario Municipal Board Reports 1973–	See Property								
Ontario Real Estate Law Guide (current)	See Property								
Ontario Reports (3d) (LR) 1882–	X	CD QL	R	—	—	—	—	—	BTR
Ontario Tax Reporter (current)	See Tax								
Ontario Trial Cases (LR) 1996–	—	CD LX IN	—	—	—	—	—	A	MAR

2. Chart B: Provincial/Territorial — *Continued*

TITLE (TYPE) YEAR-	CUM INDEX	ELECTRONIC SOURCES	REPT UNRP	STAT CASE	WORD + PH	2nd LIT	ANNO + ART	HOW USE	PUB
Workers' Compensation Appeals Tribunal Reporter	See Labour								
PRINCE EDWARD ISLAND									
Superseded law reports and digests:									
Eastern Law Reporter									
Maritime Provinces Reports									
Current publication:									
Newfoundland & P.E.I. Reports (LR) 1970–	X	CD LX IN	R	S+C	X	X	X	A	MAR
SASKATCHEWAN									
Superseded law reports and digests:									
Saskatchewan Law Reports									
Territories Law Reports									
Western Law Reporter									
Western Weekly Digests									
Current publications:									
Manitoba & Saskatchewan Tax Reporter (current)	See Tax								
Saskatchewan Decisions + Citator (D) 1975–	X	CD QL	U	Citator	—	—	—	D	WLP
Saskatchewan Reports (LR) 1979–	X	CD LX IN	R	S+C	X	X	X	A	MAR

2. Chart B: Provincial/Territorial — *Continued*

TITLE (TYPE) YEAR-	CUM INDEX	ELECTRONIC SOURCES	REPT UNRP	STAT CASE	WORD + PH	2nd LIT	ANNO + ART	HOW USE	PUB
This Week's Law (D) 1982–	X	LINE	U	S+C	—	—	—	—	5
YUKON									
Alberta, N.W.T., & Yukon Tax Reporter	See Tax								
Yukon Reports (LR) (1987–1989)	X	LX	R	S+C	X	X	X	A	MAR

3. Chart C: Business/Commerce

TITLE (TYPE) YEAR-	CUM INDEX	ELECTRONIC SOURCES	REPT UNRP	STAT CASE	WORD + PH	2nd LIT	ANNO + ART	HOW USE	PUB
Alberta Corporations Law Guide (LLF) (current)	X	—	U	—	—	—	X	L	CCH
Alberta Corporations Manual (LLF)									CAR
B.C. Corporations Law Guide (LLF) (current	X	—	U	—	—	—	X	L	CCH
B.C. Corporations Manual (LLF)									CAR
Business Law Reports (2d) (LR) 1977–	X	QL	R	S+C	X	X	X	B	CAR
Canada Corporations Law Reporter (LLF)	X	—	U	—	—	—	X	L	CCH
Canada Corporations Manual (LLF)									CAR
Canadian Bankruptcy Reports (3d) (LR) 1960–	X	QL	R	S+C	X	C	X	B	CAR
Canadian Cases on the Law of Insurance (2d) (LR) 1983–	X	QL	R	S+C	X	X	X	B	CAR
Canadian Cases on the Law of Securities	X	QL	R	S+C	X	X	X	B	CAR
Canadian Commercial Law Guide (LLF) (current)	X	—	U	—	—	—	X	L	CCH
Canadian Intellectual Property Reports (LR) 1984–1990 (Digest only 1990–1992)	X	QL	R	S+C	X	X	X	B	CAR
Canadian Patent Reporter (3d) (LR) 1942–	X	QL	R	—	—	—	X	I	CLB
Canadian Securities Law Reporter (LLF) (current)	X	CD	U	—	—	—	X	L	CCH
Canadian G.S.T. & Commodity Tax Cases (1990–)	X	—	R	S	—	—	X	L	CCH
Canadian Transport Cases (LR) 1966–	—	—	R	S+C	—	—	—	—	4
Construction Law Reports (LR) 1983–	X	QL	R	S+C	X	X	X	B	CAR
Insurance Case Law Digest (D) 1985–	X	CD	U	—	—	—	—	—	BTR
Insurance Law Digest	—	—	U	—	—	—	—	G	CAR

3. Chart C: Business/Commerce — *Continued*

TITLE (TYPE) YEAR-	CUM INDEX	ELECTRONIC SOURCES	REPT UNRP	STAT CASE	WORD + PH	2nd LIT	ANNO + ART	HOW USE	PUB
Canadian Insurance Law Reporter (LLF) (current)	X	QL	U	S	—	—	X	L	CCH
Ontario Corporations Law Guide (LLF) (current)	X	—	U	—	—	—	X	L	CCH
Ontario Corporations Manual (LLF)									CAR
Quebec Corporations Manual (LLF)									CAR
Trade and Tariff Reports (1990–)	X	—	R	S	X	—	X	—	BTR

4. Chart D: Subject — Criminal Law

TITLE (TYPE) YEAR-	CUM INDEX	ELECTRONIC SOURCES	REPT UNRP	STAT CASE	WORD + PH	2nd LIT	ANNO + ART	HOW USE	PUB
Alberta-Saskatchewan-Manitoba Criminal Conviction Cases (D) 1978–	X	QL	U	—	—	—	—	D	WLP
B.C. Decisions Criminal Cases (D) 1972–	X	CD QL	U	—	—	—	—	D	WLP
Canadian Criminal Cases (3d) (LR) 1892–	X	CD QL LX	R	C	—	—	—	I	CLB
Canadian Sentencing Digest Quantum Service (D) 1970–	—	CD	U	—	—	—	X	—	CAR
Crankshaw's Criminal Code of Canada (Citator) 1892–	—	CD	R	S	X	X	X	—	CAR
Criminal Law Digest, Revised Edition (D) 1800's–	—	CD	R	—	—	—	—	G	CAR
Criminal Reports (4th) (LR) 1946–	X	CD QL	R	S+C	X	X	X	B	CAR
Criminal Sentencing Digest (D) 1993–	—	—	U	S+C	—	—	X	—	BTR
Martin's Annual Criminal Code (Citator) 1892–	—	CD	U	S	—	—	—	—	CLB
Motor Vehicle Reports (2d) (LR) 1979–	X	QL	R	S+C	X	X	X	B	CAR
Ontario Decisions Criminal Cases (D) 1980–	X	CD QL	U	—	—	—	—	D	WLP
Weekly Criminal Bulletin (D) 1977–	X	QL LX	U	—	—	—	—	J	CLB
Young Offender's Service (D) 1985–	X	—	U	S	—	—	X	—	BTR
Young Offender's Act Manual (D) 1985–	X	—	U	S	—	—	—	—	CLB

5. Chart E: Subject — Environmental Law/Natural Resources

TITLE (TYPE) YEAR-	CUM INDEX	ELECTRONIC SOURCES	REPT UNRP	STAT CASE	WORD + PH	2nd LIT	ANNO + ART	HOW USE	PUB
Canada Energy Law Service (LLF) (current)	X	—	U	—	—	—	X	—	CAR
Canadian Environmental Law (2d) (LLF) 1970–	X	—	U	—	—	—	X	—	BTR
Canadian Environmental Law Reports (N.S.) (LR) 1972–	X	QL	R	S+C	X	X	X	B	CAR
Canadian Oil & Gas (2d) (LLF) 1906–	X	—	U	S	—	—	X	—	BTR
Digest of Environmental Law & Environmental Assessment (D) 1992–	X	—	U	—	—	—	—	C	CAR

6. Chart F: Subject — Family Law/Estates

TITLE (TYPE) YEAR-	CUM INDEX	ELECTRONIC SOURCES	REPT UNRP	STAT CASE	WORD + PH	2nd LIT	ANNO + ART	HOW USE	PUB
B.C. Family Law (D) 1983–	X	—	U	S+C	—	—	X	—	BTR
Butterworths' Ontario Family Law Quantum Service (D)	—	—	U	—	—	—	—	—	BTR
Canadian Estate Administration Guide (LLF) (current)	X	—	U	—	—	—	X	L	CCH
Canadian Family Law Guide (LLF) (current)	X	—	U	—	—	—	X	L	CCH
Estates & Trusts Reports (LR) 1977–	X	QL	R	S+C	X	X	X	B	CAR
Family Law Digest (3rd) (D) 1824–	X	CD	R	S+C	—	—	—	H	CAR
Ontario Family Law Reporter (D)	X	—	U	—	—	—	—	—	BTR
Reports of Family Law (3d) (LR) 1970–	X	CD QL	R	S+C	X	X	X	B	CAR
Weekly Digest of Family Law (D) 1982–	X	CD	U	—	—	—	—	C	CAR

7. Chart G: Subject — Human Rights

TITLE (TYPE) YEAR-	CUM INDEX	ELECTRONIC SOURCES	REPT UNRP	STAT CASE	WORD + PH	2nd LIT	ANNO + ART	HOW USE	PUB
Canadian Charter of Rights Annotated (Citator) 1982–	X	—	R	S	—	—	X	—	CLB
Canadian Human Rights Reporter (LR) 1980–	—	—	U	—	—	—	X	—	8
Canadian Native Law Reporter (JNL) 1979–	X	—	R	S	—	—	X	—	9
Canadian Rights Reporter (2d) (LR) 1982–	X	LX	R	—	—	—	X	—	BTR
Charter of Rights Decisions (D) 1982–	X	CD	U	S	—	—	—	D	WLP
Immigration Law Digest (D) 1997–	X	CD	U	S	—	—	—	D	WLP
Immigration Law Reporter (2d) (LR) 1987–	X	CD QL	U	S+C	X	X	X	B	CAR

8. Chart H: Subject — Labour/Employment

TITLE (TYPE) YEAR-	CUM INDEX	ELECTRONIC SOURCES	REPT UNRP	STAT CASE	WORD + PH	2nd LIT	ANNO + ART	HOW USE	PUB
B.C. Decisions Labour Arbitration (D) 1972–	X	CD QL	U	—	—	—	—	D	WLP
B.C. Labour Relations Board Decisions (D) 1979–	X	CD QL	U	—	—	—	—	D	WLP
B.C. Employment Standards Tribunal Decisions (D) 1996-	X	CD QL	U	—	—	—	—	D	WLP
Canada Labour Relations Board Decisions (LR) 1974–	X	QL	R	S	—	—	—	—	1
Canadian Cases on Employment Law (LR) 1983–	X	QL	R	S+C	X	X	X	B	CAR
Canadian Cases on Pension & Benefits (LR) 1994–	X	QL	R	S+C	X	X	—	B	CAR
Canadian Employment Benefits + Pension Guide (LLF) (current)	X	—	U	—	—	—	X	L	CCH
Canadian Labour Arbitration Summaries (D) 1991-	X	LX	U	—	—	—	—	J	CLB
Canadian Labour Law Reporter (LLF) (current)	X	—	U	—	—	—	X	L	CCH
Canadian Labour Relations Board Reports (2d) (LR) 1974–	X	LX	R	—	—	—	—	—	BTR
Dismissal & Employment Law Digest (D) 1986–	—	—	U	—	—	—	—	—	CLB
Employment Law Digest (D) 1996–	—	—	U	—	—	—	—	G	CAR
Labour Arbitration Cases (4th) (LR) 1948–	X	LX	R	—	—	—	—	I	CLB
Labour Law Digest (D) 1995–	—	—	U	—	—	—	—	G	CAR
Lancaster Labour Law Service (—) 1964–	X	—	U	—	—	—	X	JNL	14
Ontario Labour Relations Board Reports (LR) 1944–	X	—	R	—	—	—	—	—	2
Western Labour Arbitration Cases (LR) 1966–1985	X	—	R	S+C	—	—	—	—	3
Workers' Compensation Appeals Tribunal Reporter (Ontario) (LR)	—	—	R	—	—	—	—	—	14

9. Chart I: Subject — Property/Municipal

TITLE (TYPE) YEAR-	CUM INDEX	ELECTRONIC SOURCES	REPT UNRP	STAT CASE	WORD + PH	2nd LIT	ANNO + ART	HOW USE	PUB
B.C. Real Estate Law Guide (LLF) (current)	X	—	U	—	—	—	X	L	CCH
Digest of Municipal and Planning Law (D) 1990–	X	—	U	—	—	—	X	C	CAR
Digest of Real Property Law (D) 1990–1994	X	—	U	—	—	—	—	C	CAR
Land Compensation Reports (LR) 1971–	X	—	R	—	—	—	—	I	CLB
Municipal Law Digest (D) 1993–	—	—	U	—	—	—	—	G	CAR
Municipal & Planning Law Reports (2d) (LR) 1976–	X	QL	R	S+C	X	X	X	B	CAR
Ontario Municipal Board Reports (LR) 1973–	—	—	R	—	—	—	—	I	CLB
Ontario Real Estate Law Guide (LLF) (current)	X	—	U	—	—	—	X	L	CCH
Personal Property Security Act Cases (LR) 1977–	X	—	R	S+C	X	X	X	B	CAR
Real Property Reports (2d) (LR) 1977–	X	QL	R	S+C	X	X	X	B	CAR

10. Chart J: Subject — Tax

TITLE (TYPE) YEAR-	CUM INDEX	ELECTRONIC SOURCES	REPT UNRP	STAT CASE	WORD + PH	2nd LIT	ANNO + ART	HOW USE	PUB
Alberta, NWT, & Yukon Tax Reporter (LLF) (current)	X	CD	U	—	—	—	X	L	CCH
B.C. Tax Reporter (LLF) (current)	X	CD	U	—	—	—	X	L	CCH
Canadian GST Cases (LR) 1992–	X	—	U	S	—	—	X	—	CAR
Canada Tax Cases (LR) 1917–	X	—	R	S+C	X	—	X	—	CAR
Canada Tax Service (LLF) (current)	X	—	U	—	—	—	X	—	CAR
Canadian GST & Commodity Tax Cases (LR)	X	—	R	S	—	—	X	L	CCH
Canadian Goods & Services Tax Reporter (LLF) (current)	X	—	U	—	—	—	X	L	CCH
Canadian Tax Reporter (LLF) (current)	X	CD	U	—	—	—	X	L	CCH
Dominion Tax Cases (LR) 1920–	X	CD QL	R	S+C	X	X	X	L	CCH
Manitoba & Saskatchewan Tax Reporter (LLF) (current)	X	CD	U	—	—	—	X	L	CCH
Maritimes Tax Reporter (LLF) (current)	X	CD	U	—	—	—	X	L	CCH
Ontario Tax Reporter (LLF) (current)	X	CD	U	—	—	—	X	L	CCH
Quebec Tax Reporter (LLF) (current)	X	CD	U	—	—	—	X	L	CCH

11. Chart K: Subject — Miscellaneous

TITLE (TYPE) YEAR-	CUM INDEX	ELECTRONIC SOURCES	REPT UNRP	STAT CASE	WORD + PH	2nd LIT	ANNO + ART	HOW USE	PUB
Administrative Law Reports (2d) (LR) 1983–	X	QL	R	S+C	X	X	X	B	CAR
Apportionment of Liablity in B.C. (D) (current)	X	—	U	—	—	—	—	—	BTR
Canada Energy Law Service (current)	See Environmental								
Canadian Health Facilities Law Guide (LLF) (current)	X	—	U	—	—	—	X	L	CCH
Canadian Bankruptcy Reports (3d) 1960–	See Business								
Canadian Cases on the Law of Insurance (2d) 1983–	See Business								
Canadian Cases on the Law of Torts (2d) (LR) 1976–	X	QL	R	S+C	X	X	X	B	CAR
Canadian Insurance Law Reporter (current)	See Business								
Canadian Intellectual Property Reports 1984–1990	See Business								
Canadian Product Safety Guide (out of print)									
Canadian Securities Law Reporter (current)	*See Business*								
Carswell's Practice Cases (3d) (LR) 1976–	X	QL	R	S+C	X	X	X	B	CAR
Chitty's Law Journal (JNL) 1950–	X	—	U	—	—	—	X	—	13
Construction Law Reports 1983–	See Business								
Copyright Appeal Board Reports (LR) 1936–1989									CAR
Note: not yet published at time of writing									
Copyright Board Reports (LR) 1990–1994	X	—	R	S	—	—	—	C	CAR
Court Martial Appeal Reports 1957–	—	QL	—	C	—	—	—	—	4
Damages for Personal Injury and Death (D) 1935–	X	CD	U	—	—	—	—	—	CAR

11. Chart K: Subject — Miscellaneous — *Continued*

TITLE (TYPE) YEAR-	CUM INDEX	ELECTRONIC SOURCES	REPT UNRP	STAT CASE	WORD + PH	2nd LIT	ANNO + ART	HOW USE	PUB
Health Law Cases (D) 1880–	—	QL	—	—	—	—	—	—	15
Legal Medical Quarterly (JNL) 1977–	X	—	U	—	—	—	X	—	13
Motor Vehicle Reports 1979–	See Criminal Law								
Ontario Accident Benefit Summaries (D) 1991–	X	—	U	—	—	—	—	—	CCH
Ontario Health and Safety Law... with Digest of Cases (D)	X	—	U	S	—	—	—	—	CLB
Personal Injury Damage Assessments in Alberta	X	—	U	—	—	—	—	—	BTR
Personal Injury Damage Assessments in B.C.	X	—	U	—	—	—	—	—	BTR
Weekly Digest of Civil Procedure (D) 1985–	X	—	U	S+C	X	—	X	C	CAR

12. Chart L: Coverage of Board and Tribunal Decisions

Administrative boards and tribunals act in a quasi-judicial manner when rendering decisions. Under various subject categories below, publications are listed with the boards covered. This chart lists English language publications, while more board decision services are described in Chart M, Québec Digests. One of the most convenient means of access is through the many online databases now covering administrative boards. Many federal boards are included on the following list. Many do not offer their decisions on their Internet sites at time of writing, but may add this service at any time. Check the following Internet site: (http://canada.gc.ca/depts/major/depind_e.html).

The format for the chart below is:

(a) General publications
Publication Title Electronic availability

(b) Specific Boards and/or jurisdictions
Name of Board or single source Elcovering that Board and/or publication

Business/Commerce

(a) General publications

Canadian Cases on the Law of Securities (Carswell)	QL
Canadian Patent Reporter (Canada Law Book)	LEXIS-NEXIS, QL
Canadian Regulatory Reporter (1980-1987)	QL
Canadian Securities Law Reporter (CCH)	CD-ROM
Intellectual Property Reports (Carswell)	
McCarthy Tetrault Regulatory Reporter	QL
Trade and Tariff Reports (Butterworths)	LEXIS-NEXIS

(b) Specific Boards and/or jurisdictions

(i) Business generally

B.C. Commercial Appeals Commission	QL (1975-)
B.C. Liquor Appeal Board	QL (1978-)
Canada Competition Tribunal www.ct-tc.gc.ca	QL (1986-)
Ontario Commercial Registration Appeals Tribunal	QL (1994-)
Ontario Liquor Licence Board	QL (1994-)
Procurement Review Board of Canada	QL (1990-)

(ii) Insurance

Ontario Insurance Commission	QL (1991-)

(iii) Patents, Intellectual Property

Copyright Board Reports (Carswell)	QL (1990-)
Copyright Appeal Board Reports (Carswell)	
Trade Marks Opposition Board	QL, C.P.R., I.P.R.

(iv) Transportation/Customs/Trade

Canada Civil Aviation Tribunal	QL (1986-)
Canadian Import Tribunal	QL (1984-1988)
Canadian International Trade Tribunal (www.citt.gc.ca.menu_e.htm)	QL (1989-)
NAFTA Panel	QL, LEXIS-NEXIS
Tariff Board Reports (1937-1989)	QL (1937-1987)
Transport Commission	C.T.C.
U.S.-Canada Free Trade Agreement Panel	QL, LEXIS-NEXIS

(v) Securities Law

Alberta Securities Commission	QL (1996-)
B.C. Securities Commission (www.bcse.gov.bc.ca/new_inside.htm)	QL (1987-)
Ontario Securities Commission	QL (1983-), *O.S.C. Bulletin*

(vi) Telecommunications

CRTC	
McCarthy Tetrault Regulatory Reporter, Canadian Regulatory Reporter	QL (1980-)

CD-ROM: "Info CRTC" (1984-) available from Micromedia Ltd., Toronto
Internet site: www.crtc.gc.ca/eng/english.htm.

Environmental Law/Natural Resources

(a) General publications

Canadian Environmental Law Reports (N.S.) (Carswell).
Canada Energy Law Service (Carswell).

(b) Specific Boards

Alberta Energy and Utilities Board	*Canada Energy Law Service*
Alberta Environmental Appeal Board	QL (1994-)
Atomic Energy Control Board (http/ulysses.srv.gc.ca/aecb/docs/reporter/ecover.htm)	

British Columbia Environmental Appeal Board (www.eab.gov.bc.ca)	QL (1992-)
British Columbia Environmental Protection Compendium Appeal Decisions *Waste Management Act* (www.env.gov.bc.ca./epd/cpr/appeal.html)	
Environmental Assessment Board of Ontario (gopher://govonca.gov.on.ca/11/env/decision)	
National Energy Board	*Canada Energy Law Service*
Ontario Environmental Appeal Board	QL (1974-)

Human Rights

(a) General publications

Canadian Human Rights Reporter	
Canadian Rights Reporter	LEXIS-NEXIS
Canadian Native Law Reporter	
Immigration Law Reporter (2d)	CD-ROM, QL

(b) Specific Boards

Canadian Human Rights Tribunal	QL (1986-)
Convention Refugee Determination Division	QL (1989-)
Immigration Appeal Division	QL (1983-), I.L.R. (2d)
Indian Claims Commission (www.indianclaims.ca/english/pub/pub.htm)	
New Brunswick Human Rights Boards of Inquiry	QL (1974-)
Newfoundland Human Rights Boards of Inquiry	QL (1988-)
Nova Scotia Human Rights Boards of Inquiry	QL (1991-)
Ontario Board of Inquiry (Human Rights Code)	QL (1996-)

Labour/Employment

(a) General publications

B.C. Decisions, Labour Arbitration	QL (1982-), CD-ROM (Western Legal Publications (WLP))
Canadian Employment Benefits & Pension Guide (CCH)	
Canadian Labour Law Reporter (CCH)	
Canadian Labour Relations Boards Reports (Butterworths)	LEXIS-NEXIS

Labour Arbitration Cases and *Canadian Labour Arbitration Summaries* (Canada Law Book)	QL, LEXIS-NEXIS

(b) Specific Boards and/or jurisdictions

Alberta Grievance Arbitration Awards index	QL (1970-)
Alberta Labour Relations Board Decisions index (www.gov.ab.ca/~alrb/Decisions/DecisionsOpening.html)	QL (1952-)
B.C. Collective Agreement Arbitration Awards	QL (1996-)
B.C. Employment Standards Tribunal Decisions	WLP (and CD-ROM), QL
B.C. Labour Relations Board Decisions	WLP (and CD-ROM), QL
B.C., Workers' Compensation Board of,	*Workers' Compensation Reporter* (1973)
Canada Labour Relations Board Reports	Butterworths, QL, LEXIS-NEXIS
Canada Pension Review Board	*Pension Review Board Reports*
Canada Post Labour Arbitration Summaries	QL (1997-)
Canada Public Service Staff Relations Board	*Public Service Staff Relations Reports*, QL (1984-)
Canadian Artists and Producers Professional Relations Tribunal (homer.ic.gc.ca./capprt_e.html)	QL (1995-)
Manitoba Grievance Arbitration Decisions	QL (1993-)
Manitoba Labour Board Decisions	QL (1975-)
New Brunswick Employment Standards Decisions	QL (1986-1995)
New Brunswick Industrial Relations Board Decisions	QL (1973-1995)
New Brunswick Labour & Employment Board Decisions	QL (1994-)
Newfoundland Labour Relations Board Decisions	QL (1994-)
Ontario Employment Standards Decisions	QL (1990-)
Ontario Labour Relations Board Reports	QL (1959-)
Ontario Occupational Health & Safety Adjudication Decisions	QL (1994-)
Ontario Pay Equity Decisions	QL (1989-)
Ontario Workers' Compensation Appeals Tribunal	*Workers' Compensation Appeals Tribunal Reporter*
Saskatchewan Labour Relations Board Decisions	QL (1988-)
Unemployment Insurance Act - Umpire Decisions	*Decisions of the Umpire*

Property/Municipal

(a) General publications

Land Compensation Reports (Canada Law Book)
Municipal and Planning Law Reports (2d) (Carswell) QL (1986-)
Municipal Law Digest (Carswell)

(b) Specific Boards and/or jurisdictions

B.C. Assessment Appeal Board, Major Decisions	
Nova Scotia Utility and Review Board	QL (1993-)
Ontario Municipal Board Reports (Canada Law Book)	QL (1989-)

Miscellaneous

B.C. Information & Privacy Commissioner (http://oipcbc.org/)	QL (1994-)
Law Societies Discipline Decisions	QL (1991-)
Ontario Information and Privacy Commissioner	QL (1988-)
Ontario College of Physicians and Surgeons	QL (1992-)

13. Chart M: Québec Digests and Board/Tribunal Decisions

Below are listed Québec digests with brief annotations. The titles are those listed in the Canadian Law Information Council's *A Guide to Purchasing Law Reports* (1985) written by Doug MacEllven, Guy Tanguay, and Lorna Rees-Potter (Québec portion by Professor Tanguay). Research methods for using Québec materials are discussed in Chapter 12, Researching Québec Law. Many are available electronically, as indicated.

(a) Digests

Annuaire de jurisprudence du Québec (1935-)	This comprehensive digest arranges summaries under more than 60 areas of law, and digests cases from all of Québec's general law reports series and many specialized series. The Annuaire prints all digests in the issues of *Jurisprudence express* which may be discarded upon appearance of the new Annuaire volume.

Electronic sources: Since 1977, available in EXPRESS database (SOQUIJ).

Arbitrage — Sante et services soiaux (1983-)

Arbitration decisions are digested dealing with the establishments in the Québec social affairs system. The related law reports series is *Sentences arbitrales de l'Association des hôpitaux du Québec.*
Electronic sources: SOQUIJ (1983-).

Droit du travail express (1982-)

This comprehensive labour law digest annually summarizes approximately 1,000 cases from courts and tribunals.
Electronic sources: SOQUIJ (1982-).

Droit fiscal québécois express (1978-)

Digests of all court cases dealing with Québec taxation are included plus some tribunal decisions. The related law reports series is *Recueil de droit fiscal québécois.*
Electronic sources: Summaries available in EXPRESS database (SOQUIJ).

Fiscalité québécoise

This looseleaf reporter service on Québec taxation provides rapid digests of court cases.

Jurisprudence express (1977-)

This digest is published weekly as an update to the Annuaire and more than one-third of the cases are later reported in the *Recueils de jurisprudence du Québec* series. A microfiche edition with the full text of the judgments is available after a time lag of several weeks following the daily issue.
Electronic sources: Part of EXPRESS database (SOQUIJ) (1977-).

Jurisprudence logement (1982-)

This publication digests cases dealing with housing and landlord-tenant issues.
Electronic sources: Part of EXPRESS database (SOQUIJ) (1992-).

La Presse juridique (1993-)

Since 1993, this weekly has covered many cases from various courts in Québec. It is published as a bound volume at the end of the year.

	Electronic sources: Available as a database on QUICKLAW (LPJ).
Répertoire de jurisprudence: transport réglementé au Québec (1979-)	This digest covers transportation issues relating to the *Québec Transport Act* and the Commission of Transportation for Québec.
Résumés de sentences arbitrales (1983-)	These arbitration decisions relate to dismissal of non-unionized employees.
Résumés de jurisprudence pénale du Québec (1983-)	This is a criminal law digesting service.

(b) Board/Tribunal Decisions

Ease of access to decisions by Québec boards/tribunals varies enormously from one board to another. Board decisions can be grouped into the following categories (arranged by decreasing ease of access or use):

(i) Boards with published series of decisions and corresponding databases, usually available through SOQUIJ, such as labour, taxation, social aid, access to information, and human rights boards.
(ii) Boards without published series but offering databases of all their decisions. Many decisions are offered through *les Publications du Québec* as a stand-alone electronic product, such as education, police, and municipalities, *etc*.
(iii) Boards whose decisions are better available through a private specialized service: *i.e.*, securities, tax courts, *etc*.
(iv) Boards whose decisions are not published but are available under the various *Access to Information Statutes*.

Examples of Board and Tribunal Decision print-form sources are:

(i) *Decisions de la Commission des affaires sociales* (1975-).
(ii) *Decisions disciplinaires concernant les corporations professionnelles* (1974–).
(iii) *Decisions du Tribunal d'arbitrage* (1982-).
(iv) *Jurisprudence en sante et securite du travail* (1981-).
(v) *Recueil de decisions de la Commission des relations de travail dans la fonction publique* (1984-).
(vi) *Recueil des decisions du Bureau de revisions de l'evaluation fonciere du Québec* (1985-).
(vii) *Recueil des ordonnances de la Regie des services publics* (1970).
(viii) *Recueil des sentences de l'education; Greffe des tribunaux d'arbitrage du secteur de l'education* (1970-).
(ix) *Sentences arbitrales de l'Association des hopitaux du Québec* (1967-).
(x) *Recueil de sentences arbitrales* (1982-).

(xi) *Tribunal de l'expropriation; recueil de jurisprudence* (1972-1985).
(xii) Commission d'access a l'information
(xiii) *Bureau de revison paritaires* (1985-) and *Decisions de la Commissions d'appel en Matières de lesions professionnelles* (1986-)
(xiv) Both bodies concerned with health and safety at work.

C. SPECIFIC DIGESTS AND INDEXES: INSTRUCTIONS ON USE AND ILLUSTRATIONS

Because a particular publisher's digests or indexes may use the same classification scheme of topics and key word terminology, instructions and illustrations are given for representative titles rather than for each digest or index. Not all digests and indexes are illustrated by a representative title because some resemble the standard looseleaf textbook format or newsletter/journal format with the expected table of contents and index as main research features. Below are listed the representative titles demonstrated and the purpose for demonstrating each title.

Examples demonstrated

Example A, *Alberta Reports*
Purpose: Maritime Law Book Ltd.'s Keyword Index to Topics and Topical Index Scheme. These digests and indexes are part of Maritime's federal and provincial law reports.

Example B, *Alberta Law Reports* (2d) & (3d)
Purpose: Carswell's consolidated/cumulative law report key word indexes. These indexes are part of Carswell's provincial law reports, W.W.R., and special subject law reports (*e.g.*, *Criminal Reports*).

Example C, *Alberta Weekly Law Digest*
Purpose: Carswell's rapid digesting services. These rapid services update some of Carswell's provincial and special subject law reports.

Example D, *Alberta Decisions*
Purpose: Western Legal Publications' rapid digesting services. These federal and provincial (mostly Western) services provide updates for other publishers' federal and provincial law reports.

Example E, *Canadian Weekly Law Sheet*
Purpose: Butterworths' comprehensive digesting service for all law reports. This is particularly good for an overview of cases currently selected for law reports publication.

Example F, *Lawyers Weekly*
Purpose: Butterworths' comprehensive rapid digesting service which publishes an annual *Consolidated Digest* including law reports' cites.

Example G, *Canadian Abridgment Revised* (2nd)
Purpose: Carswell's comprehensive, over 100 volume "research system" providing all reported case digests from the early 1800s to-date, statute and case citators, secondary legal literature indexes, legislation trackers, and words and phrases.

Example H, *Canadian Current Law*
Purpose: An update to Carswell's *Canadian Abridgment* (2nd)

Example I, *Dominion Law Reports* and *Canadian Criminal Cases*
Purpose: Canada Law Book's index classification scheme concept. This index concept is now used for all of Canada Law Book's law reports (D.L.R. plus special subject reports such as C.C.C.).

Example J, *All-Canada Weekly Summaries* and *Weekly Criminal Bulletin*
Purpose: Canada Law Book's rapid digesting services to update D.L.R. and C.C.C. using the same index classification schemes as D.L.R. and C.C.C.

Example K, *Supreme Court of Canada Report Service*
Purpose: Butterworths' specialized digesting service for the Supreme Court of Canada.

Example L, *Canadian Family Law Guide*
Purpose: CCH Canadian Ltd. publishes many special subject looseleaf services with case coverage.

1. Example A: Alberta Reports

(a) Publisher:

Maritime Law Book Ltd.

Note: This is the only law publisher which makes available all of its print-form law reports in four electronic formats (diskette, online database, CD-ROM, and the Internet), and which has some law report titles produced only in electronic format. See subsection (e), Electronic sources.

(b) Other Maritime Law Book titles using the same digesting/indexing scheme:

National Reporter, Federal Trial Reports, New Brunswick Reports (Second Series), New Brunswick Reports Second Supplement, Nova Scotia Reports [1965-1969], Nova Scotia Reports (Second Series), Newfoundland and Prince Edward Island Reports, Manitoba Reports (Second Series), Saskatchewan Reports, Yukon Reports [1987-1989], Ontario Appeal Cases, British Columbia Appeal Cases, British Columbia Trial Cases Unedited, Québec Appeal Cases, Western Appeal Cases, and *Atlantic Provinces Reports.*

(c) Essential characteristics:

(i) Reported/Unreported:

The index and digests form part of these law reports; hence, the digesting is of reported cases. The advantage is that before the appearance of these provincial reports, a relatively low percentage of cases was reported from all court levels of these provinces; but now Maritime Law Book publishes more cases from the individual provinces to give researchers an opportunity to decide which cases are significant.

(ii) Scope of coverage:

The *National Reporter* reports and digests all Supreme Court of Canada and selected Federal Court of Appeal cases. The provincial reports cover civil and criminal matters by reporting all cases from a province's highest appellate court level and a large percentage from intermediate and lower court levels.

(iii) Frequency:

The reports issue weekly or biweekly paper loose parts. Reporting of cases in the *National Reporter* may be several months in advance of S.C.R, and F.C.R. Each loose part and volume has an index and digest; separate index/digest volumes covering ten volumes of each report series are issued. Note that *Atlantic Provinces Reports* are in bound volume form only (no paper loose parts) and reproduce most cases from N.B.R. (2d), N.S.R. (2d), and Nfld. and P.E.I.R.

(iv) Other features:

These report volumes and index/digest volumes contain:

(A) Tables of cases ("Index to Cases Reported"). Cumulations covering more than ten volumes are issued.

(B) Case citators ("Index to Cases Judicially Noticed") — *i.e.*, cases from any source that have been commented upon by cases in these Maritime Law Book reports.

(C) Statute citators ("Index to Statutes Judicially Noticed").

(D) Secondary literature cited ("Index to Authors and Works Judicially Noticed").

(E) "Words and Phrases Noticed".

(d) Instructions for use:

Finding case law is a three-step process (from index to digest to the case), except for the researcher familiar with the broad topic scheme who can go directly to the digest and then to the case.

STEP 1: Turn to the index of the volume (either a reports volume or index/ digest volume) which is designated as "KEY WORD INDEX TO TOPICS".

(i) After selecting key words from the framing of the legal issue, search for these key words in the index, KEY WORD INDEX TO TOPICS — see Illustration 2.

(ii) Each grouping of key words (*e.g.*, FAMILY LAW and subtopic number 1910) refers to the section in the digest (Topical Index in Step 2 below) that contains digests of cases relating to the key word.

(iii) Note that, in its indexes, Maritime Law Book uses key words that are taken from the case headnotes, as well as additional key words for greater access. In other words, a case headnote may use the phrase "escaping lawful custody" but the index's key words may additionally include "jailbreak" and "prison escape". Usually, indexes are limited to words and phrases found only in the headnotes.

STEP 2: Turn to the digest section ("Topical Index") cited with key words found in the index. That is, after finding custody, appeals, children, *etc.* in the index, turn to the TOPICAL INDEX (the digest section) — see Illustration 3.

(i) The TOPICAL INDEX Is divided into 125 major digest sections, beginning with "Actions" and ending with "Workers' Compensation". In this example, the researcher would turn to section "Family Law — Topical Index".

(ii) Each subdivision is assigned a Key Number (*e.g.,* 1910), which means that the topic "Family Law" has been assigned several hundred subtopics. The entire subtopic numbering scheme for "Family Law" allows for future subtopics by spreading the several hundred existing subtopics over 6,800 key numbers. For example, a portion of the existing sequence is:

Family Law1895 Changing child's residence
1910 Appeals, general
1940 Variation of custody and access rights, general
1941 Circumstances when applications can be made
1943 Persons entitled to apply

(iii) In each "Digests and Indexes" volume (covering ten volumes of reports), the "Topical Index" has a complete listing of present topics and key numbers (see Illustration 4). Researchers familiar with the topics and key numbers may scan the listings to find the subtopic of relevance, read the digest within the subtopic, and then fully read cited cases that appear on point, rather than beginning with the Key Word Index (Step 1).

ILLUSTRATION 2
Alberta Reports "Digest and Indexes" — Volumes 1 to 10

[STEP 1 — multiple keyword access points in "Key Word Index to Topics" leading to the topic, "Family Law 1910".]

[Page 170]

Appeals, custody of children – FAMILY LAW 4071.
Appeals, custody of children, variation of custody order on appeal – FAMILY LAW 1910.
Appeals, discipline for professional mis-
MINERALS 6144-
Appeals, juvenile delinquents, jurisdiction – CRIMINAL LAW 8882.
Appeals, leave to appeal, application for leave to appeal, form of application – PRACTICE 8871.

[Page 181]

Chattel mortages, effect of late registration of prior rights of unsecured creditors – CHATTEL MORTGAGES 2240.
Chattel mortgages, insurance proceeds, equitable assignment – CHOSES IN ACTION 363.
Children, custody, paramountcy of federal statutes, overlapping legislation – CONSTITUTIONAL LAW 3620.
Children, custody, variation of custody order on appeal – FAMILY LAW 1910.
Children, illegitimate, custody of, by

[Page 199]

ministerial acts – CROWN 2446.
Crown, reservation to, from grant of land, effect of certificate of title on - REAL PROPERTY 8015.
Crown, statutes affecting the Crown, application by necessary implication, whether provincial Crown subject to
Custody of children, paramountcy of federal statutes, overlapping legislation – CONSTITUTIONAL LAW 3620.
Custody of children, variation of custody order on appeal -FAMILY LAW 1910.
Custom, implied terms, contracts – CONTRACTS 2084.

[Page 216]

Family law, custody, paramountcy of federal statutes, overlapping legislation – CONSTITUTIONAL LAW 3620.
Family law, custody, tender years doctrine – FAMILY LAW 1884.
Family law, custody, variation of custody order on appeal – FAMILY LAW 1910.
Family law, dependents relief legisla-
maintenance, effect of a separation agreement – FAMILY LAW 4006.
Family law, divorce, corollary relief, maintenance, enforcement of payment of arrears – FAMILY LAW 4050.
Family law, divorce, corollary relief, maintenance, jurisdiction of courts – FAMILY LAW 4001.

STEP 3: After reading the digests, turn to cases which seem relevant for full study.

(e) Electronic sources or transferring research to other publications:

Maritime Law Book's editors always assign the same key number to a specific point of law no matter which report series contains the point of law. In other words, cases containing the legal concept denoted by "Family Law 1910" will have that key number assigned whether the case is in the *Alberta Reports* or *National Reporter*. Therefore, once a relevant key number has been found, search for similar cases by:

ILLUSTRATION 3
Alberta Reports "Digest and Indexes" — Volumes 1 to 10, page 541

[STEP 2 — locating a case digest under "Family Law — Topic 1910" in the "Topical Index".]

CUSTODY AND ACCESS TO CHILDREN
(1801-2200)
(continued)

FAMILY LAW – TOPIC 1889 (cont'd)
parents as guardians with generous access to the mother – Banks v Banks, 6 A.R. 421.

FAMILY LAW – TOPIC 1891
– Custody of Children – Considerations in awarding custody – Conduct of parent – Following a divorce a husband and wife both claimed custody of a 3 year old girl – The Alberta Supreme Court, Trial Division awarded custody of the girl to the father – The Trial Division stated that the evidence demonstrated "a more steadfast dedication (by the father) to the child's interests above his own than has the mother" (see paragraph 44) – B. v. B., 10 A.R. 181.

FAMILY LAW – TOPIC 1910
- Custody of children – Appeals – The Supreme Court of Canada stated that the question of the custody of an infant is a matter which peculiarly lies within the jurisdiction of the trial judge and an appeal court should not interfere unless the trial judge has clearly acted on a wrong principle or disregarded some material evidence – See paragraph 5 – Adams and Adams v. McLeod and Ramstead, 9 A.R. 1.

FAMILY LAW – TOPIC 2010
– Custody and access to children – Access - Access awards – Time limitations – Following a divorce the custody of a 9 year old boy was awarded to the boy's mother – The Alberta Supreme Court, Trial Division specified in detail the father's access or visitation rights with respect to the boy – McMillan v. McMillan, 9 A.R. 560.

FAMILY LAW – TOPIC 2095
– Custody and access – The hearing – Counsel – Representation of child's interests – The Alberta Supreme Court, Trial Division, appointed amicus curiae to represent the interests of the children in the custody aspects of a divorce hearing – The Trial Division expressed the value of having the children's interests objectively represented and noted the difficulty of even well-meaning parents to be objective about the interests of children in such circumstances – See paragraphs 1 to 3 – Copithorne v. Copithorne, 2 A.R. 431.

FAMILY LAW – TOPIC 2122
– Custody of children – Jurisdiction – Where custody order previously made in another jurisdiction – A father and mother living in Nova Scotia separated – The mother took the children with her to Alberta, where she obtained an order for custody in proceedings in which the father did not participate – At the same time the father brought an uncontested

---

(i) Examining the "Topical Index" sections in each "Digest and Indexes" volume of the other Maritime Law Book law report series (one volume for each ten volumes of reports). For example, in each volume turn directly to "Family Law 1910" to see if there are any digests.

(ii) Examining "Topical Index" sections of each individual report volume appearing after the latest "Digest and Indexes" volume (may be more than ten volumes, because of the time required to prepare such a consolidated "Digest and Indexes" volume).

ILLUSTRATION 4
National Reporter "Digest and Indexes", Volumes 11 to 20, page 500

[Listings of headings and sub-headings with topic numbers at beginning of the topic "Family Law" in the "Topical Index" section. Individual case digests are arranged under each heading as shown in Illustration 3.]

CAVEAT: The sub-headings and key numbers listed below are not intended to be exhaustive. Additional sub-headings and key numbers will be added as required in the future. The editors suggest that a searcher start with the KEY WORD INDEX unless the searcher knows which one of our numbered topic headings carries the searcher's point of law.

Summary of Headings

GENERAL PRINCIPLES (1 – 20)

MARRIAGE (150 – 350)

HUSBAND AND WIFE (600 – 999)

ADOPTION (1400 – 1800)

CUSTODY AND ACCESS TO CHILDREN (1801 – 2200)

MAINTENANCE OF WIVES AND CHILDREN (2201 – 2600)

SEPARATION AGREEMENTS (3201 – 3400)

DIVORCE (3500 – 4500)

MAINTENANCE OF WIVES, ALIMONY (4501 – 4800)

ANNULMENT OF MARRIAGE (6000 – 6200)

DEPENDENTS' RELIEF LEGISLATION (6600 – 6800)

GENERAL PRINCIPLES (1 – 20)

MARRIAGE (150 – 350)

General (150 – 165)

Prohibited marriages (166 - 180)
166 General
169 Blood relatives

HUSBAND AND WIFE (600 – 999)

General (600 – 620)

Property rights during marriage (621 – 670)

621 General
623 Transfers by husband to wife, generally
625 Title to property acquired by joint contribution or joint effort.

(iii) Maritime Law Book Ltd. publications are generally available in the following electronic versions:

(A) CD-ROMs available from the publisher in full text, full text topical case law covering seven areas of practice, easy search digests (with citations for cases listed under key numbers), and a headnote service.

(B) Online database format from LEXIS-NEXIS, and Chicago-Kent College of Law (USA).

(C) The Internet (www.mlb.nb.ca).
(D) Diskette form (MS-DOS or Windows).

Note: The following two law report titles are produced only in electronic format: *British Columbia Trial Cases Unedited* (1997-), and all cases from the British Columbia Supreme Court, without headnotes. In the *New Brunswick Reports* (2nd Supp.)(1997-), untranslated decisions are not reported in print.

2. Example B: Alberta Law Reports (Second and Third Series)

(a) Publisher:

Carswell Legal Publications

(b) Other Carswell law reports using the same digesting/indexing scheme:

Western Weekly Reports, *British Columbia Law Reports* (2d), and *Northwest Territories Reports*. *Western Weekly Digests* (1975-76) was the forerunner of Alta. L.R. (2d) and B.C.L.R. The special subject reports (*e.g.*, *Reports of Family Law)* also use this scheme:

Administrative Law Reports, Business Law Reports (Second Series), Canadian Bankruptcy Reports (Third Series), Canadian Cases on Employment Law, Canadian Cases on Pensions & Benefits, Canadian Cases on the Law of Insurance (Second Series), Canadian Cases on the Law of Securities, Canadian Cases on the Law of Torts (Second Series), Canadian Environmental Law Reports (New Series), Canadian Occupational Health & Safety Cases (1988-1995), Carswell's Practice Cases (Third Series), Construction Law Reports, Criminal Reports (Fourth Series), Estates and Trusts Reports, Immigration Law Reporter (Second Series), Motor Vehicle Reports (Second Series), Municipal and Planning Law Reports (Second Series), Real Property Reports (Second Series), Reports of Family Law (Third Series).

(c) Essential characteristics:

(i) Reported/Unreported:

The indexing and digests form part of these law reports; therefore, the digesting is of reported cases. The advantage is that Carswell's editors screen cases to determine which are significant for setting new law or serving as valuable illustration of existing law. The editors provide researchers only with cases that are considered significant, while digest access to unreported cases is provided by the advance digesting services noted below:

Law Reports	Advance Digest
Alta. L.R. (3d)	*Alberta Weekly Law Digest*
B.C.L.R. (2d)	*B.C. Weekly Law Digest*

M.P.L.R. (2d)	*Digest of Municipal and Planning Law*
R.P.R. (2d)	*Digest of Real Property Law* (discontinued)
C.P.C. (3d)	*Weekly Digest of Civil Procedure*
R.F.L. (3d)	*Weekly Digest of Family Law*
C.I.P.R. (1984-1990)	*Digest of Canadian Intellectual Property Law* (1990-1992)
C.E.L.R. (N.S.)	*Digest of Environmental Law & Environmental Assessment*

(ii) Scope of coverage:

The W.W.R.'s cover civil and some criminal cases that are considered to be of importance to all practitioners in the western provinces. The Alta. L.R. (3d) and B.C.L.R. (2d) present cases that are of particular interest to practitioners in those provinces. The special subject law reports select significant cases for full reporting, while the advance digest services provide comprehensive coverage. Cases of significance from all court levels are included.

(iii) Frequency:

The reports issue weekly (W.W.R.) or biweekly (Alta. L.R. (3d) and B.C.L.R. (2d)) paper loose parts. Each loose part and volume has a key worded index, and there are cumulative indexes for the publications.

(iv) Other features:

These report volumes and index volumes contain:

(A) Tables of cases ("Cases Reported") ("Cases Unreported")
(B) Case citators ("Cases Considered")
(C) Statute and rules citators ("Statutes Considered")
(D) Secondary literature cited ("Authorities Considered")
(E) "Words and Phrases Considered"

(d) Instructions for use:

Finding a case is a two-step process (from index to the case).

STEP 1: Turn to the index of the volume (either the report volume or cumulative index volume).

(i) After selecting key words from the legal issue, search for these key words in the index. See Illustration 5.
(ii) Note that the indexing is detailed enough to provide a brief digest of the case, but key words or key phrases are used rather than full sentences. Cases may be accessed by entry of the case under several of these key words or key phrases throughout the index (*e.g.*, the brief digest appearing alphabetically under "infants and children" and under "custody").
(iii) The "Cumulative Index" has an alphabetical listing of major key word topics used in the index. It appears at the front of the publication and

serves as a table of contents for easy scanning. A separate cumulative index volume is published annually, more or less.

STEP 2: The case citation is provided with each brief digest, and the researcher may turn directly to the page to read the full headnote.

Alternative procedure: If searching by *Canadian Abridgment* classification number, turn to the portion of each reports volume or cumulative index titled "Canadian Abridgment (2nd) classification".

(e) Electronic sources or transferring research to other publications:

Carswell's editors assign *Canadian Abridgment* classification numbers to each headnote, and those classification numbers are printed after the headnote for each case. Use the classification number to go directly to the *Canadian Abridgment* (2nd) and *Canadian Current Law* as well as to other law report volumes published by Carswell. Carswell's CD-ROM service "LawSource" is an enhancement of the contents of the *Canadian Abridgment Revised* (2nd), with separate *Abridgment* modules being added over several years. The "LawSource" product, "The Canada Reporter" collection, contains over 225,000 full-text cases. Carswell's law reports and *Canadian Abridgment Revised* (2nd) digests are available in online database format from QL Systems Ltd.

3. Example C: Alberta Weekly Law Digest

(a) Publisher:

Carswell Legal Publications

(b) Related publications:

The same indexing scheme is used in other advance digesting services for Carswell's law reports. See the following listing for relation between Carswell's advance digesting services and law reports:

Law Reports	*Advance Digest*
Alta. L.R. (3d)	*Alberta Weekly Law Digest*
B.C.L.R. (2d)	*B.C. Weekly Law Digest*
M.P.L.R. (2d)	*Digest of Municipal and Planning Law*
R.P.R. (2d)	*Digest of Real Property Law* (discontinued)
C.P.C. (3d)	*Weekly Digest of Civil Procedure*
R.F.L. (3d)	*Weekly Digest of Family Law*
C.I.P.R. (1984-1990)	*Digest of Canadian Intellectual Property Law* (1990-1992)

ILLUSTRATION 5

Alberta Law Reports (Second Series) "Cumulative Index Volumes 1-11"

[Cite is to volume and page in A.L.R. (2d).]

[Page 63]

CUSTODY — Infants and children — Jurisdiction and procedure — Wardship — Extension of wardship — Temporary wardship order — Duration — No authority in Director of Child Welfare to retain custody in absence of current wardship order.
Homenko v. Minister of Social Dev. of Alta.. ....(1977) 1-104 (T.D.)

CUSTODY — Infants and children — Welfare of child — Grandmother applying — Custody given to grandmother — Best interests of the infant considered.
Lawrence v. Lawrence. ....(1978) 5-231 (Fam. Ct.)

CUSTODY — Infants and children — Welfare of child — Guardianship of baby granted to niece and nephew of infant's father — Order reversed on appeal — Further appeal allowed — Infant's interest considered foremost — No mistake of law by trial judge awarding guardianship — His decision affirmed.
Adams v. McLeod. ....(1978) 5-391 (S.C.C.)

[Page 92]

Grandmother applying — Custody given to grandmother — Best interests of the infant considered.
Lawrence v. Lawrence. .... (1978) 5-231 (Fam. Ct.)

INFANTS AND CHILDREN — Custody — Welfare of child — Guardianship of baby granted to niece and nephew of infant's father — Order reversed on appeal — Further appeal allowed — Infant's interest considered foremost — No mistakes of law by trial judge awarding guardianship — His decision afirmed.
Adams v. McLeod. .... (1978) 5-391 (S.C.C.)

C.E.L.R. (N.S.) *Digest of Environmental Law & Environmental Assessment*

(c) Essential characteristics:

(i) Reported/Unreported:

This is designed to be a very rapidly produced digest, published upon receipt of judgments by Carswell. Many of the cases will remain unreported, with some selected for subsequent full reporting in Carswell's law reports.

(ii) Scope of coverage:

The service commenced in 1982 and covers all court levels. The other Carswell advance services also began in the 1980s.

(iii) Frequency:

Mailings are made weekly.

(iv) Other features:

(A) Table of cases

These digests include cumulating Tables of Cases for the year.

(d) Instructions for use:

The digests are arranged under fairly detailed topic headings based upon the *Canadian Abridgment* (2nd) headings, with some modification. Cumulative indexes are published four times per year for A.W.L.D. and eight times per year for B.C.W.L.D. New looseleaf volumes are issued each year to receive the releases.

Because it is a rapid service, there are no law reports citations with the digested cases. Photocopies of full judgments may be obtained from Carswell as per instructions in each issue. Other sources must be checked to see whether the cases have been reported.

(e) Electronic sources or transferring research to other publications:

A.W.L.D. and B.C.W.L.D. use *Canadian Abridgment* (2nd) topic headings, and therefore, research may be readily transferred to it. Carswell's CD-ROM service "LawSource" is an enhancement of the contents of the *Canadian Abridgment Revised* (2nd), with separate *Abridgment* modules being added over several years. The "LawSource" product, "The Canada Reporter" collection, contains over 225,000 full-text cases. Carswell's law reports and *Canadian Abridgment Revised* (2nd) digests are available in online database format from QL Systems Ltd.

4. Example D: Alberta Decisions

(a) Publisher:

Western Legal Publications

(b) Other Western Legal Publications titles using the same digesting/ indexing scheme:

Supreme Court of Canada Decisions, *Federal Court of Appeal Decisions*, *British Columbia Decisions* including its "Special Series" sub-sets, *Saskatchewan Decisions*, *Manitoba Decisions, Alberta-Saskatchewan-Manitoba Criminal Convicion Decisions*, *Charter of Rights Decisions and Ontario Decisions* (criminal only).

(c) Essential characteristics:

(i) Reported/Unreported:

This is designed to be a very rapidly produced digest, and many of the cases remain unreported.

(ii) Scope of coverage:

The service commenced in 1975.

(iii) Frequency:

Mailings are made monthly with pages being inserted in the current year's binder(s). *British Columbia Decisions* mailings are more frequent (civil cases weekly and criminal cases bi-weekly).

(iv) Other features:

(A) Table of cases:

Table of cases are produced for year to date. *British Columbia Decisions* now has a separately published cumulative Table of Cases Reported with citations for decisions which become reported.

(B) Case citator:

No printed version is available, but because the digests are quite lengthy and mention cases cited, the online database or CD-ROM versions will fulfill this function.

(C) Statute citator:

The *Alberta Decisions Citator*, a separate title, and similar citators produced for British Columbia, Saskatchewan, and Manitoba, are prepared simultaneously with the decisions services. The citators offer more complete digest summaries concerning statutes considered than are sometimes provided by the decisions services. The *Charter of Rights Decisions* contains a table of statutes considered for the *Charter of Rights* and *Bill of Rights*. *Alberta Court Rules Citator* is a separate title, and similar titles are produced for British Columbia, Saskatchewan, and Manitoba.

(d) Instructions for use:

The indexes appear at the beginning of the separate civil and criminal sections, and are very broad. The detailed subject index is the combination of broad topic and key worded subtopics printed at the top of each case digest. The update release pages are interfiled with existing looseleaf binder pages: one case digested per binder page. The researcher skims through the pages examining the running heads (headings at the top of the pages) to follow the alphabetical sequence of "broad topic-subtopic-narrow subtopic, etc."

After the 1975-1977 volume, the digests are filed in separate binders for each year. Civil and criminal digests may be in separate sections within the year's binder or in separate binders for the year. As years pass, it becomes increasingly inconvenient to search for persuasive authority case law from other provinces in the many binders. To alleviate the problem of having to search so many annual

ILLUSTRATION 6
Civil Cases Index to [1992] *Alberta Decisions*

[1992] Alta. D. 1534-02[e]

FAMILY LAW [a]

CHILDREN — CUSTODY AND ACCESS — FATHER, AWARD TO[b]

Although each parent would bc suitable as the custodial parent, joint custody is not possible as the parties are unable to communicate with each other peacefully and, on the balance, the advantages to the child are greater with the father than with the mother. The Court-appointed expert recommended custody be granted to the father; de facto custody has been with the father for some time and it seems to be working well; change in custody would involve some disruption in the child's life for no good reason; the father's plans for the future seem more stable at this time than those of the mother; the father appears to be in good health whereas the mother has some present health problems; the boy wishes to live with his father and as he is almost 10, his views should be taken into account; the father has sometimes had more to do with raising the child than in the traditional marriage; and the father is not unsuitable for custody.[c]

Sherry Lynn *S.*	Queen's Bench	July 3, 1992
v.	J.D. Edmonton	Edmonton
Roberts John *S.*[d]	4803-83706	Cote, J.

Decision: Custody of the child to the father with generous access to the mother as specified.

Facts: This decision concerns custody of a 9 year old boy. The parties had joint custody and the child lived mostly with his father, but that arrangement did not work and the mother now seeks sole custody of the son, as does the father.
Reasons: See *Headnote* above.

S.M. Mann for Petitioner
Sherry Lynn S.

M.W. Gerlach for Respondent
Robert John S.

(16 pages)

Alta. Decisions - July, 1992

[a] Running head: broad topic
[b] Running head: subtopic – narrow subtopic
[c] Case law digest
[d] Style of cause or case name
[e] Cite in *Alberta Decisions*

binders, a looseleaf volume titled *Universal Subject Locator* has been recently published. This volume contains a newly revised classification scheme which incorporates the old scheme. Pointers indicate the series and years (*i.e.*, volumes), which contain case digests for each subject.

These decisions publications are available in electronic format (online database from QL and CD-ROM from the publisher), which also alleviates the problem of having to search so many annual binders.

Because it is a rapid service, there are no law report citations with the digested cases except in the *B.C. Decisions* case table cumulation. Photocopies of full judgments may be obtained from Western Legal Publications. Instructions for ordering are found in the front of the binders.

(e) Electronic sources or transferring research to other publications:

Transferring research to other services by the publisher is facilitated by the recently created *Universal Subject Locator* discussed above in subsection (d), Instructions for use.

These decisions publications are available in electronic format ("Dart" CD-ROM products from Western Legal Publications and online databses from QL Systems Ltd.).

5. Example E: Canadian Weekly Law Sheet

(a) Publisher:

Butterworths

(b) Related publications:

The purpose of C.W.L.S. is to provide an overview of reported cases from law reports, while the purpose of Butterworths' *Lawyers Weekly* is to provide a rapid comprehensive digesting of recent unreported cases.

(c) Essential characteristics:

(i) Reported/Unreported:

This service provides digests of reported cases from 28 law reports. Supreme Court of Canada cases are digested rapidly prior to appearance in law reports. The advantage of this service is that the researcher is able to scan each issue for an overview of cases that have recently appeared in report series. Butterworths' rapid digesting service is *The Lawyers Weekly* with some of the cases being subsequently reported in law reports series and hence, later being digested in the *Canadian Weekly Law Sheet*.

(ii) Scope of coverage:

The service commenced in 1959, and generally covers existing Canadian report series.

(iii) Frequency:

Sheets are issued weekly.

(iv) Other features:

(A) Table of cases: Tables of cases appear on orange or yellow coloured sheets which cumulate groups of weekly issues throughout the year. At the end of the year, a table of cases covering the prior year is issued.

(d) Instructions for use:

Each weekly set of sheets arranges digests under approximately 30 to 40 major topic headings with the appearance of any particular heading depending on whether appropriate cases appeared in the law reports of the prior week.

Each digest is given its own key worded introductory word or phrase by which the digests are arranged under the major topic heading.

Research begins by finding a relevant digest under the desired topic, and then turning to the full text of the case, the citation of which appears at the end of the digest. As noted, Supreme Court of Canada cases will not have citations, since they have not yet been reported. The alternative method is to check the cumulative index. It consists of key words and phrases, with reference to the digest numbers. There is an interim green page cumulative index for January-June, and a cumulative annual index published at year's end.

(e) Electronic sources or transferring research to other publications:

C.W.L.S. has its own topic heading scheme (not related to other publications) and is not available electronically. Its main value is as an overview of recent reported cases.

6. Example F: Lawyers Weekly

(a) Publisher

Butterworths

(b) Related publications:

The purpose of *Lawyers Weekly* is to provide a rapid comprehensive digesting service, while Butterworths' *Canadian Weekly Law Sheet* provides an overview of cases just published in law reports series.

(c) Essential characteristics:

(i) Reported/Unreported:

This service provides digests of recent unreported cases from appellate courts across the country (selected Québec appellate cases) and of selected lower court cases. The annual *Consolidated Digest* gives law reports' citations for the cases which were reported after preparation of the weekly issue and before preparation of this annual consolidation.

(ii) Scope of coverage:

This service commenced in 1983.

(iii) Frequency:

The digests appear weekly in the newspaper titled *The Lawyers Weekly.* The digests are republished in *The Lawyers Weekly Consolidated Digest* which covers the prior year's May through the current year's April.

(iv) Other features:

(A) Tables of cases: *The Lawyers Weekly 19— Consolidated Digest* volumes have a "Table of Cases" section which cites digest location in the "Consolidated Digest" and the case's appearance in law reports.

(d) Instructions for use:

The Lawyers Weekly is a newspaper with legal stories relating to the practise of law, including reports of court cases. The weekly digest section groups digests under the newspaper's own indexing scheme of subject headings and sub-headings (*e.g.*, "Employment-Benefits-Entitlement-Employment Contract"). The case digest numbers are used for ordering full text of these recent cases from the publisher. This newspaper issues two annual bound indexes:

(i) *Lawyers Weekly 19— Consolidated Digest* which gathers the year's digests under the indexing scheme of 90 subject headings. Research is conducted in three steps by first reviewing the 90 subject headings (STEP 1). STEP 2 is turning to the appropriate subject heading section (e.g., "Employment") and scanning the sub-headings printed at the top of each digest (*e.g.*, "Benefits-Entitlement-Employment Contract"). There are cross-references from relevant keywords to the subject heading where the digest is located, *e.g.*, "Elections-Recounts. See Appeal-Timeliness-Failure to Perfect-Appeal of Election Recount". If the case has been reported, STEP 3 is using law reports' citations given at the end of each digest and to retrieve the law reports volume.

(ii) *The Lawyers Weekly Annual Index* is similar to a periodical's own index and is divided into the following sections:

(A) Subject Index to articles. This index scheme is an expansion of Library of Congress Subject Headings.

(B) Author index.

(C) Legislation Index is alphabetically arranged provincially and federally and then by statute name accompanied by cites of the articles about the legislation.

(D) Case Index lists cases commented upon by the newspaper articles. At the time of writing, *Lawyers Weekly Five-Year Cumulative*

Index (1983-1988 and 1988-1993) and the Annual Indexes are available.

(e) Electronic sources or transferring research to other publications:

The Lawyers Weekly has its own subject heading scheme (not related to other publications). After reviewing recent newspaper issues for current case law, research may be easily transferred to the newspaper's own bound "Consolidated Digest" or "Annual Indexes" for recent years. If research is being conducted by starting in the Consolidated Digests, note that the cut-off date for digests appearing in each year's Consolidated Digest is usually early May and the volume is published in late summer or fall. The 1996 *Consolidated Digest* included cases digested through May 24, 1996, so that updating research in *The Lawyers Weekly* newspaper would be from mid-May 1996 forward. *Lawyers Weekly* digests are available in electronic format (as "The Lawyers Weekly" CD from Butterworths and as an online database from QL Systems Ltd.).

7. Example G: Canadian Abridgment Revised, 2nd Edition

(a) Publisher:

Carswell (a division of Thomson Professional Publishing)

Note: The *Canadian Abridgment Revised 2nd Edition* (Can. Abr. Rev. (2nd)) encompasses a variety of research tools. At time of writing, Can. Abr. Rev. (2nd) had: case law digests in 72 main work volumes plus 65 supplement volumes; *Canadian Case Citations* (cases judicially considered) in 10 main volumes plus 10 supplement volumes; *Canadian Statute Citations* (statutes judicially considered) in 21 main work volumes plus nine supplement volumes; *Index to Canadian Legal Literature* in 14 main work volumes. Can. Abr. Rev. (2nd) has undergone extensive revision in the past decade and the process is nearing completion.

(b) Related publications:

Criminal Law Digest (Revised Edition), *Employment Law Digest*, *Family Law Digest*, *Insurance Law Digest*, *Labour Law Digest* and *Municipal Law Digest* are reprinted from Can. Abr. Rev. (2nd) case law digest volumes. *Canadian Current Law*'s several sub-titles are monthly paperbound updates to Can. Abr. Rev. (2nd). *Alberta Weekly Law Digest* and *B.C. Weekly Law Digest* use the same case law digest indexing scheme as Can. Abr. Rev. (2nd).

(c) Essential characteristics:

(i) Reported/Unreported:

The *Canadian Abridgment Revised (2nd)* has traditionally provided digests of reported decisions from all courts across Canada (federal matters from Québec courts). The advantage of this publication is the number of reports covered and the number of years of coverage, which date back to the early 1800s. With one index, a researcher can cover Canadian case law from the beginnings of Canadian courts to the most recent C.C.L. issue, which includes some recent unreported cases.

(ii) Scope of coverage:

The case law digesting extends back to 1803. The current law reports being digested are listed in an "Abbreviations" listing (see *Canadian Current Law Case Digests* for most up-to-date list). The current periodicals and other literature are listed in an "Abbreviations" listing in *Index to Canadian Legal Literature*.

(iii) Frequency:

Subtitles of Can. Abr. Rev. (2nd) are updated through re-issue of revised volumes (now completed), releases for looseleaf binder volumes, and the monthly paper loose parts comprised in *Canadian Current Law.*

(iv) Other features (see also (d), below):

(A) Table of cases: "Consolidated Table of Cases" volumes.
(B) Case citator: *Canadian Case Citations* volumes.
(C) Statute citator: *Canadian Statute Citations* volumes.
(D) Court Rules citator: "Rules Judicially Considered".
(E) Bills/Statutes/Regulations tracker: "Legislation".
(F) Secondary literature cited: "Index to Canadian Legal Literature".
(G) Words and phrases: *Words and Phrases Judicially Defined in Canadian Courts and Tribunals*.

(d) Instructions for use:

The set has several groups of volumes with titles that conceptually fall into two categories: (i) the case law digest volumes, plus volumes giving research access to the digest volumes, and (ii) volumes providing other features (outlined above in (c) (iv), "Other features").

(i) Case law digest volumes and access to them:

Case law research in Can. Abr. Rev. (2nd) may be viewed as a three step process.

STEP 1: Research access to the case law digest volumes through the *Key and Research Guide* (legal topic approach) or the *General Index* (keyword approach).

STEP 2: Reviewing the digests in the hardbound volume(s), in the soft cover volume, and in the paper loose parts.

STEP 3: Retrieving relevant cases from law reports.

1. Research access to the Case Law Digest volumes:

A case addressing several issues may be summarized in more than one digest. In Can. Abr. Rev. (2nd), several hundred thousand digests are grouped under 115 alphabetically-arranged subject titles, and each digest within a subject title is given its own number (*e.g.*, ENVIRONMENTAL LAW #545). Within each subject title, digests are grouped under sub topics. The entire listing of the subject titles with their sub topics is titled the "Key Classification System". See Illustration 7 which shows ENVIRONMENTAL LAW #545's location in the "Key Classification System" to be:

ENVIRONMENTAL LAW
- II Statutory Protection of the Environment
  - 6. Practice and procedure
    - c. Evidence
      - iv. Sufficiency of evidence
        - A. Beyond reasonable doubt

Within such a large classification system, how do you locate a narrow grouping of cases such as ENVIRONMENTAL LAW II.6.c.iv.A.?

(A) *Key and Research Guide* (Legal topic approach): This looseleaf volume lists the entire Can. Abr. Rev. (2nd), "Key Classification System" (under subject titles "Actions" to "Waters and Watercourses"). Additionally, there are many "see" cross-references from legal and fact words not used as subject titles to terms used as subjects (*e.g.*, "Compulsory Arbitration - See Arbitration"). There are "see also" references from subject titles to other locations for related subject matter. For example, "Injunctions" is a subject title, but the "Related Titles" note indicates that case digests about injunctions in certain situations are grouped with digests dealing with other subject titles (*e.g.*, "effect of injunctions on proceedings of Human Rights Tribunals - see HUMAN RIGHTS VII.1.a.").

The *Key and Research Guide* also includes a "Concordance of Subject Titles", which shows the new location of older second edition titles in the Revised 2nd Edition. Additionally, there is an Abbreviations list for law reports, journals, *etc.*

(B) The "Index" (Keyword approach): This section of the "General Index/ Caselaw Update" volume is an expansion of the subject titles, sub topics, and cross references into a keyword index. The following example shows an index entry leading to a grouping of digests numbered 541 to 560 in volume RI4B:

"Environmental Law
- Statutory Protection of the environment
  - Evidence
    - Sufficiency of evidence
      - R14B. 541-560"

(C) "Consolidated Table of Cases": If you know the name of a case in a particular subject area and want similar cases, you can look up the case name in this multi-volume sub-set of the Can. Abr. Rev. (2nd), which cites the digest number of cases. Turn to the digest which will be grouped with related case digests.

2. Case law digest volumes and loose parts:

The digests of case law are housed in different types of volumes, all of which use the "Key Classification System" to arrange the digests under the 115 subject titles.

(A) The bound volumes: Can. Abr. Rev. (2nd) has recently issued revised bound volumes. Several of the 115 subject titles can be included in one volume. See the listings of subjects on the spine of the volume (*e.g.*, the revised volume R2 spine states "Bailment & Warehousing/Banking and Banks"). Subject titles encompassing a large number of digests are included in a series of volumes which expand the original single volume (*e.g.*, Criminal law originally in volume 11 expanding to revised bound volumes R11 to R11D).

(B) The soft bound supplement volumes (digests from date of bound volume to the current year): Digests of cases decided after the publication dates of bound volumes can be found in annually published soft cover supplement volumes shelved beside the corresponding bound volumes.

(C) *Canadian Current Law — Case Digests* (digests prepared during the year): Digests prepared this current year are issued in monthly paper loose parts of *Canadian Current Law* (a separate but related publication to Can. Abr. Rev. (2nd)). These looseparts have the same "Key Classification System" as the Can. Abr. Rev. (2nd). Hence, collecting all digests under one of the 115 subject titles involves locating digests in one or more bound volumes, checking the soft cover supplement volume, and checking each monthly loose part of C.C.L. to date. A table listing those digests recently appearing under sub-topics of the "Key Classification System" is housed in the "General Index/Case Law Update" volume of Can Abr. Rev. (2nd).

Can. Abr. Rev. (2nd)'s promotional literature refers to a "new research process ... in just two simple steps", but this refers to bound volumes and soft cover volumes without considering the need to check C.C.L. loose parts. This "new ... process ... [in] two ... steps" means a great improvement over Can. Abr. Rev. (2nd)'s old system of bound main volumes, with several series of supplementing volumes and further supplementing binder volumes. The process is now simplified by the bound volume to single soft cover annual volume sequence.

(ii) Other features of the *Canadian Abridgment Revised (2nd)*:

(A) Table of cases in "Consolidated Table of Cases": This multi-volume looseleaf sub-set of Can. Abr. Rev. (2nd) is an alphabetical listing of digested cases from the 1700s to the present. Case names are listed by plaintiff, while defendant/plaintiff entries appear as "see" references to the plaintiff/defendant entries, *e.g.*, "*Bickel, Barthelmes v.*, See *Barthelmes v. Bickel*". The case name then cites:

(1) The case's location in law reports (*e.g.*, [1978] 2 W.W.R. 372).

(2) The locations of digests in the main work volumes (*e.g.*, R14B.545). Portions of a single case may have several digests appearing under different subject titles. Reported citations of each court level of all digested cases are listed. A search for a case in the "Consolidated Table of Cases" main volumes can be expanded by referring to:

   (a) The "Consolidated Table of Cases Annual Supplement" volumes which are shelved next to the main volumes.

   (b) The "Consolidated Table of Cases Quarterly Supplement" (soft cover volume).

   (c) *Canadian Current Law — Case Digests* (monthly).

(B) Case citator in the ten volume hardbound *Canadian Case Citations, 1867-1990*. Each case name is accompanied by citation to the history of the case (*i.e.*, various reported appeal levels of the case) and under each case appear later citing cases which have judicially considered the cited case. The following example shows that an 1880 case was distinguished (D) by a 1991 case.

Green v. Blackwell
32 N.J. Eq. 768 (N.J. Err. & App. 1880)
(D) *Downey v. Metropolitan Transit Commission*
(August 22, 1991)
Doc. S.C.A. 02504 (N.S.C.A.)

The citing cases are Canadian cases, while the cited cases are Canadian, British, other Commonwealth, or American. For general discussion of case citators, see Chapter 6, Statute and Case Citators. For the cited case's most recent judicial consideration by later citing cases including as yet unreported citing cases, see annual cumulative supplements shelved next to the main *Canadian Case Citations* volumes, quarterly supplements, and monthly *Canadian Case Citations* loose parts.

(C) Statute citator in *Canadian Statute Citations*: Each entry consists of a statute and a section number accompanied by a list of all Canadian cases considering the statute (reported cases since 1867, unreported Court of Appeal cases since 1987, and unreported superior court cases since 1993). The statutes are grouped under Canada federal, Canadian province or territory, international treaty, or foreign country (mostly United Kingdom). The components of this subtitle are the following volumes: Canada/International (six volumes); Alberta/North West Territories and British Columbia/Yukon (two volumes); Manitoba; New Brunswick/Newfoundland; Nova Scotia/Prince Edward Island; Ontario (three volumes); Québec (three volumes), and Saskatchewan.

The following example shows a section of a statute from the Saskatchewan volume:

Age of Majority Act, R.S.S. 1978, c. A-6, s. 2.

(c) *Hadican v. Hadican* (1984), 33 Sask. R. 89 (Q.B.)

To determine whether additional cases have considered s. 2 of the *Age of Majority Act*, the following must be checked:

- *Canadian Statute Citations* annual softcover supplement which updates to September.
- *Canadian Statute Citations* quarterly softcover supplement.
- Monthly loose parts.

For a general discussion of statute citators, see Chapter 6, Statute and Case Citators.

(D) Court Rules citator: the separate volume "Rules Judicially Considered" is arranged by jurisdiction (federal and provincial) and by statute. The following example shows a British Columbia Rule of Court.

R.41(15)(a)

(c) *Gordon v. Gordon* (June 28, 1993), Doc. new Westminster DO26980 (B.C.S.C.).

To determine whether additional cases have considered Rule 41(15)(a), the following must be checked:

(a) Annual "Rules Judicially Considered" softcover supplement volume which updates to September.

(b) *Canadian Statute Citations* quarterly softcover supplement volume ("Rules Judicially Considered" section).

(c) *Canadian Statute Citations* monthly loose parts section "Rules Judicially Considered".

(E) Bill/Statutes/Regulations tracker: the service titled "Legislation" consists of annual noncumulative volumes (*Canadian Current Law — Legislation Annual*) starting with 1989-90. During the year, there are approximately seven irregularly issued updates divided into the following sections:

(a) Progress of Bills

(b) Statutes Amended, Repealed, or Proclaimed in Force

(c) Regulations

The legislation is listed by jurisdiction and alphabetically by Act. The following example shows the amendment of a B.C. statute:

Utilities Commission Act, S.B.C. 1980, c. 60, s. 61(12), Am. 1995, c. 45, s. 60.

(F) Secondary literature cited: Can. Abr. Rev. (2nd) does not have a separate section listing secondary literature cited by cases, although many of Carswell's subject reports' cumulative indexes have such sections. Can. Abr. Rev. (2nd) does have a subset containing a feature listing cases and statute sections which have received comment in legal journals and other secondary literature. This subset is the *Index to Canadian Legal Literature* which is detailed in Chapter 8, Legal Periodicals and Legal Periodical Indexes.

This index has five sections: subject index, author index (authors of journal articles), book review index, Table of Cases (listing of cases which have received journal comment), a Table of Statutes (listing of statutes which have received journal comment). This sub-set has volumes labelled 1981 to 1984 (three volumes), 1985-1986, and annual volumes to date. Updates are the paperbound loose parts titled: *Canadian Current Law Canadian Legal Literature* (seven loose parts per year).

(G) Words and Phrases: In 1993, Carswell began publication of the eight volume set titled *Words and Phrases Judicially Defined in Canadian Courts and Tribunals*. There are approximately 50,000 judicial considerations of words and phrases. Updating is by softbound supplements shelved beside the main volumes and by the "Indexes - Words and Phrases" section of *Canadian Current Law - Case Digests*.

(e) Electronic sources or transferring research to other publications:

As noted above, the advance service for Can. Abr. Rev. (2nd) is Canadian Current Law. Can. Abr. Rev. (2nd) is a massive publication which means that computer query could facilitate research in it. Carswell now offers *Canadian Abridgment Revised 2nd Edition* case law summaries on CD-ROM (Canadian Case Digests) with a Folio search engine. The summaries are also available as an online database from QL Systems Ltd. (Boolean logic). See Chapter 10 for discussion of electronic sources and how to use them. At time of writing, the other Can. Abr. Rev. (2nd) component available on CD-ROM was *Canadian Statute Citations*.

8. Example H: *Canadian Current Law*

(a) Publisher:

Carswell

(b) Related publications:

Canadian Current Law is an advance service for the *Canadian Abridgment Revised 2nd Edition* (See 7, Example G: *Canadian Abridgment Revised (2nd)*.

ILLUSTRATION 7

Canadian Abridgment (2nd), volume R14B, p. 95, case digest #545
NOTE: Can. Abr. (2nd) has 125 main subject titles. One subject title is ENVIRONMENTAL LAW, and this illustrates case digest #545 within that title.

> **545.**[b] (II.6.c.iv.A)[a]
> Statutory protection of the environment — Practice and procedure — Evidence — Sufficiency of evidence — Beyond reasonable doubt — Tanker charged with discharging pollutant — Question of identity — Oil Pollution Prevention Regs., s. 5. An information read, "on or about the 9th day of August, 1974, the tanker barge 'Gulf Aladdin' of Canadian Registry, did discharge a pollutant". Respondent claimed that the identity of the barge was not proved beyond a reasonable doubt. Held, as two witnesses had sworn to the identity of the barge and as there was no evidence of mistaken identity, the identity was proved beyond a reasonable doubt.[c]
>
> **R. v. "Gulf Aladdin" (The)**, [1978] 2 W.W.R. 472 (B.C. Co. Ct.).[d]

---

[a] The sub-topic classification. This digest falls within the "ENVIRONMENTAL LAW II.6.c. iv.A" group of digests. A portion of the ENVIRONMENTAL LAW subject title scheme is:

I Common Law Actions
II Statutory Protection of the Environment
  1. Jurisdictions...
  2. Environment & assessment
  3. Approvals
  4. Environmental offences
  5. Availability of defences
  6. Practice and procedure
    a. General
    b. Parties
    c. Evidence
      i. General
      ii. Burden of proof
      iii. Admissibility
      iv. Sufficiency of evidence
        A. Beyond reasonable doubt

[b] This digest's individual case law digest number or index number. The digest is #545 in Vol. R14B, so its location is identified as R14B.545.

[c] The digesting of the case.

[d] Style of cause or case name with law report citation.

Can. Abr. Rev. (2nd) has been extensively revised in the past decade, which has resulted in major changes in C.C.L.

(c) Essential characteristics:

(i) Reported/Unreported:
All reported decisions of Canadian courts and tribunals are digested. Since 1987, decisions of Canadian appellate courts have been digested before they are reported in law reports series.

(ii) Scope of coverage:
More than 75 law reports are reviewed to insure inclusion of all reported cases. Listings of law reports series generally covered and a table of specific law report volumes reviewed for the C.C.L. issue are printed in each issue.

(iii) Frequency:
Canadian Current Law - Case Digests paperbound issues appear monthly. For the frequency of other paperbound subtitles, see Subsection (iv), Other features, immediately below.

(iv) Other features:
- (A) Table of cases: "Table of Cases" in C.C.L. Case Digests
- (B) Case citator: Separate paperbound loose parts titled *Canadian Case Citations* (published monthly).
- (C) Statute citator: Separate paperbound loose parts titled *Canadian Statute Citations* (published monthly).
- (D) Secondary literature cited: a feature listing literature which cites cases is *Canadian Current Law - Canadian Legal Literature* (eight paperbound loose parts published per year).
- (E) Words and phrases: "Words and Phrases" in C.C.L. - Case Digests — Indexes.
- (F) Bills/Statutes/Regulations tracker: separate paperbound loose parts titled "Legislation" (irregularly published about seven times per year).

(d) Instructions for use:

(i) *Canadian Current Law*
The paperbound loose part subscription to C.C.L. updates selected subtitles of the *Canadian Abridgment Revised 2nd.* The separately issued subtitles in the *C.C.L.* subscription are:
- (A) *Canadian Current Law — Case Digests* (published monthly) contains new material relating to "Table of Cases", "Words and Phrases", "General Index", and "Case Law Digests" sections. Lists of law reports surveyed are also featured.

(B) *Canadian Current Law — Canadian Legal Literature* (seven issues per year) is an update to Can. Abr. Rev. (2nd)'s Index to Canadian Legal Literature.

(C) *Canadian Current Law Legislation* (seven issues per year) provides current awareness with the following sections dealing with federal, provincial, and territorial legislation:

(a) the "Progress of Bills" section lists federal and provincial bills that have been the subject of legislative activity since the last issue. The present status of a bill is presented.

(b) the "Statutes Amended, Repealed or Proclaimed in Force" section lists changes for the year to-date.

(c) the "Regulations" table is an alphabetical list by jurisdiction and by enabling statute of the most recent developments regarding the making, repeal, and amendment of regulations.

There is a "Table of Gazettes Reviewed" showing specific gazette issues surveyed to prepare the issue of C.C.L. Legislation. Each fall a separately published "Legislation Annual" is issued (1989-1990, 1990-1991, 1991-1992, *etc*.).

(ii) *Canadian Case Citations* and *Canadian Statute Citations* (published monthly) provide listings of citing cases recently considering cited cases and statutes which may have been previously cited in the Can. Abr. Rev. (2nd).

(e) Electronic sources or transferring research to other publications:

C.C.L. may be used to check for very current matters, but as an advance service to Can. Abr. Rev. (2nd), most research would be an updating from Can. Abr. Rev. (2nd) to C.C.L. Material from C.C.L. is eventually absorbed into Can. Abr. Rev. (2nd), which has several electronic sources.

9. Example I: Dominion Law Reports (4th) Canadian Criminal Cases (3rd)

(a) Publisher:

Canada Law Book

(b) Related publications:

Canada Law Book issues cumulative index volumes for its law reports. In the front of each cumulative index is the "classification scheme" listing of topics and subtopics under which cases are grouped and summarized with keywords. Classification schemes have been developed for *Dominion Law Reports (3d)* and *(4th), Canadian Criminal Cases (3d), Labour Arbitration Cases (4th), Land Compensation Reports*, and *Canadian Patent Reporter (3d).*

(c) Essential characteristics:

(i) Reported/Unreported:
The indexing and keyword digests form part of these law reports; therefore, digesting is of reported cases. The advantage is that Canada Law Book's editors screen cases to determine which are significant for setting new law or serving as valuable illustration of existing law (civil cases in D.L.R. and criminal cases in C.C.C.). The editors provide researchers only with cases that are considered significant, while digest access to unreported cases is provided by the advance digesting services, *All-Canada Weekly Summaries* (civil) and *Weekly Criminal Bulletin.*

(ii) Scope of coverage:
While both D.L.R. and C.C.C. have existed since approximately the year 1900, the "Classification Scheme" as part of the cumulative index volumes and in individual volumes has appeared with the recent series. "Classification Schemes" are used for C.C.C. (3d) (1983-) and D.L.R. (4th) (1984-), and an index volume has been issued for D.L.R. (3d) (1969-1984) using the D.L.R. (4th) Classification Scheme. D.L.R. publishes civil cases from the Supreme Court of Canada, leading cases from all common law provinces, and cases of general interest from Québec. C.C.C. reports all criminal cases considered significant from all Canadian courts and jurisdictions. C.C.C. reports cases involving the *Criminal Code*, *Canada Evidence Act*, *Charter of Rights*, *Narcotic Control Act*, *Young Offenders Act*, *Competition Act*, and provincial statutes.

(iii) Frequency:
The reports issue weekly paper loose parts. Each loose part and volume has keyworded digests appearing under the law report's classification scheme.

(iv) Other features:
- (A) Table of cases: "Table of Cases"
- (B) Case citators: "Annotations" is a section of the index volumes which lists cases appearing in the series of D.L.R. or C.C.C. being indexed. Under each case citation is a listing of citing cases (from all law reports) which have considered the D.L.R. or C.C.C. cited case.

(d) Instructions for use:

Indexes appear in the law reports looseparts and bound volumes, but research likely will begin in the cumulative index volumes (e.g., D.L.R. (4th) Index, Annotations, Table of Cases: volumes 80-116). Finding a case through the cumulative index volume is a three-step process:

STEP 1: Review the volume's section titled "Classification Scheme" with its subject headings, subheadings, "see cross references", "see also cross references", and scope notes (see Illustration 8).

STEP 2: Turn to the heading/subheading in the volume's "Index" section (see Illustration 8) and read the case digests, which are concise, have keyworded entries, and include the citation to the fully reported case.

STEP 3: If the digest indicates possible relevance, turn to the full case in the cited D.L.R. or C.C.C. law reports volume.

(e) Electronic sources or transferring research to other publications:

There are advance digest services for D.L.R. and C.C.C. which use the same "Classification Scheme" as the respective law reports. The advance service for D.L.R. is *All Canada Weekly Summaries* (A.C.W.S.). The advance service for C.C.C. is *Weekly Criminal Bulletin* (W.C.B.). The advance service for L.A.C. (4th) is *Canadian Labour Arbitration Summaries* (C.L.A.S.). These publications are discussed in Section 10, Example J, following. Both LEXIS-NEXIS (offered by Butterworths) and QL Systems Ltd. carry online databases with Canada Law Book's D.L.R., C.C.C., *Canadian Patent Reporter*, *Labour Arbitration Cases*, A.C.W.S., C.L.A.S., and W.C.B. Canada Law Book offers CD-ROM collections containing D.L.R. (1956-) and C.C.C. (1898-).

10. Example J: All Canada Weekly Summaries (3d) Weekly Criminal Bulletin (2d)

(a) Publisher:

Canada Law Book

(b) Related publications:

All-Canada Weekly Summaries (3d) (A.C.W.S.) is an advance service to D.L.R. (4th), while Weekly Criminal Bulletin (2d) (W.C.B.) is an advance service to C.C.C. (3d). The advance service for L.A.C. (4th) is *Canadian Labour Arbitration Summaries* (C.L.A.S.) (see 9, Example I: *Dominion Law Reports (4th)/ Canadian Criminal Cases (3d).*

(c) Essential characteristics:

(i) Reported/Unreported:
A.C.W.S. is a rapid digesting service for civil cases, while W.C.B. is a rapid digesting service for criminal cases. Because they are rapid digesting services, the cases digested are not yet reported, and therefore, are unreported.

(ii) Scope of coverage:
The intent is to cover all written judgments from all court levels from across the country. A.C.W.S. began in 1977 and W.C.B. started in 1976. C.L.A.S. began in 1986.

ILLUSTRATION 8

Dominion Law Reports 4th "Index, Annotations, Table of Cases" volume for volumes 40-79 of *DLR 4th*

CLASSIFICATION SCHEME [section] page ix

ABORIGINAL PEOPLES[a]
(*See also* CONSTITUTION LAW — Aboriginal[c] rights; Charter of Rights — Aboriginal rights; Distribution of legislative authority — Indians; CRIMINAL LAW — Game and fisheries; Indians)
Application of human rights legislation
Application of provincial law
Crown relationship
Exemption from taxation
Hunting and fishing rights
Indian bands
Land claims
Real property
Reservations
Status[b]
ABUSE OF PROCESS *See* COURTS; TORTS[d]
ACCOUNTANTS *See* PROFESSIONS
ACTIONS *See* CIVIL PROCEDURE: *for particular kinds of action or for the existence of a cause of action see particular headings, e.g., CORPORATIONS — Derivative actions;*[e]

INDEX [section] page A-5

ABORIGINAL PEOPLES[a]

Application of human rights legislation[b]

Provision in Canadian Human Rights Act providing that Acts not affecting any provision in Indian Act or provisions made under or pursuant to Indian Act — Exception not applying to resolution of band council terminating employment of its administrator — Canadian Human Rights Act, S.C. 1976-77, c. 33, s. 63(2). *Desjarais v. Piapot Band No. 75,* 60/308[g] (F.C.A.)

Application of provincial law[b]

Aboriginal rights — Indians — Treaties — Accused members of Huron Bank charged[f] with cutting down trees, camping and making fires in provincial park contrary to Parks Act — Accused claiming that legislation not applicable to them by virtue of treaty — Document relied upon as treaty signed by general commanding British Forces during war with French — Document constituting treaty and guaranteeing Indians right to exercise religion and customs — Treaty giving Hurons right to continue carrying on customs over entire territory frequented by Hurons at time of treaty provided carrying on of customs and rights not incompatible with particular use made by the Crown of territory — Exercise of customs in provincial park not incompatible with occupancy of the park by Crown — Provincial legislation inapplicable to accused — Indian Act, R.S.C. 1970, c. I-6, s. 88 — Parks Act, R.S.Q. 1977, c. P-9, ss. 1, 11. *R. v. Sioui,* 70/427[g] (S.C.C.)

---

[a] Subject heading in "Classification Scheme" and in Index with case digest
[b] Sub-headings
[c] "See-also" cross-reference
[d] "See" cross-reference
[e] "Scope note" explaining matter covered by subject heading
[f] Case law digest in Index
[g] Cite case's location, i.e., 70 D.L.R. (4th) 427

(iii) Frequency:
Weekly paper pamphlet issues.
(iv) Other features:
(A) Table of cases: provided in cumulative index volumes.

(d) Instructions for use:

Because these digests arrange entries under the same "Classification Schemes" as D.L.R. and C.C.C., research may be readily transferred to the bound volumes and paper loose parts of A.C.W.S. and W.C.B. Remember that many A.C.W.S. and W.C.B. cases remain unreported, so research can be conducted in D.L.R. and A.C.W.S. volumes (or C.C.C. and W.C.B. volumes) covering the same time period without finding complete duplication of cases. If research is commenced in A.C.W.S. or W.C.B., the following steps are required:

STEP 1: Begin in a cumulative "Index and Table of Cases" volume for either A.C.W.S. (3d) (published annually since 1987 with each cumulative volume covering an increment of four bound volumes of A.C.W.S.) or W.C.B. (2d) (cumulative index volumes now covering volumes 1 to 28 of W.C.B. (2d)). These cumulative index volumes have an updated "Classification Scheme".

STEP 2: Look for keyword case summaries under the appropriate heading/ subheading in the Index section of the cumulative volumes and in individual bound volumes and loose parts.

You could check to see whether the case is reported in D.L.R. or C.C.C., but some types of cases will likely remain unreported. Quantum of personal injury damages and sentencing matters probably will remain unreported.

(e) Electronic sources or transferring research to other publications:

These are advance services facilitating the transfer of research from law reports to these titles. Both LEXIS-NEXIS (offered by Butterworths) and QL Systems Ltd. carry online databases with Canada Law Book's A.C.W.S., W.C.B., and C.L.A.S.

11. Example K: Supreme Court of Canada Reports Service, Second Edition

(a) Publisher:

Butterworths

(b) Related publications:

Federal Court of Canada Service, which has a purpose of providing coverage of the *Federal Court Act* with rules and orders and case digests, relevant sections of the *Income Tax Act*, courtroom procedure, forms, and practice notes.

(c) Essential characteristics:

(i) Reported/Unreported:
This service digests Supreme Court of Canada decisions, all of which appear in the Canada *Supreme Court Reports* and other law report series. As well, there are approximately 1,000 earlier decisions of the Supreme Court, which were not reported in the Supreme Court Reports but which did appear in the D.L.R.'s or other series predating the *Supreme Court Reports*. The advantage of the current service is that the digests usually appear in advance of the official reports.

(ii) Scope of coverage:
Supreme Court judgments are included back to the formation of the court. The digests to 1971 are contained in the first three volumes. Volume 4 contains the *Supreme Court Act* and Supreme Court Rules. Volumes 5 to 11 and a current service volume contain digests from 1971 to-date.

(iii) Frequency:
Current digests are issued quarterly.

(iv) Other features:
- (A) Table of cases: In volume 3 there is a main case table and a supplemental case table covering from 1969 to within the past year or two. Each year's division of digests is preceded by a table of cases for that year.
- (B) Case citator: None.
- (C) Statute citator: The statutes (both federal and provincial) considered by the Supreme Court are listed under the main index heading of "Statutes, construction of". This topic heading is continued in the annual supplement index, which is located in volume 4.
- (D) Secondary literature cited: None.
- (E) Words and phrases: None.

(d) Instructions for use:

Finding case law is partially a three-step process (from index to digest to the case), and partially a two-step process (index to the case).

(i) Finding Supreme Court cases on a particular subject prior to 1970 is a two-step process.

The first three volumes contain a detailed subject breakdown of all reported case law from the Supreme Court of Canada prior to 1970. The first step is to look up the subject or key word in the main index, which covers the first three volumes. The digests are arranged according to subject, and at the start of each major topic heading there is a listing of sub-topics. For example, the major heading "Damages" has subtopics listed as "assessment of, division of, excessive, measure of, reduction of, and right to". The case digests are arranged under the subtopics, and the digests are in the form of key words and key worded phrases.

The second step is simply to look up the case cited in the digest, in the *Supreme Court Reports.*

(ii) Finding case law decided by the Supreme Court since 1970 is a three-step process.

The first step is to look at either the annual supplement, which is a tab in volume 4, or at the index preceding each year's cases in the current service volumes.

The annual supplement is arranged in the same manner as the main index, but citations are of the *Supreme Court Reports*, other report series, and to the fuller digest which is contained in the yearly divisions from 1970 forward in the current service binder.

The other approach is to look up the key word index at the beginning of each year's divisions, which will lead to a full digest of the case within that yearly division.

Step two is to review the full digest of the decision in the yearly division tabs; these digests can run to two pages or more.

The third step is the reference to the full text of the judgment, but law report citations are not given at the end of the digests. Law report citations are given in the main index and the annual supplement index in the first three volumes.

12. Example L: Canadian Family Law Guide

(a) Publisher:

CCH Canadian Ltd.

(b) Related publications:

This title is representative of the entire line of topical law reports in looseleaf binder format by CCH.

(c) Essential characteristics:

(i) Reported/Unreported:
Some cases already reported are digested with their law reports citations given, and some very recent cases are digested before they have been fully reported.

(ii) Scope of coverage:
Looseleaf reporters are updated by removal of pages containing outdated law and insertion of new pages providing current statement of the law.

(iii) Frequency:
Update sheets are issued bi-monthly.

ILLUSTRATION 9

Supreme Court of Canada Reports Service, 1970-1981 cases index, page 3059 (Volume 3, "Annual Supplement" division tab)

[NOTE: Reference to Digest number 543.]

INFANTS

Adoption — Indian child by non-Indians under provincial legislation — Effect of Indian Act, R.S.C. 1970, c. I-6. *The Natural Parents* v. *Superintendent of Child Welfare*, [1976] 1 W.W.R. 699, 60 D.L.R. (3d) 148, 21 R.F.L. 267; affg [1974] 3 W.W.R. 363, 44 D.L.R. (3d) 718, 14 R.F.L. 396, revg [1974] 1 W.W.R. 19, 13 R.F.L. 244, Current Service, 1975, Dig. 326.

Custody — Best interests of child — Trial judge in best position to judge. *Adams and Adams* v. *McLeod and Ramstead*, Current Service, 1978, Dig. 543.

1981 Supplement

[Page 4763, Current Service, which contains Digest 543.]

[DIGEST 543]

Infants — Custody — Best interests of child — Trial judge in best position to judge

In a contest regarding the guardianship of an infant, the child had been entrusted to the mother's relatives upon the mother becoming ill when the child was four months old. A few days later the mother died and her husband thereupon took the child to his relatives. In proceedings in the Surrogate Court the husband's relatives were granted custody, but upon appeal the Appellate Division of the Supreme Court of Alberta awarded guardisnship to the mother's relatives.

Spence J., Marland, Ritchie, Dickson and Beetz JJ. concurring: "There is no need to cite any authority to delineate the task of a court upon an infant's custody issue. Time after time, and more particularly through all the latter part of this century, it has been said and repeated that the one cardinal issue is the best interest of the infant and that all else is secondary. How then is that best interest to be determined? Again our courts have been unanimous that the most authoritative pronouncement thereon is by the trial court judge who hears the evidence and assesses it."

Appeal allowed.

Adams and Adams v. *McLeod and Ramstead*, March 21, 1978.

Service Issue 26-8/78

(iv) Other features:
  (A) Table of Cases: A "Case Table" is maintained in the first tab section.
  (B) Case citator: The purpose is to give editorial comment with case digests as illustration rather than offer research tools such as case citator tables.
  (C) Statute citator: the full text of many statutes are reproduced in sections separate from the commentary portions which contain the case digests and narrative references to the statutes. The "Reference Table" lists statute sections cited by paragraphs in the work (i.e., table relating statute sections to paragraph numbers).
  (D) Secondary literature cited: The purpose is to offer secondary literature through the commentaries rather than produce tables citing other secondary authority literature.
  (E) Words and phrases: None.

(d) Instructions for use:

This three volume guide provides coverage of more than 170 federal, provincial, and territorial statutes relating to family law. The coverage is narrative commentary which cites the fully reproduced statutes in volume 2 and 3 plus case digests at the end of volume 1's subsections.

Access to the material is a two step process. First, a key word search is made in the General Topical Index in the first tab section of volume 1. Reference is to numbered paragraphs of the "Commentary" tab sections (*e.g.*, paragraph 4, 135.). A separate "Reference Table" lists statute sections with reference to the commentary paragraphs in which they appear. Second, checking for new developments is done in the Index To Recent Cases near the end of volume 1. The Index To Recent Cases is arranged numerically by paragraph number (from commentary of volume 1 or law portions of volume 2). If there are new developments, a key word description is given along with a paragraph number in the "New Developments" section where there are digests of recent court cases.

Update release pages are mailed monthly along with a blue paged Report Letter summary (pamphlet of approximately 10 pages) of the new information in the release pages. Law libraries usually keep these numbered Report Letters in pamphlet boxes on the shelf next to the looseleaf volumes.

CCH Canadian Ltd. issues a pamphlet titled "Rapid Finder Index" which lists subjects and the CCH loose part service which covers each subject.

(e) Electronic sources:

CCH Canadian Ltd. offers all of its looseleaf tax reporters in CD-ROM format. Additionally, *Canadian Securities Law Reporter* is offered in CD-ROM. The bimonthly CD-ROM title "Ontario Family Law - Electronic" is accompanied by a monthly print-form newsletter.

D. SUMMARY OF CHAPTER

With so many regional publishers expanding into national markets, and with the introduction of multiple special purpose digests/indexes by larger publishers, there is duplication of source information and competition between publishers. It is time consuming to check each digest that might have relevant cases, and within each title, to check each supplement or annual volume. On the positive side, considerable effort is now being made by publishers to simplify research methods (*e.g.*, Can. Abr. Rev. (2nd) having a newly simplified update system).

If you have a "well water drilling contract" case in Alberta, do you search each digest and index volume for *Alberta Reports*, each cumulative index in *Alberta Law Reports*, each annual volume of *Alberta Decisions*, each cumulation of *Alberta Weekly Law Digests*, etc.? How do you efficiently find similar cases that might have arisen in Saskatchewan? How do you efficiently find cases that might have been decided before each of these recent law reports or digests commenced publication? Each publisher uses its own indexing scheme. You might feel most comfortable searching the indexing scheme of one publisher, but once you find a case, should you search the indexing schemes of other publishers?

A solution to the above problem appears to be unfolding in the proliferation of electronic sources. The appearance of an increasing number of digests and services in CD-ROM and online formats allows the researcher to cover a span of sources in years without worrying about learning a variety of indexing/classification systems, and without repeating the same search in various parts of the same service. With a single query, you can search the over 100 individual volumes *Alberta Decisions, British Columbia Decisions, Manitoba Decisions,* and *Saskatchewan Decisions*. If a relevant case is found in one indexing scheme, it can be located within an indexing scheme of another publication while bypassing a search through that other indexing scheme.

An interesting development in online caselaw digests is the relation between the *Dominion Report Service* and the *Lawyers Weekly.* Since 1968, D.R.S. has digested reported cases, but in 1991, it ceased being in print form and continued only as an online database. In 1983, Butterworths' *Lawyers Weekly* commenced digesting unreported cases, some of which are later reported, and L.W. digests from 1986 to-date are an online database. If searching reported cases from 1968 and unreported cases from 1986, a query can be directed to QL System Ltd.'s online database "Summaries of Judicial Decisions, global" (SJD), which includes D.R.S. and L.W.

Before reading Chapter 10 on electronic sources and search methods, you should have a firm grasp of which digests have reported cases and which digests have rapidly prepared digests. The rapidly prepared digests (*e.g.*, *Alberta Weekly Law Digest*) may be considered as an update to a law reports series (*e.g.*, *Alberta Law Reports (3d)* or to a "digest of reported cases" publication (*e.g.*, *Canadian Abridgment Revised (2nd)*. As rapidly prepared digests become databases, you may search a span of years for such cases which never became reported. The D.R.S. and L.W. combination (QL's SJD online database) shows that you can update one publisher's reported cases digest (D.R.S.) with another publisher's update service. With the computer searching, it does not matter that Maritime Law Book Ltd. seems to have so many "index and digest" volumes and no rapid updating services. It does not matter that Canada Law Book publishes the comprehensive A.C.W.S. and W.C.B., but they update the very selective law reports D.L.R. and C.C.C. On computer, Canada Law Book's A.C.W.S. could update Maritime's *Alberta Reports*. It does not matter that Carswell's comprehensive *Canadian Abridgment Revised (2nd)* has an update with relatively brief digests in *Canadian Current Law*, while Western Legal Publications has very detailed "update" digest services (*e.g.*, *Alberta Decisions*) but no titles which are "updated" (*i.e.*, analogous to Can. Abr. Rev. (2nd)). After finding an Alberta case in Can. Abr. Rev. (2nd), you could run a manual update in A.W.L.D. and check further on computer databases such as *Alberta Decisions* or A.C.W.S. The purpose of the computer check of Alta. D. or A.C.W.S. could be to find recent cases or older cases not reported and not in Can. Abr. Rev. (2nd). You can mix and match different publishers' digests when searching and updating by computer search, and the chart below is a rough conceptual summary of the general digests as you leave this chapter and approach Chapter 10. Publications not summarized below are specialized subject digests (*e.g.*, Butterworths' *Insurance Case Law Digest*) and Supreme Court of Canada digests which are limited in content. Any of these specialized digests may be updated by the titles listed in the "updating publications" column. QL Systems Ltd. operates QUICKLAW. LEXIS-NEXIS is offered by Butterworths.

MAIN DIGEST /INDEX OR STARTING POINT	UPDATING PUBLICATIONS	ONLINE DATABASE OR CD-ROM
1. *Dominion Reports Service* (CCH: 1968-1990)	*Lawyers Weekly*	(QUICKLAW)
2. *Canadian Weekly Law Sheet* (Butterworths: 1959-)	*Lawyers Weekly*	(C.W.L.S. not on computer)
3. *Lawyers Weekly* may be starting point for 1983-		(LEXIS-NEXIS and QUICKLAW)
4. Can. Abr. Rev. (2nd) (Carswell: 1800-)	*Canadian Current Law* B.C.W.L.D., Alta. W.L.D.	(QUICKLAW) or CD-ROM

5. *Dominion Law Reports* *Canadian Criminal Cases* (Canada Law Book: 1900-)	*All-Canada Weekly Summaries* *Weekly Criminal Bulletin* (Canada Law Book: mid-1970s)	(LEXIS-NEXIS or QUICKLAW or CD-ROM)
6. *All-Canada Weekly Summaries* or *Weekly Criminal Bulletin* may be starting point mid-1970s-		(LEXIS-NEXIS or QUICKLAW)
7. Maritime Law Book Ltd. law reports for all provinces (1970s-) *e.g., Alberta Reports*	Canada Law Book Ltd.'s *A.C.W.S.* or *W.C.B.*	(LEXIS-NEXIS)
8. Western Legal Publications decisions may be starting point for 1970s-		(QUICKLAW or CD-ROM)

Research examples:

1. A water well drilling case may have been decided decades ago, so Can. Abr. Rev. (2nd) might be a starting point. You could update with C.C.L., but relevant cases may not be reported. Updating could be in *Alberta Decisions* which has digests of many cases which never became reported.
2. Lack of seat belt use as contributory negligence would have arisen since the 1960s or 1970s, so a starting point could be D.R.S. or Can. Abr. Rev. (2nd) with updating in A.C.W.S., L.W., or Western Legal decisions online databases.
3. Sky-diving cases are probably 1970s or later, and search could commence in any of the starting points except *Lawyers Weekly* (1983-) and use any updating.
4. Fax machine cases are probably 1980s or later and could commence in any of the starting points and use any updating.
5. Charter of Rights cases are 1980s or later and could commence in any of the starting points and use any updating. Specialized report and digest titles from this Chapter 3 are also relevant.
6. Ocean fishing boat cases may not have been heavily reported in older series of law reports, so a start might be in Maritime Law Book Ltd. reports which commenced publication in the Atlantic provinces in the 1970s but did not begin publication in British Columbia until the 1990s. A further search could be made in *B.C. Decisions.*
7. Building contracts involving high-rise office towers may yield starting points of Can. Abr. Rev. (2nd) and/or D.L.R. with updating in any of the sources listed.

Final Note before leaving this chapter and approaching the chapter on electronic sources and search methods:

Manual research starting points are a matter of choice when in a law library holding all resources. Starting points on computer systems may be determined by the publications available in electronic format. Check the "ELECTRONIC SOURCES" column in the charts beginning on p. 43 to determine which publications are available online, on the Internet and/or CD-ROM. Note that some publications' online availability is through LEXIS-NEXIS, through QL, or through both.

Chapter 4

Statutes

Statutes are primary authority law passed by the federal Parliament or by provincial legislatures. The legislatures may enact entirely new statutes during a legislation session, or they may amend existing statutes by adding new wording and/or repealing existing wording. The basic starting point for statutory research is the latest sets of revised statutes federally and for each province. The set of revised statutes for each jurisdiction is a multivolume collection of statutes with wording current as of a certain date. When a statute revision is enacted into law, reference to earlier statutes is unnecessary for current research, except for some statutes which may not have been repealed by and not included in the statute revision. New statutes and amendments to existing statutes are found in sessional volumes issued at the end of each legislative session. Research in revised statutes must be updated by use of sessional volumes or in annual volumes. Legislative bills that are enacted into statutes are available in paperbound form before the appearance of the hardbound sessional volumes.

A. OVERVIEW OF STATUTORY RESEARCH

Important considerations in researching statutes are being familiar with index access to statutes, knowing how to update statutory research, and locating case law comment upon statutes.

1. Statute Indexes

True statute indexes may be a collection of individual Act indexes, a listing of subject headings under which are cited statutes dealing with the subjects, or a combination of both. Some listings may recite only sections of Acts and are more detailed "tables of contents" than true indexes.

A law library is filled with multi-volume sets having lengthy indexes. You will note that some provincial statute sets have no index. How can this be?

Cases from other provinces have persuasive authority in the courts of your province, hence at some point every researcher may be using law reports covering, for example, P.E.I. Statutes from other jurisdictions have no authority outside their own boundaries. Statute index preparation is a large task known to this text's original author and spouse, who read 10,000 pages of Saskatchewan statutes and prepared an 1,800-page index (photo-reduced for printing). How can a private publisher economically justify such an effort for the relatively small-sized market of a P.E.I. index? Federal and provincial government-produced statute indexes are rare.

The solution of the 1980s was the comprehensive indexing prepared by CLIC, which dissolved. By mid-1997, the only subject indexes being produced were: *Index to Federal and Ontario Statutes 199-* (by Mary McLean; issued annually by Carswell), *Index to the Statutes of Saskatchewan* (issued biennially by the Law Society of Saskatchewan), and a subject index for each New Brunswick legislative session (issued by Maritime Law Book Ltd. of Fredericton). An index for British Columbia is in the planning stages.

Why do you need a statute index when you can make a computer keyword search on the full text of a collection of statutes (CD-ROM collection or online database)? For specific terms, both computer keyword searching and printed indexes can be satisfactory. For example, one province may call an Act the *Beekeepers Act* while another province may name a similar Act the *Apiaries Act.* One printed index may give you a "see reference" from "apiaries" to "beekeepers", while the other province may "see reference" from "beekeepers" to "apiaries". A computer keyword search may be satisfactory if you use alternate search terms to include different terminology used for the same concept. But what if the usual phrasing of the concept is not used as terminology in one or more statutes or even statute collections?

To illustrate this point, the concept "interprovincial agreements" is a subject heading in the printed *Index to the Statutes of Saskatchewan.* A random check of four of the statutes cited under this subject heading shows that none of the four statutes actually uses the wording "interprovincial agreement(s)", which might be a specific keyword phrase used in searching the electronic versions of the statutes. This concept of "interprovincial agreements" is expressed in the four statutes (enacted in different years) with the following different and very general wording:

> Chapter D-12.11: "enter into agreements on behalf of..." is found in the first paragraph of the section, but "the government of any other province" is in a subclause below.
>
> Chapter S-8: "reciprocal agreement with any other province..." is a concept not split between paragraphs as in c. D-12.11.
>
> Chapter S-23: "agreement with the Government of any other province... providing for a reciprocal arrangement..." This links "reciprocal" with "arrangement" rather than "agreement" as in c. S-8.
>
> Chapter W-6: "arrangements or agreements with any province or provinces". If you required the search to contain the term "reciprocal" (found in chapters S-8 and S-23), the query would not yield chapters W-6 or D-12.1.

With such general terminology used to describe a concept and without a uniform manner of phrasing the concept, a computer keyword search would yield uncertain results. However, a printed index, prepared by a person looking for concepts stated in different ways, would collect all of the statutes under the subject heading, "interprovincial agreements".

2. Updating statutory research

Updating of statutes for each jurisdiction may vary, but it usually involves locating amendments in a Table of Public Statutes (or Table of Statutes) which shows changes since the last statute revision and then being certain that no bills recently enacted into law have made changes since the issuance of the last Table of Public Statutes.

An important consideration is the date on which the statute comes into force. The steps a bill takes in federal Parliament to become a statute is first, second, and third reading in both the House of Commons and the Senate. If it is approved at third reading, the bill receives Royal Assent from the Governor General, the Queen's Representative. After the Royal Assent the bill is a statute, but the statute may not be effective or "in force" if the wording of the statute states a date other than Royal Assent date for the statute to come into force.

The wording of the statute may call for it to come into force on the date of Royal Assent, on a specified date, or upon proclamation by the Governor General. Coming into force on a future date to be proclaimed by the Governor General allows the administrative machinery time to consider the bill before it is brought into force. If the wording of the statute does not state a date for it to come into force, the *Interpretation Act* states that the statute will come into force on the date of Royal Assent.

The procedure for passing provincial bills into statutes is similar to the federal structure, with Royal Assent being given by the Lieutenant Governor. Some jurisdictions publish statutes in looseleaf format so that the existing set can be kept current without the necessity of checking changes in wording due to amendments in the various sessional volumes since the last statute revision.

3. Cases considering statutes

Statute citators provide access to case law interpreting statutes; similarly, there are some publications which are annotated codes listing sections of specific statutes with cases considering them. There are a number of annotated Criminal Codes, and some annotated legislation services and hardbound texts for specific federal and provincial Acts. Statute citators often provide listings of statute amendments as well as cases considering statute sections. Statute citators are discussed in Chapter 6.

B. FEDERAL STATUTES

1. Revised Statutes of Canada, 1985 (R.S.C. 1985)

(a) The main volumes

Volumes 1 through 8 of the hardbound set of R.S.C. 1985 contain the full texts of the statutes as they were in force on December 31, 1984. Statutes appear in both

English and French versions in parallel columns. They are arranged in alphabetical sequence according to the short titles of the statutes. The full title of statute may be quite lengthy, but in these instances, a shortened title is cited in one of the first sections of the Act. The numbering system consists of alphanumeric combinations with the alpha designation from the first letter of the first word of the Act and the numeric designation being the number of the statute as it falls in alphabetic order within the letter, *e.g.*, the *Canadian Pension Plan Act* is chapter C-8.

(b) The "Table of Concordance", and the Supplements to R.S.C. 1985

R.S.C. 1985, with its law stated as of December 31, 1984, did not come into force until December 12, 1988. Obviously, there was legislation passed during 1985, 1986, 1987, and 1988. This legislation appears in "Supplement" volumes to R.S.C. 1985:

1st Supplement volume: federal legislation through 1985.
2nd Supplement volume: federal legislation through 1986.
3rd Supplement volume: federal legislation through 1987.
4th Supplement volume: federal legislation to December 12, 1988.
5th Supplement volume: the *Income Tax Act*.

After 1988, federal legislation appears in sessional volumes, Statutes of Canada (S.C.); see Section C, Updating the R.S.C. 1985. The Acts in the original eight volumes of R.S.C. 1985 each had an alphanumeric designation (*e.g.*, c. A-2 for the *Aeronautics Act*). A new Act which appears in a supplement volume is cited in the following format: R.S.C. 1985, c. 17 (lst Supp.), R.S.C. 1985, c. 3 (2nd Supp.), R.S.C. 1985, c. 15 (3rd Supp.), and so on. A new Act in a Statutes of Canada volume is cited, *e.g.*, S.C. 19—, c. 14. Each Act is given a chapter number ("c." in the cite).

R.S.C. 1985 has a separately published booklet titled "Table of Concordance", which shows where Acts in the old R.S.C. 1970 now appear in the R.S.C. 1985 (*i.e.*, their new chapter numbers).

(c) Other elements of R.S.C. 1985

(i) The "History and Disposal of Acts Table" in the 5th Supplement lists former legislation by chapter and section number (*e.g.*, R.S.C. 1970 and sessional volumes to 1985). Cross reference cites show how the older sections were repealed or repealed and replaced before R.S.C. 1985, or how they were consolidated into, omitted from, or not consolidated (not repealed and not consolidated) into R.S.C. 1985.

(ii) Schedules to R.S.C. 1985 (in Appendix I) and to each Supplement showing Acts and portions of Acts repealed as of the coming into force of the R.S.C. and Supplements.

(iii) Appendix II to R.S.C. 1985: 47 Constitutional Acts and documents. These are English and Canadian statutes ranging from the *Constitution Act, 1867* (U.K.), formerly known as the *British North America Act,*

1867; to the *Canada Act 1982*, including the *Constitution Act 1982* (U.K.); to the Proclamation bringing into force the *Constitution Act 1982* (Canada).

(iv) Appendix III to R.S.C. 1985: the *Canadian Bill of Rights*, S.C. 1960, c. 44.

(d) Index to R.S.C. 1985 and the Supplements

Before its demise, the Canadian Law Information Council (CLIC) produced a comprehensive keyword index to R.S.C. 1985 and its Supplements (to 1988). Annually, Carswell publishes a cumulative index titled *Index to Federal and Ontario Statutes*.

C. UPDATING THE R.S.C. 1985

1. Statutes of Canada

Statutes of Canada (S.C.) are sessional volumes of statutes published subsequent to the statute revision. The statutes amending prior legislation and new statutes enacted during each session of Parliament are reproduced in full text in both English and French in the bound sessional volumes. The Table of Contents shows that Public General Acts are printed in Part I while Local and Private Acts are reproduced in Part II. The statutes classified as "Public General Acts" have general application while "Local and Private Acts" are applicable to certain locales, groups, or individuals. Local and Private Acts are not included in statute revisions.

The features and tables of each sessional volume are:

(a) "Proclamations of Canada" which have been made during the session covered by the volume. Acts proclaimed are listed alphabetically with the date on which they came into force and with citation to the proclamation in the *Canada Gazette Part II*. Part II's non-cumulative quarterly index lists most recent proclamation dates with updating to be accomplished in individual issues of Part II.

(b) "Table of Public Statutes" listing Acts from R.S.C. 1985, unconsolidated Acts from 1907 to the present, and new Acts from January 1, 1985 that have been amended. Beside each section of an amended Act is the citation to the amending Act. This table supersedes all such tables in earlier sessional volumes.

(c) The "Index to Public General Acts" is a collection of indexes to the individual new Acts and Acts amending prior legislation which are contained in that sessional volume only.

2. Canada Gazette Part III and Canada Statute Citator

Canada Gazette Part III publishes the statutes passed during the parliamentary session after they receive Royal Assent, but before all of the session's statutes are cumulated into the *Statutes of Canada* bound sessional volume. Like the *Statutes of Canada* sessional volume, some issues of Part III have proclamation dates from the beginning of the session. Some Part III issues have a Table of Public Statutes (see Illustration 10), which supersedes the Table in the latest sessional volume.

For federal statutes excluding the *Criminal Code*, the *Canada Statute Citator* lists the text of amendments. It is a looseleaf publication that approximates the currency of the *Canada Gazette Part III*.

3. Electronic and index access to the R.S.C. 1985 and S.C. sessional volumes

A particular Act in R.S.C. 1985 subsequently may have been amended by each session of Parliament, and the researcher is usually concerned about the current wording of that Act. The researcher may search through each sessional volume and note changes, but this may be cumbersome. Statutory research is facilitated by an annually updated index and three electronic versions of current federal statute wording.

(a) The CD-ROM Edition

The CD-ROM edition of the *Consolidated Statutes and Regulations of Canada* was introduced in 1996 to replace the looseleaf edition, which was discontinued. The current wording of both the statutes (R.S.C. 1985 as amended by all subsequent sessional volumes of S.C.) and regulations (see Chapter 5) is contained on one CD-ROM, and the CD-ROM is updated with a replacement CD-ROM twice yearly. Unconsolidated Acts in force are slowly being added. The "Table of Public Statutes" is included in the CD-ROM. CD-ROM versions are available from Canada Law Book and Justice Canada.

The CD-ROM consolidation, like the old looseleaf version, has no official sanction and is prepared for the convenience of reference only. There is no index access to the CD-ROM consolidation, though keyword searches can be performed on the full text of the statutes and regulations. In addition to the consolidation, annual statutes are grouped separately under their respective years.

When new Acts are placed in the CD-ROM edition, the Statute Revision Commission assigns an alphanumeric designation (*e.g.,* c. M-3.2), so that the entire CD-ROM set will have alphanumeric designations. Because the CD-ROM set does not have official sanction, the official cite to a new Act might be S.C. 19—, c. 21, while the Commission might assign c. D-3.6. The "3.6" indicates that the original R.S.C. 1985 had chapters D-3 and D-4, but now there are six new Acts fitting alphabetically between D-3 and D-4 (*i.e.*, D-3.1, D-3.2, D-3.3, D-3.4, D-3.5, and D-3.6).

(b) Online databases

R.S.C. 1985 as amended to the current year is available as a database from LEXIS-NEXIS (access code CANADA: "CANSTA") and from QL Systems Ltd. (access code "RSCC"). R.S.C. 1970 as amended to 1985 is available at access code "RC70". Keyword searches may be made of the full text.

(c) Internet database

R.S.C. 1985 and subsequent sessional volumes are available as the *Consolidated Statutes of Canada* Internet database provided by the Department of Justice. There is a search engine for searching the text of the statutes. The statutes database is available at the Internet address:

(http://canada.justice.gc.ca/loireg/index_enhtml).

(d) Index to Federal and Ontario Statutes 199-

This index by McLean contains over 600 subject headings with some pertaining only to federal statutes, some only to Ontario, and some to both sets of Acts. There are hundreds of "see references" from terms not used as subjects to the appropriate subject headings. Carswell annually publishes McLean's updated indexes.

4. Table of Local and Private Acts, Statutes of Canada, 1867 to 1979. Supplements 1979-

This table published under authority of the *Statute Revision Act*, S.C. 1974-76, c. 20, lists all federal local and private Acts, other than those dealing with divorce. Amendments and sections repealed have been considered in this table which groups Acts alphabetically under the headings; Banks, Board of Trade, Bridges, Harbours, Insurance, Patents, Pipelines, Railway Bridges and Tunnels, Railways, Religious and Charitable Organizations, Trust and Loan Companies, and Miscellaneous. Supplementary tables are published periodically, and at the time of writing, the most recent table was dated December 31, 1990.

5. Legislative bills

Legislative bills from the House of Commons and Senate are published after the first and third readings. A subject matter index to the bills is found in the House of Commons Debates index. To check the progress of a bill through Parliament, the researcher may check any of the following sources:

(a) Journals of the House of Commons and Senate.
(b) *Status of Bills Report* published weekly by the Library of Parliament.
(c) The "Progress of Bills" section in *Canadian Current Law Legislation*.
(d) The *CCH Ottawa Letter* section, "Progress of Legislation" under the "Federal Legislative Record" Tab.

(e) *Canada Statute Citator* "Monthly Bulletin Service".
(f) *Canada Legislative Index* published by the B.C. Courthouse Library Society.
(g) Electronic version through QL's database, "Canada Status of Bills" (access code "CSB").

6. Proclamation dates

If the Act states that it will come into force on a date to be proclaimed rather than upon a date mentioned in the Act or upon Royal Assent, proclamation dates may be checked in the following sources:

(a) "Proclamations of Canada" tables in sessional volumes and in *Canada Gazette Part III*, and as announced in the *Canada Gazette Part II*.
(b) The "Statutes Amended, Repealed or Proclaimed in Force" section of *Canadian Current Law Legislation*.
(c) *Canada Statute Citator* under the listing for each individual Act.
(d) The *CCH Ottawa Letter*: "Progress of Legislation".
(e) *Status of Bills Report* (Library of Parliament).
(f) *Canada Legislative Index* published by the B.C. Courthouse Libraries Society.

The entire statute may come into force at one time, may have different sections come into force on different dates, and may have the statute or portions thereof come into force in various jurisdictions within the country at different times.

7. Annotated statutes/statute citators

Updating statutory research also requires searching for case law considering statutes. Statute citators and annotated statute publications are discussed in Chapter 6. The *Canada Statute Citator* covers most federal statutes, while there are many *Criminal Code* and tax citators. Publications in this area can be as comprehensive as the *Canadian Statute Citations* element of the *Canadian Abridgment Revised 2nd Edition*, or as specific and focused as Carswell's *Annotated Immigration Act of Canada*.

D. CONSTITUTIONAL DOCUMENTS AND LITERATURE

A nation's constitution may be either a set of fundamental laws and principles found in a number of documents, or a single, supreme document. Canada and the United Kingdom are in the former category; the United States is in the latter.

ILLUSTRATION 10

Statute Index example; Table of Public Statutes updating example
Index to the *Statutes of Saskatchewan* (to Nov. 1, 1990)

APIARIES ACT, c. A-22[a]
*Apiary
- Definition, 2(b)
- Equipment imported from outside Saskatchewan, 6
*Appeal of registration cancellation, 4
*Beekeepers
- Definition, 2(c)
- Disease, concealing, 8(2)
- Equipment see *Equipment, beekeeping
- Immovable broodcombs, 5
- Registration of see *Registration of beekeepers
*Bees
- Definition, 2(e)

Page 26

EQUIPMENT[b]
*Beekeeping, c.A-22, ss.6-9, 12
*Electrical equipment, defective or unapproved c. E-6.2, ss. 2(j), 18, 20-21
*Fuel-burning equipment under Clean Air Act c. C-12.1, ss. 2(h), 5-20
*Gas Inspection Act and gas, c. G-3.1, ss. 2(j), 15, 19, 21

Page 170

[a] "Individual Act" subject heading in a Type 1 - Type 2 statute index
[b] "General Topic" subject heading in a Type 1 - Type 2 statute index

---

Canada Gazette Part III Ottawa, Friday, October 2, 1992
Statutes of Canada, 1992
Table of Public Statutes

Arctic Waters Pollution Prevention – R.S., 1985, c. A-12
(Prévention de la pollution ...)

s. 2, 1992, c. 40, s. 49[a]
s. 2.1, added, R.S., c. 6 (3rd Supp.), s. 91

Page 11

[a] Shows that Section 2 of the Arctic Waters Pollution Act, R.S.C. 1985, chapter A-12 has been amended by S.C. 1992, chapter 40, section 49

1. The Constitution Acts, 1867 to 1982 and other constitutional documents

The *Canada Act, 1982*, c. 11 (U.K.) contains schedule B (*Constitution Act, 1982*) which was enacted for and has the force of law in Canada. The *Constitution Act, 1982* was proclaimed in force on April 17, 1982 (section 15, Equality rights, came into force on April 17, 1985), and section 60 states that "the Constitution Acts, 1867 to 1975 (No. 2) and this Act may be cited together as the *Constitution Acts, 1867 to 1982*." The *Constitution Act, 1982* Schedule 1 (Modernization of the Constitution) lists constitutional statutes enacted by English and Canadian Parliaments from 1867 and gives the new names of the Acts. For example, the new name of *The British North American Act, 1867*, 30-31 Vict., c. 3 (U.K.) is *Constitution Act, 1867*. The text of The *B.N.A. Act* (*Constitution Act, 1867*) and amendments are reproduced in R.S.C. 1985, Appendix II.

In 1867, The *B.N.A. Act* established the "Dominion" of Canada and, among other features, the Act enumerated the powers of the Parliament in section 91 and listed the exclusive powers of provincial legislatures in section 92.

The *Statute of Westminster, 1931* enacted the principle that no law made by the English Parliament would extend to Canada other than at the request and consent of Canada. Other of the *Constitution Acts* mark such significant events as the admission of new provinces to the Dominion.

A broader interpretation of the term "constitution" beyond the *Constitution Acts 1867 to 1982* would be inclusion of the Canadian *Bill of Rights*, S.C. 1960, c. 44 (R.S.C. 1985, Appendix III). A very broad view of what documents are considered constitutional may be surveyed in Wiktor and Tanguay, *Constitutions of Canada*, Federal and Provincial (Dobbs Ferry, N.Y.: Oceana Publications). A more recent publication is Funston and Meehan, *Consolidated Canadian Constitutional Documents* (Toronto: Carswell, 1994), which includes statutes, orders in council and proclamations (some predating Confederation). Other landmarks in Canadian political and judicial history include the abolition of appeals from the Supreme Court of Canada to the Judicial Committee of the Privy Council in England.

The *Constitution Act, 1982* has a profound impact on the legal system through litigation of such concepts as the guarantee of rights expressed in Part I: *Canadian Charter of Rights and Freedoms*. The Charter has some provisions similar to the *Canadian Bill of Rights, 1960* (no sections repealed by the *Constitution Act, 1982*) and to the American *Bill of Rights* (first ten amendments to the United States *Constitution*). There is a large and growing body of case law and secondary literature interpreting and explaining the *Canadian Charter of Rights and Freedoms*. For a checklist of research sources, see Chapter 11, N. *Canadian Charter of Rights and Freedoms* (and Constitution Acts, 1867 onward).

E. TREATIES

Treaty is defined (Yogis, *Canadian Law Dictionary*, 214) as "a compact made between two or more independent nations", and "other words used as a synonym for treaties, or for particular types of treaty, are agreement, pact, protocol, charter, statute, act, convenant .... ". The definition further notes that by *R. v. Syliboy*, [1929] 1 D.L.R. 307 (N.S. Co. Ct.) a treaty, "when in conflict with a statute, must follow the statute."

While the *British North American Act, 1867*, did not mention treaties, Canada became more involved in negotiations affecting Canada until the Imperial Conference of 1926 concluded that treaty negotiations power "initially reserved for the Sovereign was now to be exercised by the Governor General on the advice of the Canadian Minister of State for External Affairs" (Bishop, *Canadian Official Publications*, at 195).

The *Canada Treaty Series* has been published by the Department of Foreign Affairs and International Trade since 1928, which publishes treaties to which Canada may be one of two parties or one of a number of signatories. Various cumulative indexes for increments of years have been published by the official government printer, and recently *Treaties in Force for Canada: A List of Treaties of Canada in force as of January 1, 1988* was published. This is presently updated by an annual publication titled *Treaty Action*, and an index is in preparation. Treaties are part of the indexing for the *Government of Canada Publications: Quarterly Catalogue* (updated by reference to the *Weekly Checklist of Canadian Government Publications*), and the *Canadian Yearbook of International Law* covers treaties.

The *Canadian Treaty Calendar 1928-1978* by Christian Wiktor, Professor of Law at Dalhousie University, is published by Oceana Publications, Dobbs Ferry, New York. Volume 1 has a chronological index listing treaties by date plus a numerical list by *Canada Treaty Series* number. Volume 2 has a country index including multilateral treaties and a subject index. The index includes treaties prior to 1928 which involved Canada.

Butterworths publishes the looseleaf service entitled *Canada's Tax Treaties* in three volumes which contain full text of and commentary on existing and proposed tax treaties between Canada and other nations.

Copies of individual treaties can be ordered by CTS number at (819) 956-4800.

F. PROVINCIAL STATUTES

In addition to current provincial statutes applying to a province, older English statutes, which were applicable to a province at the province's entry into Confederation, were part of the province's law and are still primary authority excepting legislative change. The old English *Statute of Frauds* is still primary authority in some provinces, while others have enacted their own statutes. A "Table of English Statutes in Force in Canada" is listed in Jean Cote, "Introduction of English Law into Alberta" (1964), 3 *Alberta Law Review* 262. Research in English material should be in the Chronological Table of the Statutes (see Chapter 13), focusing on the year of entry into Confederation.

The mechanics of research in provincial statute law is similar to methods employed in federal research. The basic elements in updating provincial statutes are given below by province and territory.

1. Alberta

(a) Latest statute revision: R.S.A. 1980 (eight volumes).
(b) Looseleaf statutes edition available: Yes.
(c) Index format: At time of writing, there was a CLIC index to 1985 as well as a supplement for Acts from 1986-1990.
(d) Updating the revision: Examine the "Table of Public Statutes" in the latest annual or sessional volume, or the paperbound Interim Edition.
(e) Status of bills: *Alberta Hansard*, *Alberta Legislative Summary* (Legal Education Society of Alberta), *Canadian Current Law Legislation, Alberta Parliamentary Digest,* or *CCH Provincial Legislative Record.*
(f) Proclamation dates: Latest sessional volume, *Alberta Gazette Part I, Alberta Parliamentary Digest, CCH Provincial Legislative Record,* or *Canadian Current Law Legislation.*
(g) Statute citators: *Statutes of Alberta Judicially Considered, Alberta Decisions Citator, Alberta Reports* "Statutes Judicially Noticed" section, or *Canadian Statute Citations.*
(h) Electronic sources:
    (i) Internet: Full text of statutes (www.gov.ab.ca/qp/acts.html). There is no search engine, and the Acts are accessed alphabetically.
    (ii) Online: Statutes, regulations, and the *Alberta Gazette* are available from the Queen's printer with a search engine (ISYS). The statutes are also available on QL.
    (iii) CD-ROM: Statutes, regulations, and the Gazette are available as "QP Source" from the Queen's Printer. Search engine (ISYS).

2. British Columbia

(a) Latest statute revision: R.S.B.C. 1996 (15 volumes).
(b) Looseleaf statutes edition available: Yes.
(c) Index format: At time of writing, an index was in preparation
(d) Updating the revision: Check the "Table of Statutes" in latest sessional volume or the *British Columbia Statute Citator.* Check third reading bills "Public Acts of British Columbia", which are issued after each legislative session.
(e) Status of bills: *Votes and Proceedings, Canadian Current Law Legislation, CCH Provincial Legislative Record* or *B.C. Legislative Digest* (B.C. Courthouse Library Society).
(f) Proclamation dates: *British Columbia Gazette* Part I and Part II, *Canadian Current Law Legislation, British Columbia Statute Citator,* CCH Provin-

cial Legislative Record or *B.C. Legislative Digest* (B.C. Courthouse Library Society).

(g) Statute Citators: *British Columbia Statute Citator, Statutes of British Columbia Judicially Considered, British Columbia Appeal Cases* "Statutes Judicially Noticed" section, *B.C Decisions Citator,* or *Canadian Statute Citations*.

(h) Electronic sources:
  - (i) Internet: Full text of statutes (www.qp.gov.bc.ca/stat_reg/statutes). Search engine. Progress of Bills and Provisions in Force (enactments, amendments, and repealed) are also provided.
  - (ii) Online: QL Systems Ltd.
  - (iii) CD-ROM: Available from the Queen's Printer.

3. Manitoba

(a) Latest statute revision: The Acts of Manitoba were re-enacted pursuant to the decision of the Supreme Court of Canada in *Re Manitoba Language Reference* (1985), 1 S.C.R. 721. "R.S.M." is "Re-enacted Statutes of Manitoba", and the R.S.M. volumes are: R.S.M. 1987 (five volumes plus Supplement); R.S.M. 1988 (one volume); R.S.M. 1989 and 1990-Municipal (one volume); R.S.M. 1990 (two volumes). Acts in bilingual format commencing with the sessional volume S.M. 1986-87 will not need to be re-enacted. The looseleaf set, *Continuing Consolidation of the Statutes of Manitoba* (C.C.S.M.), includes the R.S.M. Acts plus the S.M. 1986-87 and later Acts.

(b) Looseleaf statutes edition available: Yes, *Continuing Consolidation of the Statutes of Manitoba* (C.C.S.M.).

(c) Index format: Index for each Act.

(d) Updating the revision: Table of statutes in annual volume or tables in the C.C.S.M.

(e) Status of bills: *Votes and Proceedings, Canadian Current Law Legislation* or *CCH Provincial Legislative Record.*

(f) Proclamation dates: *Manitoba Gazette Part I*, latest annual volume, *CCH Provincial Legislative Record,* or *Canadian Current Law Legislation.*

(g) Statute citators: *Statutes of Manitoba Judicially Considered, Manitoba Decisions Citator, Manitoba Reports* "Statutes Judicially Noticed" section, or *Canadian Statute Citations*.

(h) Electronic sources:
  - (i) Online: QL Systems Ltd.

4. New Brunswick

(a) Latest statute revision: R.S.N.B. 1973 (six volumes).

(b) Looseleaf statutes edition available: Yes.

(c) Index format: There is a "Descriptive Word Index" in R.S.N.B. 1973, and

Maritime Law Book publishes a *Subject Matter Index to Public and Private Statutes of New Brunswick.*

(d) Updating the revision: Check the "Table of Public Statutes" in the latest sessional volume.

(e) Status of bills: *Canadian Current Law Legislation,* or *CCH Provincial Legislative Record.*

(f) Proclamation dates: *New Brunswick Royal Gazette,* schedules in the sessional volumes, *CCH Provincial Legislative Record*, or *Canadian Current Law Legislation.*

(g) Statute citators: The *New Brunswick Reports (Second Series)* reports a high percentage of cases, and the "Statutes Judicially Noticed" section of the Digest and Indexes volumes and individual reports volumes serve as statute citators. Also *Canadian Statute Citations.*

(h) Electronic sources:
   (i) Online: QL Systems Ltd., but at the time of writing, it was current only to 1986.

5. Newfoundland

(a) Latest statute revision: R.S.N. 1990 (10 volumes).

(b) Looseleaf statutes edition available: No.

(c) Index format: No index available at the time of writing.

(d) Updating the revision: Examine the "Table of Public Statutes" in the latest sessional volume or in a separately published pamphlet.

(e) Status of bills: *Canadian Current Law Legislation,* or *CCH Provincial Legislative Record.*

(f) Proclamation dates: *Newfoundland Gazette Part II, CCH Provincial Legislative Record,* or *Canadian Current Law Legislation.*

(g) Statute citators: The *Newfoundland & Prince Edward Island Reports* publish a high percentage of cases, and the "Statutes Judicially Noticed" section of the Digest and Indexes volumes and individual reports volumes serve as statute citators. Also see *Canadian Statute Citations.*

(h) Electronic sources:
   (i) Internet: Listing of Acts only (www.gov.nf.ca/just/jus_regHTM).

6. Nova Scotia

(a) Latest statute revision: R.S.N.S. 1989 (12 volumes).

(b) Looseleaf statutes edition available: Yes.

(c) Index format: 46 page "Subject Guide" is in the last volume of the statute revision.

(d) Updating the revision: Check the "Table of Public Statutes" in the latest sessional volume.

(e) Status of bills: *Standing of Bills Index* published by the Legislative Library, *Canadian Current Law Legislation*, and *CCH Provincial Legislative Record.*

(f) Proclamation dates: *Canadian Current Law Legislation, CCH Provincial Legislative Record, Nova Scotia Royal Gazette Part II.*

(g) Statute citators: *Nova Scotia Reports, Second Series* "Digest and Indexes" volumes and individual reports volumes; "Statutes Judicially Noticed". The index to *Nova Scotia Law News* and N.S.C.L. Also *Canadian Statute Citations*.

(h) Electronic sources:

(i) Internet: At the time of writing, a consolidation of the full text of the statutes was being placed on the Internet (www.gov.ns.ca/legi/legc/legislat.htm).

7. Ontario

(a) Latest statute revision: R.S.O. 1990 (13 volumes).

(b) Looseleaf statutes edition available: No.

(c) Index format: index included in the final volume of the revision. Carswell publishes annually updated index, *Index to Federal and Ontario Statutes 1990-*.

(d) Updating the revision: Examine the "Table of Public Statutes" in the latest sessional volume or the *Ontario Statute Citator* including its "Weekly Bulletin Service" and "Current Bills Service".

(e) Status of bills: "Status of Bills" in *Votes and Proceedings, Ontario Statute Citator* "Weekly Bulletin Service", *Canadian Current Law Legislation, CCH Provincial Legislative Record*, Carswell's *Ontario Legislative Digest Service*, or QL's Online database "Ontario Status of Bills" (access code OSB).

(f) Proclamation dates: *Ontario Gazette, Ontario Statute Citator* "Weekly Bulletin Service", *Canadian Current Law Legislation, CCH Provincial Legislative Record*, or the table in the latest sessional statute volume.

(g) Statute citators: *Ontario Statute Citator* and bound volume *Ontario Statute Annotations, Ontario Appeal Cases* or *Ontario Trial Cases* "Statutes Judicially Noticed" sections, or *Canadian Statute Citations*.

(h) Electronic sources:

(i) Internet: Full text of statutes (legis.acjnet.org/Ontario/en/Laws/Search.html). Includes a search engine.

(ii) Online: LEXIS-NEXIS (access code CANADA, "ONTSTA"); QL Systems Ltd. (access code RSO).

(iii) CD-ROM: Available from the Queen's printer at (www.gov.on.ca//MBS/english/publications).

8. Prince Edward Island

(a) Latest statute revision: R.S.P.E.I. 1988 (three volumes).
(b) Looseleaf statutes edition available: Yes, with annual updating.
(c) Index format: At time of writing, there was a CLIC index dated 1988.
(d) Updating the revision: Check the "Table of Public Acts" in the latest sessional volume.
(e) Status of bills: *Canadian Current Law Legislation, CCH Provincial Legislative Record.*
(f) Proclamation dates: *Royal Gazette of Prince Edward Island Part I*, latest sessional volume, *CCH Provincial Legislative Record, Canadian Current Law Legislation.*
(g) Statute citators: *Newfoundland & Prince Edward Island Reports* Digest and Index volumes and individual reports volumes: "Statutes Judicially Noticed". Also *Canadian Statute Citations.*
(h) Electronic sources: No.

9. Québec

(a) Latest statute revision: R.S.Q. 1977 (10 volumes).
(b) Looseleaf statutes edition available: Yes, *Revised Statutes of Québec.*
(c) Index format: Index for each Act, and General Index all in one volume.
(d) Updating the revision: Examine the annual volumes of Québec Statutes or, if using looseleaf, the *grey pages* in the Documentation volume.
(e) Status of bills: *Canadian Current Law Legislation*, or Law Clerk's Office (418) 643-2840. Electronic sources: Bills in first reading are available on the internet at (http://www.assnat.qc.ca/eng/publications/Projets-loi/publics/index.htm).
(f) Proclamation dates: *Gazette officielle du Québec Part II*, Laws and Regulations, *Canadian Current Law Legislation.*
(g) Statute citators: *Table de la législation citée* (1965-1977; 1978-1987; 1988-1993) completed by tables in (annual) *Annuaire de jurisprudence et de doctrine du Québec* and (three times a year) in *Jurisprudence express* or Can. Abr. Rev. (2nd) in part. Same in *La Presse juridique* since 1993.
(h) Electronic sources: The R.S.Q. are available as a SOQUIJ online database (=LAWS) and as the SOQUIJ CD-ROM titled, "Lois et reglements du Québec".

10. Saskatchewan

(a) Latest statute revision: R.S.S. 1978 (11 volumes).
(b) Looseleaf statutes edition available: Yes.
(c) Index format: produced biennially by the Law Society of Saskatchewan.
(d) Updating the revision: Check the latest "Table of Public Statutes" in the

publication entitled *Tables to the Statutes of Saskatchewan and Saskatchewan Regulations* and *This Week's Law.*

(e) Status of bills: *Votes and Proceedings, Canadian Current Law Legislation, CCH Provincial Legislative Record, This Week's Law.*

(f) Proclamation dates: *Saskatchewan Gazette Part I, CCH Provincial Legislative Record, Canadian Current Law Legislation, This Week's Law.*

(g) Statute citators: *Saskatchewan Decisions Citator, Statutes of Saskatchewan Judicially Considered, This Week's Law, Saskatchewan Reports* "Statutes Judicially Noticed" section, or *Canadian Statute Citations.*

(h) Electronic sources:
   (i) Internet: Full text of statutes and regulations (www.qp.justice.gov.sk.ca). Search engine available. Subscription necessary.
   (ii) Online: QL Systems Ltd. At time of writing, updated to mid-1995.

11. Northwest Territories

(a) Latest statute revision: *Revised Statutes of the Northwest Territories, 1988* (four volumes plus supplements).

(b) Looseleaf statutes edition available: No.

(c) Index format: CLIC index dated 1988.

(d) Updating the revision: Check "Table of Public Acts" in the latest annual volume.

(e) Status of bills: *Debates of the Legislative Assembly* (end of session), *Canadian Current Law Legislation,* or *CCH Provincial Legislative Record.*

(f) Proclamation dates: *Northwest Territories Gazette Part I,* latest sessional volume, *Canadian Current Law Legislation,* or *CCH Provincial Legislative Record.*

(g) Statute citators: *Northwest Territories Reports* "Statutes Judicially Considered" section or *Canadian Statute Citations.*

(h) Electronic sources:
   (i) Internet: Full text of statutes. (legis.acjnet.org/ACJNet/TNO/1988_en.html). MS Word / WP format.

12. Yukon

(a) Latest statute revision: *Revised Statutes of the Yukon, 1986* (two volumes).

(b) Looseleaf statutes edition available: *Revised Ordinances of the Yukon Territory, 1978* (three binders).

(c) Index (table of contents) format: "Index of Section Headers".

(d) Updating the revision: "Tables of Public Statutes" in the latest sessional volume.

(e) Status of bills: *Government Bills: Progress of Bills, Canadian Current Law Legislation, CCH Provincial Legislative Record.*

(f) Proclamation dates: *The Yukon Gazette Part I, Canadian Current Law Legislation, CCH Provincial Legislative Record.*

(g) Statute Citator: *Canadian Statute Citations.*

(h) Electronic sources:
  - (i) Internet: Annual statutes 1994-. MS Word / WP format.
  - (ii) Online: QL Systems Ltd. At time of writing, updated to end of 1989.

Chapter 5

Subordinate Legislation

Subordinate legislation is primary authority law in the form of regulations, orders, rules, by-laws, municipal by-laws, *etc.*, which have been issued by official persons or bodies pursuant to authority granted by enabling statutes. Each item of subordinate legislation may be referred to as a statutory instrument. Regulations may be issued by a ministry to supply needed detail for broad administrative functions defined by Parliament or a provincial legislature, *e.g.*, Air Regulations are issued by the Department of Transport pursuant to the *Aeronautics Act.* While regulations have wide application, orders may be issued for narrower purposes.

Indexing for regulations is usually a listing, rather than a true index. Enabling statutes are listed alphabetically, with regulations titles and cites listed under each statute. Federal regulations and some provincial regulations have become available electronically.

A. FEDERAL REGULATIONS

1. Canada Gazette Part II

"Consolidated Index of Statutory Instruments", a quarterly issue of the *Canada Gazette Part II*, is the source in which to initiate a search for federal regulations. This quarterly publication lists regulations printed in the *Consolidated Regulations of Canada, 1978;* lists regulations in their locations in the *Canada Gazette Part II* to update the C.R.C. 1978; lists regulations not included in the C.R.C. 1978; and lists statutes for which regulations are exempt from publication.

Regulations are cited by year and number, *e.g.*, S.O.R./82-37, "S.O.R." is an abbreviation for "Statutory Orders and Regulations", while "S.I." indicates statutory instruments other than regulations or orders.

The specific tables comprising the "Consolidated Index of Statutory Instruments" are:

(a) Table I - Table of Regulations

This is an alphabetical listing of the titles of the regulations and other statutory instruments, and is not a listing by subject matter. This listing by short title includes the enabling statute under which the regulation was made.

(b) Table II - Table of Regulations by Statute

This is an alphabetical listing of enabling statutes with a listing of locations of regulations made pursuant to them. If the regulation is contained in the C.R.C. 1978, it will provide citation of the C.R.C. location. For regulations not consolidated in or having appeared since the C.R.C. 1978, the citation will be a location in the *Canada Gazette Part II*.

The *Canada Gazette* does not contain a subject matter index to regulations, so the researcher must know the name of the enabling statute under which relevant regulations might have been made.

(c) Table III - Table of Regulations Exempt from Publication

Table III is a listing of statutes for which regulations are exempt from publication. By the *Statutory Instruments Act,* R.S.C. 1985, c. S-22, s. 11(2), no person can be convicted of an offence contravening an unpublished regulation unless the situation falls within the listed exceptions.

Updating search in the quarterly issue "Consolidated Index of Statutory Instruments" requires searching through each *Canada Gazette, Part II* to date. The index in the back of each Part II lists regulations within the issue but does not give the portion of the old regulations affected which necessitates examination of each amending regulation.

2. Consolidated Regulations of Canada 1978

The *Consolidated Regulations of Canada 1978* (C.R.C. 1978) publishes the full text of all generally applicable federal regulations in force on December 31, 1977. Volumes 1 to 18 publish the regulations grouped under an alphabetical arrangement of enabling statutes. There is no subject matter index for the C.R.C. 1978, and access is through the "Table of Contents" and "Schedule" (volume 19).

(a) "Table of Contents" is an alphabetical list of enabling statutes. Under each statute appear the regulation titles and the regulations' location in the main volumes of the C.R.C. 1978.

(b) The "Schedule" is a list of regulations and parts of regulations revoked by the C.R.C. 1978.

3. The Canada Gazette Part II, 1978, Special Issue

This two-volume issue provides a partial update to the C.R.C. 1978 by publishing regulations made during 1978 that amended regulations contained in the C.R.C. 1978. The *Special Issue* publishes the full text of the amending regulations and includes a table listing the chapters in the C.R.C. that were affected by amending regulations. This set prints only amending regulations, rather than entirely new regulations issued during 1978. The new regulations for 1978 are published in regular issues of the *Canada Gazette Part II* for 1978.

ILLUSTRATION 11

Consolidated Regulations of Canada, 1978, "Table of Contents", page 7

[Showing regulations under the *Arctic Waters Pollution Prevention Act*.]

Chapter	Subject	Page	Chapter	Subject	Page
	APPROPRIATION ACTS – *Conc.*			ARCTIC WATERS POLLUTION PREVENTION ACT	
971	General Adjustment Assistance Regulations	7603	353	Arctic Shipping Pollution Prevention Regulations	2237
326	Home Insulation Regulations	2053	354	Arctic Waters Pollution Prevention Regulations	2275
327	Hospital Insurance (Outside Canada) Regulations	2055	355	Governor in Council Authority Delegation Order	2281
328	Indian Economic Development Regulations	2061	356	Shipping Safety Control Zones Order	2283
329	Indian Off Reserve and Eskimo Housing Regulations	2069			

The Canada Gazette Part II, "Consolidated Index of Statutory Instruments", January 1, 1955 to June 30, 1992, page 78

[Showing regulations under the *Arctic Waters Pollution Prevention Act*.]

ARCTIC WATERS POLLUTION PREVENTION ACT, *RSC 1985, c. A-12*

Arctic Shipping Pollution Prevention Regulations (s. 12) .... CRC, Vol. III, c. 353, p. 2237

23/ 2/78	SOR/78-180	24/ 2/78	8/ 3/78	798
4/ 5/78	SOR/78-430	8/ 5/78	24/ 5/78	2230

4. Commercial print sources of access to federal regulations

(a) The "Regulations" table in *Canadian Current Law Legislation* lists, by enabling statute, all new and amending regulations recently promulgated. Gazette citations are given as well as sections of regulations affected.

(b) The three-volume looseleaf *Canada Regulations Index* by Carswell Ltd. is not a keyword comprehensive subject index to the federal regulations, but it is the most comprehensive method for tracking changes to regulations.

The service provides alphabetical tables of statutes which have had regulations promulgated under their authority and tables of regulations and statutory instruments with authorizing statutes for each. The "Regulation Title Index" alphabetically lists regulation names, under which the authorizing statutes are given. The "Statute Index" alphabetically lists statute names, under which are listed regulations or statutory instruments made pursuant to the statutes.

Issues are mailed monthly to maintain the timeliness of this service.

5. Electronic sources of access to federal regulations

(a) Internet: Full text of federal regulations (http://canada.justice.gc.ca./Loireg/index_en.html).

(b) Online: LEXIS-NEXIS' database titled "Consolidated Regulations of Canada"; LEXIS-NEXIS access code CANADA: "CANREG"; Table of Contents access code CANADA: "CNRGTC" and QL Systems Ltd.'s database titled "Statutory Orders and Regulations of Canada"; QL access code "SOR"; SOR Table of Contents access code "SORT".

(c) CD-ROM: "Consolidated Statutes and Regulations of Canada" available from Justice Canada or Canada Law Book.

B. FEDERAL ORDERS IN COUNCIL

Richard De Boo Ltd. began and Carswell continued a subscription service listing federal Orders in Council. The full title of the publication is "Orders In Council: A Weekly Listing of Federal Cabinet Orders In Council". Included is a semi-annual cumulative subject index and Table of SOR and SI Registration Numbers for Orders in Council.

The Editor's preface of the publication notes that in 1984, there were about 4,000 Orders in Council with about a third of them appearing in the *Canada Gazette*. Orders exempt from publication include orders having very limited affect, affecting national security or international relations, or affecting individual's privacy. In the weekly listing, gazetted orders are asterisked, and a phone number is given to obtain copies of other orders.

Federal Orders In Council require Federal Cabinet and Governor General approval. Ministerial orders (about 230 in 1984) may be made directly by Ministers and agencies empowered to make and amend orders and regulations. Proclamations are given by the Governor in Council. As a supplement to the Orders In Council listings, this publication lists Ministerial orders and Proclamations which have been gazetted.

C. PROVINCIAL REGULATIONS

Provincial regulations are published in official government gazettes, but access is usually only in the form of listings under enabling statutes. There are some commercial sources for regulations research and some provincial regulations are available electronically.

Sources for provincial regulations research are:

1. Alberta

(a) Text of regulations printed in: *Alberta Gazette, Part II*; looseleaf version.
(b) Listing by enabling statute: Cumulative listing in the gazette and annual bound volume of regulations.
(c) Commercial sources: *Canadian Current Law Legislation*: "Regulations".
(d) Electronic sources:
  (i) Internet: Full text of regulations (www.gov.ab.ca/qp/regs.html). There is no search engine, and the regulations are accessed alphabetically.
  (ii) Online: Statutes, regulations, and the *Alberta Gazette* are available from the Queen's Printer with a search engine (ISYS).
  (iii) CD-ROM: Statutes, regulations, and the Gazette are available as "QP Source" from the Queen's Printer. Search engine (ISYS).

2. British Columbia

(a) Text of regulations printed in: *British Columbia Gazette, Part II*; *Consolidated Regulations of British Columbia* (looseleaf).
(b) Listing by enabling statute: cumulative listing in I*ndex of Current British Columbia Regulations* (semiannual); cumulative listing in the gazette.
(c) Commercial sources: listing in *British Columbia Statute Citator*; *Canadian Current Law Legislation*: "Regulations"; *B.C. Legislative Digest* (B.C. Courthouse Library Society).

3. Manitoba

(a) Text of regulations printed in: *Manitoba Gazette, Part II*; selected regulations appear in the looseleaf *Continuing Consolidation of the Statutes of*

Manitoba. Regulations have been reenacted pursuant to the Supreme Court of Canada order. Begin research by consulting the most recent quarterly index in the *Manitoba Gazette Part II*.

(b) Listing by enabling statute: cumulative in the bound annual volume, *Manitoba Regulations*.

(c) Commercial sources: Canadian *Current Law Legislation*: "Regulations".

4. New Brunswick

(a) Text of selected regulations printed in: *New Brunswick Royal Gazette*; the looseleaf *Consolidated Regulations of New Brunswick* (1985-).

(b) Listings by enabling statute: cumulative listing in the gazette annual bound volume or in the last volume of the looseleaf consolidation.

(c) Commercial sources: *Canadian Current Law Legislation*: "Regulations".

5. Newfoundland

(a) Text of regulations (subordinate legislation) printed in: *Newfoundland azette Part II*. Subordinate legislation was re-gazetted in 1978-1979, and any regulations not republished were void.

(b) Listing by enabling statute: The cumulative index of subordinate legislation in the Gazette.

(c) Commercial sources: *Canadian Current Law Legislation*: "Regulations".

6. Nova Scotia

(a) Text of regulations printed in: *Nova Scotia Royal Gazette, Part II* since 1977.

(b) Listing by enabling statute: "Cumulative Index" annual issue of the *Royal Gazette, Part II* (listing for current year). A cumulative index for 1942-1970 appeared in S.N.S. 1970-1971; annual indexes in 1972 and 1973 sessional volumes; 1973-1977 Regulations of Nova Scotia "Red Binder" index.

(c) Commercial sources: *Canadian Current Law Legislation*: "Regulations".

(d) Electronic sources:

  (i) Internet: Full text of regulations (www.gov.ns.ca/just/publish/registry/index.htm).

7. Ontario

(a) Text of regulations printed in: *Revised Regulations of Ontario 1990*; *Ontario Gazette*.

(b) Listing by enabling statute: cumulative listing in the gazette; Table of Regulations in sessional statute volumes, which lists regulations both in and not in the revision; Carswell: *Ontario Regulation Service.*
(c) Commercial sources: Carswell's *Ontario Regulations Service*; *Canadian Current Law Legislation*: "Regulations."
(d) Electronic sources:
    (i) Internet: Full text of regulations (http://legis.acjnet.org/Ontario/en/index.html). Includes a search engine.
    (ii) Online: At time of writing, QL's database "Ontario Regulations, A to H" has an access code "RO" and is updated to mid-1994.

8. Prince Edward Island

(a) Text of regulations printed in: *Royal Gazette of Prince Edward Island, Part II*; the *Revised Regulations of Prince Edward Island* (two volumes, looseleaf).
(b) Listing by enabling statute: Annual listing in gazette; *Revised Regulations of Prince Edward Island.*
(c) Commercial sources: *Canadian Current Law Legislation*: "Regulations".

9. Québec

(a) Text of regulations printed in: *Revised Regulations of Québec*, 1981 (11 volumes with two volumes supplement); *Gazette officielle du Québec Part 2: Laws and Regulations.*
(b) Listing by enabling statute: *Tableau des modifications et index sommaire des réglements refondus du Québec* (french only) published twice a year by the regulation service of the Direction de la refonte (Justice).
(c) Commercial sources: *Canadian Current Law Legislation*: "Regulations".
(d) Electronic sources: Revised regulations are available in English as a SOQUIJ online database (=REGU). The CD-ROM "Lois et reglements" provides only French language text.

10. Saskatchewan

(a) Text of regulations printed in: *Saskatchewan Gazette, Part II* (revised regulations appearing as prepared) and *Part III* (new regulations). The *Revised Regulations of Saskatchewan* (looseleaf edition) are in nine volumes.
(b) Listing by enabling statute: The organization of the looseleaf regulations set is in this format. *Tables to the Statutes of Saskatchewan and Saskatchewan Regulations* also uses this format.
(c) Commercial sources: *Saskatchewan Decisions Citator* (listing); *Canadian Current Law*; *This Week' s Law.*
(d) Electronic sources:

(i) Internet: Full text of regulations.
(www.qp.justice.gov.sk.ca)
Search engine. Subscription fee.

11. Northwest Territories

(a) Text of regulations printed in: *Revised Regulations of the Northwest Territories 1990*; *Northwest Territories Gazette, Part II.*
(b) Listing by enabling statute: cumulative listing in annual bound *Northwest Territories Gazette, Part II*; table in sessional statute volumes (beginning in 1979-80).
(c) Commercial sources: *Canadian Current Law Legislation*: "Regulations".

12. Yukon

(a) Text of regulations printed in: *Yukon Regulations* (nine looseleaf binders); *Yukon Gazette, Part II* (1982-).
(b) Listing by enabling statute: "Table of Contents" to *Yukon Regulations.*
(c) Commercial sources: *Canadian Current Law Legislation*: "Regulations".

D. COURT RULES

Current versions of the Supreme Court of Canada Rules and the Federal Court Rules may be found respectively in Butterworths' *Supreme Court of Canada Reports Service* and *Federal Court of Canada Service*. *Supreme Court of Canada Practice* (annual editions by Carswell) includes rules and case digests. *Supreme Court of Canada Manual* (Canada Law Book; looseleaf).

Provincial court rules may be found in provincial bound volumes or looseleaf consolidations.

Some court rules publications are annotated with cases considering the rules and derivation of the rules from English rules. If an English rule is cited as the origin of a provincial court rule, the *Supreme Court Practice* (English "White Book") may be referred to for English cases construing the phrasing used in the current provincial rules.

Annotated court rules include:

1. Alberta: *Alberta Rules of Court Annotated* (Carswell); *Civil Procedure Handbook/Guide* (Juriliber).
2. British Columbia (and Yukon Supreme Court): *British Columbia Practice*, 2d ed. (looseleaf, Butterworths); *British Columbia Rules Citator* (Western Legal Publications) does not reproduce the text of the rules.
3. Manitoba: *Manitoba Queen's Bench Rules Annotated* (Carswell).
4. Nova Scotia: *Nova Scotia Annotated Rules of Practice* (Carswell).
5. Ontario: *Holmested & Watson Ontario Civil Procedure* (Carswell) gives

coverage to Ontario's *Courts of Justice Act* and *Rules Of Civil Procedure* proclaimed on January 1, 1985; the textbook *Ontario Civil Practice* by Watson and McGowan published by Carswell; *Ontario Annual Practice* (Canada Law Book); *Annotated Rules of Criminal Practice* (Carswell).

6. Saskatchewan: *The Queen's Bench Rules of Saskatchewan: Annotated.* (Law Society of Saskatchewan Libraries).

Many law reports and many case digest publications have tables listing statutes judicially considered, and often these tables include court rules. The charts in Chapter 3, section B note whether the law reports and digests listed include statutes considered. Chapter 6 discusses statute citator publications, many of which include court rules considered (*e.g.*, *Canadian Abridgment Revised 2nd* volume "Rules Judicially Considered").

Chapter 6

Statute and Case Citators

Statute sections, or clauses and words within statute sections, may be construed by case law. Statute citators list the cases that consider statutes. Regulations and court rules may also be considered by cases. Cases are often cited by later cases under the principle of *stare decisis*. Case citators list these later citing cases under the earlier cited cases.

A. CANADIAN ABRIDGMENT REVISED 2ND COMPONENTS, CANADIAN STATUTE CITATIONS AND CANADIAN CASE CITATIONS

The most comprehensive sets of statute citators and case citators are subtitles within the digest publication, *Canadian Abridgment Revised 2nd edition*, which was discussed in Chapter 3. The subtitles are *Canadian Statute Citations* and *Canadian Case Citations.*

1. Canadian Statute Citations

In *Canadian Statute Citations*, each entry consists of a statute and section number accompanied by a listing of all Canadian cases considering the statute (reported cases since 1867; unreported court of appeal cases since 1987; unreported superior court cases since 1993). The statutes are grouped under Canada federally, provincially or territorially; international treaty; or foreign country (mostly the United Kingdom). The components of this subtitle are the following volumes: Canada/International (six volumes); Manitoba; New Brunswick/Newfoundland; Nova Scotia/Prince Edward Island; Ontario (three volumes); Québec (three volumes); and Saskatchewan.

The following example shows a section of a statute from the Saskatchewan volume:

Age of Majority Act, R.S.S. 1978, c. A-6, s.2
(c) *Hadican v. Hadican* (1984), 33 Sask. R. 89 (Q.B.).

To determine whether additional cases have considered section 2 of this Act, the following must be checked:

(a) *Canadian Statute Citations* annual softcover supplement which updates to the prior September.

(b) *Canadian Statute Citations* quarterly softcover supplement.
(c) monthly loose parts.

2. "Rules Judicially Considered" volume

A separate volume of the *Canadian Abridgment Revised (2nd)* serves as a court rules citator. The separate volume "Rules Judicially Considered" is arranged by jurisdiction (federal and provincial), and by statute. The following example shows a British Columbia Rule of Court.

R. 41(15)(*a*)
(c) *Gordon v. Gordon* (June 28, 1993), Doc. New Westminster DO26980 (B.C.S.C.).

To determine whether additional cases have considered Rule 41(15)(*a*), the following must be checked:

(a) Annual "Rules Judicially Considered" softcover supplement volume which updates to the prior September.
(b) *Canadian Statute Citations* quarterly softcover supplement volume "Rules Judicially Considered" section.
(c) *Canadian Statute Citations* monthly loose parts section "Rules Judicially Considered".

3. Canadian Case Citations

The main volumes of the case citator component are the 10 volume *Canadian Case Citations, 1867-1990.* Each case name is accompanied by citation to the history of the case (*i.e.*, various reported appeal levels of the case) and under each case appear later citing cases which have judicially considered the case. The following example shows that an 1880 case was distinguished (D) by a 1991 case.

Green v. Blackwell
32 N.J. Eq. 768 (N.J. Err. & App. 1880)
(D) *Downey v. Metropolitan Transit Commission*
(August 22, 1991)
Doc. S.C.A. 02504 (N.S.C.A.)

The citing cases are Canadian cases while the cited cases are Canadian, British, other Commonwealth, or American.

For updating, see annual cumulative supplements shelved next to the main *Canadian Case Citations* volumes, quarterly supplements, and monthly *Canadian Case Citations* loose parts.

B. STATUTE CITATORS FOR CIVIL STATUTES

1. Common features

There are two types of coverage offered by statute citators. Some citators list only reported cases (cases from full-text reports series), while others list cases from rapid reporting digests, which contain all cases from the jurisdiction whether they later become reported or not. The span of years covered is also a consideration because of the recent appearance of a number of citators, which usually include unreported and reported cases.

Notification of changes to statute sections is accomplished by two methods. One method is by means of a "scope note" which is found at the beginning of the listing of cases for each statute and shows the changes to sections of the statutes. The other method is by means of a table of changes to statutes given in a separate section of the citator.

In addition to statutes being considered, most separately published citators list regulations and court rules considered. There are many types of publications which may be considered as statute citators, and they fall roughly into the following groupings:

(a) *Canada Statute Citator* covering most federal statutes (*Criminal Code* and *Income Tax Act* being notable exceptions). See Section C. 1. below.
(b) Citators for the *Criminal Code*. See Section D. below.
(c) Citators for the *Income Tax Act*. See Chapter 11's research checklist for Tax (section 0.8).
(d) Citators for provinces' statutes. See Sections C.2., C.3., and C.4. below.
(e) Digests and indexes publications with statute citator sections. See Section C.5. below.
(f) Annotated legislation series and citators for specific statutes such as the *Canadian Charter of Rights and Freedoms*. See Section C.6. below.

2. Jurisdictions covered

The separately published citator for federal statutes is the *Canada Statute Citator* (R.S.C. 1985 ed.). Companion bound volumes, *Canada Statute Annotations,* list pre-1985 cases considering pre-1985 statutes that were incorporated into R.S.C. 1985.

Looseleaf statute citator services giving reported cases are available for Ontario, British Columbia, Alberta, Saskatchewan, Manitoba, and Nova Scotia. Comprehensive statute citators listing unreported as well as reported cases are available for British Columbia, Alberta, Saskatchewan, and Manitoba. Many reports, digests, encyclopedias, and textbooks have tables of statutes considered by the cases reported, digested, or discussed within the publications. British Columbia is covered by three publications listed in the next section, while Saskatchewan is covered by *Saskatchewan Decisions Citator* (listed in the next section) plus *This Week's Law* (published by the Law Society of Saskatchewan Libraries).

C. INSTRUCTIONS FOR USE — STATUTE CITATORS

Because all of a publisher's citators usually use the same format, instructions and illustrations are given for representative titles. See the cross-reference table below for a representative example of each statute citator. Each example includes an illustration with numbered highlights and features a brief listing of material digested, relationship to other publications, etc.

Publication Title	*Representative Title Demonstrated*	*Example No.*
Canada Statute Citator	*Canada Statute Citator*	1
Ontario Statute Citator	*British Columbia Statute Citator*	2
British Columbia Statute Citator	*British Columbia Statute Citator*	2
Nova Scotia Statute Citator (R.S.N.S. 1989)	*Statutes of British Columbia Judicially Considered*	3
Statutes of British Columbia Judicially Considered	*Statutes of British Columbia Judicially Considered*	3
Statutes of Alberta Judicially Considered	*Statutes of British Columbia Judicially Considered*	3
Statutes of Saskatchewan Judicially Considered	*Statutes of British Columbia Judicially Considered*	3
Statutes of Manitoba Judicially Considered	*Statutes of British Columbia Judicially Considered*	3
British Columbia Decisions Statute Citator	*Saskatchewan Decisions Statute Citator*	4
Alberta Decisions Statute Citator	*Saskatchewan Decisions Statute Citator*	4
Saskatchewan Decisions Statute Citator	*Saskatchewan Decisions Statute Citator*	4
Manitoba Decisions Statute Citator	*Saskatchewan Decisions Statute Citator*	4

1. Canada Statute Citator example

(a) Features

(i) Title demonstrated: *Canada Statute Citator* (R.S.C. 1985 ed.).
(ii) Publisher: Canada Law Book.
(iii) Scope of coverage: Reported cases taken from law reports that cover R.S.C. 1985 and later Acts.

The volume *Canada Statute Annotations* (R.S.C. 1985 ed.) is a compilation of case annotations to the *Revised Statutes of Canada* between 1971 and 1988 (R.S.C. 1985 published in 1988). This volume lists Acts in force in the 1985 federal statute revision and gives cases considering versions of the revised statutes as they existed prior to 1985. Only those pre-1988 cases still relevant appear in this publication. Sections of the older statutes may have been repealed or amended prior to or in the 1985 statute revision, and cases considering such repealed legislation were not included in this publication.

The volume *Canada Statute Annotations* (R.S.C. 1970 ed.) is a compilation of case annotations to the *Revised Statutes of Canada* between 1941 and 1971. This volume lists Acts in force in the 1970 federal statute revision and gives cases considering versions of the revised statutes as they existed prior to 1970. Only those pre-1970 cases still relevant in 1970 appear in this publication. Sections of the older statutes may have been repealed or amended prior to or in the 1970 statute revision, and cases considering statute wording changed before or by 1970 were not included in this publication.

Hence, to find cases considering a statute in existence from 1941 to the present, research must be conducted in three publications: *Canada Statute Citator* (R.S.C. 1985 ed.) in looseleaf, in the bound *Canada Statute Annotations* (R.S.C. 1985 ed.) for cases 1971-1988, and in bound *Canada Statute Citations* (R.S.C. 1970 ed.) for cases 1941-1971.

(iv) Changes to statute sections: The history of the statute sections, including proclamation dates, is given in the main body of the work. The wording of new statute sections or amended versions of statute sections is provided in the main text.

(v) Regulations and rules considered: Cases considering federal regulations or court rules are not included.

(b) Instructions for use

The statutes are listed alphabetically by short title. Amendments are listed by giving the text of the amendments. If sections have been repealed since the 1985 statute revision, they are noted. The ministry that administers the Act is listed for all statutes. This format is similar to that of *British Columbia Statute Citator* - see Illustration 12.

Cases are listed under the section number of the statute, and a brief digest of the portion of the case construing the statute is presented. Citations are given for all law reports in which the case appears. If cases between 1971 and 1988 occur in the *Canada Statute Annotations* (R.S.C. 1985 ed.) volume, note is made in the *Canada Statute Citator* to that effect.

Cases construing the *Criminal Code* are not included in this publication, but are found in separate publications (*Criminal Code* citators, as discussed in the next section). Cases construing the *Income Tax Act* are not included, but are found in separate publications such as the annual Stikeman *Income Tax Act Annotated* (see Chapter 11's research checklist for Tax).

If there are not any cases or amendments to a particular statute section, the section is not listed. If there are no cases or amendments to an Act, the Act is listed with the note that there is no material to report on that Act.

This publication is available along with the full text of the federal statutes on Canada Law Book's "Canada Statute Service on CD-ROM".

2. British Columbia Statute Citator example

(a) Features

(i) Title demonstrated: *British Columbia Statute Citator* (R.S.B.C. 1979 ed.). Note: At time of writing, R.S.B.C. 1996 had been published, and a new edition of this demonstrated title (based on R.S.B.C. 1979) was anticipated.

(ii) Publisher: Canada Law Book.

(iii) Related publications: *Ontario Statute Citator* (R.S.O. 1990 ed.) and *Ontario Statute Annotations* for older statute revisions. A binder was provided into which pages from the *British Columbia Statute Citator* considering R.S.B.C. 1960, could be transferred.

(iv) Scope of coverage: Cases are taken from full-text law reports series, plus *Weekly Criminal Bulletin* and *All-Canada Weekly Summaries* (also published by Canada Law Book). For cases construing statutes from the prior statute revision, including statutes retained in force by the 1979 B.C. statute revision, refer to the citator for the prior statute revision.

(v) Changes to statute sections: Notification of amendments and appeals are given, but for the text of all amendments noted, see the official text of the annual *Statutes of British Columbia.*

(vi) Regulations and rules considered: There is a regulations table listing the Acts in R.S.B.C. 1979, under which are listed regulations titles, regulations numbers from the *British Columbia Gazette,* and gazette dates. Cases considering regulations are not given in the regulations table. The table is simply a list of regulations made pursuant to the statutes.
Cases considering court rules are not listed.

(vii) Note that the *Ontario Statute Citator* has a "Weekly Service Bulletin" which has information about current legislation.

(b) Instructions for use (refer to Illustration 12)

The statutes are listed alphabetically by short title. Amendments and repeals by section number are given. The ministry that administers the Act is noted for all statutes.

Cases are listed under the section number of the statute. A brief digest of the portion of the case construing the statute is given. Citations for all law reports or digests in which the case is reported or digested are presented.

An explanation of the use of the regulations table precedes the table, but the key point is that the table is an alphabetical listing of regulation titles under the alphabetical listings of statutes, rather than being a regulations case citator or key word index to regulations. The date of the table should be checked to determine what updating research is required.

3. Statutes of British Columbia Judicially Considered example

(a) Features

(i) Title demonstrated: *Statutes of British Columbia Judicially Considered.* Note: At time of writing, R.S.B.C. 1996 had been published, and a new edition of this demonstrated title (based on R.S.B.C. 1979) was anticipated.

(ii) Publisher: Carswell.

(iii) Related publications: *Statutes of Alberta Judicially Considered, Statutes of Saskatchewan Judicially Considered,* and *Statutes of Manitoba Judicially Considered.* See bound volumes for earlier statute revisions - *e.g., Statutes of British Columbia Judicially Considered* 1960-1978 for R.S.B.C. 1960, and *Alberta Rules of Court Judicially Considered* 1970-1981. Carswell, also publishes *Nova Scotia Statute Citator* (R.S.N.S. 1989).

(iv) Scope of coverage: Reported cases considering R.S.B.C. 1979. Cases considering prior statute revisions are printed in bound volumes.

(v) Changes to statutes sections: The "Table of Public Statutes" at the back of these citators lists changes to statutes, and this section is similar to tables published by provincial governments. The researcher should check the date of the table to determine what updating research is required.

(vi) Regulations and Rules considered: There is a separate tab for rules of court judicially considered. There is an alphabetical chart of regulations made pursuant to statutes accompanied by the regulation number from the official government gazette.

(b) Instructions for use (refer to Illustration 13)

Statutes are listed alphabetically by short title. The R.S.B.C. 1979 edition of *Statutes of British Columbia Judicially Considered* has "Statutes Considered" and "Court Rules Considered" sections.

4. Saskatchewan Decisions Citator example

(a) Features

(i) Title demonstrated: *Saskatchewan Decisions Citator.*

(ii) Publisher: Western Legal Publications.

(iii) Related publications: *British Columbia Decisions Citator, Alberta Decisions Citator, Manitoba Decisions Citator.*
(iv) Scope of coverage: Includes unreported as well as reported cases that interpret statutes. This publication gives coverage back to the late 1970s.
(v) Changes to statute sections: This publication does not provide this service.
(vi) Regulations: The regulations tab lists new and amending regulations under alphabetically arranged statutes. The regulation number and prior regulations affected are listed. The listing is updated each month.

(b) Instructions for use

Statutes are listed alphabetically by short title. Digests of the portions of cases interpreting the statutes are printed on looseleaf pages and interfiled by statute section number within the statute title. There are separate tab sections or binders for digests from each year.

5. Digests and indexes publications with statute citator sections

Many law reports and/or digests including looseleaf reporter services have sections that specifically list statutes judicially considered. Some of these publications list English statutes that have been considered by Canadian courts. Such publications include: *Canadian Abridgment Revised 2nd* component titled *Canadian Statute Citations* (discussed in the first section of this chapter), *National Reporter,* CCH and Carswell looseleaf reporter services, other Maritime Law Book law reports ("Statutes Judicially Noticed" sections), and Carswell law reports ("Statutes Judicially Considered" sections). For a listing, see the column labelled "STAT-CASE" in the charts of Chapter 3, Section B. Encyclopedias and textbooks may have "Table of Statutes" upon which comment has been made. *This Week's Law* (Saskatchewan) also has "Statutes Considered" sections.

6. Annotated legislation series and citators for specific statutes

There are citator publications dealing generally with federal (*Canada Statute Citator*) and provincial (discussed above) statutes, and there are general law reports with citator sections. In addition, some publications act as citators for specific statutes or groups of statutes:

(a) Citators for the *Criminal Code* and related statutes are covered in the next section, D.
(b) Citators for the *Income Tax Act* and tax publications with citator sections are listed in Chapter 11's research checklist for tax.
(c) Citators for statutes other than the criminal and tax areas include:
  (i) Business/Commerce
  Annotated Bank Act (Carswell).

Annotated Bankruptcy and Insolvency Act (Carswell).
Annotated Canada Business Corporations Act (Carswell).
Annotated Canada Shipping Act, The (Butterworths).
Annotated Competition Act (Carswell).
Annotated Copyright Act (Carswell).
Annotated Customs Act (Carswell).
Annotated ... Trade-Marks Act (Carswell).
Bank Act Annotated (Butterworths).
Canadian Business Corporations Acts Annotated (Butterworths text).
Canadian Patent Act Annotated (Canada Law Book).
Canadian Trade-Marks Act — Annotated (Carswell).
National Trade and Tariff Service: i.e., Customs Act, etc. (Butterworths).

(A) Alberta
Annotated Business Corporations Act of Alberta, 3rd ed. (Carswell).

(B) British Columbia
Annotated British Columbia Company Act, 2nd ed. (Carswell).
Annotated British Columbia Insurance (Motor Vehicle) Act, 2nd ed. (Carswell).

(C) Ontario
Annotated Insurance Act of Ontario (Carswell, three volumes).
Annotated Ontario Business Corporations Act (Canada Law Book).
Annotated Ontario Business Corporations Act, 1994 (Carswell).
Annotated Ontario Construction Liens Act (Carswell).
Annotated Ontario Personal Property Security Act (Carswell).
Annotated Ontario Securities Act (Carswell).
Insurance Act of Ontario Annotated (Butterworths).
Ontario Business Corporations Act, Annotated (Butterworths).

(ii) Environment / Natural Resources
Annotated B.C. Environmental Law Statutes, (Carswell).
Annotated Canadian Environmental Assessment Act (Carswell).
... Annotated Guide ... Forest Practices Code & Forest Act, British Columbia (Canada Law Book).
Annotated Ontario Environmental Protection Act (Carswell).
Annotated Ontario Water Resources Act (Carswell).
Canadian Environmental Law, 2nd ed. (Butterworths, seven volumes).
Canadian Oil and Gas, 2nd ed. (Butterworths, 10 volumes).
Ontario Environmental Protection Act Annotated (Canada Law Book).

(iii) Family Law
Annotated Divorce Act (Carswell).

Canadian Divorce Law and Practice, 2nd ed. (Carswell, two volumes, looseleaf).
Divorce Act Manual (Canada Law Book).

(A) Alberta and British Columbia
Alberta Family Law — Annotated Legislation (Butterworths).
British Columbia Family Law (Butterworths, two volumes).

(B) Ontario
Annotated Child and Family Services Act, (Carswell).
Annotated Ontario Estates Statutes (The 1997) (Carswell).
Annotated Ontario Family Law Act, 1997 (Carswell).
Ontario Annotated Family Law Service (Butterworths).
Ontario Family Law Act Manual, 2nd ed. (Canada Law Book).

(iv) Human Rights
Annotated Canadian Human Rights Act (Carswell).
Annotated Citizenship Act (Carswell).
Annotated Immigration Act (Carswell).
Annotated Indian Act (Carswell).
Annotated Ontario Human Rights Code (Carswell).
Canadian Charter of Rights Annotated (Canada Law Book).
Canadian Human Rights Reporter.
Charter of Rights Decisions (Western Legal Publications).
Practical Guide ... Ontario Human Rights Code (Canada Law Book).

(v) Labour Law/Employment
Annotated British Columbia Labour Relations Code (Butterworths).
Annotated Canada Labour Code (Carswell).
Annotated Employment Insurance Statutes (Carswell).
Annotated Ontario Employment Standards Act (Carswell).
Annotated Ontario Labour Relations Act (Carswell).
British Columbia Annotated Industrial Relations Act (Butterworths, two volumes).
Canada Labour Relations Board: An Annotated Guide (Canada Law Book).

(vi) Property/Municipal
Annotated Landlord and Tenant Act (Ontario) (Carswell).
Secured Transactions in Personal Property in Canada, 2nd ed. (Carswell, three volumes, looseleaf).

(A) Ontario
Annotated Municipal Act of Ontario (Carswell).
Annotated Ontario Condominium Act (Carswell).
Annotated Ontario Development Charges Act (Carswell).
Annotated Ontario Landlord and Tenant Act (Carswell).
Ontario Planning Practice: Annotated Statutes and Regulations (Canada Law Book).

(vii) Health and Medical
Annotated Ontario Mental Health Statutes (Carswell).
Regulated Health Professions Act ... Guides/Ontario (Canada Law Book).

D. STATUTE CITATORS FOR THE CRIMINAL CODE AND RELATED STATUTES

The *Criminal Code* and related statutes form the basis of a number of specialized statute citators. Searching for *Criminal Code* sections is especially effective on computer databases devoted to criminal law. Qualifying key words may be connected to the section number and sub-number. Annotated Criminal Codes and related publications are:

1. Martin's Annual Criminal Code 19—, with Annotations by Edward L. Greenspan (Canada Law Book)

(a) Statutes reproduced: *Criminal Code*, *Canada Evidence Act*, *Food and Drugs Act, Young Offenders Act*, and *Canadian Charter of Rights and Freedoms.*
Note: *Martins Criminal Code, Counsel Edition* is a looseleaf version of this citator.
Note: The companion volume, *Martin's Related Criminal Statutes*, covers the *Canada Evidence Act, Canadian Bill of Rights, Competition Act, Contraventions Act, Corrections and Conditional Release Act, Criminal Records Act, Customs Act, Extradition Act, Federal Court Act, Firearms Act, Fisheries Act, Fugitive Offenders Act, Identification of Criminals Act, Income Tax Act, Interpretation Act, Mutual Legal Assistance in Criminal Matters Act, Official Secrets Act, Prisons and Reformatories Act, Proceeds of Crime Act, Seized Property Management Act, Supreme Court Act*, and *Transfer of Offenders Act.*
(b) Coverage: Digests of reported and selected unreported cases follow each statute section.
(c) Format: Single bound volume, while the Counsel Edition is in looseleaf.
(d) Index and tables: "Index", "Table of Cases", "Table of Concordance" between R.S.C. 1985 and prior existing section numbers.
(e) Forms: "Appendix" with suggested forms of charges for the offences most commonly encountered.

2. Crankshaw's Criminal Code of Canada, R.S.C. 1985, edited by Gary P. Rodrigues (Carswell)

(a) Statutes reproduced: *Canada Evidence Act, Canadian Bill of Rights, Charter of Rights and Freedoms, Corrections and Conditional Release Act, Constitu-*

tion Acts, Criminal Code, Criminal Injuries Compensation Acts, Criminal Records Act, Extradition Act, Food and Drugs Act, Fugitive Offenders Act, Identification of Criminals Act, Mutual Legal Assistance in Criminal Matters Act, Official Secrets Act, Prison and Reformatories Act, Transfer of Offenders Act, Young Offenders Act, and many others.

(b) Coverage: Digests of reported cases from Canada and older cases from other jurisdictions of relevance follow each statute section. There is also a legislative history of each section, a listing of related *Criminal Code* sections and related statutes, and citation of relevant periodical articles and law reports annotations.

(c) Format: This nine-volume looseleaf service is updated with page insert releases and a quarterly Cumulative Case Law Supplement. After consulting the main work, consult the supplement under the relevant section to bring your search up to date.

(d) Index and tables: "Index", "Table of Cases", "Table of Concordance" between R.S.C. 1985 and all antecedents back to 1892.

(e) Forms: Part XXV in Volume 5.

3. Snow's Annotated Criminal Code by D.R.H. Heather, Q.C. (Carswell)

(a) Statutes reproduced: *Constitution Act, Controlled Drugs and Substances Act, Criminal Code, Canada Evidence Act, Food and Drugs Act, Young Offenders Act, Criminal Records Act, and Identification of Criminals Act.*

(b) Coverage: Digests of reported cases follow each statute section. A tab division has cites to articles, annotations, and practice notes appearing in the four series of the *Criminal Reports*.

(c) Format: This single looseleaf volume is updated with page insert releases.

(d) Index and tables: "Keyword Index" and "Table of Cases".

(e) Forms: A tab division has suggested wordings of charges for *Criminal Code* offences.

4. Annotated 199— Tremeear's Criminal Code by Mr. Justice David Watt and Michelle Fuerst

(a) Statutes reproduced: *Canada Evidence Act, Constitutional Act 1982, Controlled Drugs and Substances Act, Criminal Code, Firearms Act, Food and Drugs Act, Interpretation Act, Young Offenders Act.*

(b) Coverage: Digests of reported cases follow each statute section.

(c) Format: Bound annual of approximately 2,000 pages.

(d) Index and tables: Keyword index.

(e) Forms: A separate part containing forms.

5. Statute citators for related statutes

(a) *Canadian Charter of Rights and Freedoms* (much of criminal law practice affected by the Charter).
 (i) *Canadian Charter of Rights Annotated* (Canada Law Book).
 (ii) *Charter of Rights Decisions* (Western Legal Publications).
(b) *Young Offenders Act.*
 (i) *Young Offenders Service* (Butterworths).
 (ii) *Young Offenders Act Manual* (Canada Law Book).
(c) *Canada Evidence Act.*
 (i) *Annotated Canadian Evidence Acts* (Carswell).

E. CASE CITATORS

Cases may consider earlier cases in a number of ways, and case citators provide a list of abbreviations to indicate in what manner the citing (later) cases treat the cited (earlier) cases. The later report or digest may be the same case but in the appeal process, and the case citator abbreviations show how the history of the case evolves in the appeal process. The individual publications should be checked, but common abbreviations are as follows:

History of a case through the appeal process

Aff. (affirmed)	Decision affirmed on appeal.
Am (amended)	Decision altered on appeal.
Q. (quashed)	Decision set aside by appellate court for lack of jurisdiction.
Rev. (reversed)	Decision reversed on appeal.
Var. (varied)	Part of decision affirmed or reversed.

Treatment of the earlier cited case by later citing cases

Apld. (applied)	Principle of law from cited case was applied by the citing case.
Dist. (distinguished)	Citing case distinguishes itself from cited case on either essential facts or on a narrow point of law, even though the case may have appeared similar in many respects.
Folld. (followed)	Citing case follows cited case as being a leading case in the subject area.
Over. (overruled)	Decision of the citing case overrules the principle of law as stated in the cited case.

The *Canadian Case Citations* of the *Canadian Abridgment Revised (2nd)* provides a selected listing of significant citing cases considering the earlier cited cases from the early 1800s to the present. *Canadian Case Citations* was discussed in section 1 of this chapter.

Many law reports and digests providing jurisdictional or special subject coverage include cases judicially considered/noticed. For a listing of publications offering this function, see the column labelled "STAT-CASE" (note the "C"'s indicating a cases considered feature) in the "Charts" in Chapter 3, Section B. *CanCite* was a multi-volume case citation service published in the early 1990s by an established publisher. The publisher did not have a large customer base within the legal profession, and the project was not continued. *Canadian Case Citations* carries on as the comprehensive printed source.

For electronic means of finding cases judicially considered, see Chapter 10.

ILLUSTRATION 12
British Columbia Statute Citator (R.S.B.C. 1979 Edition)

[Coverage of the *Motor Carrier Act*, pages 91-1, 91-2]

MOTOR CARRIER ACT
R.S.B.C. 1979, Chap. 286

Amended 1980, c. 60, ss. 152 to 153; proclaimed in force September 11, 1980, by B.C. Reg. 384/80, *B.C. Gaz., Part II*, September 30, 1980
Amended 1981, c. 15, s. 128; proclaimed in force November 26, 1981 by B.C. Reg. 468/81, *B.C. Gaz., Part II*, December 15, 1981
Amended 1981, c. 21, s. 53; in force June 30, 1981

Administered by the Ministry of Transportation and Highways

For the text of all amendments noted see the official text of the Annual Statutes of British Columbia.

Section 31

Subsec. (2) amended, subsec. (3) repealed and subsecs. (3) to (12) substituted 1980, c. 60, ss. 152 and 153.

Section 33

Subsec. (1) repealed 1981, c. 15, s. 128.

Section 52

Re Gray Line of Victoria Ltd. and Chabot et al. (1981), 125 D.L.R, (3d) 197, [1981] 5 W.W.R. 385, 29 B.C.L.R. 168 (S.C.).

The appellate jurisdiction of the Lieutenant-Governor in Council does not violate s. 96 of the *British North America Act, 1867.*

Subsec. (1) *Re Gray Line of Victoria Ltd. and Chabot et al.* (1980), 117 D.L.R. (3d) 89. [1981] 2 W.W.R. 636 (B.C.S.C.).

The Lieutenant-Governor in Council is defined in the *Interpretation Act* (B.C.) as the Lieutenant-Governor acting with advice of the Executive Council. By convention, the Executive Council may act through a committee of one or more of its members. The rules of natural justice required that the real decision be made only by a majority of the members of the Executive Council who heard the appeal.

Subsec. (1)(*b*) *Re Gray Line of Victorian Ltd. and Chabot et al.*, see s. 52(l), *supra.*

Subsec. (7) amended 1981, c. 21, s. 53.

ILLUSTRATION 13
Statutes of British Columbia Judicially Considered May 1980-1982

[Coverage of the *Motor Carrier Act*, pages 146, 147]

MOTOR CARRIER ACT
R.S.B.C. 1979, c. 286

Nat. Freight Consultants Inc. v. Motor Tpt. Bd., [1980] 4 W.W.R. 67, 7 M.V.R. 42, 112 D.L.R. (3d) 32, 22 A.R. 54, 31 N.R. 26, reversing [1979] 2 W.W.R. 534, 96 D.L.R. (3d) 278, 4 A.R. 252, which reversed [1978] 2 W.W.R. 230, 84 D.L.R. (3d) 504, 10 A.R. 408 (S.C.C.)

Gray Line of Victoria v. Chabot; *Gray Line of Victoria Ltd. v. McClelland* (1981), 29 B.C.L.R. 168, [1981] 5 W.W.R. 385, 125 D.L.R. (3d) 197 (S.C.). - This Act is intra vires the province.

Sections 3, 5.

Gray Line of Victoria Ltd. v. Chabot; *Gray Line of Victoria Ltd. v. McClelland* (1981), 29 B.C.L.R. 168, [1981] 5 W.W.R. 385, 125 D.L.R. (3d) 197 (S.C.). - The creation of a right of appeal to the Lieutenant-Governor in Council or to any provincially designated tribunal from the decision of the Motor Carrier Commission is intra vires the province, because the appeal function is to regulate motor transportation and is not a judicial function.

Sections 31, 36.

Re C.P. Tpt. Co. (1979), 20 B.C.L.R. 127, 107 D.L.R. (3d) 384 (C.A.). - Although the requirement that a commission under the *Energy Act* have a quorum of two is incorporated by reference into the *Motor Carrier Act*, such a requirement does not preclude the Motor Carrier Commission from delegating to one of its members all of its powers and duties in hearing a particular application.

Chapter 7

Legal Encyclopedias

Legal encyclopedias are secondary authority legal literature which summarize existing statutory and case law in narrative commentaries arranged by subject. The format of legal encyclopedias is similar to that of general encyclopedias, except that there may be many more footnotes. The text often consists of one-line summaries of cases or statutes, and such sentences footnote to case or statute citations.

The two current encyclopedias covering the Eastern and Western regions are *Canadian Encyclopedic Digest* (Western 3rd edition) and *Canadian Encyclopedic Digest* (Ontario 3rd edition) by Carswell. Carswell offers both editions on one CD-ROM as "Canadian Encyclopedic Digest on CD-ROM".

A. CANADIAN ENCYCLOPEDIC DIGEST (ONTARIO 3RD EDITION)

Carswell publishes this legal encyclopedia in 40 looseleaf volumes. To broaden the coverage beyond Ontario law for federal and common law subjects, decisions from other provinces, from England, and from other common law jurisdictions have been included where appropriate. The basic format is the division of the work into 160 topics which are called "titles". Each title has its narrative paragraphs numbered to facilitate access.

1. Access through the keys

Main access to the work is through the looseleaf volume entitled *Research Guide and Key*. The *Key* is a starting point which provides the following sections:

(a) "Contents Key", contains a list of subject titles showing the volumes in which they appear.

(b) "Statutes Key", which is a statute citator. It lists statutes alphabetically, interfiling federal statutes with Ontario statutes. In this Key, statute section numbers are accompanied by the encyclopedia paragraph numbers that discuss the statute sections. Each title has its own "Table of Statutes".

(c) "Rules and Regulations Key" lists rules and regulations in a format similar to the "Statutes Key".

(d) "Index Key" which acts as an index to the entire set. References from the key words are to volume numbers and title numbers.

The looseleaf *Research Guide and Key* is updated through yellow supplement pages at the beginning of each section.

2. Updating and relation to other research sources

Updating is accomplished by yellow coloured supplement pages filed at the beginning of each title. If there are major changes to the law, the main white coloured looseleaf pages are replaced. Research may be transferred to the *Canadian Abridgment Rev. (2nd)* by mention of the appropriate *Canadian Abridgment Rev. (2nd)* title following the table of contents for each C.E.D. (Ont. 3rd) title. While this encyclopedia may include some citations of cases from other jurisdictions, notation of the cases cited within other digests, such as the *Canadian Abridgment Rev. (2nd)*, will lead to additional cases on point from other jurisdictions.

3. Tables of Statutes Concordance

A potential major problem is a change in statute revision while the main white-pages of a title cite to the old statute revision. There are tables of concordance cross-referencing from old revision cites in the white pages to current revision location of the statutory phrasing. Recent revision changes have been R.O. 1980 to R.O. 1990 and R.S.C. 1970 to R.S.C. 1985.

B. CANADIAN ENCYCLOPEDIC DIGEST (WESTERN 3RD EDITION)

The Canadian Encyclopedic Digest (Western 3rd edition)(C.E.D) is similar in concept to Carswell's other encyclopedia, C.E.D. (Ontario 3rd edition), but C.E.D. (Western 3rd) more recently began the replacement of its hardbound 2nd edition by a new looseleaf 3rd edition. C.E.D. (Western 3rd) stresses: federal law; provincial law for British Columbia, Alberta, Saskatchewan, Manitoba, and territorial law for the Northwest Territories and the Yukon. There are 159 titles arranged alphabetically in 43 looseleaf binders, plus the key volume. All reported cases and significant unreported cases are considered for inclusion in the narrative or footnotes. The intent is for each "title" to be complete in itself with its own Classification of Title (Table of Contents), Table of Cases, Table of Statutes, an Index, and if applicable a Table of Rules and Regulations. Pages are numbered within each title, and paragraphs are numbered to facilitate access. The tables and index for each title cite paragraph numbers. General access to the set is through the keys.

1. Access through the keys

The Key volume contains the following sections providing access to the titles:

(a) "Contents key" contains a list of subject titles showing the volumes in which they appear.

(b) "Statutes key", which consolidates the Table of Statutes from all titles. References are from cited sections of acts to paragraph numbers in the titles. For example:

STATUTES KEY

Accountants (Chartered) Act,
R.S.B.C. 1979, c. 2 s. 1 .... 28-119 s. 59.

For example, Section 1 is discussed in Volume 28, Title 119, paragraph 59.

(c) "Rules key" and "Regulations key", which consolidate tables from all titles.

(d) "Index" which cites from keyword terms to paragraph numbers within the titles. The index has many "see" cross-references. For example:

INDEX
INFANTS AND CHILDREN

juvenile delinquency. See YOUNG OFFENDERS
legal representations 18-77 ss. 557, 558
limitation of actions 18-77 ss. 150, 151

2. Updating and relation to other research sources

Yellow supplement pages are provided annually for each title's narrative text plus the title's tables. The yellow supplement entirely replaces the prior year's supplement, and if major changes occur in the subject matter, the whole title (white and yellow pages) may receive a new white-page, main article. The front page of the yellow supplement itemizes the latest dates of sources *(e.g.*, date of latest *Canadian Current Law* issue consulted used to prepare the supplement's narrative). Research may be transferred to Carswell's *Canadian Abridgment Revised (2nd)* by finding the "C.E.D.-cited" case in the Can. Abr. Rev. (2nd) "Table of Cases". The Can. Abr. Rev. (2nd) "Table of Cases" will show the location of the case's digest within a Can. Abr. Rev. (2nd) group of similar case digests (*i.e.*, one "C.E.D.-cited" case leading to a grouping of similar cases in Can. Abr. Rev. (2nd)). The Can. Abr. Rev. (2nd)'s "Key Classification System" number can be researched up to the latest issue of *Canadian Current Law Case Law Digests.*

Chapter 8

Legal Periodicals and Legal Periodical Indexes

A. TYPES OF PERIODICALS AND COMMON FEATURES OF INDEXES

1. Types of legal periodicals

The traditional definition of legal periodical literature would encompass law reviews and similar journals. This definition could be expanded to include material indexed in periodical indexes such as collections of essays, annotations in law reports series, and audio cassette tapes. The contents of all of the foregoing types of literature are not contained in a law library's card or online catalogue, and subject access is provided by periodical indexes.

Legal periodicals of a journal nature fall into three categories: law school reviews, bar association publications, and special subject journals. The function of law school reviews, which are produced by an editorial board of law students, is to provide legal research and writing experience for outstanding law students as well as providing articles by practising lawyers in areas of current interest. These articles may either be theoretical in nature or critical of existing law. They provide footnotes to cases and statutes, as do legal encyclopedias and other finding aids for primary law.

Bar association journals generally provide news of local bar activities, but there also may be valuable articles concerning practical points of law.

Special subject journals may be produced by law schools, associations, or private publishers, with articles directed toward a specific topic. Law report annotations are included in this category.

Journals may contain broad-ranging articles, comments upon a particular case, and book reviews. Some Canadian journals, which specialize in a non-legal field, frequently contain legal articles, and the legal contents are indexed in Canadian legal periodical indexes.

2. Common features of legal periodical indexes

Periodical literature is accessed through periodical literature indexes, not through the card catalogues or other book holdings listings of law libraries. When using a periodical index, note the number of journals indexed and the number of years covered by the index. While journal articles often deal with matters of current interest, the time lag in preparation of periodical indexes can be relatively lengthy.

Common features appearing in many periodical indexes are:

(a) A subject index, which arranges articles and case comments in subject order.
(b) An author index, which alphabetically lists authors with the titles and citations of their articles.
(c) A table of cases, which alphabetically lists cases with citations for the case comments.
(d) A book review index, which alphabetically lists book authors with their book titles, persons reviewing the books, and citations for the book reviews.

Periodical articles and other secondary literature are sometimes cited by case law. The journal article citator function is not filled by legal periodical indexes, but rather by case law digest publications and law report indexes. These digest and report tables are given such titles as "Authorities Cited" or "Index to Authors and Works Judicially Noticed". See the "2nd LIT" (secondary literature cited by cases) column in the "charts" in Chapter 3, Section B.

Some legal periodical indexes now form databases on computer systems.

3. Expanded functions of legal periodical indexes

The traditional view of legal periodical indexes is as a library research tool since individual journal articles do not appear in the library's card catalogue. With the growing body of legal literature, it would be valuable for the law office to have a research tool indexing various types of literature in addition to journal articles. Some indexes have expanded beyond merely indexing periodical literature. Some materials discussed in Chapter 9 (textbooks and CLE materials) and in Chapter 18 (government publications) are now indexed in such publications as the *Canadian Abridgment Revised (2nd)*'s component *Index to Canadian Legal Literature.*

B. PERIODICAL INDEXES FOR CANADIAN LEGAL LITERATURE

There are several Canadian and American periodical indexes providing coverage of Canadian legal periodical literature. Each publication has its own advantages: number of journals indexed, rapidness of publication, depth and detail of indexing, and span of years.

Individual legal periodical indexes are:

ILLUSTRATION 14
Index to Canadian Legal Periodical Literature, 1978, page A-41

[NOTE: For the time period covered, there were no case comments on the 1978 Supreme Court of Canada case used as an example in Illustrations 1-5, 8, 9.]

INFANTS

Adolescents who kill a member of the family. B.M. Corimer and others (1978) Violence 466-478

Alternatives to the judicial process: court avoidance in child neglect cases. D. Cruikshank (1978) 12 UBC L Rev 248-275

Child abuse: the problem. A.J. Solnit. (1978) Violence 243-252

The child and the court. J. Wilson (1977) 1 Can lawyer 2:23-25

Child care or protection racket? J.A. Scutt (1978) 1 Family L R 48-57

Child law and religious extremists: some recent developments. F. Bates (1978) 10 Ottawa L R 299-312

Children in the courts: a selected empirical review. K. Catton. (1978) 1 Can J Fam 329-362

Children's suicide. M. Rood de Boer. (1978) Violence 441-459

The international kidnapping of children: common law, Canada. R. Anderson. (1975) 13 Col I Dr Comp 123-139

The international kidnapping of children: comparative summing-up. J.A. Clarence Smith. (1975) 13 Col I Dr Comp 192-196

sion). Ontario. Ministry of the Attorney General. (1976) 29 Rrep Fam L 134-154

La représentation de l'efant vs les tribunaux de la jeunesse, de droit commun et d'appel; explication du théme. P.A. Champagne. (1978) 38 R du B 515-517

La représentation de l'enfant vs les tribunaux de la jeunesse, de droit commun et d'appel; rapport d'atelier. A. Mondor. (1978) 38 R du B 517-519

Sibling violence. S. K. Steinmetz (1978) Violence 460-465

The unsworn evidence of children and mutual corroboration E. Gertner. (1978) 16 Osgoode Hall L 495-513

See also
ADOPTION
CHILD ABUSE
INFANTS (CIVIL LAW)
JUVENILE COURTS
JUVENILE DELINQUENCY
PARENT AND CHILD

Cases

Liffiton et al. and Campbell, [1972] 2 O.R. 592. (1978) 3 F.L.A.S. side 1

R. v. Tennant and Naccarato, (1975) 23 C.C.C. (2d) 80, (1978) March C.L.A.S. side 1, pt. 1 – side 2, pt. 1

---

1. Index to Canadian Legal Periodical Literature (ICLPL)

(a) Analysis

(i) Publisher: Published by Index to Canadian Legal Periodical Literature.

(ii) Scope of coverage: 1961 to date; law reviews, bar association journals, special subject journals including those with only partial legal contents, audio cassette series, and collections of essays.

(iii) Frequency and time lag: Issues are released approximately every three months. While there was a time lag problem, the time lag from receipt of the issue by the subscriber back to date of some entries is down to about four months.

(iv) Features:
 (A) Subject Index: Yes, including good coverage of Québec topics.
 (B) Author index: Yes.
 (C) Table of cases: Yes.
 (D) Book review index: Yes.

(b) Instructions for use

The ICLPL is issued in June and September in loose part form, with each loose part being cumulative from January. Bound volumes are issued for the full year, and there are cumulations for 1961-70 and each five year period thereafter.

Near the front of the Index, there is a listing of subject headings used, with references from French legal terms to the English headings used. Articles are listed alphabetically by title under each subject heading in the "Subject Index", with any case comment citations assigned to the subject heading appearing after the article citations.

If there is an article citation referring to a collection of essays or to another irregular or unfamiliar publication, book ordering information is provided near the front under the listing "Collection of Essays" (following the listing of "Periodicals").

A case comment is listed in the "Subject Index" in the sublisting entitled "Cases" at the end of the listing of articles under each subject heading as noted above. Case comments are also listed under the commentator's name in the "Author Index", and in the "Table of Cases", which gives case comments alphabetically by name of the first party in the style of cause.

2. Index to Canadian Legal Literature

(A separately published component of the *Canadian Abridgment Revised (2d)* and also published in a bound annual Library Edition.)

(a) Analysis

(i) Publisher: Carswell

(ii) Scope of coverage: The written index policy in the publication states:

 "Coverage: ICLL is both a periodical index and a bibliography of Canadian secondary legal literature. In addition to articles, case comments and annotations from more than 140 Canadian legal and law-related periodicals, ICLL indexes monographs, individual essays from edited collections, federal and provincial government publications, and the publications of law faculties and legal research institutes and associations, including theses. For the practitioner, it indexes publications from the law societies and associations, including continuing legal education (CLE) materials. For the lay[person], ICLL indexes popular legal works and public legal education (PLE) materials, including audio-visual materials."

Both English language and French language materials are indexed.

(iii) Frequency and time lag: Paper loose parts are issued eight times per year under the title, *Canadian Current Law Canadian Legal Literature*. Annual volumes are published under the title, *Index to Canadian Legal Literature*. Some of the entries have a time lag of only several months.

(iv) Features:

(A) Subject Index: The English subject headings are a combination of Library of Congress Subject Headings and National Library of Canada Subject Headings. The sub-headings are subject, form (cases, seminars, etc.), or jurisdictional. "See" cross-references are included.

(B) Author Index: If a publication has multiple authors, the work is entered under each author's name.

(C) Table of Cases: Cases are only included if they have received substantial comment in case comments, annotations, or articles.

(D) Table of Statutes: Statutes are only included if they received substantial comment by the literature.

(E) Book Review Index: A work is entered under its title, author, and reviewer.

(b) Instructions for use

There are five access points to information as noted in the above description of the five features. The publication appears in paper loose part form eight times per year under the title, *Canadian Current Law Canadian Legal Literature*. Annual volumes titled *Index to Canadian Legal Literature* have been issued since 1987. Two volumes covered 1985-1986. There was an initial three-volume set which covered to 1984 and which updated and replaced a feature of the Can. Abr. (2nd) begun in the 1950s. With more than 15 bound volumes at time of writing, it seems likely that the consolidation process within the Can. Abr. Rev. (2nd) may extend to this component.

(c) Electronic sources

(i) Internet: Micromedia Limited (www.mmltd.com/voyageur/icll_sht.html).

(ii) Online: QL Systems Ltd.'s databases:
"Index to Canadian Legal Literature, global" (ICLL); journal articles, texts, case comments (ICLJ), book reviews (ICLB).

(iii) CD-ROM: Micromedia Limited (Toronto).

3. Current Law Index (CLI)

(a) Analysis

(i) Publisher: Information Access Company, Foster City, California, U.S.A.

(ii) Scope of coverage: This relatively new index began publication in 1980, and it covers more than 700 law periodicals published in English throughout the world. The exception of coverage of journals published in English is the inclusion of some Québec journals. There are no restrictions as to the minimum number of pages an article must cover before it is indexed.

(iii) Frequency and time lag: It is intended to be a comprehensive yet rapidly produced index. There are eight monthly issues, three quarterly cumulations, and a single annual cumulation.

(iv) Features:

(A) Subject Index: The "Subject Index" contains detailed subject headings with many references from terminology not used as subject headings to actual subject headings, and from one subject heading to a related subject heading. If there are more than 15 articles per subject heading, the subject heading is subdivided.

(B) Author Index: There is a combined "Author/Title Index".

(C) Table of Cases: There are separate tables of cases listing cases including case comments by both plaintiffs' and defendants' names, and a "Table of Statutes" index, listing statutes alphabetically within jurisdiction.

(D) Book Review Index: Book reviews are assigned a letter grade (on a scale of A to F) according to the response of the book reviewer. They are contained within the "Author/Title Index", rather than being a separate listing.

(b) Instructions for use

This American index has a substantial number of Canadian titles indexed, and more may be added. With the great number of subject headings used in cross-references, it is not practical to have a listing of subject headings at the front of the publication. Search of the subject index should be made by key word, similar to searching digest indexes.

To locate an article that reviews a book, use the author/title index by searching for the reviewer of the book, the author of the book, or the title of the book.

CLI covers many Commonwealth legal periodicals, which is advantageous because of the suspension of the *Index to Commonwealth Legal Periodicals*.

(c) Related publication: Legal Resource Index (LRI)

This research tool is published in conjunction with CLI but has the added features of indexing popular periodicals (*e.g., Macleans*) and some books, government documents, and newspapers.

(d) Electronic sources for Legal Resource Index

Online sources are: LEXIS-NEXIS, library LEXREF, file name LGLIND; WESTLAW (through QL Systems Ltd.), identifier LRI. Check with Micromedia Ltd. (Toronto) about CD-ROM and Internet availability.

4. Index to Legal Periodicals

(a) Analysis

(i) Publisher: H.W. Wilson Company, Bronx, New York, U.S.A.
(ii) Scope of coverage: 1908 to date. More than 400 legal journals from Canada, the United States, England, Ireland, Australia, and New Zealand are indexed. Articles must be five pages in length before they are indexed.
(iii) Frequency and time lag: Issues are produced 11 times per year and are cumulated quarterly, annually, and triannually. The time lag may be six months or more from time of publication of the article to receipt of the index by the subscriber.
(iv) Features:
  (A) Subject Index: There is a combined "Subject and Author Index".
  (B) Author Index: There is a combined "Subject and Author Index".
  (C) Table of Cases: There is a "Table of Cases Commented Upon", and a "Table of Statutes Commented Upon" which lists statutes by country and province.
  (D) Book Review Index: The "Book Review Index" provides a listing, by author, of the material being reviewed.

(b) Instructions for use

The cumulative issues provide a list of subject headings with references from terminology not used as subject headings to wording used as subject headings, and from one related subject heading to another. Articles are alphabetically arranged under subject headings, with no subject heading subdivisions. Case comments are listed at the end of each subject heading.

(c) Electronic Sources

Online sources are: LEXIS-NEXIS, library LEXREF, file name ILP; WESTLAW (through QL Systems Ltd.), identifier ILP. Check with Micromedia Ltd. (Toronto) about CD-ROM and Internet availability.

5. Legal periodicals' own indexes and other indexes

Some individual journals provide their own cumulative indexes, *e.g.*, *The Canadian Bar Review Index*, *The Criminal Law Quarterly Index*, *The Law Society of*

Upper Canada Special Lectures Index and Tables, and *The University of British Columbia Law Review Index.*

A basic caution is that no single source covers all English language legal journal articles in the countries tracing their legal heritage to Great Britain.

Other legal periodical literature indexes include:

(a) Index to Periodical Articles Related to Law

This index covers periodicals with some legal contents which are not covered by *Current Law Index or Index to Legal Periodicals.*

(b) Index to Foreign Legal Periodicals

This index is primarily designed to cover English language articles which are not from the Commonwealth or the United States. It is particularly useful for international law and comparative law. It is available electronically on WESTLAW (through QL Systems Ltd.), identifer IFLP. Check with Micromedia Ltd. (Toronto) for CD-ROM and Internet availability.

(c) Legal Journals Index

This index covers more than 250 journals from Great Britain and began in 1986. The separate indexes include: subject, author, case, legislation, and book review. Sweet and Maxwell law publishers (Carswell as agent), incorporates *Legal Journals Index* and *European Legal Journals Index* into a single CD-ROM.

(d) Current Index to Legal Periodicals

This serves as an advance service to the *Index to Legal Periodicals* and is published by the University of Washington, Marian G. Gallagher Law Library, Seattle, Washington. The most recent eight weeks are available electronically on WESTLAW (through QL Systems Ltd.), identifier CILP.

(e) Index to Commonwealth Legal Periodicals

This index was published from 1974 to 1981 and covered more than 150 periodicals from throughout the Commonwealth. Almost half of the journals indexed were not covered by the *Index to Canadian Legal Periodical Literature* or the *Index to Legal Periodicals*. This publication predates *Current Law Index.*

(f) Australian Legal Literature Index

The LEXIS-NEXIS online system of databases includes the Australian library, AUST, with the ALLI file (*Australian Legal Literature Index*, 1985-).

(g) Bibliography of legal periodicals in electronic format

The Bora Laskin Law Library at the University of Toronto provides a listing of legal periodicals available online or through the Internet. The Internet address for this bibliography is: www.law-lib.utoronto.ca/

Chapter 9

Other Secondary Literature Research Sources

The largest category of secondary legal literature not covered by other chapters is the textbook area, including continuing legal education (CLE) material and looseleaf services. Form and precedent sets are a useful source of prescribed forms for court work and for drafting legal documents. "Words and phrases" publications and dictionaries offer quick access to legal terminology. Directories are useful when contacting lawyers for assistance in other cities.

A. TEXTBOOKS

1. Common features

Legal textbooks may perform functions similar to legal encyclopedias by providing narrative discussion of an area of law with footnotes to cases and statutes, but they are able to provide more in-depth discussion than the relatively short encyclopedia or journal articles. The most in-depth discussion of existing law will be found in textbooks that are not law school casebooks. If a casebook is the only textual treatment of an area, a casebook's index will provide access to limited discussion and comment on sub-areas of the law. Textbooks may not only be a digest or narrative of existing law; they may also be the author's forum for suggesting changes that should be made in current law.

Common features of textbooks include a table of cases discussed in the narrative, a table of statutes discussed, and sometimes forms which are useful drafting aids for lawyers. There may be means for updating the volume by insertion of looseleaf pages if the publication is in binder format, by placement of a pocket part inside the front or back cover of the book, or by publication of separate paperbound or hardbound supplements. Textbooks are sometimes cited by court cases as persuasive authority statements. For law reports which have tables of texts and other "secondary literature" cited by cases, see the "2nd LIT" column in the "charts" in Chapter 3, section B.

The major Canadian legal textbook publishers are Butterworths, CCH, Canada Law Book, Carswell, and Emond Montgomery. Provincial legal education societies and continuing legal education offices as well as Insight Educational Services Ltd. produce textbook-like binder materials after seminars. Law offices may place themselves on the mailing lists for these publishers and may subscribe to the new acquisition listings from law school libraries. From review of these acquisition listings, law offices may discover other publishers from which they wish to receive regular mailings.

2. Arrangement of texts in law libraries

(a) Cataloguing books

While smaller court house libraries may have textbooks arranged alphabetically by author, larger law libraries usually have their textbook collections catalogued, classified, or both. If a library has been catalogued, the library staff has made a listing of all the library's books and included information such as author, title, general publishing data, and subject headings or the areas of law a book covers.

The listing may be made on cards filed in the trays of the library's catalogue. Under this arrangement, the master card for each book is reproduced several times, with the author appearing at the top of one card, the title placed at the top of another card, and the various subject headings assigned to the book at the tops of other cards. These cards are then filed alphabetically in the trays of the catalogue so that lawyers may locate books by author, title, or subject heading.

Rather than using card catalogues, some libraries may produce the listings in microcopy such as microfilm or microfiche. Users should receive instructions from library staff on how to use these tools. The library may also provide the listings in a computer printout of the library's holdings arranged by author, title, and subject heading.

Many law libraries have implemented computer "online" catalogues, which provide access to patrons via terminals in the libraries' reader services areas. The effectiveness of online catalogues depends on the software used for compilation. Software can range from simply off-the-shelf database computers to complex systems which integrate all library operations, including book ordering, circulation, and cataloguing.

In recent years, the online catalogue has become the preferred option even for small libraries and law firm collections. Except for the smallest collections, cataloguing now relies almost exclusively upon electronic sources available online and on CD-ROM.

(b) Classifying books with call numbers

The library is "classified" if the books are grouped on the shelves accordingly to subject. There are several classification schemes in use throughout larger libraries, but all of them assign alphanumeric designations to sub-areas of law. This subject designation is used in conjunction with an additional alpha numeric abbreviation for the author's name. This combination of alphanumeric designations provides a unique call number for each book. The call number is placed on the spine of the book so that it may be placed on a library shelf by author's name within a very narrow subject grouping. For example, John D. Whyte's book, *Canadian Constitutional Law*, has the call number KM70W629 in the classification scheme used by the Law Society of Saskatchewan. KM70 places the book in the constitutional law section, while W629 places the book alphabetically by author within the constitutional law grouping.

Arranging books on the shelf by subject makes it more convenient for lawyers to browse through all of the library's holdings in a particular area, especially when the particular book the lawyer wants is currently on loan. Lawyers should not only rely upon browsing in a particular shelf location, but should also use the card catalogue or other listing, because while books may have only one shelf location, they may have several subject headings. The library shelf containing books on taxation may not be the library's complete textbook coverage of the subject, since the card catalogue's subject-heading division on taxation may yield additional material — such as a book primarily dealing with agriculture which has a small portion on taxation and has been shelved in the agricultural law location.

B. LOOSELEAF SERVICES

1. Format

Looseleaf services are published in binder format so that the subscriber receives pages covering new developments in the law on a frequent basis. The new pages are inserted in place of obsolete pages which are removed. Looseleaf services are published in fields that are rapidly changing and growing with the issuance of regulations, rulings, and interpretations by governments, commissions, boards, and associations. The looseleaf services gather this regulatory and miscellaneous matter in one source and publish it along with relevant statutes, cases or digests, and editorial commentary.

Depending on the area of law, the arrangement of the service may be by section of a particular statute or in a topic arrangement chosen to fit several statutes to the particular field. In addition to insert pages to be placed in the main body of the text, summaries or current reports are also sent to the subscribers so that they may survey changes in the law since the prior issuance of updating material.

The looseleaf services that fully report court cases and board decisions provide for permanent cumulation of cases through either bound volumes or transfer binders. At the end of each year, the annual cumulation of cases and decisions is removed from the main binders and placed in a transfer binder as a permanent housing of the year's cumulation, or is removed to be replaced by a bound volume containing the cases or decisions. An example is the *Canadian Insurance Law Reporter* CCH Canadian Ltd. A current binder holds recent decisions which, after a few years, are rebound in transfer binders.

2. Research approaches

(a) The general search by key word or phrase

The general index, which may be called a topical index, gives key word access to the main body of the looseleaf service. References in this main index may lead to a page number in the service or a paragraph number. Some services use paragraph numbers so that cross-references will remain constant within the work, even though page numbers change as new material is added. The major sections of the work are usually divided by tab dividers, and sections contain the text of appropriate Acts followed by relevant regulations, cases or case digests, and editorial commentary.

The most recent material on a topic is initially collected in a current or "new matters" section which often has its own index. Some services facilitate transition from the main body to the new matter by cross-referencing the new matters' index to the pages or paragraph numbers of the main body. Periodically the contents of the new matters section is incorporated into the body of the main work.

The current report or summary will provide the subscriber with an overview of the most significant material contained in the latest update releases.

CCH gives subscribers a "Rapid Finder Index" which cross-references from subtopics of law to the CCH looseleaf publication that covers the subtopic.

(b) Tables search

The other method of entry into the looseleaf services is by table of cases, table of regulations, tables of bulletins, *etc.* When a specific case or document is known, it may be researched in one of the tables or finding aids. The main table may have a supplementary table which is incorporated into the main table periodically. For instructions on how to use a looseleaf service, see Example L in Chapter 3, C. 12.

C. FORMS AND PRECEDENT SETS

Forms and precedents sets provide models to be used or adapted to a lawyer's particular needs when drafting agreements, court documents, etc. These sets may concentrate on court work or on general or specialized non-litigation areas.

In the early 1990s two major Canadian forms sets began publication in looseleaf form. At time of writing, the 11th edition of *O'Brien's Encyclopedia of Forms* (Canada Law Book) has published nine divisions in 20 volumes, while *Canadian Forms & Precedents* (Butterworths) has published three modules in eight volumes. These two publishing projects both cover the commercial area, corporations, banking, real estate, and wills. *O'Brien's* also covers a variety of other specialized situations, and both publishers offer court forms. Carswell produces several "wills" titles, the specialized *Criminal Law Precedents,* and two four-volume corporate precedent sets.

Form books are idea books to be adapted, and if a narrow, particular point cannot be located in the Canadian forms and precedents sets, reference can be made to forms and precedents of other jurisdictions where some sets are 30 volumes or more. Forms and precedents books from England are discussed in Chapter 13; from the United States in Chapter 14; and from Australia and New Zealand in Chapter 15.

The major Canadian forms and precedents sets are:

1. Comprehensive Forms Sets

(a) Canadian Forms and Precedents (Butterworths):

This looseleaf forms and precedents series is published in modules, and subscriptions may be placed for any or all of the modules. Each module has its own consolidated index, table of cases, and table of statutes. Each title within a module has a table of contents, commentary, and checklists where appropriate. The modules and contents are:

Module 1: "Banking and Finance" (four volumes)

The titles and major sub-titles are: basic account and business forms; treasury and central banking agreements; interbank agreements, Euroloans; commercial paper; credit facilities (loan agreements, financing arrangements, loan extension & renewal, notices and demands); interlender agreements; legal opinions; resolutions, bylaws & certificates; receiverships and collections; security documentation (real property security, security agreements, debentures, trust indentures, additional forms of security, *e.g.*, guarantees and indemnities); private placements; derivatives and related agreements; equity financing.

Module 2: "Commercial Transactions" (three volumes)

The titles are: patents; trade-marks; industrial design; copyright; distribution of goods and services; computer contracts; entertainment agreements; equipment leasing; sale of a business; manufacture and sale of goods, transport and storage of goods.

Module 3: "Debtor/Creditor" (one volume plus computer diskette of forms)

The major areas are: bankruptcy, receivership, restructuring, construction liens, and levying execution. Diskettes are available.

(b) O'Brien's Encyclopedia of Forms, 11th edition (Canada Law Book):

This 11th edition was published in looseleaf over several years in the early 1990s and now consists of nine main divisions in 20 volumes. There are cross-references between forms and optional clauses are presented with many of the forms. Subscriptions may be placed for any or all of the divisions. Each division has its own index. WordPerfect disks containing the forms are available free with purchase of the printed volumes. The disks are of value to busy practitioners, who can increase productivity. The divisions and contents are:

Division I: "Commercial and General" (five volumes)

The approximately 50 chapters include: Affidavits, Agreements, Agriculture, Arbitration, Assignments, Building Contracts, Clubs and Associations, Computers, Dealerships, Franchises, Gifts, Hospitals, Powers of Attorney, Promissory Notes, Sales, and Secured Transactions.

Division II: "Corporations" (four volumes)

The four parts are: General Corporate Documents, Banking and Borrowing, Securities Law, and Corporate Acquisitions.

Division III: "Conveyancing and Mortgages" (one volume)

Designed for the general practitioner or specialist, the forms extend from listing agreements to complex joint venture agreements.

Division IV: "Leases" (one volume)

Designed for the general practitioner or commercial real estate specialists. Relevant provincial statutes are noted when they require specific wording.

Division V: "Wills and Trusts" (one volume)

A wide array of complete wills and portable clauses, arranged under subject headings.

Division VI: "Ontario Family Law" (one volume)

The volume includes litigation documents and letters of suggested communication to clients. The domestic contracts include statutory requirements regarding income tax and corporate law.

Division VII: "Labour Relations" (two volumes)

Labour and employment subjects include human rights, labour standards, trade unions, health and safety, unemployment insurance, workers compensation, pay equity, and industrial action and discipline. Federal, Alberta, B.C., and Ontario contexts are considered.

Division VIII: "Ontario-Court Forms" (three volumes)

This subset provides checklists, office forms and letters, and civil action court forms.

Division IX: "Municipal Corporations" (one volume)

Commentary and agreements including administration, finances, facilities, and planning and development.

Master Subject Index, Divisions I-IX (one volume)

Includes a master table of contents and cross references.

2. Civil Actions Forms Sets

(a) Williston and Rolls' Court Forms (Butterworths)

This four volume looseleaf set attempts to include 2,000 civil action forms ranging from the beginning of court work with retainer and change of solicitors, through other preliminary matters, commencement of proceedings, discovery, originating motions, extraordinary remedies, judgments and orders, costs, and to appeals. The material follows a chronological format parallelling the structure of the Ontario *Rules of Civil Procedure*. The set is available on a single CD-ROM with access by Rule Heading, form name or number, or keyword search.

(b) British Columbia Court Forms (Butterworths)

This five volume set by McLachlin and Taylor is a looseleaf which is maintained by the insertion of replacement pages. The forms are presented as they would be encountered chronologically in a civil action, and the set includes examples of completed forms. The set includes commentary, Table of Cases, Table of Statutes, and subject index. It is included with *British Columbia Practice, 2nd Edition* on a CD-ROM titled "British Columbia Civil Practice Library".

(c) O'Brien's Encyclopedia of Forms (Canada Law Books)

"Division VIII: Ontario — Court Forms" (three volumes)

3. Criminal Law Forms Sets

(a) Criminal Law Precedents (Carswell)

This two-volume looseleaf set has the stated purpose of being "offered not so much out of a desire to achieve a standardization of form in the endless variety of individual cases governed by the same statutory provisions but rather in hopes that some assistance may be afforded in drafting the documentation necessary to achieve a proper and just result in those cases."

The contents cover warrants and orders, procuring the attendance of witnesses, judicial interim release, the *Protection of Privacy Act,* institution of proceedings, trial procedure on evidence, appellate remedies (indictable offences), extraordinary remedies, summary conviction proceedings, and material on statutes other than the *Criminal Code,* but related to criminal matters. The appendices have rules respecting appeals from each of the provinces and territories.

Diskettes are available.

4. Specialty Forms Sets: Wills

(a) Butterworth publishes:

McIntryre, *Practical Wills Drafting*
This book contains checklists, questionnaires, and sample clause precedents.

(b) Carswell publishes:

(i) Scott-Harston, *Tax Planned Will Precedents*, 3rd Edition
The volume contains annotated precedents, master will, will instruction checklist, alternative clauses, relevant legislation, and discussion of trusts. There are "How to Use" guides for each section. A collection of three computer diskettes containing the text of the wills precedents is optionally available. Diskettes are available.

(ii) Sheard, Hull, and Fitzpatrick, *Canadian Forms of Wills*, 4th edition, 1982, 402 pages. (Out of print).

(iii) Histrop, *Estate Planning: A Solicitor's Manual*
This volume also includes domestic contract precedents, trust deed documents, estate planning forms, checklists, and signing instructions. Optional computer diskettes are available to increase productivity.

(c) Canada Law Book publishes:

Wills forms and precedents are included in *O'Brien's Encyclopedia of Forms, Division V*, "Wills and Trusts".

5. Specialty Forms Sets: Corporations, Banking, and Securities

(a) Butterworths publishes:

Canadian Forms & Precedents, Module "Banking and Finances".

(b) Carswell publishes:

Partners of the firm Davies, Ward, & Beck (Toronto) prepare the contents of the following looseleaf precedent sets for Carswell. Each set has five volumes:

(a) *Canadian Corporation Precedents, 3rd edition* (diskettes available).

(b) *Canadian Securities Law Precedents* (diskettes available).

(c) Canada Law Book publishes:

O'Brien's Encyclopedia of Forms, Division II: Corporations (three volumes)
Banking and securities law included.

D. WORDS AND PHRASES SETS AND LEGAL DICTIONARIES

Legal dictionaries define words and Latin phrases as they are used in the legal context. Often the definition has been taken from a definition given as part of a judge's opinion, and the dictionary gives the case citation. The definition given is one of general usage in the legal community if a relevant court decision has not provided a definition.

Words and phrases publications are listings of court decisions that have defined words and phrases. Words or phrases not defined by court decisions will not be found in these sets. Separately published words and phrases sets include brief digests of the portions of cases defining the words or phrases. Sections of law reports or digests listing words and phrases usually only provide case citation where the definitions can be found, rather than providing a digest of the case.

Specific publications with Canadian coverage are:

1. Legal Dictionaries

(a) The Dictionary of Canadian Law 2nd Edition (by Dukelow and Nuse)

Published by Carswell in 1994, this is the first comprehensive (1,560 pages) dictionary based on primary Canadian law. The definitions are based upon frequency of use in primary law sources and in Canadian textbooks. Authorities are cited. It is a complete dictionary, and if reliance upon another dictionary was necessary, the source was *Jowitt's Dictionary of English Law.* Latin terms and maxims are included. The preface states: "The unique character of Canada is strongly reflected in the large number of entries which relate to the regulation of our country's natural resources, to agriculture and related industries".

(b) Pocket Dictionary of Canadian Law 2nd Edition (by Dukelow and Nuse)

Published by Carswell in 1995 and prepared by the authors of the *Dictionary of Canadian Law 2nd Edition* (1,560 pages), this briefer work (562 pages) is directed at a general audience. Definitions are based upon primary Canadian law.

(c) Canadian Law Dictionary 2nd Edition (by John A. Yogis, Q.C.)

In the late 1970s, Barron's Educational Series, Inc. (a publisher with offices in New York and Toronto), asked John A. Yogis, Q.C. (Professor of Law, Dalhousie University) to adapt for Canadian audiences a law dictionary which had been prepared for the American beginning law student or layperson.

With considerable revision of American terminology, and additions of Canadian concepts (*Charter of Rights, etc.*), this book defines over 2,000 terms. The second edition was published in 1990.

2. Words and Phrases Sets

(a) Words and Phrases Judicially Defined in Canadian Courts and Tribunals (Carswell)

This is a comprehensive, eight volume publication containing approximately 50,000 judicial considerations of words and phrases. Entries include extracts from the considering judgments. It is affiliated with the *Canadian Abridgment Revised (2nd) edition* and is updated by softcover supplements.

(b) Words and Phrases, Legal Maxims (4th edition) (Carswell)

This three-volume set is a relatively complete treatment of Canadian words and phrases, and it provides digests of portions of the cases defining the words and phrases. This looseleaf set is a new edition of the title published by De Boo for many years.

(c) Canada Tax Words, Phrases & Rules (Carswell)

This looseleaf volume has two tab sections: "Words & Phrases" and "Rules". English and French language cases are covered from 1917 to the present.

(d) Insurance Law Words & Phrases (Carswell)

This looseleaf volume contains approximately 1,300 insurance law definitions taken from Carswell's comprehensive set, *Words and Phrases Judicially Defined in Canadian Courts and Tribunals.*

(e) Crankshaw's Criminal Code of Canada R.S.C. 1985: "Words and Phrases" volume (Carswell)

This looseleaf volume contains over 4,000 criminal law definitions from cases, from Law Reform Commission Reports, and from the *Criminal Code* and related statutes.

(f) Words and Phrases Legally Defined (3rd ed.) (Butterworths)

The English publication gives selected digests of Canadian cases defining words and phrases.

E. DIRECTORIES

Directories list lawyers alphabetically by name and by city within province. There is accompanying biographical data and sometimes a listing of preferred areas of practice, which is not necessarily the same as certified specialties.

Canadian legal directories include:

1. Canadian Law List (Canada Law Book)

The main listing is of all lawyers in Canada by province, municipality, and firm. Another section lists lawyers alphabetically with firm and location. This reference of over 2,000 pages is issued annually. Also available on CD-ROM.

2. Canada Legal Directory (Carswell)

This annual reference of over 1,500 pages lists law firms by city within each province. There is a separate finding list by lawyer's name. Fax numbers are included. Lawyers' E-mail addresses are accessed through Carswell's E-mail Directory at the Internet address: www.carswell.com/LawDir/.

3. Martindale-Hubbell Law Directory

This annual, multi-volume American publication has a selective Canadian sections within the "International Law Directory" volumes. Preferred areas of practice are noted, and biographical data is relatively complete.

The LEXIS-NEXIS online computer database service (available through Butterworths) contains 800,000 listings broken down by geographical area and by area of practice. The LEXIS-NEXIS library is "MARHUB", and there are almost 100 files within this computer database library. Among the 100 file names are CBIO (Canadian professional biographies listings for law firms and corporate legal departments), IBADIR (International Bar Association Directory), PATENT (combined U.S. and international patent and trademark listings), ASDIG (Asian law digests), and EURDIG (European law digests).

4. Association directories

(a) "Directory of Law Teachers" (Canadian Association of Law Teachers). Internet site: (www.droit.umontreal.ca/en/index.html).
(b) *Canadian Association of Law Libraries Directory* (Carswell).

5. Almanacs and administrative directories

The annual *Canadian Almanac and Directory* (Copp-Clark Pitman) and the annual *Corpus Almanac and Canadian Sourcebook* (Corpus Information Services) supply directory information for federal and provincial governments. In looseleaf form, the *Corpus Administrative Index* provides detailed access to government departments and officials. Carswell's *The Legal Desk Book* includes many addresses useful to Ontario lawyers. Carswell also publishes the *Directory of Canadian Accounting Firms*, which includes listings by geographical location and by preferred area of practice.

6. Legal telephone directories

Canada Law Book Ltd. produces legal telephone directories for Ontario, Alberta, Atlantic region, and British Columbia. Canada Law Book Ltd. also publishes the *Canadian Legal Fax and E-mail Directory.*

7. West's Legal Directory

West Publishing provides a North American and international directory through the Internet address: www.wld.com.

Chapter 10

Computer-Assisted Legal Research

A. SEARCHING ELECTRONIC SOURCES

The use of computer technology in legal research is not new. Since the late 1970s researchers have accessed online services to complement their manual research of hardcopy sources. Since that time there has been a significant increase in the volume and nature of legal materials available in electronic format, with online services appearing, amalgamating, and occasionally disappearing. CD-ROM entered the scene in the mid-1990s with an explosion of highly useful products, after a decade of slow development. At about the same time, the Internet became a key information source to researchers in terms of both ease of access and, increasingly, scope of content. Today electronic sources are available in three formats: online database providers, CD-ROM, and the Internet. These formats are defined mainly by differing search methods and/or hardware/software requirements, and are somewhat arbitrary (*i.e.*, the internet is really a type of online access). They are, however, convenient categories for practical discussion. The term "computer-assisted legal research", once confined to online sources, now encompasses all of these options.

It is now generally accepted that thorough research must include electronic legal research tools. There are several reasons for this:

(a) An electronic product cannot be thought of simply as a substitute for the hardcopy version(s). Although the same data appears in both, the access methods differ significantly. The user of the electronic product will usually have additional access options including free-text searching (*i.e.*, the ability to retrieve cases, statutes, or other documents which contain specified combinations of words), and hypertext maneuverability (*i.e.*, the ability to jump from a case citation embedded in a summary or discussion to the full text of the case). These options are provided in the search engine which accompanies the product. They can reduce research time, but perhaps more importantly, they can assist in locating information which is otherwise extremely difficult to locate. In other words, they can provide a significant advantage, and are ignored at one's own peril.

(b) Electronic formats can be updated more conveniently than hardcopy, resulting in more up-to-date information, particularly in online and Internet sources.

(c) Large volumes of information can be accessed from office or home, and storage concerns are eliminated.

(d) Because information costs are based on access rates rather than ownership of paper, costs can be reduced and selective access can result in significant savings for the researcher.

Nevertheless, the new research methods bring new concerns. As formats and options multiply, researchers must raise practical questions: what is available on each of the electronic formats? Is one of the Internet, CD-ROM, or online provider enough, or are all three required? How efficient are the search engines provided by various publishers offering services in each of the three formats? Throughout this book, the reader will find "electronic sources" notations alongside the descriptions of hardcopy legal publications. The aim in this chapter is to: (a) provide an overview of electronic legal resources, and (b) examine the technology available to access these resources. Detailed listings of publishers, services, and titles are found in Appendix B. The analysis proceeds on the assumption that the two essential requirements for effective computer-assisted legal research are: (a) a comprehensive collection of legal materials accessible electronically, and (b) a good understanding of search methods.

1. Search Engines

Vast amounts of legal information are now stored in electronic format. In order to access this information, users must rely on software developers who hopefully have a good appreciation of the materials and the users who must access them. As more legal materials become available in alternative formats, new search engines are introduced, some of which contain significant enhancements. In order to evaluate the results of computer-assisted research, one must have an understanding of the basic types of search engines and enhancements. Search engines may typically employ either Boolean (exact match) or natural language (near-match) retrieval methods, with various enhancements and added features depending on the publisher/distributor. Most CD-ROM products employ Boolean-based engines. Online database providers vary: QL Systems Ltd. employs an enhanced Boolean version, while LEXIS-NEXIS offers a choice between enhanced Boolean and natural language (free style) engines. WESTLAW also offers a natural language option (WIN). Internet search engines (Yahoo, Excite, Alta Vista — see below) permit a variety of near natural language approaches which sometimes defy classification. Although they are designed for universal searching in an Internet environment and are not specifically designed for legal materials, they require attention because they open the door to the growing body of Internet legal resources. An examination of the two basic categories of search engines follows, with examples of typical variations and enhancements.

(a) Boolean search engines (examples are from QUICKLAW)

QL Systems Ltd.'s QUICKLAW will be used as an example of a system using Boolean search commands. A basic understanding of these commands is necessary even when using QL's enhanced Version 7.1 and Query Wizard or any of the enhanced Boolean engines provided on CD-ROM or on the Internet.

(i) Boolean connectors: and/or/butnot; dates; proximity; field

(A) AND/OR/BUTNOT

When using Boolean language, the searcher will retrieve cases containing word combinations which exactly match not only the words in the query, but also the precise word relationships established by the connectors used to join the words in the query ("and", "or", "not"). Thus the query *sentence & heroin & trafficking* retrieves only cases which contain all three words. If, for example, a case contained the words sentencing (rather than sentence), heroin and trafficking, the case would not be retrieved. Most Boolean engines provide truncation operators, *i.e., sentenc! & heroin & trafficking.* QL will automatically search plurals if the searcher has indicated this option. A wildcard feature similar to truncation permits the searcher to specify multiple substitutes for one or more letters in a word; *privati*ation* covers both privatization and privatisation. Searches are expanded by including alternative expressions separated by "or". When typing a query on QL, a space indicates the "or" function used for alternate expressions. Thus, the query *slander defamation* retrieves all cases which contain either of these words. Note: The searcher would type in the term "or" only when it is required to divide the entire query. *Slander defamation & politician* retrieves cases containing the following combinations: Slander and politician; defamation and politician. But *slander or defamation & politician* retrieves all cases containing the term slander plus all cases containing both the terms defamation and politician. The occurrence of words can be totally excluded. Thus *assault butnot officer* retrieves only cases which contain the word assault but not the word officer (or by extension, the phrase peace officer). If a Boolean *and* follows a Boolean *butnot*, the *and* will cancel the *butnot*.

(B) DATE SEARCHING

Searches may be confined to a specified date or date range. Thus *murder & @date after 1993* retrieves all cases containing the word murder and dated subsequent to 1993. Additional options are:

murder & @date 1993/07/19
murder & @date 1993/07
murder & @date 1993
murder & @date before 1993
murder & @date after 1993/07/19
Before and *after* can be used with days, months, or years in the above format.
murder & @date 1993/07/19 - 1994/06/28
murder & @date 1993/07 - 1994/06
murder & @date 1993 - 1994

(C) PROXIMITY CONNECTORS

Boolean searching can be a precise and valuable instrument. For example, if a term or terms expressing a legal concept are joined with fact words (*i.e.*, *negligence & "ski instructor"*), the percentages of relevant documents retrieved can be high. Conversely, if no documents are retrieved, immediate conclusions can be drawn. Likewise, if the searcher wants to locate all occurrences of a word or phrase regardless of context, Boolean searching is 100 per cent relevant. Thus "*res ipsa loquitor*" locates all cases in which the phrase occurs. Proximity connectors can be used to specify that search terms must be within a given number of words from each other. Thus *negligence /5 "ski instructor"* retrieves only cases in which the word negligence occurs within five words of the phrase "ski instructor". Likewise, *negligence /p "ski instructor"* retrieves only cases where both terms are in the same paragraph.

(D) FIELD SEARCHING

If the online database contains documents with data divided into separate fields, a Boolean engine may permit field searching. Thus *@6 negligence & "ski instructor"* retrieves only cases in which the words occur in field 6, which is the keyword section of a headnote.

(ii) Boolean connectors: specific examples

(A) CASES JUDICIALLY CONSIDERED

Where field 7 is the body of the headnote, the query could be *@7 Bailey /2 Jones.* An alternative and more convenient way to locate cases on QL is to locate the earlier cited case (*e.g.*, *Bailey v. Jones*) for which later considerations are sought (*@2 Bailey /2 Jones*, where field 2 is the name or style of cause of the case), and then use the *Cite* command to generate a list of judicial considerations along with a complete history of the case through the courts. The *Cite* option is an example of the present trend to introduce more sophisticated search facilities to complement or replace basic Boolean techniques.

(B) STATUTES JUDICIALLY CONSIDERED

@7 Narcotics / Act /7 72 would be a query for considerations of the *Narcotics Act*, s. 72.

(C) LOCATING STATUTES AND STATUTE SECTIONS BY SUBJECTS

@1 marriage would be a query where field one is the title of the statute. *@1 marriage & @ infants* where @ alone reverts to a search of all fields in the document in order to locate sections in the *Marriage Act* dealing with the marriage of infants. Note however, that free text searching of statutes is hampered by the characteristic peculiarities of statutory language. For example, the above search would not succeed if the statute refers to minors rather than infants.

(D) JUDICIAL APPROACH

@6 "gross negligence" & @4 beagle is an example of a query where all decisions of Judge Beagle involving gross negligence are sought.

(E) INDEX SCHEME SEARCHING

Some case reports employ detailed index schemes to classify decisions. The Maritime Law Book Ltd. scheme is an example. A QL query searching for a topic within the Maritime Law Book scheme could be *labour/law/3 7000* where the searcher has consulted the Maritime classification scheme before drafting the query and knows that the classification "Labour Law — 7000" probably contains cases on the point.

(F) EXPERT WITNESSES

Retaining an expert witness, or challenging one, involves investigating past retainers. In this instance, an effective Boolean search is possible on full-text cases because a name is a singular item which does not occur in a variety of contexts. *@7 Peter / Pan* is an example of a query seeking cases in which the expert witness, Mr. Peter Pan, is mentioned.

(iii) Disadvantages of Boolean search engines

Boolean search logic permits precision searching, but it also places a heavy burden on the searcher. Legal research is concept-oriented, but Boolean searching requires a technical approach separate from legal concepts: what combination of words is likely to occur in the document sought? In formulating a query, it is usually possible to identify certain words or phrases which will almost certainly be present. These may be called anchor terms. Thus, formulating a query to retrieve cases dealing with possession of drugs might begin by identifying the word "possession" as an anchor term. However, although the searcher is looking for cases involving possession of drugs generally, the word "drugs" will not function as an anchor word because it is a generalization representing many potential expressions including narcotics, heroin, cocaine, marijuana, marihuana, *etc*. There is a large variety of words which may occur in cases dealing with one legal issue: *i.e.*, what constitutes possession of drugs? The search can be expanded by using the "or" connector, but the searcher cannot always be confident that the list is exhaustive.

In recent years, full-text cases have replaced the headnotes and summaries which accompanied the introduction of Boolean engines. The full-text of journals and even the occasional textbook is now beginning to appear on QUICKLAW. These developments further complicate the search process by increasing the likelihood that search terms will appear in irrelevant context, and proximity searching does not always address the problem. Consider the following search for cases/articles on well water drilling contracts: *well & water & drill drilling & contract.* The query might retrieve a case containing the following sentence: "The government asserted that the defendant clothing manufacturer's DRILL cloth uniforms did not repel WATER nearly as WELL as CONTRACT specifications required for DRILLING military personnel in the rain". The problem could have been avoided by providing a proximity connector (*well/water*), but not without risk. Although occurrences of the words "well" and "water" are predictable, the searcher cannot be certain that the phrase "well water" would occur in all relevant documents.

The demands of Boolean searching can place the inexperienced searcher at a disadvantage. The ability to draft effective queries comes with practice, and many lawyers are too busy to invest the necessary time. This critique applies in varying degrees to all systems and search engines.

(iv) Enhanced Boolean searching

Online database providers and CD-ROM manufacturers have recently added numerous features to Boolean systems. One such feature is QL's Cite command, which generates a list of considerations of retrieved cases (see above subsection (E) Cases judicially considered). Also, Version 1.7 of QUICKLINK for Windows provides a full Windows-based graphical user interface which makes searching easier by leading the user step-by-step through query formulation. Version 1.7 is available free from QL, along with a supporting product called QUICKLAW Wizard. These products do not eliminate the problems inherent in Boolean searching, but can be of assistance to inexperienced users. Version 1.7 converts QL commands to point-and-click options, and jump-markers provide hyperlinks from citations within cases to full-text cases, digests, and citator records, thus approximating CD-ROM and Internet attributes previously unavailable on QL. Speedbars containing point-and-click command buttons allow rapid and effective selection of case law, statutes, and general databases. There is also a speedbar command for WESTLAW, a major American system accessible through QUICKLAW.

Folio software has been used exclusively on CD-ROM by Canadian legal publishers and is now the most common search engine for accessing major publications such as the *Canadian Abridgment Revised (2nd) edition*. We are now witnessing a migration of these publications to the Internet, and it appears that an Internet version of Folio is part of the move. Folio employs an enhanced Boolean engine, with copious hyperlinks and a Windows interface which prompts the user to enter search words in designated fields.

(b) Natural language search engines

Natural language search engines permit the researcher to enter searches in the form of simple questions which state the issue(s). There is no need to apply Boolean logic and connectors to exactly match word combinations and word relationships. Instead, the search engine itself performs the match, locating documents which best match the query in terms of occurrence of search words. An example of a natural language query might be: "what is the test for gross negligence where a gratuitous passenger is injured in a motor vehicle accident?"

Another example, containing a mixture of fact and concept words might be: "is a ski instructor liable for death or injury where s/he fails to warn a student of dangerous trail conditions?"

An advantage of natural language search engines is ease of search formulation. Nevertheless, care must be taken to include essential words, and to exclude extraneous ones. Lawyers are trained to precisely state issues and can draw on this experience while avoiding the need to learn complicated technical rules.

Disadvantages of natural language search engines include the large number of irrelevant documents which are normally retrieved. Natural language search engines employ ranking algorithms designed to present retrieved documents in order of "relevancy". These algorithms are useful, but relevant documents are frequently found at the middle to lower end of the list of retrieved documents. Searchers must approach search results judiciously in deciding how far down the "relevancy scale" they should go in examining documents.

2. Formats

(a) Online database providers

Online database providers include the earliest electronic sources available to researchers. They are accessible by direct telephone connection to local dialports provided by the vendor, datapac, or recently, via Internet. The user must obtain a password, and billing is usually on a time-spent basis, although limitless time contracts are often available. Online sources are convenient ways to access legal information because updating is accomplished at source by the provider, unlike CD-ROM, which requires on-site replacement at frequent intervals, making currency the responsibility of the user. If CD-ROM products are loaded on network server hard drives, updating can become labour-intensive. Finally, because online sources can be updated more frequently than CD-ROM by direct data input at source, the information they contain is often more current than CD-ROM. Among the disadvantages is the constant dependence on telephone communication, downtime and bad lines. Linespeeds of some graphics-intensive products can be slower than CD-ROM, just as a standard Internet connection can be slower than CD-ROM, but these are not major problems and are expected to be eliminated soon.

(i) QL Systems Ltd.'s QUICKLAW

QUICKLAW is a major Canadian online legal information service, offering access to Canadian case law (full text and summaries), administrative tribunal decisions, statutes, regulations, law journals (full text), summary and citator services, legal literature indexes, newspapers, and wire services. A listing of QL databases appears in Appendix B. QL provides very good coverage of full-text primary legal sources (court and tribunal decisions, statutes, and regulations) as well as citators and legal literature indexes, although some problems still plague the updating of statute compilations. Electronic versions of major secondary sources (textbooks, subject services, and looseleafs) are generally not found on QL. However, these are appearing on CD-ROM and slowly migrating to the Internet, where they will likely be marketed by the major legal publishers.

The QL search engine employs basic Boolean connectors (and, or, not) and requires exact word matches (see above section 1(a) Boolean search engines, for a detailed description of QUICKLAW commands). This functions reasonably well for primary materials, though experienced searchers tend to do better than occasional users, due to the literal nature of basic Boolean searching. QL has recently introduced Version 1.7 of QUICKLINK for Windows, which provides a full Windows-based graphical user interface which makes searching easier. Significant recent enhancements such as hypertext links to related items are valuable additions because they approximate CD-ROM and Internet-based attributes previously unavailable on QL. The QUICKLAW Query Wizard guides the user through a series of steps in formulating queries.

(ii) LEXIS-NEXIS

LEXIS-NEXIS is a major online source for legal materials covering Canada, the United States and United Kingdom, and Commonwealth countries, and a range of other countries worldwide. Separate groups of databases (Libraries) are maintained for each jurisdiction: the Canada Library provides access to Canadian legal, news, company and country information. Federal and Ontario statutory and regulatory material is currently available with additional jurisdictions in progress. A full complement of federal and provincial case law is also online (see contents list in Appendix B). In addition to legal sources, an impressive list of international news sources and specialist journals is contained in a 492 page "Directory of Online Services" which is published annually. Of special interest is the LEXIS-NEXIS search engine, which offers the user a choice between Boolean and natural language searching. Powerful research features include:

(a) LEXSEE, a citation-based full-text retrieval service which permits retrieval of case law and secondary sources at any point during a search.
(b) LEXSTAT, which permits retrieval of the full text of a code or statute section.
(c) LEXCITE, which locates the citations to case law and statutes.
(d) AUTO-CITE and SHEPARD's Citator Services, for validation of citations, location of judicial considerations, and appeals.

(iii) Maritime Law Book Ltd.

Maritime Law Book Ltd. publishes provincial and federal jurisdictional case reports, and offers both in print form and in a service called "National Reporter System Online" (see the contents list in Appendix B). This service is accessible only via the Internet but is included here because of its classification as an online service. Users can subscribe to this service for a basic flat fee. Considering the breadth of case coverage, this feature will appeal to researchers, especially those located in jurisdictions covered by the service. The search engine is Boolean with search prompts to assist the inexperienced user.

(iv) Other Canadian sources

Sources not accessible by direct telephone line but available on the Internet are discussed separately below in subsection (c), Internet Sources.

(v) American online sources

The major American online services are LEXIS-NEXIS (see (ii), LEXIS-NEXIS, above) and WESTLAW. Both services offer coverage of American state and federal case law and statutory materials. Natural language search options are included in standard subscriptions. Subscription to one of these services is the obvious choice for firms which require occasional access to American primary materials.

(b) CD-ROM sources

In 1994, Justice Canada discontinued the looseleaf consolidation of the *Revised Statutes of Canada (1985)* and chose to continue the publication solely on CD-ROM and the Internet. This came as a surprise to the Canadian legal community, because at the time there was, with the exception of a few fill-in-the-blank legal forms, nothing else being published on CD-ROM. This situation changed quickly in 1995 when major Canadian legal publishers began to invest heavily in conversion of key research titles to CD-ROM. By 1996, and after a decade of relative non-use, CD-ROM was established as an essential format for legal information. At about the same time, the Internet had outgrown its early academic origins and was promising even greater changes in information delivery. As publishers and researchers approach the comfort level with CD-ROM formats, legal resources on the Internet continue to multiply. The reader should keep this dual development in mind when examining both.

(i) Advantages of CD-ROM

Most CD-ROM products are supplied with Boolean search engines enhanced by Windows technology and hypertext maneuverability (see (a), Boolean search engines, above.) Compact disks are portable and can be copied to a hard drive or accessed directly from a CD-ROM drive. There is no need for telephone jacks or good telecommunication lines and no multi-user congestion unless the application is networked. They can, therefore, be accessed by counsel in court or wherever a laptop computer can be carried. Unlike many online services which charge by the amount of time spent online, CD-ROM usage involves a one-time layout: costs are predictable. Although most CD-ROM products are designed to become inoperable after a few months of manufacture, many publishers now sell "archive" copies at regular periods for a moderate sum; online systems offer only access.

(ii) Disadvantages of CD-ROM

As already noted, a CD-ROM subscription resembles a hardcopy looseleaf subscription: updates arrive in the mail and must be loaded/interfiled. Ultimately it is the subscriber who must ensure that the most recent update has been properly installed. Users of hardcopy looseleaf materials know this is not as simple as it sounds: to err is human. Online and Internet sources are updated centrally by the provider, eliminating this concern. They are also normally updated more frequently, often daily. Finally, disks can be misplaced or stolen, particularly in multiple-user applications such as libraries and large firms.

(iii) Materials available on CD-ROM

A wide assortment of primary and secondary materials is now available on CD-ROM (see list of Publishers in Appendix B). Due perhaps to the coincidental development of CD-ROM and more powerful search engines, secondary sources and major legal research tools such as the *Canadian Abridgment Revised (2nd) edition* and the *Canadian Encyclopedic Digest* have been marketed on CD-ROM and are generally well received. Research packages of primary and secondary materials covering a legal field (criminal law, family law, practice, *etc.*), have also been recently introduced: these make good use of hypertext links (see 1(*a*)(iv), Enhanced Boolean searching), enabling the searcher to jump from a reference or citation to full text or alternate treatments. This capability saves time but also assists the reasoning process by providing instantaneous information links both forward and backward.

An example of a CD-ROM Folio product is Carswell's "Family Law Partner". It is updated quarterly by replacement CD-ROMs and monthly by a print-form digest service of new family law cases. The CD-ROM "Family Law Partner" contains the following material:

(a) *Reports of Family Law* (1971 to present), plus an extensive collection of family law cases gleaned from a Carswell sister product, the comprehensive *Canada Reporter*. The total is over 8,500 cases.

(b) Quantum digests of reported and unreported cases describing support awards and property distribution, categorized by income level, nature of asset, *etc.*

(c) Digests of reported and unreported cases derived from the *Weekly Digest of Family Law.*

(d) Relevant federal legislation plus provincial statutes and regulations from Alberta, British Columbia, Ontario and Saskatchewan.

(e) Commentary consisting of MacDonald and Ferrier, *Canadian Divorce Law and Practice*; McLeod, *Child Custody Law and Practice;* MacDonald and Wilton, *Law and Practice under the Ontario Family Law Act;* McLeod and Mamo, *Matrimonial Property in Canada;* Wilton and Miyauchi, *Enforcement of Family Law Orders and Agreements,* and more.

The following illustration shows a computer screen from the CD-ROM "Family Law Partner". This is a standard Folio screen used in almost all CD-ROM products. Note the following: (a) the tool belt which runs along the top of the screen composed of point-and-click buttons, (b) Template 1, Template 2, Template 3, and Query buttons assist in search formulation, and (c) search terms appear in light bars (user can jump from one occurrence to the next). (Folio screen and templates 1, 2, and 3: Reprinted by permission of Carswell, a division of Thomson Canada Limited.)

ILLUSTRATION 15
Folio Screen

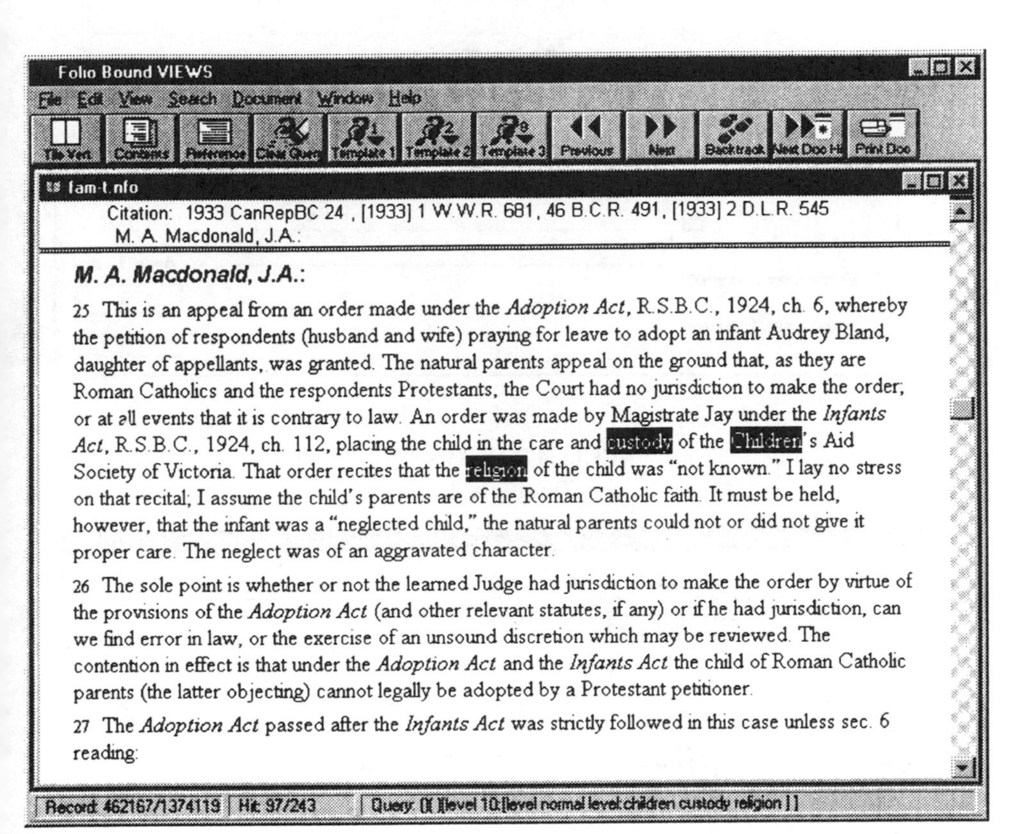

The three search templates are illustrated as follows:

ILLUSTRATION 16
Template 1

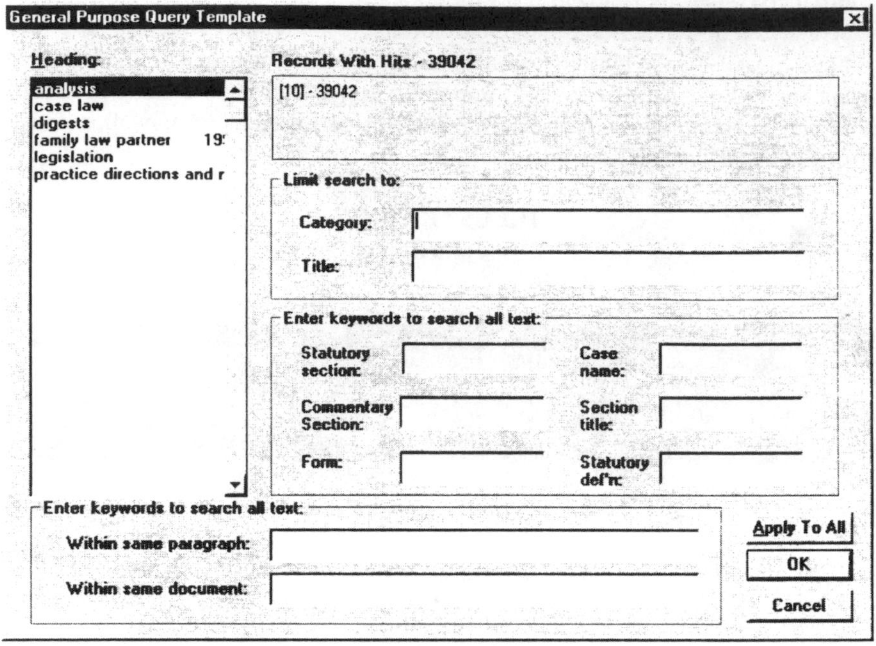

General Purpose Query Template

Heading:
analysis
case law
digests
family law partner 19
legislation
practice directions and r

Records With Hits - 39042
[10] - 39042

Limit search to:
Category:
Title:

Enter keywords to search all text:
Statutory section:
Case name:
Commentary Section:
Section title:
Form:
Statutory def'n:

Enter keywords to search all text:
Within same paragraph:
Within same document:

Apply To All
OK
Cancel

ILLUSTRATION 17
Template 2

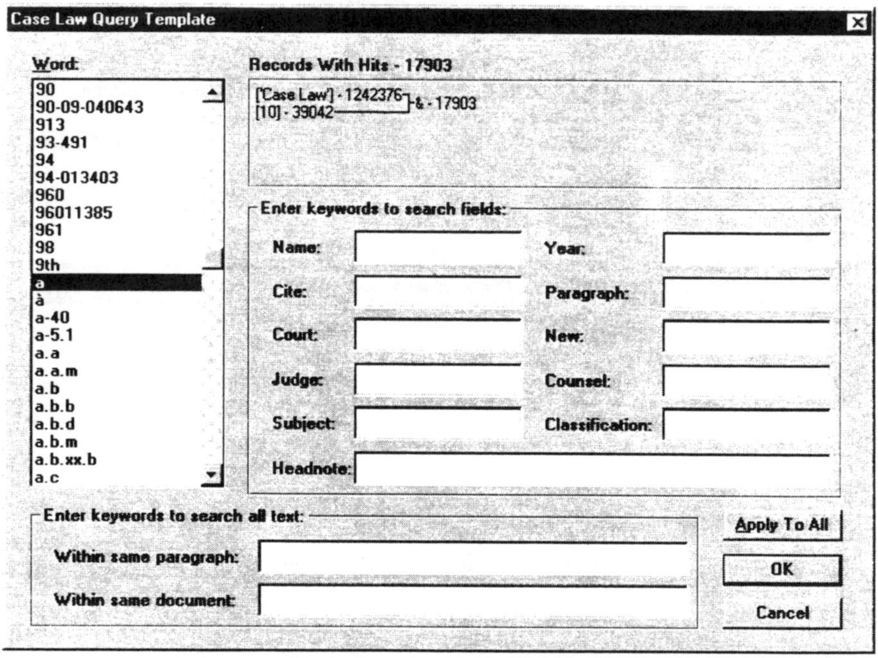

Case Law Query Template

Word:
90
90-09-040643
913
93-491
94
94-013403
960
96011385
961
98
9th
a
à
a-40
a-5.1
a.a
a.a.m
a.b
a.b.b
a.b.d
a.b.m
a.b.xx.b
a.c

Records With Hits - 17903
['Case Law'] - 1242376 & - 17903
[10] - 39042

Enter keywords to search fields:
Name:
Year:
Cite:
Paragraph:
Court:
New:
Judge:
Counsel:
Subject:
Classification:
Headnote:

Enter keywords to search all text:
Within same paragraph:
Within same document:

Apply To All
OK
Cancel

ILLUSTRATION 18
Template 3

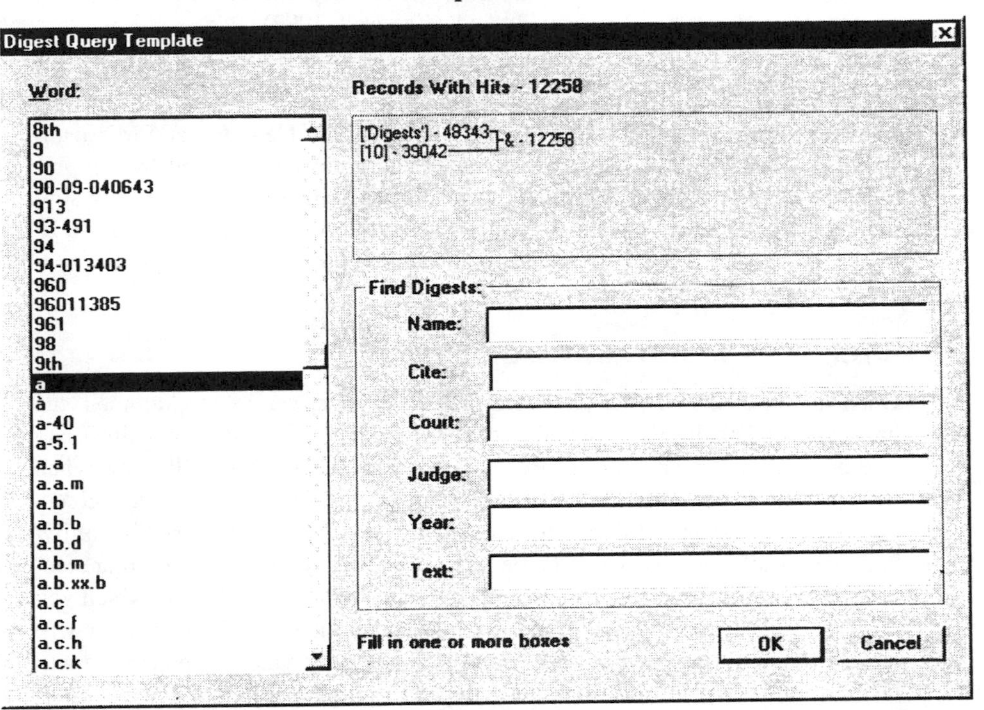

(c) Internet sources

(i) Preliminaries for Internet neophytes

(A) INTERNET PROVIDERS

Access to the Internet begins by choosing an Internet provider, which might be your local telephone company, cablevision company, or one of many commercial providers which advertise locally. A provider is a gateway which provides access to the Internet. While specialized uses raise many technical considerations in choosing a provider, we are assuming that your principal use of the Internet will be to access legal research resources. Because congestion and communication speeds can seriously hamper the most perfectly conceived search strategy, you should at least ask around before contracting with any provider, or obtain from the provider a list of major clients. Be wary of providers which offer abnormally low rates. If you intend at some point to set up a homepage or utilize large amounts of storage space, you should consult a detailed analysis of the subject such as *Canadian Lawyers' Internet Guide* or Jackson and Taylor, *The Internet Handbook for Canadian Lawyers*, 2nd ed. (Carswell, 1997).

(B) INTERNET BROWSERS

The two most popular browsers at time of writing are Netscape and Microsoft Explorer. While both of these are adequate and are often supplied by the provider, be careful to obtain the most recent version so that your system will support new technological advances as they are introduced. If you intend to use E-mail, check to see if this is included. Your Internet provider will supply the necessary passwords to sign on to its gateway.

(C) GETTING ON TO THE INTERNET

Once you have entered your password (automatic entry can be programmed) the browser will default to a preset address (which can be changed). An address can also be referred to as a Uniform Resource Locator (URL). You will know when you are there because the URL will appear on the "Address" box on your screen. For example, using Microsoft Explorer, the default address is http://home.microsoft.com. This is a home page provided by the browser's manufacturer; it tells you that you are signed on. If you have the URL of a site which you wish to contact, type it in the address box and push Enter. The browser will inform you of the progress of your connection to the site you have entered; it will take several seconds or several minutes depending on the degree of congestion. If it appears to be taking too long, you can terminate the connection. Connect to a new site at any time during the session by changing the URL in the "address" box and pushing Enter.

The browser screen contains point-and-click buttons. One of these, labelled "Favourites" in Explorer permits you to save the URL of any site you visit by simply clicking and choosing the ADD option while connected to the site. Once saved, the URL becomes a hypertext link to the site it represents. Soon your list of URLs will include sources for judgments, statutes, regulations and secondary materials, many of which are accessed free of charge. The typical Internet user is a collector of URLs, many of which are collected from sites maintained by other collectors who compile lists of hypertext links - just click on the URL and you are there. Some of the most valuable URLs in your Favourites list will be those which lead to these sites containing legal resource links.

Most of the resources which we will examine are found on the World Wide Web (WWW), the rapidly-expanding Internet mega-host. A typical WWW URL begins with "http:" which denotes the required protocol (hypertext client-server); then two forward slashes, "//"; then introduction of the host, "www"; followed by the directory path and resource name. Example:

http://www.excite.com.

(ii) Internet search engines generally

There is no universal index to all information on the Internet. Instead, there is a variety of search engines available, each of which provides partial coverage and each of which overlaps the others. A site may be easily accessible on all, or only one. Internet search engines have colorful names and tend to look alike, though they are not alike in breadth of coverage or available enhancements. They tend to employ as a common denominator the same advanced Boolean mechanics as the CD-ROM Folio engine with various further refinements as the HTML Internet environment permits. For example, in Yahoo! documents need not contain all search words to be retrieved, but documents containing more search words are ranked higher than documents containing fewer. Other Yahoo! ranking factors are: (a) matches which occur in the title of documents are ranked higher than matches occuring in the body or text; and (b) words denoting general categories are ranked higher. These ranking factors occur in various combinations and variations in other search engines.

You can obtain information on search commands and ranking for most search engines by clicking on the appropriate word(s) (*i.e.*, "options") usually located near the box provided to enter a specific search. Another particularly powerful enhancement is Intelligent Concept Extraction (ICE) which, in the words of Excite Search, "finds relationships that exist between words and ideas". To the extent that this technology succeeds in accomplishing its claims, the first rule of Boolean searching (search words not concepts) can be forgotten. Indeed Excite encourages its users to "search for ideas and concepts instead of just key words". For example, with ICE the query *elderly people financial concerns* locates sites mentioning the economic status of retired people and the financial concerns of senior citizens. The general lesson here is that Internet search engines are rapidly moving far beyond the basic search concepts of only a few years ago into new applications which resist airtight categories such as Boolean and natural language. Once the new user has gained even a brief familiarity with the point-and-click hypertext environment of the Internet, searching becomes a series of choices aided by a type of intuition which accommodates advance and change.

(iii) Illustration of searching on Yahoo! (http://www.yahoo.com)

On connecting to Yahoo! the user is presented with two options: (1) you may search by general subject by clicking on any of the broad categories listed on the introductory page, or (2) you may formulate a specific word search by clicking the search box at the top of the page. (See illustration Yahoo! 1).

ILLUSTRATION 19
Yahoo! 1

Yellow Pages - People Search - Maps - Classifieds - Personals - Chat - Email
Shopping - My Yahoo! - News - Sports - Weather - Stock Quotes - **more...**

- **Arts and Humanities**
  Architecture, Photography, Literature...
- **News and Media** [Xtra!]
  Current Events, Magazines, TV, Newspapers...
- **Business and Economy** [Xtra!]
  Companies, Finance, Employment...
- **Recreation and Sports** [Xtra!]
  Sports, Games, Travel, Autos, Outdoors...
- **Computers and Internet** [Xtra!]
  Internet, WWW, Software, Multimedia...
- **Reference**
  Libraries, Dictionaries, Phone Numbers...
- **Education**
  Universities, K-12, College Entrance...
- **Regional**
  Countries, Regions, U.S. States...
- **Entertainment** [Xtra!]
  Cool Links, Movies, Music, Humor...
- **Science**
  CS, Biology, Astronomy, Engineering...
- → **Government**
  Military, Politics **[Xtra!]**, Law, Taxes...
- **Social Science**
  Anthropology, Sociology, Economics...
- **Health** [Xtra!]
  Medicine, Drugs, Diseases, Fitness...
- **Society and Culture**
  People, Environment, Religion...

What's New - Weekly Picks - Today's Web Events - Yahoo! Internet Life
Yahooligans! for Kids -Visa Shopping Guide - Yahoo! Style - 3D Stock Viewer

World Yahoos Australia & NZ - Canada - Denmark - France - Germany - Japan - Korea
Norway - SE Asia - Sweden - UK & Ireland
Yahoo! Metros Atlanta - Austin - Boston - Chicago - Dallas / Fort Worth - Los Angeles
Get Local Miami - Minneapolis / St. Paul - New York - S.F. Bay - Seattle - Wash D.C.
Smart Shopping with VISA

Suggest a Site - Company Info - Openings at Yahoo! - Contributors - Yahoo! How-To

(A) TO SEARCH BY GENERAL SUBJECT.

Click on Law, which is a subcategory of Government. The following list of subject-links appears:

ILLUSTRATION 20
Yahoo! 2

Yahoo! - Government:Law Page 1 of 1

Top:Government:Law

Search Options

● Search all of Yahoo Search only in **Law**

- **Yahoo! Net Events: Law** - today's chats and programs.
- **Indices** *(49)*

- **Arbitration and Mediation** *(24)*
- **Business Law** *(34)*
- **Cases** *(215)* NEW!
- **Companies and Firms@**
- **Constitutional** *(44)*
- **Consumer** *(19)*
- **Continuing Legal Education** *(20)* NEW!
- **Countries** *(25)*
- **Criminal Law and Justice@**
- **Disabilities@**
- **District Attorneys@**
- **Elder Law** *(11)*
- **Employment Law** *(26)*
- **Entertainment** *(12)*
- **Environmental@**
- **Estate and Probate** *(7)* NEW!
- **Events** *(8)*
- **Federal** *(15)*
- **General Information** *(57)*
- **Health** *(11)*
- **Immigration** *(73)*
- **Indigenous Peoples@**
- **Institutes** *(28)*
- **Intellectual Property** *(166)* NEW!
- **International Law** *(38)*
- **Journals** *(87)*
- **Judiciary and Supreme Court@**
- **Law Enforcement@**
- **Law Schools** *(239)*
- **Lawyer Jokes@**
- **Legal Ethics** *(3)*
- **Legal Research** *(63)*
- **Lesbian, Gay and Bisexual Resources@**
- **News and Media** *(44)* NEW!
- **Organizations** *(154)*
- **Privacy** *(21)*
- **Property** *(5)*
- **Self-Help** *(8)*
- **Sexuality@**
- **Software Companies@**
- **Tax** *(11)*
- **Telecommunications** *(5)*
- **U.S. States** *(26)*
- **Women's Resources@**
- **Usenet** *(9)*

(B) TO RESTRICT THE SEARCH TO CANADIAN LAW.

Choose Countries, and the following list appears:

ILLUSTRATION 21
Yahoo! 3

Yahoo! - Government:Law:Countries Page 1 of 1

Top:Government:Law:Countries

Search Options

● Search all of Yahoo   Search only in **Countries**

- **Argentina@**
- **Australia@**
- **Austria@**
- **Brazil@**
- **Canada@**
- **China@**
- **Estonia@**
- **France@**
- **Germany@**
- **Ireland@**
- **Israel@**
- **Japan@**
- **Mexico@**
- **Mongolia@**
- **Peru@**
- **Portugal@**
- **Russia@**
- **Singapore@**
- **Slovenia@**
- **Spain@**
- **Sweden@**
- **Switzerland@**
- **Uganda@**
- **Ukraine@**
- **United Kingdom@**

Yahoo! Internet Life shows you the way to the best sites!
Click here to try it Free

Choose Canada, and the following list of sites appears:

ILLUSTRATION 22
Yahoo! 4

Yahoo! - Regional:Countries:Canada:Government... Page 1 of 2

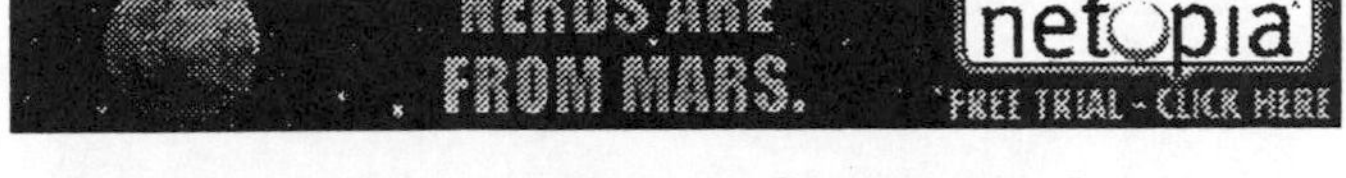

Top:Regional:Countries:Canada:Government:Law

Search Options

● Search all of Yahoo   Search only in **Law**

- **Indices** *(3)*

- **Companies and Firms@**
- **Constitutional** *(3)*
- **Consumer** *(1)*
- **Documents@**
- **Health** *(1)*
- **Immigration** *(16)*
- **Intellectual Property** *(1)*
- **Journals** *(4)* NEW!
- **Law Schools** *(13)*
- **News and Media** *(3)* NEW!
- **Organizations** *(9)*
- **Regional** *(7)*
- **Young Offenders Act** *(9)*

- World Wide Legal Information Association - USA and Canadian legal information, a legal dictionary, a crime prevention Police Station, International Legal News, legal who's who and directories.

- ARVIC'S Guide to Intellectual Property in Canada
- Canada Law - Osgoode Hall Law School's comprhensive index of Canadian law and law-related sites on the internet.
- Canadian Aboriginal Law
- Canadian Association of Elizabeth Fry Societies - works to develop and maintain policies, programs and services for women who have come into, or who are at risk of coming into conflict with the law.
- Canadian Law: A History
- Canadian Legal and Government Resources
- Canadian Legal Information Centre
- Canadian Legal Network - CANLAW - provides lawyers with access to their peers, legal resources and research, and provides the general public with access to the legal community.
- Canadian Legal Resources
- Canadian Statutes & Regulations - (ACJNet) Canada
- CAPIC Position Paper - Canadian Association of Photographers & Illustrators in Communications. This paper is a response to the Cdn Government Information Highway Advisory Council.
- Community, Contract and Aboriginal Policing Services Directorate - to communicate and heighten awareness about our services and promote community policing. information on crime

prevention, victim services, aboriginal policing and contract policing services.

- Construction Law Letter - Canadian newsletter containing summaries of construction-related court decisions, case comments and relevant articles.
- Contract Law Page - provides a chance for interactive study of primarily Canadian contract law.
- Copyright Reform in Canada - examines problematic aspects of copyright and digital media.
- Equality Rights Law under the Charter of Rights & Freedoms
- General and Aboriginal Law
- Judith Bowers Law Links - resources for Canadian lawyers.
- Law-on-the-Web Project Master Index to Legal Resources
- **Legislation - Department of Justice@**
- **Solicitor General@**
- **Supreme Court of Canada@**
- Virtual Canadian Law Library
- FAQ - Canadian Legal FAQs
- Usenet - can.legal

Note that the descriptions which accompany the links vary in length and detail and in some cases are non-existent. This is because format and classification of links is left to the discretion of the website operator; therefore do not expect consistency. With this caveat in mind, new users of the Internet can take full advantage of the hypertext links to explore and become familiar with each site. As an example, we will click on the link described as "Canada Law - Osgoode Hall Law School's comprehensive index of Canadian law and law-related sites on the internet". We are presented with a "URLs court of (mainly) Canadian (mostly) legal links":

ILLUSTRATION 23
Yahoo! 5

Osgoode Hall Law School - Canada Law: an URLs... Page 1 of 1

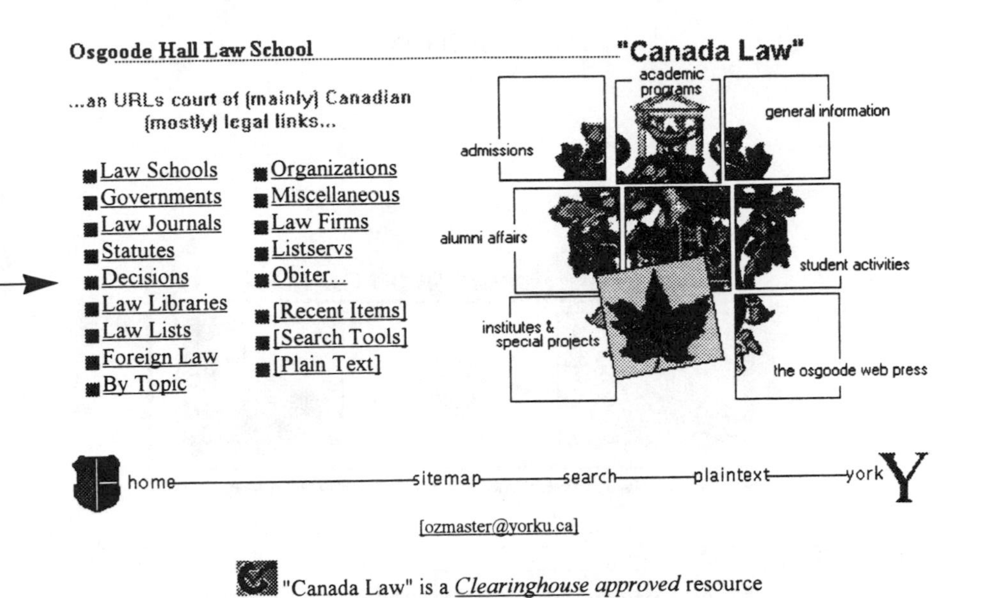

Clicking on Decisions, the following appears:

ILLUSTRATION 24
Yahoo! 6

Osgoode Hall Law School - Canada Law: judicia... Page 1 of 1

- Recent Supreme Court rulings
  - indexed by year
  - searchable
- Summaries of selected British Columbia judgments -- *New!*
- Summaries of some 1995 judgments in maritime law -- ditto 1996 -- *New!*

<<<< **Back to Canada Law table of contents**

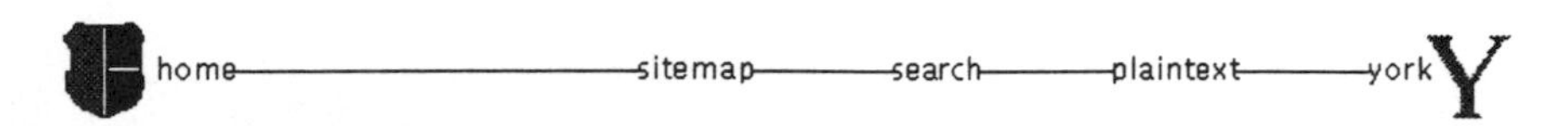

Are these all the Canadian decisions on the Internet? Not necessarily: there are numerous other cites to examine, among them those located back in Illustration Yahoo! 4. But to proceed with our illustration, we will choose Recent Supreme Court Rulings indexed by year. At the time of writing, the next screen provides us with a change of address for the Supreme Court of Canada cite:

ILLUSTRATION 25
Yahoo! 7

La Cour suprême du Canada Page 1 of 1

Décisions de la *Cour suprême du Canada.*

Le document que vous désirez obtenir n'est pas disponible sur le serveur.
Nous en avons pris bonne note.

Nouvelle adresse : http://www.droit.umontreal.ca/doc/csc-scc/index.html

The file that you want to reach is not available on this server.
This problem have been taken care of.

New location : http://www.droit.umontreal.ca/doc/csc-scc/en/index.html

This temporary link will in time be eliminated. For the present, we follow instructions and click on the new address:

ILLUSTRATION 26
Yahoo! 8

Français English

This experimental service is brought to you thanks to a joint project between the **Supreme Court of Canada** and the **Centre de Recherche en Droit Public** at University of Montreal. The Supreme Court rulings are available from 1993 and are in various formats.

Disclaimer information related to the published documents

Press releases (Subscribing to press releases)

Current press release 1997 1998

Recent rulings

Recents until January 22, 1998

Reports

1989: volume 1 volume 2
1990: volume 1 volume 2 volume 3
1991: volume 1 volume 2 volume 3
1992: volume 1 volume 2 volume 3
1993: volume 1 volume 2 volume 3 volume 4
1994: volume 1 volume 2 volume 3
1995: volume 1 volume 2 volume 3 volume 4
1996: volume 1 volume 2 volume 3
1997: volume 1 volume 2

Weekly bulletins

Current bulletin 1994 1995 1996 1997 1998

Search in the documents

Searching in decisions

Submit Cancel

You can also use the fielded search

You are the 653852 th visitor of this site since july 15, 1994.

Published by the Centre de recherche en droit public of
the Faculty of Law, University of Montreal

We are now at the Supreme Court of Canada cite. Note that the decisions can be accessed directly or searched much in the same way as on QL. A search for res & ipsa & loquitur retrieved the following:

ILLUSTRATION 27
Yahoo! 8a

Retrieval results

Page 1 of 1

Help	**Retrieval results**	*NaturelNet Navigation*
Full text: *res & ipsa & loquitur*		

Searching in decisions

res & ipsa & loquitur | Submit | Cancel

1) Hollis v. Dow Corning Corp.

1995: February 2; 1995: December 21. (165666 bytes)

English: HTML, Text, RTF, WordPerfect 5.1 (DOS),

French: HTML, Text, RTF, WordPerfect 5.1 (DOS),

[100 % relevant]

2) snell v. farrell

1989: December 6; 1990: August 16. (58506 bytes)

English: HTML, Text, RTF, WordPerfect 5.1 (DOS),

French: HTML, Text, RTF, WordPerfect 5.1 (DOS),

[100 % relevant]

3) tock v. st. john's metropolitan area board

1989: January 31; 1989: December 7. (104931 bytes)

English: HTML, Text, RTF, WordPerfect 5.1 (DOS),

French: HTML, Text, RTF, WordPerfect 5.1 (DOS),

[90 % relevant]

Documents	**1 to 3**	

Note: National Yahoos devoted to specific countries are also available. An alternative approach would have been to begin by choosing the Canada "national Yahoo!" on the introductory page (see again illustration 1), then proceeding to the Law category. Similar options exist on other search engines: Webcrawler contains a Lawcrawler which can be further narrowed to focus exclusively on Canadian legal materials. The user is cautioned however not to rely exclusively on such narrowly focused options.

(C) TO SEARCH BY SPECIFIC WORDS:

The optional search method is to enter specific words into the Search box provided at the top of the introductory screen. A space denotes "and" (unlike QL where it means "or"). Note that it is not necessary for all search words to occur in retrieved documents; however, those which contain the highest number of search words will be retrieved and presented first. As noted above, matches occuring in titles and words denoting general categories will be ranked higher. Basic Boolean searches are also possible. A phrase is indicated by quotes, thus "*Osgoode Hall*". To require that words must all be present in documents in order for them to be retrieved, separate the search words with a plus sign, thus *Canadian + Cases*. A minus sign denotes BUTNOT, thus *court - tennis*.

Example: Assume we are trying to locate decisions from British Columbia. We may choose to search the "National Yahoo!" and specify Canada on the introductory page (see again Illustration 19 Yahoo! 1, p. 190). The following example uses the general Yahoo! option.

Enter British Columbia Decisions. The following appears:

ILLUSTRATION 28
Yahoo! 9

Yahoo! Search Results Page 1 of 1

YAHOO! Help - Personalize **Yahoo! Mail** - Stock Quotes - Yahoo! Chat

Categories **Web Sites** AltaVista News Stories Net Events

Found **0** categories and **1** site for **british columbia decisions**

Yahoo! Site Matches (1 - 1 of 1)

amazon.com
Find
Related Books
merchants with
related products

Regional: Countries: Canada: Provinces and Territories: **British Columbia**: Government: Law

- **British Columbia** Superior Courts - posts BC Court of Appeal and Supreme Court **decisions** online.

Go to AltaVista

british columbia decisions | Next Search | options - help

Other Search Engines

AltaVista - WebCrawler - HotBot - Lycos - Infoseek - Excite -- Image Surfer - DejaNews - More...

Yellow Pages - People Search - City Maps - Get Local - Today's Web Events & Chats - **More Yahoos**

Copyright © 1994-98 Yahoo! Inc. - Company Information - Help

One link has been retrieved: British Columbia Superior Courts. Clicking on this link, the following appears:

ILLUSTRATION 29
British Columbia Superior Courts
Home Page

BRITISH COLUMBIA SUPERIOR COURTS

Welcome to the British Columbia Superior Courts Home Page!
Visited [illegible] times since August 01, 1996.

Information...

- About the B.C. Superior Courts
- About the Web Site - Online August 01, 1996
- Search the Reasons for Judgment Database
- Court of Appeal for British Columbia
- B.C. Court of Appeal Registry - Address
- → Supreme Court of British Columbia
- B.C. Supreme Court Registries - Addresses

Other Links...

Supreme Court of Canada

Comments regarding Web page via email to: ag_jud_help@titan.gov.bc.ca
Permission 1996 BC Superior Courts Judiciary

Choosing for example Supreme Court of British Columbia, the following appears:

ILLUSTRATION 30
Supreme Court of British Columbia
Home Page

HOME
APPEAL
SEARCH

B.C. Supreme Court

Table of Contents...

Welcome to the Supreme Court Home Page

The Supreme Court of British Columbia is the province's superior trial court. It is a court of general and inherent jurisdiction. There are 100 Supreme Court judges who sit in eight judicial districts, travelling on circuit through the year. There are also 14 Supreme Court masters who deal with pre-trial matters. The Supreme Court hears both civil and criminal cases and also hears appeals from the Provincial Court.

| Home | Court of Appeal | Supreme Court |

Comments regarding Web page via email to: ag_jud_help@titan.gov.bc.ca

(iv) Other search engines:

The researcher should experiment with the various major search engines available. One should keep abreast of new developments, and there is no better source than the Internet for a complete list of Internet search engines. Try Yahoo! and enter *internet search engines* to access over 100.

(v) Electronic mail lists and discussion groups

The ability to communicate with people who share the same subject interests is a valuable research tool in itself. In addition to the free exchange of Internet addresses and information resources, list members with similar information needs can engage in E-mail discussions and share proposed solutions. If you wish to subscribe to a list, you will require an E-mail address on a mail server. Ask your provider for available E-mail options. The address will be in the form of userID@domain; that is, you will be assigned a User ID which, when joined to the domain name of the computer holding the mail server that collects your mail, becomes your E-mail address. To subscribe to a list, you must send: (a) your E-mail address and (b) a short subscription message, to the list address which the list has specified for subscribers. If the list(s) you subscribe to are large, be prepared to receive a large number of messages daily. Most E-mail programs provide various convenient ways to access and sort incoming messages. There are two types of lists: moderated lists combine and edit raw messages before they are forwarded to individual subscribers; unmoderated lists forward raw messages as they arrive.

3. Planning Computer-Assisted Research

Choosing the resources appropriate for a particular research task can be confusing, given the variety of formats and search engines. There are however certain basic considerations.

(a) Should you use hardcopy or computer-assisted methods?

Initial consideration should be given to the use of manual and/or computer resources. The question is usually one of timing and degree, not whether one or the other should be used exclusively.

(i) Computer-assisted methods are normally more productive if the researcher is generally familiar with the area in which the issue occurs. Texts remain the best source for general coverage of an area, and at present most are still in hardcopy only. For this reason, research often begins with books.

(ii) Even where the researcher is familiar with the area, both formats should be carefully considered. Full-text treatises and looseleafs are beginning to appear in CD-ROM in subject packages like "Butterworths' British

Columbia Civil Practice Library" (*British Columbia Practice, 2nd ed.*). Nevertheless, there remains a wealth of secondary sources which are not in electronic format, and to these we must apply the same addage we applied to the new technology - ignore them at your own risk.

(iii) Some issues lend themselves to the precision of Boolean searching. The earlier example of a case involving a negligent ski instructor applies to illustrate the usefulness of narrow wordmatch searches where a combination of fact and concept words emerge in formulating the search. Many hours of manual research would probably be required to locate negligent ski instructor cases, while a search for negligen! /p "ski instructor" takes about 20 seconds on QL. The results of the search might then be used to locate similar cases by locating judicial considerations or by consulting hardcopy classification schemes via Tables of Cases.

(b) Should you use online, CD-ROM, or the Internet?

Consideration must be given to the contents of the three electronic formats discussed above in order to choose an appropriate source/service/database. Undoubtedly the existence of electronic sources in three separate formats, each requiring its own separate technology, is, at best, inconvenient.

(i) Statutes

If, for example, federal statutes must be consulted, all three formats are useful: LEXIS-NEXIS and QUICKLAW each contain a federal statutes database, and the R.S.C. 1985 is available on CD-ROM. Several sources on the Internet provide access to federal statutes, bills, and bill tracking services (see Chapter 4). However, in terms of currency, which varies with each of these sources, the Internet provides the most up-to-date information with, *inter alia*, access to the Journals of the House and Senate.

(ii) Case law

Large volumes of case law, in full text or summary form covering all Canadian jurisdictions can be searched on LEXIS-NEXIS's CANADA library and on QUICKLAW. When planning a search, consideration must be given to which databases are most appropriate. Examples:

(A) A search on a criminal issue would usually include the *Canadian Criminal Cases* (LEXIS-NEXIS CCRIM, QL CCC), *Criminal Reports* (QL CR), and *Weekly Criminal Bulletin* (LEXIS-NEXIS and QL WCB) databases. These could then be updated by searching a full-text rapid-update service such as the CANCAS file on LEXIS-NEXIS or the *Canadian Judgments* (CJ) database on QL.

(B) A search involving an action against the Crown would include Exchequer and Federal court databases.

(C) Research contemplating a civil action for assault might begin with a search on the *All Canada Weekly Summaries* (LEXIS-NEXIS and QL:ACWS), which contains only civil cases and avoids the irrelevant criminal cases which would be contained in a mixed database of civil and criminal cases.

(D) A search for the name of an expert witness would be done on a Canada-wide full-text database such as CANADA, CANCAS on LEXIS-NEXIS or Canadian Judgments (CJ) on QUICKLAW.

(E) Where references to a subject are common even though the subject is not at issue (*i.e.*, damages may be referred to in the text of cases though not at issue), a summary database might be preferred.

(iii) Legal subject categories

If the issue falls conveniently into a legal category covered by a CD-ROM subject package, the researcher has the advantage of accessing selected primary and secondary sources joined by hypertext links and updated regularly. For example, Carswell's "Labour Law Partner" contains the *Annotated Canada Labour Code* (Snyder); the *Annotated Unemployment Insurance Act* (Rudner); Federal, Ontario, Alberta, and British Columbia labour law legislation (more provinces to be added); the full text of all *Canada Reporter* labour law decisions; treatises including *Evidence and Procedure in Canadian Labour Arbitration* (Gorsky) and *The Law of Collective Bargaining* (Raynor). "Labour Law Partner" is updated every three months.

(iv) Jurisdicational requirements

Jurisdictional considerations may narrow the sources considerably: a search for cases under the *Limitation of Civil Rights Act*, R.S.S. 1978 c. L-16 would be confined to LEXIS-NEXIS's CANADA library "SASKR" file or QUICKLAW's SJ, SASK, and regionals databases where only considerations by Saskatchewan courts are sought. The same search could be conducted on the Case Summaries or Fulltext databases on LINE, the Saskatchewan Law Society Libraries' *Legal Information Network Extension*.

(v) Currency and time coverage

Currency and time coverage requirements affect all searches, often requiring the same search to be repeated on several databases or other sources. For example, a search on QL's *Dominion Law Reports* (DLR) database might be repeated in the *Canadian Judgments* (CJ) database because the CJ database is updated more frequently while the DLR database covers a much longer time period. Alternatively or perhaps additionally, the search might be done on a CD-ROM product: Carswell's "Canada Reporter" which contains over 220,000 full-text decisions and is updated monthly. Internet sources might also be consulted for very recent decisions of the Supreme Court of Canada or the decisions of some provinces (B.C. Superior Courts at time of writing).

4. Formulating the Search Query

The following techniques are useful when formulating a search for use with Boolean search engines. They may also be used when formulating natural language search statements to make sure that all relevant terms are included.

(a) Frame the issue and select key words

Frame the issue for the problem in the same way as you would before beginning manual research (see Chapter 1), and include key words and phrases that would form the basis for initial manual searching. Do not use full sentences, but include legal phrases that will not appear in a variant form (*i.e.*, *res ipsa loquitur*). For example, where a restaurant patron sustains injuries by sitting on a restaurant chair which collapsed, the terms might be:

restaurant
chair
"res ipsa loquitur"

(b) "And" connectors

Since all terms searched should be in the same case for it to be on point, join the terms identified in example (a) with "and", thus: restaurant and chair and "res ipsa loquitur". The complete formulation of the query probably will include more than the terms initially identified. The Boolean search is literal, so the query should perhaps include the word "stool", in order to retrieve relevant cases involving a customer injured by a collapsing stool in a restaurant, and should include "cafeteria" in case the accident-prone eating place is referred to as such. As additional words are added to the query, its formulation is made easier by using a chart, which assists the thought process in recording the relationship between key words. First, replace the "ands" by vertical lines:

restaurant | chair | "res ipsa loquitur"

(c) "or" connectors

Now add each alternate expanding term like "stool" and "cafeteria" under the term which it expands:

restaurant	chair	"res ipsa loquitur"
cafeteria	stool	

Each vertically-listed word has an "or" relationship to the word above it (*i.e.*, the spaces between terms arranged vertically in columns mean "or"). Different legal concepts could also be listed beneath "res ipsa loquitur" to expand the search to cover occupiers liability situations:

restaurant	chair	"res ipsa loquitur"
cafeteria	stool	"occupiers liability"

Now convert back to simple English, continuing to use a space to represent "or":

restaurant cafeteria & chair stool &
"res ipsa loquitur" "occupiers liability"

(d) Rules for expanding the query

(i) Variant forms
Truncation should be used routinely wherever variant forms are a possibility (see 1(*a*)(i), Boolean searching). For example:
(A) Plurals: Add plurals unless the system automatically searches them: tort torts.
(B) Spelling variations: Add "marihuana" under "marijuana" or use a wildcard; *i.e.*, "mari*uana" on QUICKLAW.
(C) Suffixes: Add "expropriated" under "expropriation" or use a truncation feature, *i.e.*, expropriat! on QUICKLAW.

(ii) Synonyms and Antonyms
Use dictionaries and a thesaurus for adding synonyms and antonyms as alternates. An example of synonyms and near-synonyms: "automobile, car". An example of antonyms: "voluntary confession", "involuntary confession". Inclusion of both phrases separated by an "or" (represented by a space on QL) would probably yield more relevant cases than inclusion of just one of them.

(iii) Analogous words
Use textbooks, legal encyclopedias, indexes, and headnotes from cases already known to add analogous words as alternates which would retain the original concepts of the issue. By using analogous alternates, the search for "automobile car" could be expanded to "automobile car van truck vehicle". An analogous alternative for "nursing home" might be "day care centre". Obviously, the question of whether a term is an analogous alternate depends on the legal and factual issues of each case.

(e) Butnot

Use "butnot" to refine your search. The "butnot" connector will exclude what follows it: "discrimination butnot racial" would retrieve all cases containing the word "discrimination" except those containing the word "racial", thus excluding cases containing reference to "racial discrimination". Add butnot at the end of your query. Chart as follows:

(butnot)
damages | discrimination | race
racial

(f) Phrases and proximity connectors

A phrase can be searched on QL and most other systems by including it surrounded by quotation marks. Before using a phrase in a query, consider the various possible ways of expressing the concept. For example, "right to counsel" could appear as "right to retain counsel", "right to legal counsel", *etc.* If a phrase is not as static and frozen as "res ipsa loquitur", use a proximity connector ("/" means next word, "/3" means within three words, *etc.*). For example, right /5 counsel.

(g) Review your query to eliminate too-broad and too-narrow terms

For a document to be retrieved, at least one word from each column must be in it. Hence, more "ands" mean that a single document must contain many words before it is retrieved; this means that you run the risk of excluding documents which you would like to see but which are not retrieved because they do not contain one of the words that you have included in the query. More "ors" mean that a document need contain only one of the words separated by "or" before it is retrieved; this means you could be inundated with irrelevant documents. On this final review, carefully eliminate terms which artificially narrow or broaden your search.

B. BOOLEAN CHARTING EXAMPLES

Expertise in formulating queries does take time to develop and is a skill separate from framing the legal issue for a problem. But until natural language searching becomes the norm (and to some degree, after), researchers must continue to logically chart legal issues. Even lawyers who prefer to engage others to do computer-assisted research will benefit from the following examples, which illustrate proper search formulation.

Examples are given below to illustrate a variety of research situations in which the computer may be of assistance. The format used for the examples is:

(Number) (Categorization of the search)

Problem — A brief note about the legal issue

Charting — The charting of the problem to yield the proper formulation of the question for input to the computer. The vertical lines represent

"&s" and words arranged in vertical columns would be connected by "ors". For example:

Newspaper	libel defamation

would be written as: "newspaper & libel or defamation". In each example, vertical lines (&s) may be replaced by proximity connectors. See Formulating the Search Query (f).

Analysis — An explanation of the charting and possible noting of the problem as an illustration of a particular computer research technique.

Examples of charting:

1. Narrow, straightforward problem

Problem — A gas station site is to be expropriated.

Charting —

gas	station	expropriation
gasoline	shop	compensation
filling	garage	value
repair		valuation

Analysis — Because it is a narrow point, the vocabulary may be increased to ensure all variations are searched without concern about too many combinations of search terms yielding irrelevant cases. The combinations searched will include:

(a) "gas & station & expropriation" which should retrieve relevant cases;

(b) "gas & shop & expropriation" which is meaningless and will retrieve no cases since "gas shop" is not a commonly used phrase. "Shop" is included in the question to be combined with "repair" to yield "repair shop";

(c) consider using proximity connectors to link the columns, *i.e.*, gas/station/10 expropriation.

2. Very broad search

Problem — To compile a list of statute sections about duties relating to sheriffs.

Charting — sheriff
sheriffs

Analysis — In a matter of minutes, a complete printout of all statute sections using the terms "sheriff" or "sheriffs" is obtained.

3. Personal injury damages

Problem — A complete printout of unreported as well as reported cases giving quantum of damages for causing or aggravating phlebitis and causing a sprained ankle.

Charting — damages | phlebitis
quantum |

Analysis — Usually it is best to select the most severe injury yielding the highest likely damages award. Combining injuries may narrow the search to exclude significant cases considering one but not both or more of the injuries. Search should be made in databases having a high percentage of cases digested or reported, such as D.R.S., A.C.W.S., W.L.P., and A.P.R., which are good sources of damages awards.

4. Criminal Code citator

Problem — Cases considering *Criminal Code* s. 380(1) as it relates to defrauding senior citizens in home repairs.

Charting — 380(1) | age
elderly
senior
home
repair
improvement

Analysis — This charting would yield cases considering s. 380(1) in conjunction with senior citizens and home repairs. The question would be searched in the C.C.C. and W.C.B. databases to insure that section 380(1) will be associated with the *Criminal Code* in the headnotes. The terms, "crim. cr. criminal & code", could be added when searching D.R.S. and W.L.P. so that 380(1) will probably be linked with the *Criminal Code*. The proximity connector could be used in this example: "criminal / code".

5. Criminal sentencing

Problem — Finding cases giving lengths of sentences imposed for trafficking heroin.

Charting — sentenc! | heroin | trafficking

Analysis — By searching the W.C.B. or W.L.P. databases, many unreported sentencing cases are retrieved. If searching CJ, consider using proximity connectors.

6. Narrowing the above search to a specific jurisdiction

Problem — Only cases from a particular jurisdiction are wanted.

Charting — sentenc! | heroin | trafficking | Ontario

Analysis — This charting requires "Ontario" to appear in the document so that only some of the cases retrieved in example 5 above will now be retrieved.

Note that it is also possible to limit "Ontario" to the part of the document that refers to court or jurisdiction. This would be especially useful if searching CJ. Also, see Example 11 below.

7. Finding cases on new, unreported developments

Problem — Cases on the recent developments in television dishes receiving satellite signals.

Charting —

television	satellite
t.v.	dish
broadcasting	dishes

Analysis — This question may be asked of databases such as A.C.W.S., and C.J., which have very recent cases that have not yet or may never be fully reported.

8. Truncation

Problem — Cases dealing with negligence by insurance agents.

Charting —

insurance	agent	negligen!
	agents	

Analysis — The "!" indicates that the word has been truncated to pick up any variation with the stem of "negligen" — *e.g.*, negligence, negligent, negligently, etc. This is a broad question which will yield many cases, so the computer researcher may choose to print only the boldface key words portion of the headnote to save the lawyer time in scanning the printout.

9. Phrase search

Problem — Cases concerning professional misconduct by a lawyer.

Charting — "professional misconduct" | lawyer

Analysis — The question searched will be "lawyer & professional misconduct" which will ensure that "professional" and "misconduct" will appear next to each other in the headnote. An alternative charting would be:

"professional misconduct"	barrister
	solicitor

10. Two phrases

Problem — The same problem as in Example 9, but with the addition of the phrase "conduct unbecoming".

Charting —

"professional misconduct" "conduct unbecoming"	lawyer barrister solicitor

11. Civil statute citator

Problem — Cases discussing dissipation of property in connection with *Matrimonial Property Act.*

Charting and Analysis — There are several considerations when searching for statutes in headnotes.

(a) "Matrimonial Property Act" | Saskatchewan

The Act as a phrase connected to the jurisdiction is sufficient if a low number of retrieved cases is anticipated.

(b)

"Matrimonial Property Act"	28 28(1)	Saskatchewan

If a high number of retrievals is expected, the general section number and subsection as an alternate may be added to the query to narrow the search. Irrelevant cases may be retrieved if the section numbers retrieve statutes other than the desired statutes.

(c)

@5"Matrimonial Property Act"	28 28(!

The search may be restricted to particular segments or elements of the headnote such as the statutes judicially noticed segment of Maritime Law Book Ltd.'s headnotes in the *National Reporter System.* The symbol, "@5", in the query for the N.R.S. database designates that the 5th segment (statutes judicially noticed) be searched. The researcher might not be certain how the statutes are cited in the headnote segment — *i.e.*, R.S.S. for *Revised Statutes of Saskatchewan,* S.S. for *Statutes of Saskatchewan* if the Act came in force subsequent to the statute revision, Saskatchewan or Sask., or Saskatchewan *Matrimonial Property Act.*

(d) matrimonial | property | dissipation

Using key words rather than section numbers avoids the problems inherent in the approaches illustrated above and allows for retrieval of cases considering statutes from other provinces which probably use different numbers for the sections dealing with the concept in question.

(e) Proximity connectors can be very effective:

-"Matrimonial Property Act" /7 28(!

12. Case citator

QL Systems provides a case citation/history feature which generates a list of considering cases as well as a history of most cases which appear in QL databases. To use this service, retrieve the case by searching significant words in the style of cause (*i.e.*, @2 Jones & Stevens), then enter "cite".

The following comments apply to instances where this feature is not available.

Three types of problems are presented below to illustrate use of the computer to find cases judicially considered by cases stored in the databases. For the unreported cases stored in QL's W.L.P. and C.J. databases, the only source for prior cases cited by these unreported cases is the computer search — *i.e.*, non-existence of commercially printed tables.

(a) For styles of cause containing an unusual name, use the most distinctive word or words. For example, *R. v. Therens* would result in a query of simply Therens.

(b) For very common names, subject key words may be added to narrow the search:
Smith & custody & access

If the case had been *Smith v. Smith,* it is only necessary to enter Smith once in the query since the computer only recognizes the need for the term to appear once in a stored document.

(c) Never use abbreviations, but rather use uncommon names or common names with subject key words. The problem with abbreviations is that they may appear in so many variants. For example, "Board of School Trustees of School District No. 57 (Prince George)" may appear as "Prince George Board of School Trustees", "Bd. of School Trustees of S.D. 57 (Prince George)", "S. Dist. No. 57 (Prince George)", plus many more.

(d) It is possible to limit a cases judicially considered search to the appropriate segment of the document, thus avoiding retrieval of the case itself. The @ command is used to do this: "@7 Therens".

13. Finding trends in cases decided by a particular judge

Problem — Finding cases on matrimonial property determined by Judge Smith of Saskatchewan.

Charting —matrimonial | property | @4 Smith | Saskatchewan
marital

Analysis — Many headnotes will contain matrimonial property and Smith, so the search may be narrowed by requiring that Smith and Saskatchewan appear only in the court/judges segment of the headnote (*e.g.*, segment @4 in this example). All key words after the segment symbol will be required to be in that segment. Matrimonial & property & @4 Smith & Saskatchewan is a properly phrased search, but @4 Smith

& Saskatchewan & matrimonial & property is not proper because the statement requires matrimonial property to be in segment 4.

14. Searching for elements of indexing schemes used in digests and headnotes

Problem — The researcher has located a *Saskatchewan Reports* case with a point of law classified as "Labour Law — Topic 7000" (Maritime Law Book classification scheme) and wants other cases discussing this narrow point of law.

Charting — "Labour Law | "Topic 7000"

Analysis — This search would be asked of all databases taken from Maritime Law Book's publications including the *National Reporter System* database.

15. Retrieving zero documents

Problem — The lawyer specified the two search terms church and copyright, but no cases were retrieved with the computer's response being "zero documents".

Charting — church | copyright

Analysis — This narrow search required both words of this unusual combination to be in one headnote. With such specific words, the lawyer may be confident that no cases in the databases discuss this matter, therefore a zero documents retrieval can be informative.

16. Current awareness search

Problem — The lawyer wants a weekly update on "oil and gas leases" cases from across the country.

Charting — lease | oil
| gas

Analysis — Each week, this query may be made to the A.C.W.S. database, asking for reverse chronological order which enables the researcher to print out only the cases that are new since the last printout.

Note that both LEXIS-NEXIS and QL automatically add the plural (*i.e.*, leases).

If the search is to be done on a full text such as CJ which is updated daily, the occurrence of irrelevant retrievals can be reduced by using a proximity connector in place of "&". (See Formulating the Search Query (f)).

Chapter 11

Research Checklists: Master, Federal, Provincial, Territorial & Subject-Areas

The master research checklist is presented as a general overview of Canadian legal research, and it may be adapted for the particular needs of the researcher. Subject areas for checklists have been determined largely by areas covered by law reports and digests, and the checklists present specific titles as well as directions for locating other sources. The subject checklists give representations, while exhaustive bibliographies are beyond the scope of this book. General research for federal law and the law of each province and territory is covered by individual checklists. Because these are brief checklists, they will be most helpful for researchers approaching the law of a province other than the researcher's own jurisdiction.

The area of professional conduct has been included because this is an area of concern to younger lawyers who may want guidance as specific situations of uncertainty arise.

The final checklist is an aid to finding citations for reported and unreported Canadian cases, English and Commonwealth cases, and American cases.

These checklists are designed primarily for common law research, while approaches to Québec law are covered in Chapter 12.

Electronic sources are noted.

A. MASTER RESEARCH CHECKLIST

While these are general overviews, more in-depth bibliographic awareness is now possible from your office by using the Internet to search law school library book holdings. An example of a law library website is Osgoode Hall Law School's Internet address: www.library.yorku.ca/.

1. Background information

(a) Researcher: .... Date:..

(b) Research for: .... File No.: .... Deadline: ....

(c) Facts:..

....

(d) Legal issue: ....
(e) Key words, legal and fact: ....
(f) Electronic sources search to be made initially: Yes .... No ....
Charting of the key words for an electronic search: ....
Sources to be searched: ....

2. Research in secondary authority material as background reading

(a) Legal encyclopedias

For encyclopedias, use either the key word search approach (index) or legal topic approach (Table of Contents) as discussed in Chapter 1. The Table of Cases approach may be used if one or more relevant cases are initially known.

Note: Both C.E.D. Ontario (3rd) and C.E.D. Western (3rd) are available on a single CD-ROM from Carswell.

(1) C.E.D. (Ontario 3rd)
  a) KEY Part V key words Index
  b) update with Can. Abr. Rev. (2nd) and C.C.L. by the cross-reference from the C.E.D. title to Can. Abr. (2nd) titles (in each C.E.D. titles' Table of Contents).

(2) C.E.D. (Western 3rd)
  a) KEY words Index
  b) update with Can. Abr. Rev. (2nd) and C.C.L. by the cross-reference from the C.E.D. titles to Can. Abr. (2nd) titles (in each C.E.D. titles' Table of Contents).

(3) *Halsbury's Laws of England*
  a) 3rd edition with Canadian Converters
  b) 4th edition with much of the change being in statutory law.

(4) *American Jurisprudence 2d* (CD-ROM from Carswell)
Corpus Juris Secundum (Insurance and tax portions available online from WESTLAW through QL Systems Ltd. identifiers CJS-INS and CJS-FTX).

(5) *Halsbury's Laws of Australia* (selected titles available online through LEXIS-NEXIS from Butterworths: library AUST and files HALTOC for table of contents or HALSAU).
The Laws of Australia (CD-ROM from Carswell).

(b) Legal periodical indexes

The Table of Cases approach may be used to look for case comments.

(1) *Index to Canadian Legal Periodical Literature* (subject index).
(2) *Index to Canadian Legal Literature* (part of Can. Abr. Rev. (2nd)). (QL 1987-).
(3) *Current Law Index* and *Legal Resources Index*
(LEXIS-NEXIS from Butterworths: library LEXREF and file LGLIND).

Index to Legal Periodicals (LEXIS-NEXIS from Butterworths: library LEXREF and file ILP) and (WESTLAW through QL: identifier ILP).
Index to Foreign Legal Periodicals (WESTLAW through QL: identifier IFLP).

(c) Other secondary legal literature sources
 (1) Textbooks (key word in index, legal topic in Table of Contents, or Table of Cases approach) including continuing legal education material and government documents (see Chapters 9 and 18).
  (a) Check library's catalogue (see Chapter 9, part A).
 (2) Looseleaf services
  (a) Check library's catalogue which may be online.
  (b) "Rapid Finder Index" by CCH Canadian Ltd.

(d) Social science, business, and science literature as background for litigation (see Chapter 18 but one must consider an electronic search as a supplement to this manual research).

(e) Publications' supplements should be checked for updating.

3. Case law indexes and digests: national and regional materials

(a) Key word search approach
National (all courts but often selective coverage of Québec) and Regional.
 (1) Reported
Atlantic Provinces Reports
Canadian Abridgment Revised (2nd)
Canadian Current Law (QL and CD-ROM)
Canadian Weekly Law Sheet
Dominion Law Reports/Canadian Criminal Cases indexes (LEXIS-NEXIS and QL)
Dominion Report Service (on QL only)
"National Reporter System" on LEXIS-NEXIS (includes *National Reporter*, *Federal Trial Reports*, and provincial reports from Maritime Law Book)
Western Appeal Cases (LEXIS-NEXIS)
Western Weekly Reports (QL)
 (2) Unreported
All Canada Weekly Summaries (LEXIS-NEXIS and QL)
Canadian Current Law
Lawyers Weekly (QL)
Weekly Criminal Bulletin (LEXIS-NEXIS and QL)

(b) Legal topic approach
This approach may be used for digests with detailed Table of Contents such as the Can. Abr. Rev. *(2nd)* volume titled: "Key and Research Guide".

(c) Words and phrases approach
This approach may be used with the words and phrases publications listed in Chapter 9, part D (such as *Words and Phrases Judicially Defined in Canadian Courts and Tribunals*), and with titles listed as having Words and Phrases features (see Chapter 3's Charts). Also, *The Dictionary of Canadian Law (2nd ed.)*.

(d) Table of Cases approach may be used in separately published digests such as the Can. Abr. Rev. (2nd) to locate a grouping of cases related to a case initially known.

(e) Cases judicially considered tables should be checked as an update.

4. Statutes and regulations: indexes, listings, and updating

(a) Statutes: federal and provincial revisions and sessional/annual volumes
  - (1) Index or computer database
  - (2) Updating in Table of Public Statutes
  - (3) Proclamation dates
  - (4) Legislative Bills
  - (5) Statutes judicially considered

(b) Regulations: federal consolidations and provincial revisions for some jurisdictions plus Gazette issues
  - (1) Indexing is usually poor with table form listings of regulations by enabling statute being the most common access
  - (2) Electronic search available for some jurisdictions

5. Search of other sources

If manual research of Canadian law has not yielded as complete a memorandum as anticipated, then:

(a) Consider electronic research if such has not already been made

(b) Consider search of other jurisdictions' law
  - (1) English law, Chapter 13
  - (2) Australian and New Zealand law, Chapter 15
  - (3) American law, Chapter 14

Note: Case law searches noted in federal, provincial, and territorial lists below are assumed to include research in the national and regional law reports and digests cited in the Master checklist above.

B. FEDERAL MATERIALS CHECKLISTS

1. Federal case law

(a) Federal (in approximate order of reporting/digesting timeliness for each court)

(1) Supreme Court of Canada
QL's LAW/NET online databases (access code LNET)
Supreme Court of Canada Summaries
Supreme Court of Canada Cases (LEXIS-NEXIS)
Supreme Court of Canada Decisions (QL 1980-)
The Lawyers Weekly (CD-ROM, QL, LEXIS-NEXIS)
National Reporter (LEXIS-NEXIS)
Supreme Court of Canada Reports Service
Canada Supreme Court Reports (no current cumulative index)(QL)

(2) Federal Court
Federal Court of Appeal Decisions (QL)
National Reporter/Federal Trial Reports (LEXIS-NEXIS)
Federal Court of Canada Service
Federal Court Reports (QL)
Federal Court of Appeal Cases (LEXIS-NEXIS)
Federal Court Trial Division Cases (LEXIS-NEXIS)

2. Federal statute law

(a) Federal statutes

(l) Statute research and update
R.S.C. 1985 Index/*Index to Federal and Ontario Statutes 199+* (Carswell)
Statutes of Canada (index for new acts in sessional volumes)
Canada Gazette Part III issues including Table of Public Statutes issues (LEXIS-NEXIS online database, access code CANSTA (Canada library))
QL online database: access code RSCC
CD-ROM: Canada Law Book
Internet: http://canada.justice.gc.ca/Loireg/index_enhtml

(2) Proclamation dates: *Canada Gazette Part I, Canada Statute Citator*

(3) Citators
Canada Statute Citator and *Annotations*
Crankshaw's Criminal Code, Martins Criminal Code, etc., *Stikeman Income Tax Annotated,* and looseleaf tax services
Canadian Statute Citations (Carswell, 19 volumes)
Statutory time limitations: *Federal Limitation Periods,* Butterworths looseleaf

3. Federal regulations

(a) Text of regulations
Consolidated Regulations of Canada, 1978
Canada Gazette Part II

LEXIS-NEXIS online database access code CANREG (Canada library)
QL online database: access code SOR
CD-ROM: Canada Law Book
Internet: http://canada.justice.gc.ca/Loireg/index_enhtml

(b) Index/tables of regulations
Canada Gazette Part II Consolidated Index of Statutory Instruments
Canada Regulations Index (by Carswell)

4. Case citators

(a) Federal statutes citators
Canada Statute Citator/Annotations (not *Criminal Code* or *Income Tax Act*)
Canadian Abridgment Revised (2nd) "Canadian Statute Citations" (has all federal statutes)

(b) Cases Judicially Considered by federal cases
Can. Abr. Rev. (2nd) Canadian Case Citations volumes (Carswell, 10 volumes)
National Reporter's "Cases Judicially Noticed" section

C. ALBERTA CHECKLIST

1. Case law

(a) Reported
Alberta Law Reports (3d)(QL)
Alberta Reports (LEXIS-NEXIS)

(b) Unreported
Alberta Weekly Law Digest
Alberta Decisions

2. Statute law

(a) Statute research and updating
R.S.A. 1980 (looseleaf)
S.A. including Table of Public Statutes
Hansard, *Canadian Current Law Legislation, CCH Provincial Legislative Record, Alberta Parliamentary Digest, Alberta Legislative Summary*

(b) Proclamation dates
Alberta Gazette Part I, Canadian Current Law Legislation, CCH Provincial Legislative Record, Alberta Parliamentary Digest

(c) Citators
Statutes of Alberta Judicially Considered, Alberta Decisions Citator, Alberta Reports "Statutes Judicially Noticed" section, *Canadian Statute Citations*

(d) Statutory time limitations: *Alberta Limitations Manual,* looseleaf, Butterworths
(e) Electronic sources: Internet, Online (QP and QL), CD-ROM

3. Regulations

(a) Text of Regulations
Alberta Gazette Part II
(b) Access/Indexing/Listing
Cumulative listing in the *Gazette*
Canadian Current Law Legislation
(c) Electronic sources: Internet, Online (QP and QL), CD-ROM

4. Case citators

Alberta Decisions on CD-ROM or QL
Alberta Law Reports (3d) "Cases Judicially Considered"
Alberta Reports "Cases Judicially Noticed"
Canadian Case Citations

D. BRITISH COLUMBIA CHECKLIST

1. Case law

(a) Reported
British Columbia Appeal Cases (LEXIS-NEXIS)
British Columbia Law Reports (2d) (QL)
(b) Unreported
British Columbia Weekly Law Digest
British Columbia Decisions
British Columbia Trial Cases

2. Statute law

(a) Statute research and updating
R.S.B.C. 1996 (looseleaf)
S.B.C. including Table of Statutes (also in *B.C. Statute Citator), Votes and Proceedings, B.C. Legislative Digest, Canadian Case Law Legislation, CCH Provincial Legislative Record*
(b) Proclamation dates
B.C. Gazette Parts I and II, Canadian Case Law Legislation, B.C. Statute Citator, B.C. Legislative Digest, CCH Provincial Legislative Record
(c) Citators
B.C. Statute Citator, Statutes of B.C. Judicially Considered, B.C. Deci-

sions Citator, B.C. Appeal Cases "Statutes Judicially Noticed" sections, *Canadian Statute Citations*

(d) Electronics sources: Online, CD-ROM, Internet

3. Regulations

(a) Text of regulations
British Columbia Gazette Part II
Consolidated Regulations of British Columbia

(b) Access/Indexing/Listing
Index of Current British Columbia Regulations
British Columbia Statute Citator
Canadian Current Law Legislation
B.C. Legislative Digest

4. Case citators

B.C. Appeal Cases "Cases Judicially Noticed" sections
B.C. Decisions on CD-ROM or QL
B.C. Law Reports "Cases Judicially Considered"
Canadian Case Citations

E. MANITOBA CHECKLIST

1. Case law

(a) Reported
Manitoba Reports (2d) (LEXIS-NEXIS)

(b) Unreported
Manitoba Decisions

2. Statute law

(a) Statute research and updating
Re-enacted Statutes of Manitoba in series 1987 through 1990. Looseleaf is *Continuing Consolidation of the Statutes of Manitoba* (C.C.S.M.).
S.M. and C.C.S.M.'s "List of Statutes in Continuing Consolidation", *Canadian Case Law Legislation, CCH Provincial Legislative Record*

(b) Proclamation dates
Manitoba Gazette Part I, Canadian Case Law Legislation, S.M., *CCH Provincial Legislative Record*

(c) Citators
Statutes of Manitoba Judicially Considered
Manitoba Decisions Citator

Manitoba Reports "Statutes Judicially Noticed" section
Canadian Statute Citations
(d) Electronic sources: Online (QL)

3. Regulations

(a) Text of regulations
Manitoba Gazette Part II
(b) Access/Indexing/Listing
Manitoba Regulations
Canadian Current Law Legislation

4. Case citators

Canadian Case Citations
Manitoba Decisions on CD-ROM or QL
Manitoba Reports "Cases Judicially Noticed"

F. NEW BRUNSWICK CHECKLIST

1. Case law

New Brunswick Reports (Second Series) (reported) (LEXIS-NEXIS)

2. Statute law

(a) Statute research and updating
R.S.N.B. 1973 (looseleaf) and Maritime Law Book Ltd.'s *Subject Matter Index to Public and Private Statutes of New Brunswick.*
S.N.B. including Table of Public Statutes
Canadian Case Law Legislation, CCH Provincial Legislative Record
(b) Proclamation dates
N.B. Royal Gazette, Canadian Case Law Legislation, CCH Provincial Legislative Record
(c) Citators
Canadian Statute Citations, N.B.R. (2d) "Statutes Judicially Noticed section"

3. Regulations

(a) Text of regulations
New Brunswick Royal Gazette, Consolidated Regulations of N.B.
(b) Access/Indexing/Listing
Cumulative listing in gazette bound annual
Canadian Current Law Legislation

4. Case citators

New Brunswick Reports (Second Series) "Cases Judicially Noticed"
Canadian Case Citations

G. NEWFOUNDLAND CHECKLIST

1. Case law

Newfoundland & Prince Edward Island Reports (reported) (LEXIS-NEXIS)

2. Statute law

(a) Statute research and updating
R.S.N. 1990
S.N. including Table of Public Statutes
Canadian Case Law Legislation, CCH Provincial Legislative Record

(b) Proclamation dates
Newfoundland Gazette Part II, Canadian Case Law Legislation, CCH Provincial Legislative Record

(c) Citators
Canadian Statute Citations
Newfoundland and Prince Edward Island Reports "Statutes Judicially Noticed" section

(d) Electronic sources: statute listing on Internet

3. Regulations

(a) Text of regulations
Newfoundland Gazette Part II

(b) Access/Indexing/Listing
Cumulative Index in Gazette
Canadian Current Law Legislation

4. Case citators

Canadian Case Citations
Newfoundland and Prince Edward Island Reports "Cases Judicially Noticed"

H. NORTHWEST TERRITORIES CHECKLIST

1. Case law

Northwest Territories Reports (reported) (QL)

2. Statute law

(a) Statute research and updating
Revised Statutes of N.W.T. 1988
Sessional volumes including Table of Public Acts
Debates of the Legislative Assembly, Canadian Case Law Legislation, CCH Provincial Legislative Record

(b) Proclamation dates
Northwest Territories Gazette Part 1, sessional volume, *Canadian Case Law Legislation, CCH Provincial Legislative Record*

(c) Citators
Canadian Statute Citations
Northwest Territories Reports "Statutes Judicially Considered"

(d) Electronic sources: Internet

3. Regulations

(a) Text of regulations
Revised Regulations of the Northwest Territories 1990
Northwest Territories Gazette Part II

(b) Access/Indexing/Listing
Cumulative Listing in annual bound *Northwest Territories Gazette Part II,* sessional statute volumes
Canadian Current Law Legislation

4. Case citators

Northwest Territories Reports "Cases Judicially Considered"
Canadian Case Citations

I. NOVA SCOTIA CHECKLIST

1. Case law

(a) Reported
Nova Scotia Reports (Second Series) (LEXIS-NEXIS)

(b) Unreported
Nova Scotia Law News

2. Statute law

(a) Statute research and updating
R.S.N.S. 1989 (looseleaf consolidations including Table of Contents), S.N.S. including Table of Public Statutes

Standing of Bills Index, *Canadian Case Law Legislation, CCH Provincial Legislative Record*

(b) Proclamation dates
Canadian Case Law Legislation, Nova Scotia Royal Gazette Part II, CCH Provincial Legislative Record

(c) Citators
N.S.R. (2d), "Statutes Judicially Noticed" section, index to *Nova Scotia Law News, Canadian Statute Citations*

(d) Electronic sources: Internet

3. Regulations

(a) Text of regulations
Nova Scotia Gazette Part II

(b) Access/Indexing/Listing
"Cumulative Index" annual issue of the *Royal Gazette Part II, Canadian Current Law Legislation*

(c) Electronic sources: Internet

4. Case citators

Nova Scotia Reports (Second Series), "Cases Judicially Noticed"
Canadian Case Citations

J. ONTARIO CHECKLIST

1. Case law

(a) Reported
Ontario Appeal Cases (LEXIS-NEXIS)
Ontario Reports (Third Series) (QL)
Ontario Trial Cases (LEXIS-NEXIS, QL)

(b) Unreported
Lawyers Weekly (QL)

(c) Ontario subject reports/digests
Butterworths Ontario Family Law Quantum Service
Ontario Decisions (criminal)
Ontario Labour Relations Board Reports
Ontario Municipal Board Reports
Weekly Digest of Civil Procedure

2. Statute law

(a) Statute research and updating
R.S.O. 1990
S.O. including Table of Public Statutes
Votes and Proceedings, Ontario Statute Citator's Weekly Service Bulletin, *Canadian Case Law Legislation, CCH Provincial Legislative Record*
Index to Federal and Ontario Statutes (updated annually)

(b) Proclamation dates
Ontario Gazette, "Weekly Service Bulletin", *Canadian Case Law Legislation*, S.O., *CCH Provincial Legislative Record*

(c) Citators
Ontario Statute Citator and *Annotations, Ontario Appeal Cases*' "Statutes Judicially Noticed" sections, *Canadian Statute Citations*

(d) Statutory time limitations
Ontario Limitation Periods, looseleaf, Butterworths

(e) Electronic sources: Internet, LEXIS-NEXIS, QL, CD-ROM

3. Regulations

(a) Text of regulations
Revised Regulations of Ontario 1990
Ontario Gazette

(b) Access/Indexing Listing
Cumulative listing in the gazette
Sessional statute volumes
Carswell's Ontario Regulations Service
Canadian Current Law Legislation

(c) Electronic sources: Internet, QL

4. Case citators

Ontario Appeal Cases "Cases Judicially Noticed"
Canadian Case Citations

K. PRINCE EDWARD ISLAND CHECKLIST

1. Case law

Newfoundland and Prince Edward Island Reports (reported) (LEXIS-NEXIS)

2. Statute law

(a) Statute research and updating
R.S.P.E.I. 1988 (looseleaf)

S.P.E.I. including Table of Public Statutes
Canadian Case Law Legislation
CCH Provincial Legislative Record

(b) Proclamation dates
Royal Gazette of Prince Edward Island Part II, S.P.E.I., *Canadian Case Law Legislation, CCH Provincial Legislative Record*

(c) Citators
Newfoundland and Prince Edward Island Reports "Statutes Judicially Noticed" sections
Canadian Statute Citations

3. Regulations

(a) Text of regulations
Royal Gazette of Prince Edward Island
Revised Regulations of Prince Edward Island

(b) Access/Indexing/Listing
Annual listing in gazette
Revised Regulations of Prince Edward Island
Canadian Current Law Legislation

4. Case citators

Newfoundland and Prince Edward Island Reports "Cases Judicially Noticed"
Canadian Case Citations

L. SASKATCHEWAN CHECKLIST

1. Case law

(a) Reported
Saskatchewan Reports (LEXIS-NEXIS)

(b) Unreported
This Week's Law
Saskatchewan Decisions

2. Statute law

(a) Statute research and updating
R.S.S. 1978 (looseleaf)
S.S., *Tables to the Statutes of Saskatchewan, Votes and Proceedings, Canadian Case Law Legislation, CCH Provincial Legislative Record, This Week's Law*

(b) Proclamation dates
Saskatchewan Gazette Part I, Canadian Case Law Legislation, CCH Provincial Legislative Record, This Week's Law

(c) Citators
Statutes of Saskatchewan Judicially Considered, Saskatchewan Decisions Citator, This Week's Law, Saskatchewan Reports "Statutes Judicially Noticed" section

(d) Electronic sources: Internet, QL

3. Regulations

(a) Text of Regulations
Saskatchewan Gazette Part III
Revised Regulations of Saskatchewan

(b) Access/Indexing/Listing
Tables to the Statutes of Saskatchewan and Saskatchewan Regulations
Saskatchewan Decisions Citator
Canadian Current Law Legislation

(c) Electronic sources: Internet

4. Case citators

Saskatchewan Reports "Cases Judicially Noticed" section
This Week's Law (for unreported cases)
Saskatchewan Decisions on CD-ROM on QL
Canadian Case Citations

M. YUKON CHECKLIST

1. Case law

The Yukon does not have a separately published law reports series (except *Yukon Reports,* 1987-1989). Some cases are found in the D.L.R.'s and W.W.R.'s, but more complete sources would be national unreported digesting services such as *Lawyers' Weekly*, A.C.W.S. and W.C.B., which are easily accessed by QUICKLAW or LEXIS-NEXIS online search. QL's YJ database has Yukon judgments starting with 1986.

2. Statute law

(a) Statute research and updating
Revised Statutes of the Yukon, 1986, sessional volume including Tables of Public Statutes, *Canadian Case Law Legislation*, *CCH Provincial Legislative Record*, Government Bills: Progress of Bills

(b) Proclamation dates: *Yukon Gazette Part I, Canadian Case Law Legislation, CCH Provincial Legislative Record*
(c) Citators
Canadian Statute Citations
(d) Electronic sources: Internet

3. Regulations

(a) Text of regulations
Yukon Regulations
Yukon Gazette
(b) Access/Indexing/Listing
"Table of Contents" to *Yukon Regulations*
Canadian Current Law Legislation

4. Case citators

Canadian Case Citations

N. CANADIAN CHARTER OF RIGHTS AND FREEDOMS (and Constitution Acts, 1867 +)

1. Law reports

Canadian Rights Reporter (2nd) (LEXIS-NEXIS 1994-)
Canadian Human Rights Reporter

2. Digests

Charter of Rights Decisions

3. Citators

Annotated Canadian Charter of Rights and Freedoms (Carswell)
Canadian Charter of Rights Annotated (Canada Law Book)

4. Textbooks

Atrens, *The Charter and Criminal Procedure: Section 7 and 11,* 1989, Butterworths
Bayefsky, *International Human Rights Law: Use in Canadian Charter of Rights and Freedoms Litigation,* 1992, Butterworths
Beaudoin, *Canadian Charter of Rights and Freedoms,* 2d ed., 1989, Carswell

Charles et al, *Evidence and the Charter of Rights and Freedoms,* 1989, Butterworths
Cooper-Stephenson, *Charter Damages Claims,* 1990, Carswell
Davis, *Canadian Constitutional Law Handbook - Leading Statements,*
Principles, and Precedents, 1985, Canada Law Book
Gibson, *The Law of the Charter: Equality Rights*, 1990, Carswell
Hogg, *Constitutional Law of Canada,* 3rd ed., 1991, Carswell
McDonald, *Legal Rights in the Canadian Charter of Rights and Freedoms,* 2d ed., 1987, Carswell
Risk, *Canadian Constitutional Law,* (two volumes), 1994, Emond Montgomery Publications
Roach, *Constitutional Remedies in Canada*, looseleaf, 1994, Canada Law Book
Schabas, *International Human Rights Law and the Canadian Charter (2d)*, 1996, Carswell
Schneiderman, *Freedom of Expression and the Charter*, 1991, Carswell
Sharpe, *Charter Litigation,* 1987, Butterworths
Sproat, *Equality Rights and Fundamental Freedoms*, looseleaf, 1996, Carswell
Stratas, *The Charter of Rights in Litigation,* looseleaf, Canada Law Book
Strayer, *The Canadian Constitution and the Courts,* 1988, Butterworths
Stuart, *Charter Justice in Canadian Criminal Law,* 1991, Carswell
Trakman, *Reasoning with the Charter,* 1991, Butterworths

See also checklists for Criminal Law and Human Rights.
Check also with provincial Continuing Legal Education Centres for seminar publications and audio cassettes.

5. Periodical literature

Charter of Rights Newsletter (Canada Law Book)
National Journal of Constitutional Law (Carswell)
Also, see the "Charter" as a legal periodical index subject heading.

O. SUBJECT-AREA RESEARCH CHECKLISTS

The following subject checklists first list law reports and digests from Chapter 3. The *Index to Canadian Legal Periodical Literature* subject headings are only representative with many more in the publications and other headings in other periodical indexes. Encyclopedia article titles in C.E.D. (Western 3rd) and C.E.D. (Ontario 3rd) are frequently the same, but, of course, the emphasis of the contents is on different regions. C.E.D. (Western 3rd) and C.E.D. (Ontario 3rd) are available on a single CD-ROM from Carswell.

The listing of textbooks is very selective with only recent titles indicating broad topic coverage being included. The checklists of texts began in the first edition of this textbook when CLIC still had identified a "literature gap list in areas of substantive Canadian law". The "gap list" was terminated as many more Canadian texts were published in the 1980s. The textbook listings below are selective in the following sense: books on a broad sub-area are included (*e.g.*, *The Law of Interest in Canada)* while texts on very narrow areas (*e.g.*, tax sub-areas) are excluded; where several publishers' texts cover the same subject matter, all texts are listed; books under 200 pages are generally excluded (usually "guide" books rather than in-depth discussion of substantive law). The text listings are samplings and are generally from the following publishers listed with their abbreviations used in the listings below: Butterworths (BTR), Carswell (CARS), Canada Law Book (CLB), and Emond Montgomery (E-M). Other publishers' abbreviations used are: WLP for Western Legal Publications and CCH for Commerce Clearing House, Canadian Ltd. Some of the texts are in looseleaf format, indicated by "llf". The subject groupings below are relatively few, and there was some difficulty determining the appropriate category for some specific titles. I subjectively placed each text into an existing category and did not include a "miscellaneous" or "other" category. Of course, each year will see more texts published in all areas, and these lists are current to mid-1997. Publisher's catalogues (including smaller publishers) and representatives should be consulted for a complete survey of the titles available.

Casebooks, reprints from legal encyclopedias, and provincial continuing education and bar admission material are not included.

The "other sources" selectively list looseleaf services, annotated legislation services, and samples of other publications. These checklists present representative titles, and exhaustive bibliographies are beyond the scope of this book. The holdings of local law school or law society libraries should be checked to gather more complete information.

1. Business/Commerce

(a) Corporations and partnerships

(1) Case Law

Business Law Reports, CARS(QL 1986-)
Canada Corporations Law Reporter, CCH
British Columbia Corporations Law Guide, CCH
Ontario Corporations Law Guide, CCH
Canadian Commercial Law Guide, CCH

See also Chapters 3, and 12. Chart L ...Tribunal Decisions ... Business/ Commerce

See also Chapter 6, C. 6. Annotated Legislation ... Business/Commerce

(2) *Index to Canadian Legal Periodical Literature* subjects:

Anti-Trust Law	Business
Commerce	Commercial Law
Consolidation & Merger	Corporate Liquidation

Corporation Reorganization	Corporations
Dividends	Franchising
Partnerships	Unfair Competition

(3) *Canadian Encyclopedia Digest* title: Corporations

(4) Selected list of textbooks

Aird and Berus, *Business Acquisition Agreements: An Annotated Guide*, 1992, CLB

Bourgeois, *Law of Charitable and Nonprofit Organizations 2nd, The*, 1996, BTR

Campbell, *Merger Law and Practice,* 1997, CARS

Canadian Franchise Guide, llf, CARS

Ellis, *Fiduciary Duties in Canada,* llf, CARS

Harris, *Annotated Business Agreements,* llf, CARS

Hepburn, *Limited Partnerships,* llf, CARS

Kerr, *Procedures for Meetings and Organizations 3d*, 1996, CARS

Kwaw, *Law of Corporate Finance in Canada, The,* 1997, BTR

Manzar, *Practical Guide to Canadian Partnership Law, A,* llf, CLB

McCarthy, Tétrault, *Directors' and Officers' Duties and Liabilities in Canada,* 1997, BTR

Nathan, *Corporate Meetings: Law and Practice,* llf, CARS

Peterson, *Shareholder Remedies in Canada*, llf, BTR

Phillips, *Personal Remedies for Corporate Injuries,* 1992, CARS

Rossiter, *Business Legal Adviser,* llf, CARS

Sarna, ed., *Corporate Structure, Finance, and Operations,* nine volumes, 1980-, CARS

Shareholder's Agreements: An Annotated Guide, 1997, CLB

Sutherland and Horsley, et al., *Fraser & Stewart Company Law of Canada 6th,* 1993, CARS

Welling, *Corporate Law in Canada: The Governing Principles 2d,* 1991, BTR

(5) Other

British Columbia Corporation Manual, CARS

Canada Corporation Manual, llf, three volumes, CARS

Canadian Business Law Journal, CLB

"Corporate Law Partner" CD-ROM collection, CARS

Ontario Corporation Manual, CARS

Québec Corporation Manual, CARS

(b) Insurance

(1) Case Law

Canadian Cases on the Law of Insurance, CARS (QL 1984-)

Canadian Insurance Law Reporter, CCH

Insurance Case Law Digest, BTR

Insurance Law Digest, CARS

See also Chapter 6 C.6. Annotated Legislation... Business/Commerce

(2) *Index to Canadian Legal Periodical Literature* subjects:

Fire Insurance	Indemnity
Insurance	Life Insurance
Marine Insurance	

(3) *Canadian Encyclopedic Digest* title: Insurance

(4) Selected list of textbooks

Fire Loss Litigation in Canada: A Practical Guide, llf, CARS
Guide to Effective Insurance, 2nd ed., A, 1992, BTR
Insurance Law in Canada, 2d ed., 1991, CARS
Liability Insurance Law in Canada, 2nd ed., 1996, BTR
Norwood on Life Insurance Law in Canada 2nd ed., 1993, CARS
Residential Insurance Policies, Annotated, llf, CARS

(5) Other

Canadian Insurance Law Review, CARS
Canadian Journal of Insurance Law, BTR (LEXIS-NEXIS)
Insurance Law Words and Phrases, CARS

(c) Patents, Intellectual Property

(1) Case Law

Canada Patent Reporter (3d), CLB (LEXIS-NEXIS, QL)
Intellectual Property Reports, CARS (QL 1984-1989)

See also Chapter 3, 12. Chart L, Tribunal Decisions ... Business/Commerce
See also Chapter 6 C.6., Annotated Legislation... Business/Commerce

(2) *Index to Canadian Legal Periodical Literature* subjects:

Authors & Publishing	Patents
Copyright	Trade Marks & Trade Names

(3) *Canadian Encyclopedic Digest* titles:

Copyright, Trade Marks & Industrial Designs

(4) Selected list of textbooks

Barrigar, *Canadian Patent Act Annotated 2nd,* llf, CLB
Hughes, *Hughes on Copyright and Industrial Design,* llf, BTR
Hughes, *Hughes On Trade Marks,* llf, BTR
Hughes and Woodley, *Hughes & Woodley on Patents,* llf, BTR
Richard, et al. eds, *Canadian Trade Marks Act Annotated,* llf, CARS

(5) Other

Intellectual Property Journal, CARS

(d) Transportation/Customs/Trade/Contracts

(1) Case Law

Trade and Tariff Reports, BTR (LEXIS-NEXIS)
Canadian Transport Cases (no cumulative index)

See also Chapter 3, 12. Chart L, Tribunal Decisions ... Business/Commerce
See also Chapter 6, C.6, Annotated Legislation ... Business/Commerce

(2) *Index to Canadian Legal Periodical Literature* subjects:

Contracts	Exports & Imports
International Trade	Tariff & Customs Laws

(3) *Canadian Encyclopedia Digest* titles:

Customs & Excise

(4) Textbooks

Addy, *Competition Law Service,* llf, CLB
Affleck, *Canadian Competition Law*, annual subscription, CARS
Appleton, *Navigating NAFTA: A Concise User's Guide to the North American Free Trade Agreement,* 1994, CARS
Estey, *Legal Opinions in Commercial Transactions,* 1997, BTR
Fernandez, *Transportation Law*, llf, CARS
Fridman, *Sale of Goods in Canada 4th ed., The,* 1995, CARS
Fridman, *Law of Contract in Canada 3rd ed., The,* 1994, CARS
Johnson, *North American Free Trade Agreement: A Comprehensive Guide, The*, 1994, CLB
Klotz, *International Sales Agreements: An Annotated Drafting and Negotiating Guide,* 1997, CLB
Livingston, *Livingston's Canadian Customs Guide,* annual subscription, CARS
Livingston, *Livingston's NAFTA Handbook: Canadian Customs Procedures,* 1994, CARS
Paterson, *International Trade and Investment Law in Canada 2nd ed.,* llf, CARS
Roberts, *Roberts on Competition/Antitrust: Canada and the United States 2nd ed.*, 1992, BTR
Waddams, *Law of Contracts 3rd ed., The,* 1993, CLB

(5) Other

Canadian Transportation Reporter, llf, CARS
Free Trade Agreement - Panel Review Decisions (LEXIS-NEXIS)
National Trade and Tariff Service, llf, BTR
"NAFTA on CD-ROM", Micromedia Ltd. Toronto
North America Free Trade Agreement (LEXIS-NEXIS)
North America Free Trade Agreement Panel Decisions (LEXIS-NEXIS)
U.S.-Canada Free Trade Agreement *Implementation Act* (LEXIS-NEXIS)

(e) Other: Banking/Bankruptcy/Construction/Securities

(1) Case Law

Canadian Bankruptcy Reports (N.S.), CARS (QL 1983-)
Canadian Cases on the Law of Securities, CARS (QL 1992-)
Canadian Securities Law Reporter, CCH: print or CD-ROM
Construction Law Reports, CARS (QL 1985-)

See also Chapter 3, 12. Chart L, Tribunal Decisions Business/Commerce... Securities Law

See also Chapter 6, C.6, Annotated Legislation, Business/Commerce

(2) *Index to Canadian Legal Periodical Literature* subjects:

Bankruptcy	Bonds
Construction Contracts	Investments
Securities	Stocks

(3) *Canadian Encyclopedic Digest* titles:
Bankruptcy and Insolvency
Building Contracts
Securities, Stocks, and Grain Exchanges

(4) Selected list of textbooks

(i) Banking
Manzer, *Bank Act Annotated, The,* 1993, BTR
McGuinness, *Law of Guarantee 2nd ed., The,* 1996, CARS
Ogilvie, *Canadian Banking Law,* 1991, CARS
Sarna, *Letters of Credit: The Law and Current Practice,* llf, CARS

(ii) Bankruptcy
Bennett, *Bennett on Creditors' and Debtors' Rights and Remedies 4th ed.,* 1994, CARS
Dunlop, *Creditor-Debtor Law in Canada 2nd ed.,* 1995, CARS
Edmunds, *Canadian Credit and Collection Guide 2nd ed.,* llf, CARS
Fraser, *Debt Collection: A Step by Step Legal Guide,* llf, CLB
Honsberger, *Debt Restructuring: Principles and Practice,* llf, CLB
Houlden, *Bankruptcy Law of Canada 3d ed.,* llf, CARS
McLaren, *Canadian Commercial Reorganization: Preventing Bankruptcy,* llf, CLB

(iii) Construction
Goldsmith, *Goldsmith on Canadian Building Contracts 4th ed.,* llf, CARS
Kirsch and Roth, *Annotated Construction Contract (CCDC2-1994), The,* 1997, CLB
Macklem and Bristow, *Construction Builders' and Mechanics' Liens in Canada 6th ed.,* llf, CARS
McLachlin and Wallace, *Canadian Law of Architecture & Engineering 2nd ed., The,* 1994, BTR
Scott and Reynolds, *Scott and Reynolds on Surety Bonds*, llf, CARS
Wise, *Manual of Construction Law,* llf, CARS

(iv) Securities
Albioni, ed., *Securities Law and Practice*, 10 volumes, llf, CARS
Gillen, *Securities Regulation in Canada,* 1992, CARS

(5) Other
"Bankruptcy Partner" CD-ROM collection, CARS
Canadian Securities Law Reporter, llf, CCH: print or CD-ROM
Commercial Insolvency Reporter, BTR (LEXIS-NEXIS)
National Banking Law Review, BTR (LEXIS-NEXIS)

National Insolvency Review, BTR (LEXIS-NEXIS)
Nelligan Power Condo Law Newsletter (QL 1992-)
"Securities Partner Plus" CD-ROM collection, CARS

2. Criminal Law/Motor Vehicles

(a) Case law
(1) Reported
Canadian Criminal Cases (3d), CLB (LEXIS-NEXIS, QL)
Criminal Law Digest, CARS
Criminal Reports (4th), CARS: CD-ROM (QL 1984-)
Motor Vehicle Reports, CARS (QL 1984-)
See Also Chapter 6. C.6, Annotated Legislation ... Criminal Law
(2) Unreported
Alberta-Saskatchewan-Manitoba Criminal Conviction Cases, WLP: print or CD-ROM (QL 1980-)
B.C. Decisions Criminal Cases, WLP: print or CD-ROM (QL 1980-)
Canadian Sentencing Digest, CARS: print or CD-ROM
Crankshaw's Criminal Code, CARS: print or CD-ROM
Criminal Sentencing Digest, BTR
Martin's Annual Criminal Code, CLB: print or CD-ROM
Ontario Decisions Criminal Cases, WLP: print or CD-ROM
Snow's Annotated Criminal Code, CARS
Tremeear's Criminal Code, CARS
Weekly Criminal Bulletin, CLB (LEXIS-NEXIS, QL)
Young Offender's Act Manual, CLB
Young Offender's Service, BTR

(b) *Index to Canadian Legal Periodical Literature* subjects:
Arrest
Arson
Assault & Battery
Bail
Blood Tests
Burglary
Child Abuse
Criminal Law
Criminal Responsibility
Criminal Statistics
Criminology
Drunkeness
Juvenile Delinquency
Lie Detection
Narcotics
Police Power
Search & Seizure
Sex Crimes
Victims of Crime
War Crimes
White Collar Crime

(c) *Canadian Encyclopedic Digest* titles:
Criminal Law
Narcotic Control
Sentencing

(d) Selected lists of textbooks

(1) Charter and Procedure

Atrens, et al, eds., *Criminal Procedure: Canadian Law & Practice*, llf, BTR

Cameron, ed., *Charter's Impact on the Criminal Justice System,* 1996, CARS

Chayko et al., eds., *Forensic Evidence in Canada,* 1991, CLB

Cooper, *Crown Privileges,* 1990, CLB

Cox, *Criminal Evidence Handbook,* biennial editions, CLB

Ewaschuk, *Criminal Pleadings and Practice in Canada, 2nd ed.*, llf, CLB

Fontana, *Law of Search and Seizure in Canada 4th ed., The*, 1997, BTR

Gibson, *Criminal Law Evidence, Practice, and Procedure*, llf, CARS

Hutchison, *Search and Seizure Law in Canada,* llf, CARS

Judicial Interim Release (Bail Manual), llf, BTR

LaForest, *LaForest's Extradition to and from Canada 3rd ed.,* 1991, CLB

Levy, *Examination of Witnesses in Criminal Cases 3rd ed.,* 1994, CARS

Marin, *Admissibility of Statements 9th ed.*, llf, CLB

McLeod, *Canadian Charter of Rights: The Prosecution and Defence of Criminal and Other Statutory Offences,* llf, CARS

McWilliams, *Canadian Criminal Evidence 3rd ed.,* llf, CLB

Salhany, *Canadian Criminal Procedure 6th ed.,* llf, CLB

Segal, *Disclosure and Production in Criminal Law,* llf, CARS

Stuart, *Charter Justice in Canadian Criminal Law,* 1996, CARS

Trotter, *Law of Bail in Canada, The,* 1992, CARS

(2) Motor vehicles and driving

Hamilton, *Impaired Driving and Breathalyzer Law,* llf, BTR

McLeod, *Breathalyzer Law in Canada: The Prosecution and Defence of Drinking and Driving Offences 3rd ed.,* llf, CARS

McLeod, *Criminal Code Drive Offences,* llf, CARS

Segal, *Manual of Motor Vehicle Law 3rd ed.,* llf, CARS

Law of Speeding and Radar 2nd ed., The, 1991, BTR

(3) Sentencing

Clewley, *Sentencing: The Practitioner's Guide,*, llf, CLB

Ruby, *Sentencing, 4th ed.,* 1994, BTR

(4) General and miscellaneous

Bay, Bloom, eds., *Practical Guide to Mental Health, Capacity and Consent Law of Ontario,* 1996, CARS

Burns, *Criminal Injuries Compensation 2nd ed.,* 1992, BTR

Der, *Jury: A Handbook of Law and Practice, The*, llf, BTR

Gibson, *Canadian Criminal Code Offences,* llf, CARS

Granger, *Criminal Jury Trial in Canada 2nd ed,* 1996, CARS

Grant, *Law of Homicide, The,* llf, CARS
Harris, *Weapons Offences Manual,* llf, CLB
Harvey, *Sexual Offences Against Children and the Criminal Process,* 1993, BTR
Henderson, *Commercial Crime in Canada,* llf, CARS
Kenkel, *Defence Lawyer's Trial Book, The,* llf, BTR
MacFarlane, *Drug Offences in Canada 3rd ed.,* llf, CLB
Marin, *Guide to Investigations and Prosecutions,* 1995, CLB
Martin, *Essays on Aspects of Criminal Practice*, 1997, CARS
Mewett and Manning, *Mewett and Manning on Criminal Law 3rd ed.,* 1994, BTR
Meyers, *Criminal Lawyer's Commonplace Book,* llf, BTR
Nightingale, *Law of Fraud and Related Offences, The,* llf, CARS
Pink, *Expert: A Practitioner's Guide, The,* llf, CARS
Platt, *Young Offenders Law in Canada,* 1995, BTR
Prowse, *Working Manual of Criminal Law,* llf, CARS
Salhany, *Criminal Trial Handbook,* llf, CARS
Stuart, *Canadian Criminal Law: A Treatise 3d ed.,* 1995, CARS
Tolefson, *Mental Disorder in Criminal Proceedings,* 1993, CARS

(e) Other
"Canada Practice Guides — Criminal Series": 15+ guide books of 100-200 pages, CARS
Canadian Criminal Law Review, CARS
Criminal Law Finder, an index of criminal law publications, CLB
"Criminal Law Partner" CD-ROM collection, CARS
Criminal Law Quarterly, CLB
Drinking and Driving Law newsletter, CARS
Gold, *Annual Review of Criminal Law,* CARS
Watt, *Criminal Law Precedents,* CARS
See also the checklist above in this chapter: "N, Canadian Charter of Rights and Freedoms"

3. Environment/Natural Resources

(a) Case Law
Canadian Environmental Law, BTR
Canadian Environmental Law Reports, CARS (QL 1986-)
Canadian Oil & Gas, BTR
Canadian Native Law Reporter
McCarthy Tetrault Digest of Environmental Law and Environmental Assessment, CARS
See also Chapter 3, 12. Chart L, Tribunal Decisions... Environmental Law/ Natural Resources

See also Chapter 6. C.6. Annotated Legislation... Environment/Natural Resources

(b) *Index to Canadian Legal Periodical Literature* subjects:

Air Pollution
Birds (protection of)
Energy Resources
Environmental Control
Fish and Game
Forests and Forestry
Natural Resources
Nuclear Energy
Oil and Gas
Pollution
Water and Water Courses

(c) *Canadian Encyclopedic Digest* titles:

Environmental Law
Oil & Gas

(d) Selected list of textbooks

Berger, *Prosecution and Defence of Environmental Offences, The,* llf, E-M
Cameron, *Environmental Concerns in Business Transactions: Avoiding the Risks,* 1993, BTR
Esrin, *Business Guide to Environmental Law,* llf, CARS
Faieta, et al., *Environmental Harm: Civil Actions and Compensation,* 1996, BTR
Jeffery, *Environmental Approvals in Canada: Practice and Procedure,* llf, BTR
Lucas and Hunt, *Oil and Gas Law in Canada,* 1990, CARS
McConnell, Gerlock, eds., *Environmental Spills: Emergency Reporting, Clean-up, and Liability,* llf, CARS
Pardy, *Environmental Law: A Guide to Concepts,* 1996, BTR
Poch, *Corporate and Municipal Environmental Law,* 1989, CARS
Saxe, *Environmental Offences: Corporate Responsibility and Executive Liability,* 1990, CLB
Swaigen, *Regulatory Offences in Canada: Liabilities and Defences,* 1992, CARS
Thompson, *Environmental Law and Business in Canada,* 1993, CLB
Vanderzwagg, ed., *Canadian Ocean Law and Policy,* 1992, BTR

(e) Other

Canada Energy Law Service, llf, CARS
Dictionary of Environmental Law and Science, The, 1994, E-M
"Environmental Law Partner" CD-ROM collection, CARS
Environmental Policy & Law, monthly, CARS
Journal of Environmental Law and Practice, CARS

4. Family Law/Estates

(a) Case Law

(1) Reported

Family Law Digest, CARS, CD-ROM
Reports of Family Law (3rd ed.), CARS, (CD-ROM; QL 1984-)

(2) Unreported
B.C. Family Law (Revised Edition), BTR
Butterworths' Ontario Family Law Quantum Service
Canadian Family Law Guide, CCH
Ontario Family Law Reporter, BTR (LEXIS-NEXIS)
Weekly Digest of Family Law, CARS

(3) Estates
Canadian Estate Administrative Guide, CCH
Estates & Trust Reports, CARS
See also Chapter 6 C.6, Annotated Legislation... Family Law

(b) *Index to Canadian Legal Periodical Literature* subjects:

Alimony and Maintenance
Annulment
Bigamy
Birth Control
Child Abuse
Common Law Marriage
Community Property
Estate Planning
Infants
Inheritance & Succession
Married Women
Parent and Child
Trusts & Trustees
Wills

(c) *Canadian Encyclopedic Digest* titles:
Devolution of Estates, Family Law (Divorce), Family Law (General), Husband and Wife, Infants and Children, Wills

(d) Selected list of textbooks

(1) Children
Berstein, et al., *Child Protection Law in Canada,* llf, CARS
Leonoff and Montague, *Practical Guide to Custody and Access Assessments*, 1997, CARS
McLeod, *Child Custody Law and Practice,* llf, CARS
Phillips, et al., *Adoption Law in Canada,* llf, CARS
Wilson, *Wilson on Children and the Law,* llf, BTR

(2) Marriage
Bissett-Johnson and Holland, eds., *Matrimonial Property Law in Canada,* llf, CARS
Cole and Freeman, *Property Valuation and Income Tax Implication of Marital Dissolution,* llf, CARS
Hainsworth, *Divorce Act Manual,* llf, CLB
Holland and Poutney, eds., *Cohabitation: The Law in Canada,* llf, CARS
MacDonald, et al., *Canadian Divorce Law and Practice 2nd ed.,* llf, CARS
Pask and Hass, *Division of Pensions,* llf, CARS
Patterson, *Pension Division and Valuation: Family Lawyers' Guide,* llf, CLB
Payne, *Payne on Divorce 4th ed.,* 1996, CARS
Stark, *Domestic Contracts,* llf, CARS
Wilton, *Enforcement of Family Law Orders and Agreements,* llf, CARS

(3) Wills

Allen, *Estate Planning Handbook 2nd ed.,* 1991, CARS

Armstrong, *Estate Administration: A Solicitor's Reference Manual,* llf, CARS

Christopoulos, *Taxation of Trusts and Beneficiaries,* llf, CARS

Cullity, *Taxation and Estate Planning,* llf, CARS

de Villars, *Estate Administration in Alberta: A Solicitor's Reference Manual,* llf, CARS

Hull, *Challenging the Validity of Wills,* 1996, CARS

Jenset, *Guide to Estate & Trust Accounting,* llf, CARS

Law Society of Upper Canada Special Lectures, *Estates: Planning, Administration, and Litigation,* 1996, CARS

Macdonnell, et al., *Macdonell, Sheard, & Hull on Probate Practice 4th ed.,* 1996, CARS

McIntyre, *Practical Wills Drafting,* 1992, BTR

Rintoul, *Solicitor's Guide to Estate Practice in Ontario 2nd ed., The,* 1990, BTR

Schnurr, *Estate Litigation,* llf, CARS

Sokol, *Mistakes in Wills in Canada,* 1995, CARS

Waters, *Law of Trusts in Canada 2nd ed.,* 1984, CARS

(4) General

Gordon, *Adult Guardianship Law in Canada*, llf, CARS

Hainsworth, *Ontario Family Law Act Manual,* llf, CLB

Klotz, *Bankruptcy and Family Law,* 1994, CARS

Law Society of Upper Canada Special Lectures, *Family Law: Roles, Fairness, and Equality*, 1994, CARS

MacDonald, *Law and Practice Under the Family Law Act of Ontario*, llf, CARS

Ontario Annotated Family Law Service, llf, BTR

Rashkis, *Income Tax and Family Law Handbook,* llf, BTR

(e) Other

Alberta Family Law - Annotated Legislation, llf, BTR

Annual Review of Family Law, CARS

Canadian Family Law Quarterly, CARS

"Estates Partner (Ontario)" CD-ROM collection, CARS

"Family Law" topic and associated key numbers in the "Digest and Indexes" volumes for all Maritime Law Book Ltd.'s law report series

"Family Law Partner" CD-ROM collection, CARS

Money and Family Law newsletter, CARS

Nelligan Power Family Law Newsletter (QL 1992-)

Reports of Family Law, (Reprint Series), 1824-1970 (as predecessor to *Reports of Family Law* 1970 - Carswell)

See also Chapter 6, C "FORMS AND PRECEDENTS SETS" including subsection 4 "Specialty Forms Sets: Wills"

5. Human Rights

(a) Case Law

(1) *Canadian Charter of Rights and Freedoms*
Canadian Rights Reporter, BTR (LEXIS-NEXIS 1994-)
Canadian Charter of Rights Annotated, CLB
Charter of Rights Decisions, WLP

(2) General and other
Canadian Human Rights Reporter
Canadian Native Law Reporter and *Canadian Native Law Cases*
Immigration Law Reporter (2d), CARS (QL 1987-)
See also Chapter 3, 12. Chart L, Tribunal Decisions... Human Rights
See also Chapter 6, C.6. Annotated Legislation... Human Rights

(b) *Index to Canadian Legal Periodical Literature* subjects:

Aged	Civil Rights
Freedom of Assembly	Freedom of Association
Handicapped	Homosexuality
Human Rights	Japanese in Canada
Mental Health	Native Rights
Women	

(c) *Canadian Encyclopedic Digest* title:
Human Rights

(d) Selected list of textbooks
Bagambiire, *Canadian Immigration and Refugee Law,* 1996, CLB
Bevan, *Employment Equity Manual, The,* llf, CARS
Casswell, *Lesbians, Gay Men, and Canadian Law,* 1996, E-M
Chotalia, *Human Rights Law in Canada,* llf, CARS
Gilbert, *Entitlement to Indian Status and Membership Codes in Canada,* 1996, CARS
Hathaway, *Law of Refugee Status, The,* 1991, BTR
Keene, *Human Rights in Ontario 2nd ed.,* 1992, CARS
McDowell, *Human Rights in the Workplace: A Practical Guide,* llf CARS
Mendes, ed., *Racial Discrimination-Law and Practice,* llf, CARS
Tarnopolsky, *Discrimination and the Law in Canada,* llf, CARS
Waldman, *Immigration Law and Practice,* llf, BTR
Wildsmith, *Aboriginal Peoples and Section 25 of the Canadian Charter of Rights and Freedoms*, 1988, Native Law Centre, University of Saskatchewan
Woodward, *Native Law,* llf, CARS
Zinn, *Law of Human Rights in Canada: Practice and Procedure*, 1996, CLB
See also checklist above in this chapter: "N, Canadian Charter of Rights and Freedoms"

(e) Other
"Canada Practice Guides — Immigration Series", 5+ publications of 200-300 pages, CARS

Charter cases/Human Rights Reporter element of *Lancaster Labour Law Service*

"Immigration Law Partner" CD-ROM collection, CARS

6. Labour Law/Employment

(a) Case Law

(1) Labour

(A) General

Canadian Labour Law Reporter, CCH

Labour Law Digest, CARS

Lancaster Labour Law Service

(B) Arbitration

B.C. Decisions, Labour Arbitration, WLP: CD-ROM (QL 1982-)

Canadian Labour Arbitration Summaries, CLB (LEXIS-NEXIS, QL)

Labour Arbitration Cases (3rd ed.), CLB (LEXIS-NEXIS, QL)

(C) Labour Relations Boards

B.C. Labour Relations Board Decisions, WLP: CD-ROM, (QL 1979-)

Canada Labour Relations Board Decisions

Canadian Labour Relations Boards Reports, BTR, (LEXIS-NEXIS)

Ontario Labour Relations Board Reports

See also Chapter 3, 12. Chart L. ...Tribunal Decisions... Labour/ Employment

See also Chapter 6, C.6, Annotated Legislation ...Labour Law/ Employment

(2) Employment

Canadian Cases on Employment Law, CARS

Canadian Cases on Pensions and Benefits, CARS

Canadian Employment Benefits & Pension Guide, CCH

Decisions of the Umpire (Unemployment Insurance)

Dismissal and Employment Law Digest, CLB

Employment Law Digest, CARS

(b) *Index to Canadian Legal Periodical Literature* subjects:

Arbitration & Award | Industrial Arbitration
Industrial Relations | Master & Servant
Pensions | Strikes & Boycotts
Unemployment | Unemployment Insurance
Wages

(c) *Canadian Encyclopedic Digest* titles:

Arbitration

Labour Law

Unemployment Insurance

(d) Selected list of textbooks

(1) Arbitration

Brown, *Canadian Labour Arbitration 3rd ed.,* llf, CLB
Corry, *Collective Bargaining and Agreement,* llf, CLB
Gorsky, *Evidence and Procedure in Canadian Labour Arbitration,* llf, CARS
Palmer, *Collective Agreement Arbitration in Canada 3rd ed.,* 1991, BTR
Rayner, *Law of Collective Bargaining,* llf, CARS

(2) Employment

Aggarwal, *Sex Discrimination: Employment Law and Practices,* 1994, BTR
Aggarwal, *Sexual Harassment in the Workplace 2nd ed.,* 1992, BTR
Ball, *Canadian Employment Law,* llf, CLB
Bolland and Mole, *Employment Policies That Work,* llf, CARS
Christie, *Employment Law in Canada,* 1993, BTR
Echlin and Thomlinson, *For Better or Worse: A Practical Guide to Canadian Employment Law,* 1996, CLB
Elliott, *Ontario's Equity Laws,* llf, CLB
Harris, *Wrongful Dismissal,* llf, CARS
Levitt, *Law of Dismissal in Canada 2nd ed., The*, 1992, CLB
Mercer Pension Manual, The, llf, CARS
Mole, *Butterworths Wrongful Dismissal Practice Manual,* llf
Sproat, *Employment Law Manual: Wrongful Dismissal, Human Rights, and Employment Standards,* llf, CARS
Stikeman and Elliott, *Executive Employment Law,* llf, BTR

(3) General

Kerr, *Labour Relations Board Remedies in Canada,* llf, CLB
MacNeil, *Trade Union Law in Canada,* llf, CLB

(e) Other

Canadian Employment Law Guide, llf, CCH
Canadian Labour and Employment Law Journal, CARS
Employment and Labour Law Reporter newsletter, BTR, (LEXIS-NEXIS)
Employment Bulletin: Legal Issues in the Workplace, The, CLB
Employment in Alberta, llf, BTR
Employment in British Columbia, llf, BTR
Employment in Ontario, llf, BTR
"Employment Law Partner" CD-ROM collection, CARS
"Labour Law" topic and associated key numbers in Maritime Law Book Ltd.'s CD-ROM "Headnote" Service; also online through LEXIS-NEXIS
"Labour Law Partner" CD-ROM collection, CARS
Nelligan Power Employment Law Newletter (QL 1990-)
"Ontario Practice Guide Labour/Employment Series" 2+ titles (100-200 pages), CARS

"The Practical Guide Series" 7+ titles (100-200 pages) on Ontario Labour and Employment Law (Canada Law Book)

See also this chapter's checklist "11, Health and Medical"

7. Property/Municipal

(a) Case Law

(1) Property

B. C. Real Estate Law Guide, CCH
Ontario Real Estate Law Guide, CCH
Personal Property Security Act Cases, CARS
Real Property Reports, CARS (QL 1978-)

(2) Municipal, Assessment, and Expropriation

B.C. Assessment Appeal Board, Major Decisions
B.C. Assessment Authority Stated Cases
Digest of Municipal and Planning Law, CARS
Land Compensation Reports, CLB
Municipal and Planning Law Reports, CARS (QL 1986-)
Municipal Law Digest, CARS
Ontario Municipal Board Reports, CLB

(b) *Index to Canadian Legal Periodical Literature* subjects:

Adjoining Landowners
Chattel Mortgages
City Planning
Condominium & Cooperative
Easements
Expropriation
Housing
Landlord & Tenant
Leases
Municipal Corporations
Personal Property
Public Lands
Real Estate Agents
Real Property
Regional Planning
Secured Transactions
Torrens System
Zoning

(c) *Canadian Encyclopedic Digest* titles:

Boundaries
Condominiums
Easements
Expropriation
Income Tax
Landlord & Tenant
Mortgages
Municipal Corporations
Municipal & School Taxes
Municipal Transportation
Planning and Zoning
Real Property
Revenue
Sale of Land
Secured Transactions

(d) Selected list of textbooks

(1) Condominiums

Baker, *Condominium Law in Ontario,* 1991, CLB
Loeb, *Condominium Law and Administration 2nd ed.,* Ontario, llf, CARS

Nelligan Power Condo Law Newsletter (QL 1992-)

(2) Contaminated Land

Coburn, *Toxic Real Estate Manual,* llf, CLB

Griffiths, ed., *Contaminated Property in Canada,* llf, CARS

(3) Expropriation

Boyd, *Expropriation in Canada: A Practitioner's Guide,* 1988, CLB

Coates, *New Law of Expropriation,* llf, CARS (hardcover editions available for Alberta, B.C., and Ontario)

Todd, *Law of Expropriation and Compensation in Canada 2nd ed., The,* 1992, CARS

(4) Landlord / Leases

Balfour, *Landlord and Tenant Law,* 1991, E-M

Haber, *Commercial Lease: A Practical Guide 2nd ed., The,* 1994, CLB

Haber, *Landlord's Rights and Remedies in a Commercial Lease: A Practical Guide,* 1996, CLB

Lamont, *Residential Tenancies 4th ed.,* 1983, CARS

Williams and Rhodes Canadian Law of Landlord and Tenant 6th ed., llf, CARS

(5) Municipal

Law Society of Upper Canada, *Ontario Municipal Board Index to Applications* and *Ontario Land Compensation Board Index to Applications*

Rogers, *Canadian Law of Planning and Zoning,* llf, CARS

Rogers, *Law of Canadian Municipal Corporations 2nd ed., The,* llf, CARS

(6) Real Estate Transactions

DiCastri, *Law of Vendor and Purchaser 3d ed.,* llf, CARS

DiCastri, *Registration of Title to Land,* llf, CARS

Lamont, *Lamont on Real Estate Conveyancing,* llf, CARS

Perell, *Remedies and the Sale of Land,* 1988, BTR

Price, *Conducting a Foreclosure Action,* 1996, CARS

Rayner, and McLaren, *Falconbridge on Mortgages 4th ed.,* 1977, CLB

Roach, *Canadian Law of Mortgages of Land, The,* 1993, BTR

Salvatore, *Agreements of Purchase and Sale*, 1996, BTR

(7) Taxes (Income, Property)

Atlas, *Taxation of Real Estate in Canada,* llf, CARS

Canadian Real Estate Income Tax Guide, llf, CCH

Ontario Property Tax Reporter, CARS

Walker, *Ontario Property Tax Assessment Handbook*, 1993, CLB

(8) General

Anger & Honsberger's Law of Real Property 2nd ed., two volumes, 1985, CLB

Fields and Gershman, eds., *Canadian Commercial Real Estate Manual,* llf, CARS
McLaren, *Secured Transactions in Personal Property in Canada 2nd ed.*, llf, CARS
Reiter, *Real Estate Law 4th ed.,* 1992, E-M

Note: Carswell publishes a number of additional titles specifically dealing with Ontario real estate law.

See also: Chapter 6, C.6. Annotated legislation series... Property/Municipal

8. Tax

(a) Case Law
Alberta, N.W.T. & Yukon Tax Reporter, CCH: CD-ROM
British Columbia Tax Reporter, CCH: CD-ROM
Canada GST Cases, CARS
Canadian GST & Commodity Tax Cases, CCH
Canada Tax Cases — Canada Tax Service, (llf, 14 volumes) CARS (Carswell online)
Dominion Tax Cases — Canadian Tax Reporter, CCH: CD-ROM (QL 1920-)
Manitoba & Saskatchewan Tax Reporter, CCH: CD-ROM
Maritime Tax Reporter, CCH: CD-ROM
Ontario Tax Reporter, CCH: CD-ROM
Québec Tax Reporter, CCH: CD-ROM

(b) *Index to Canadian Legal Periodical Literature* subjects:
Capital Gains Tax
Corporations: Taxation
Double Taxation
Income Tax: Deductions
Inheritance Estate and Gift Taxes
Property Taxes
Tax Havens
Taxation

(c) *Canadian Encyclopedic Digest* titles:
Municipal and School Taxes, Income Tax, Revenue

(d) Selected list of textbooks
(1) General Texts and Annotations
Canadian Master Tax Guide, annual, CCH
Hogg, *Principles of Canadian Income Tax Law,* 1995, CARS
Krishna, *Fundamentals of Canadian Income Tax Act: An Introduction 3rd ed., The,* 1995, CARS
Sherman, *Practitioner's GST Annotated, The,* annual, CARS
Sherman, *Practitioner's Income Tax Act,* annual, CARS
Stikeman, *Income Tax Act Annotated,* annual, CARS

Introduction to Federal Income Taxation in Canada annual editions, CCH

(2) Looseleaf Services — comprehensive/general

Canada Income Tax Guide, llf, CCH: CD-ROM
Canada Income Tax & Policy, five volumes, CARS
Canada Income Tax Guide, CCH: CD-ROM
Canadian Income Tax Act, Regulations and Rulings, three volumes, CCH: CD-ROM
Canadian Tax Reporter, 11 volumes, CCH: CD-ROM
Sherman, *Tax for Non-Lawyers*, CARS
Slutsky, *Tax Adminstration Reports,* five volumes, CARS
Slutsky, *Tax Regulation Reports,* two volumes, CARS
Stikeman, *Canada Tax Manual,* two volumes, CARS
Stikeman, *Canada Tax Service*, 14 volumes, CARS

(3) Looseleaf services — topical

Bergen, *Practitioner's British Columbia Taxes Annotated,* annual bound editions, CARS
Boyle, ed., *Canadian Tax Objection and Appeal Procedure,* CCH
Brown and Snother, *Taxation of Aboriginal Peoples in Canada,* CARS
Campbell, *Income Tax Administration in Canada,* CARS
Canada GST Service, seven volumes, CARS
Canada Tax Planning Service, llf (four volumes), CARS
Canada's General Anti-Avoidance Rule: A Practical Guide, CARS
Canada's Tax Treaties, llf, BTR
Canadian Goods & Services Tax Reporter, llf, CCH: CD-ROM
Drache, *Canadian Taxation of Charities and Donations,* CARS
Drache, *Charity and Not-for-Profit Sourcebook, The,* CARS
Federal Income Tax Litigation in Canada, llf, BTR
Gamble and Sinclair, *Taxation of Canadian Mining Income,* llf, (one volume), CARS
Innes, *Tax Avoidance,* CARS
Innes, *Tax Evasion,* CARS
McDonald, *Canadian Current Tax,* llf, BTR
Tari, *Federal Income Tax Litigation,* BTR

(4) Newsletters

Canadian Tax News, CARS
GST Times, CARS
Pound's Tax Case Notes, CARS
Taxpayer, CARS

(5) Research Tools

Canada Tax Words, Phrases, and Rules, llf, CARS
Dominion Tax Cases Consolidated Findings Lists, llf, CCH

Note: For income tax, there are two guides that relate sections of the Act to textbooks, periodical articles, portions of looseleaf services, Interpretation

Bulletins, Information Circulars, Income Tax Rulings, Income Tax Regulations, and case law:

Income Tax References, by Andre Yelle (Carswell), in looseleaf and CD-ROM

Canadian Income Tax Research Index (CCH), in looseleaf

(6) Electronic sources for tax from Canada's private legal publishers and legal online services

(A) CCH Canadian Ltd.:

(i) All of CCH's federal tax services are available as "Electronic Tax Library Combinations" of titles.

(ii) *Dominion Tax Cases* on CD-ROM. Note that it is available online from QL.

(iii) *Window on Canadian Tax* on CD-ROM gives commentary on internal documents from Revenue Canada.

(iv) All of CCH's "provincial tax reporters" are available as CD-ROM including savings through "combination subscriptions".

(v) CCH Canadian's On-line Bulletin Board "CCH Protos" supplements both their print and CD-ROM services by providing tax material from the past six months. Unlimited use subscriptions are sold.

(B) Carswell

(i) "Canadian Tax Online" has over 60 bulletin boards and databases covering income tax, GST, and other sales and commodity taxes.

(ii) "GST Partner: CD-ROM collection including *Canada GST Service* and *Canada GST Cases.*

(iii) "The Income Tax Act in transition" CD-ROM for awareness of new and proposed changes to the Act and regulations.

(iv) "Provincial TaxPartner - British Columbia" CD-ROM

(v) "Provincial TaxPartner - Ontario" CD-ROM

(vi) "Revenue Canada Views on disc" CD-ROM to enable you to keyword search Revenue Canada's own file of unpublished tax interpretations, internal memoranda, and responses at conferences.

(vii) Various levels and numbers of sources available on CD-ROM (comprehensive and monthly updates for $3,000 annually in 1997 to quarterly and fewer sources for $500 annually): "TaxPartner", "TaxPartner Basic+", and "TaxPartner Basic".

(C) QL Systems Ltd. (online services): databases and bulletin boards including Revenue Canada publications, court decisions, a collection of material from CCH Canadian Ltd., a GST Bulletin Board, and a federal sales tax bulletin board.

(D) LEXIS-NEXIS (online services): a selection of Tax Court of Canada cases in the CANTCT file in the CANADA library.

(7) Electronic sources for tax information from Revenue Canada's Internet site: www.rc.gc.ca.

9. Personal Injury/Negligence

(a) Case Law

Apportionment of Liability in British Columbia, llf, BTR

British Columbia Decisions, "Special Series on Personal Injury Damages Cases", WLP

Canadian Cases on the Law of Torts, CARS (QL 1983-)

Damages for Personal Injury and Death, CARS: CD-ROM

Personal Injury Damage Assessments in Alberta, BTR

Personal Injury Damage Assessments in British Columbia, BTR

(b) *Index to Canadian Legal Periodical Literature* subjects:

Collisions at Sea	Contributory Negligence
Damages	Explosions
Industrial Accidents	Last Clear Chance
Liability	Master and Servant
Negligence	Personal Injuries
Torts	Workers' Compensation

(c) *Canadian Encyclopedic Digest* titles:

Damages

Negligence

(d) Selected lists of textbooks

Bruce, *Assessment of Personal Injury Damages 2nd ed.,* 1992, BTR

Cooper-Stephenson, *Personal Injury Damages in Canada 2nd ed.,* 1996, CARS

Feldthuson, *Economic Negligence: The Recovery of Pure Economic Loss 3rd ed.,* 1994, CARS

Fridman, *Law of Torts in Canada, The,* 1989, CARS

Fridman, *Restitution 2nd ed.,* 1992, CARS

Gross, ed., *Injury Evaluation, Medicolegal Principles,* 1991, BTR

Hoffman, *Emotional Consequences of Personal Injury, The,* 1992, BTR

Klar, *Tort Law 2nd ed.,* 1996, CARS

Linden, *Canadian Tort Law 6th ed.,* 1997, BTR

Rainaldi and Klar, *Remedies in Tort,* llf (five volumes), CARS

Smith and Sefton, *Accounting for Damages: A Framework for Litigation Support 2nd ed.*, llf, CARS

Waddams, *Law of Damages, The,* llf, CLB

Principles and Proofs in the Law of Remedies, Law Society of Upper Canada Special Lectures, 1995

(e) Other

Some general digests and reports, which cover a high percentage of cases, have specific headings for personal injuries awards. The sources are now available as computer databases. Because the electronic source query can be very specific for personal injury damages, one of the computer's highest capabilities is searching these damages awards.

Digest access in book or electronic form to quantum awards and applied principles is provided by:

(1) Summaries (Canada Law Book)
All-Canada Weekly Summaries. Most efficiently searched in its electronic format: LEXIS-NEXIS or QL.

(2) Decisions (Western Legal Publications): CD-ROM
(also LEXIS-NEXIS)
Alberta Decisions
British Columbia Decisions
Manitoba Decisions
Saskatchewan Decisions
Topic heading: Personal Injury Damages (Specific Injuries-Quantum)

(3) Reports (Maritime Law Book Ltd.: "Headnotes" on CD-ROM)
(also QL)
Alberta Reports
British Columbia Appeal Cases
Manitoba Reports
New Brunswick Reports
Newfoundland and Prince Edward Island Reports
Nova Scotia Reports
Ontario Appeal Cases
Ontario Trial Cases
Saskatchewan Reports
Yukon Reports

(4) Carswell's CD-ROM collection, which includes *Damages for Personal Injury and Death,* is "Personal Injury Damages Partner".

10. Practice and Procedure/Administrative Law

(a) Case Law
Administrative Law Reports, CARS (QL 1983-)
Carswell's Practice Cases, CARS (1986-)
Weekly Digest of Civil Procedure, CARS

(b) *Index to Canadian Legal Periodical Literature* subjects:

Abuse of Rights	Administrative Law
Administrative Procedure	Appellate Procedure
Civil Procedure	Costs
Cross-Examination	Declaratory Relief Actions and
Discovery	Defences

Evidence	Injunction
Pretrial Procedure	Writs

(c) *Canadian Encyclopedic Digest* titles:

Actions	Injunctions
Administrative Law	Practice

(d) Selected list of textbooks

(1) Administrative Law

Anisman and Reid, eds., *Administrative Law: Issues and Practice,* 1995, CARS

Blake, *Administrative Law in Canada,* 1992, BTR

Jones, *Principles of Administrative Law 2nd ed.,* 1994, CARS

Law Society of Upper Canada Special Lectures 1992, *Administrative Law: Principles, Practice, and Pluralism,* 1993, CARS

Law Society of Upper Canada, *Practice and Procedure Before Administrative Tribunals,* llf, four volumes, CARS

Moskoff, ed., *Administrative Tribunals: A Practice Handbook for Legal Counsel,* 1989, CLB

Mullan, *Administrative Law 3rd ed.,* 1996, CARS

(2) Practice

Cass, *Discovery: Law, Practice, and Procedure in Ontario,* 1993, CARS

Castel, *Canadian Conflict of Laws 3rd ed.*, 1994, BTR

Cooper, *Crown Privilege,* 1990, CLB

Crane, et al., *Supreme Court of Canada Practice,* semi-annual, CARS

Cudmore, *Choate on Discovery 2nd ed.,* llf, CARS

Cudmore, *Civil Evidence Handbook,* llf, CARS

Fraser, *Conduct of Civil Litigation in British Columbia, The,* llf, BTR

Goldstein, *Visual Evidence: A Practitioner's Manual,* llf, CARS

Holmstead and Watson, Ontario Civil Procedure, llf, five volumes, CARS

Huberman, *Ontario Orders and Judgments Annotated,* llf, CARS

Maddaugh, *Law of Restitution, The,* 1990, CLB

Manes, Organized Advocacy: A Manual for the Litigation Practitioner, Revised edition, llf, CARS

Manes, Solicitor-Client Privilege in Canadian Law, 1993, BTR

Marin, *Admissibility of Statements 9th ed.*, llf, CLB

Meehan, et al., *Supreme Court of Canada Manual: Practice and Advocacy,* llf, CLB

Mew, *Law of Limitations, The,* 1991, BTR

Mewett, *Witnesses,* llf, CARS

Muldoon, *Law of Intervention: Status and Practice,* 1989, CLB

Ontario Manual of Civil Litigation, llf, CARS

Orkin, *Law of Costs 2nd ed.,* llf, CLB

Palmer, *Law of Set-off in Canada, The,* 1993, CLB
Rochon, Terry *Interlocutory Proceedings Strategy and Practice,* 1996, BTR
Schiff, *Evidence in the Litigation Process,* 1993, CARS
Sgayias, et al., *Federal Court Practice,* annual, CARS
Sharpe, *Injunctions and Specific Performance 2nd ed.,* llf, CLB
Sopinka, *Conduct of an Appeal, The,* 1993, BTR
Sopinka, *Law of Evidence in Canada, The,* 1992, BTR
Sopinka, *Trial of an Action 3rd ed., The,* 1994, BTR
Stockwood, *Civil Litigation, 3rd ed.,* 1992, CARS
White, *Art of Discovery,* 1990, CLB
Zuker, *Ontario Small Claims Court Practice,* annual, CARS

(e) Other
Administrative Agency Practice, newsletter, CARS
Alberta Limitations Manual, llf, BTR
British Columbia Appellate Practice, llf, CARS
British Columbia Practice, llf, BTR
Canadian Journal of Administrative Law and Practice, CARS
"Civil Practice Partner" CD-ROM collection for Ontario, CARS
"Civil Practice Partner (Alberta)" CD-ROM collection, CARS
Federal Limitations Manual, llf, BTR
Guide to Alberta and Federal Limitations Periods, llf, CARS
Guide to B.C. and Federal Limitations Periods, llf, CARS
Guide to Ontario and Federal Limitations Periods, llf, CARS
Leon, *Ontario Civil Court Forms,* llf, CARS
Practice Guides — Civil Litigation Series", 15+ titles of 100-275 pages for individual provinces (*e.g.*, nine for Alberta, four for Ontario, and B.C.), CARS
Reid's Administrative Law, newsletter, CARS
Williston and Rolls Court Forms 2nd ed., llf, four volumes, BTR: CD-ROM
See also Chapter 5, D. "Court Rules"

11. Health and Medical

(a) Case Law
Canadian Occupational and Safety Law Cases, (1988-1995), CARS
Health Facilities Law Guide (CCH)
Health and Safety Law element of Lancaster Labour Law Service
"Health Law Cases" (1880-1990s; prepared by U. of Alberta), QL Systems Ltd. online database
Legal Medical Quarterly
Ontario Accident Benefit Case Summaries, CCH

Ontario Health & Safety Law: A Complete Guide to the Law and Procedures with Case Summaries, CLB

(b) *Index to Canadian Legal Periodical Literature* subjects:

Euthanasia	Health
Hospitals	Medical Jurisprudence
Mental Health	Nurses and Nursing
Physicians and Surgeons	

(c) *Canadian Encyclopedic Digest* titles:
Hospitals
Medicine
Workers' Compensation

(d) Selected list of textbooks
Arboleda-Florez, *Mental Health Law and Practice,* llf, CARS
Berry, *Canadian Pharmacy Law,* 1995, CLB
Canadian HIV/AIDS Policy & Law Newsletter (QL 1994-)
D'Andrea et al., *Illness and Disability in the Workplace: How to Navigate Through the Legal Minefield,* llf, CLB
Garth, *Butterworths Workers' Compensation in Ontario Service*, llf
Gilbert, *Guide to Workers' Compensation in Ontario 2nd ed.*, 1995, CLB
Health Law in Canada, quarterly issues, BTR (LEXIS-NEXIS)
Meagher, *Doctors and Hospitals: Legal Duties*, 1991, BTR
Nelligan Power Health Law Newsletter (QL 1993-)
Picard, *Legal Liability of Doctors and Hospitals in Canada 3rd ed.*, 1996, CARS
Robertson, *Mental Disability and the Law in Canada 2nd ed.*, 1994, CARS
Rozovsky, *Aids and Canadian Law,* 1992, BTR
Rozovsky, *Canadian Dental Law,* 1987, BTR
Rozovsky, *Canadian Health Information, 2nd ed.*, 1992, BTR
Rozovsky, *Canadian Law of Consent to Treatment,* 1997, BTR
Sharpe, *Law and Medicine in Canada 2nd ed., The*, 1987, BTR
Steinecke, *Complete Guide to the Regulated Health Professions Act, A,* Ontario, llf, CLB

P. PROFESSIONAL CONDUCT

The area of professional conduct and related areas of discipline and negligence are covered by a variety of book and non-book sources:

1. The Canadian Bar Association's *Code of Professional Conduct* supplements the rules with illustrative commentary and carefully selected footnotes to literature throughout the common law world.
2. The provincial Law Society's handbook should be consulted for Benchers' professional conduct rulings. The lawyer should determine whether the

Law Society has adopted the CBA *Code of Professional Conduct* and/or other rules of conduct in addition to rules of discipline.

3. The Law Society may have advisory services such as the Practice Advisory Service and Mentor System utilized by the Law Society of Upper Canada. Secretaries of the Law Societies and Benchers may be contacted for advice in some instances. The LSUC Practice Advisory Service's publication is entitled the *Adviser.*
4. The province's Continuing Legal Education office should be contacted for seminar material on the subject as well as for Bar Admission Course material.
5. Subject headings (*e.g.,* ethics) may be traced through the *Index to Canadian Legal Periodical Literature* and other legal periodical indexes.
6. Canadian textbooks and booklets like Smith, *Professional Conduct for Canadian Lawyers,* 1989, Butterworths; Lund, *Lectures on Professional Conduct and Etiquette* (reproduced by the Law Society of Upper Canada, 1950), 1956, Carswell; and Perell, *Conflicts of Interest in the Legal Profession,* 1995, Butterworths; Hamilton, *Self-Governing Professions: Digests of Court Decisions,* looseleaf, Canada Law Book; "Law Societies Discipline Decisions" online database from QL Systems Ltd. (1991-), access code "LSDD"; MacKenzie, *Lawyers & Ethics: Professional Responsibility and Discipline,* looseleaf, Carswell.
7. English textbooks such as *Cordery's Law Relating to Solicitors,* 9th ed., Butterworths; *A Guide to the Professional Conduct of Solicitors,* 1974, The Law Society; Bird and Weir, *The Law, Practice, and Conduct of Solicitors,* 1989, Waterlow; and Flenley and Leach, *Solicitors' Negligence,* 1997, Butterworths.
8. American sources like the *Digest of Bar Association Ethics Opinions* (American Bar Foundation — a continuing series); *Legal Ethics in the Practice of Law,* Zitrin and Langford, 1995, available through Butterworths; legal ethics law review articles in the LEXIS-NEXIS library "LAWREV" at file "ETHICS" (available through Butterworths); about 40 WESTLAW broad and narrow databases online databases dealing with ethics (available through QL Systems Ltd.).
9. Statutory language for such extreme actions as professional misconduct or conduct unbecoming may be used for key word searches of printed digest and reports indexes, or as the basis of an online query.

Q. LOCATING CASE CITATIONS

When only the style of cause is known for a case, the following methods may be employed to locate the citation(s) for the case:

1. Citations for Canadian cases

The *Canadian Abridgment Revised (2nd)* component *Consolidated Table of Cases* lists case names accompanied by law report citations (including parallel citations in different law reports and for each court level of the case). Citation is also made for digest locations in the Can Abr. Rev. (2nd). The set encompasses reported cases from Canadian law reports and unreported decisions of appellate courts (1987-). Access is by plaintiff or defendant name. The set consists of four hardbound volumes with each volume supplemented by an annual softcover volume. *Canadian Current Law - Case Digests* provide quarterly and monthly updates. *Consolidated Table of Cases* is included in Carswell's CD-ROM version of *Canadian Abridgment Revised (2nd).*

Case citations are available through QL Systems Ltd. "QUICKCITE" Case Citator (access code QC) and through QL's "Canadian Abridgment Citator" (Canadian Case Citations) with an access code of ABRC (cases 1867 to date). QL Systems Ltd. databases with unreported cases can be helpful for unreported cases before 1987 (commencement of unreported case coverage by Can. Abr. Rev. (2nd)'s *Consolidated Table of Cases): Lawyers Weekly, All Canada Weekly Summaries, Weekly Criminal Bulletin,* and Western Legal Publication's decisions services (*e.g., Saskatchewan Decisions*).

2. Citations for English and Commonwealth cases

The Digest (formerly *English and Empire Digest)* may be used. The LEXIS-NEXIS database library "ENGGEN" at file "CASES" has cases since 1936 with parallel citation. There are many files (databases) within the LEXIS-NEXIS "Commonwealth Cases Library" (COMCAS).

3. Citations for American cases

The Decennial Digests within the American Digest System have "Tables of Cases" volumes. When using the updating "General Digest" volumes, each volume's "Table of Cases" must be examined because there are no separate "Tables of Cases" cumulations for the "General Digest". The most practical method is using the WESTLAW computer system through QL as a gateway.

Chapter 12

Researching Québec Law*

The purpose of this chapter is to present Québec legal research concepts to common law lawyers and law students. The focus will thus be on issues and areas that are different from common law approaches; similarities between the two systems will of course be outlined when appropriate. The structure of this chapter follows closely that of the book itself, so that it can be read in the context of the research process of other jurisdictions. We have, however, added an overview that helps understand Québec's system from a comparative law perspective. For more particulars on Québec legal research, see *La recherche documentaire en droit* by D. Le May and D. Goubau (Montreal: Wilson et Lafleur Ltée, 1994).

A. OVERVIEW OF THE QUÉBEC LEGAL SYSTEM

Contrary to common belief, much of Québec Law is very similar in feature to what one finds in a Common Law jurisdiction.

1. Definition and scope of Québec Law

Québec law is, first of all, the law applicable in Québec; this implies some common features and some differences when compared with other systems.

(a) Like other systems of law, Québec law:

- (i) originates from different sources: statutes, regulations, case law, custom, contracts and doctrine (opinions of legal scholars)
- (ii) includes the federal statutes that are almost always applicable to Québec except as otherwise mentioned. These are excluded from the scope of this chapter.
- (iii) covers both private and public law.
- (iv) is bilingual since all legislative texts are published in French and English, following s. 133 of the *Constitution Act, 1867.* But note the importance of subsection 40(2) of the Québec *Interpretation Act,* R.S.Q. 1977, c. 1-16, which states:

---

* Denis Le May, B.A., LL.B., LL.M. (Laval), M.L.S. (Montreal). Member of the Bar of Québec, Law Librarian, Université Laval, Québec. This chapter is kept up-to-date at the author's website: http://www.bibl.ulaval.ca/ress/droit.

> In case of doubt, the construction placed on any act shall be such as not to impinge on the status of the French language.

(b) Unlike other systems of law, Québec law:

(i) is a mixed system of law and a living laboratory of comparative law since the civil law system and the Common Law system co-exist. Why are there two systems in Québec? History answers: the British conquest of 1760 changed automatically the public law of the land according to prevalent doctrine (see *Campbell v. Hall,* (1774) I Cowp 204; 98 E.R. 1045). After a period of turmoil, the British Parliament clarified the situation as to private law (that of public law was legally unquestioned): the old French laws would be applicable in Québec.

> [...] and that in all Matters of Controversy, relative to Property and Civil Rights, Resort shall be had to the Laws of Canada, as the Rule for the Decision of the same [...]

Section 8 of *The Québec Act, 1774,* 14 George III, c. 83 (U.K.); R.S.C. 1985 (App. II, No. 2).

This is the legal basis on which the civil law system is still used in Québec.

(ii) is codified, as far as private law is concerned. Thus, most of the private law is in the *Civil Code* (see section C, the *Civil Code*, for further particulars on the matter). Without adding to confusion, let us remember that the Code is not exhaustive in terms of private law. Private law outside of the code can indeed be found in statutes and in the body of decisions on the Code.

2. Applicability of English or French law

The duality of the Québec legal system has led to the oft-made assumption that Québec is different because "they use the Code Napoleon out there". On the negative side, let us first state firmly, that since Québec participates fully in the Canadian sovereignty, no laws of another country are applicable directly to Canada and this covers French law as well. The use of French law in Québec is even more restricted than a comparable use of the laws of the countries of the Commonwealth by a Common Law lawyer. The Québec lawyer would first have to decide whether the matter under consideration is one of public or of private law. If public law is the answer, then the research is done as by Common Law approaches (looking first to the local jurisdiction's law and then to the law of other common law jurisdictions such as other provinces, England, other Commonwealth countries, the U.S., *etc.*). If private law, then the use of French authorities may be suitable in certain cases (see chart). Note that the following chart is a simplification which has exceptions such as the frequent practice of the Québec legal profession citing other provinces, American, and English cases dealing with insurance (a "private law problem").

QUÉBEC'S SUPPLETIVE LAW:
SYNOPTIC/SYNTHETIC CHART

Kind of problem: Private or public	*Direct suppletive law: Persuasive*	*Indirect suppletive law: Reasons*
PRIVATE Law problem: look for Québec solution:	Look for solution applied in French law;	Look for solution compatible with the ecosystem of Civil Law*
If NONE →	If NONE →	
PUBLIC LAW problem: look for Québec or Canada solution:	Look for solution applied in English Law;	Look for solution compatible with the ecosystem of Common Law*
If NONE →	If NONE →	

* If NONE: Look into the other system for comparative reasons.

This chart shows: a) where to start to solve a problem;
b) when to resort to French law;
c) how French and English law are both suppletive and comparative following the "time" when they are referred to.

This is discussed in more detail in Section C, *The Civil Code*.

3. Summary of Québec's substantive law

The best summary available in English on Quéebec's substantive law, albeit short, is still the Québec Law Digest in the latest edition of the *Martindale Hubbell Law Directory.*

B. STATUTES

Québec statutes are very similar to statutes all across Canada with the only additional feature being that there is a permanent revision which is also official. For the remaining, the introductory remarks of Chapter 4, Statutes are valid for Québec as well.

1. Revised Statutes of Québec 1977 (the current statute revision)

(a) The main volumes: The hardcover edition of R.S.Q. 1977 appeared in volumes 1 through 10 containing the full text of the statutes in force on December 31, 1977. Statutes appear in separate French and English editions. They are arranged in alpha numerical sequence according to the first substantive word of the French version.

(b) Index volume: An index has been published that covers the content of the R.S.Q. 1977. So far there has been no updating of the index.

(c) Documentation: A separate volume called "Documentation and Index" (although containing no index) is published with the revision. It gives tables of contents, both alphanumerical and alphabetical (in English), presents the R.S.Q.'s, and ends with tables of Repeals and General Concordance.

(d) The looseleaf edition: The Revised Statutes are also available in looseleaf format with updates twice a year (cut off dates: March 1st and September 1st). Offices and libraries planning a light or irregular use of the Québec Statutes may consider not buying the looseleaf edition which takes time to keep up to date and rely upon the traditional system, *i.e.*, bound volumes, annual volumes and separate bills.

Electronic sources: The Revised Statutes are offered by the Québec Department of Justice as an online database (=LAWS) available through SOQUIJ (Société québécoise d'information juridique). The Revised Statutes are also available from SOQUIJ on CD-ROM (Lois et reglements au Québec), which provides full updated bilingual text of statutes and regulations.

(e) The *Editeur officiel du Québec* (Official Printer) regularly publishes separate chapters of the most important Acts. As they are excerpts from the permanent R.S.Q.'s, they are both up to date and official, and have an index in most cases. To receive the catalogue of new releases from *l'Editeur officiel,* write to Les Publications du Québec, C.P. 1005, Québec (Québec) G1K 7B5, phone (418) 643-5150 or 1-800-463-2100 or fax (418) 643-6177 or 1-800-561-3479. (Note that this is valid for consolidated acts only and not for regular subscriptions to bills and debates available from the Clerk of the House). See 2(c) for more details.

Electronic sources: You may also access statutes on the Internet: (http://www.lois.gouv.qc.ca). Browsing to see what titles are available is free, but you will need an account number to download any Act you want. Note that you cannot select a section or a chapter, but rather you must download an Act as a whole. This option will please occasional users with an urgent request. This option is entirely different from the usual online database searches because you cannot search for terms within the text of the statute (you may only download, for a price, a text you know you want). *Les Publications du Québec* is a trademark for the Québec Government publications sold in bookstores, or in this case, electronically. For an overview of its offerings, visit its Internet site: (http://www.doc.gouv.qc.ca/publications).

(f) Electronic sources: Since January 1998, the French version only of the R.S.Q.s is available for free on the Internet at the following URL: http://205.236.113.155/cgi-bin/foliocgi.exe/gratnet.nfo. You may find some statutes under the government departments' Internet sites (presently very limited). Check the Québec government site (http://www.gouv.qc.ca/introa.htm), and click on "Departments and Institutions". At least, most of the departments will provide a list of the statutes for which they are responsible.

2. Updating the R.S.Q. 1977

(a) *Statutes of Québec* (S.Q.) are annual (since 1969; before that they were sessional) volumes of statutes published subsequent to the revision. Prior to their publication in the annual volume, statutes are published separately as legislative bills (French and English editions) and also in *Gazette officielle du Québec: Part 2, Laws and Regulations.*

Electronic sources: Acts after the R.S.Q. 1977 are not available online or on the Internet. These Acts can be purchased through *Les Publications du Québec*. These statutes can also be downloaded from the electronic edition of the *Gazette officielle du Québec, Part II,* provided one has a Gazette subscription: see Internet site (http://www.gazette.gouv.qc.ca/indexe.html). To subscribe or to buy a specific issue, you need to fill out and submit a form, and you will electronically receive an access code and password within minutes. However, there is one difficulty: Gazettes are retrievable only by the issue's number. There is no concordance between the Bill number and the Gazette issue number. The solution to this problem is to look in the index at the end of the Internet web page. This is rather slow and cumbersome because the website index provides the Bill number and Gazette issue number only. To find the page number at which the Bill starts, you must then search the individual index of the cited Gazette issue.

(b) The most recent volume contains a cumulative list of amendments (on yellow pages) and should be checked to note any change brought to legislation. One problem may arise when the researcher does not have the alphanumerical identification of the Chapter. This will surely be the case when one does not subscribe to the looseleaf edition. To avoid this problem, check in the annual volume, in the yellow pages, the Equivalence Table of Chapters consolidated to [date]. This will give the alphanumerical reference to the new chapter in R.S.Q. and will allow for an easy use of the table of amendments.

(c) This step should be completed by the *Répertoire législatif de l'Assemblée Nationale;* published annually around February, which gives a summary of enacted legislation during the preceding year with table of amendments for the year. This is the best tool to use until the annual volume is published. The *Répertoire* is available in French only, free from the Clerk of the House. Write to Assemblée Nationale, Distribution des documents parlementaires, 5 Place Québec, bureau 195, Québec (Québec) G1R 5P3, phone (418) 643-2754 or fax (418) 528-0381. This is also the port of entry to subscribe to bills and debates of the House.

(d) The looseleaf edition. If you are using the looseleaf edition, the texts are up to date as indicated both on the binder labels of the book and on the last page of the text of all chapters.

To complete your data with what happened between that date and a more recent one, turn to the *Table of amendments that came into force between* [date] and [date] (grey pages) in the volume "Documentation and index". This table will tell what changes have been made even though the updates are not published yet. Of course, in all cases, a final check should be made for separate current bills. The looseleaf edition of the statutes is supposed to be brought up to date twice yearly, but at times the updating has been more than a year behind.

(e) Telephone information service. The Québec *Service de la refonte* (Statutes and Regulations revision office) offers a unique telephone service that helps bring one's information up to date, especially since the last distribution. This service gives information on the state of the R.S.Q.'s as they stand on the day of the phone call, on proclamation dates affecting sections or parts previously not in force, and on amendments brought to any section in the revision. Phone: (418) 643-4808, fax (418) 646-1696 or write: Ministère de la justice, Direction de la refonte, 1200 route de l'Eglise, Sainte-Foy (Québec) G1V 4M1.

(f) Current bills in first reading are available in print form either as part of a subscription or by individual purchase. Note that they are not published in the *Gazette officielle du Québec*. More often, recent bills introduced in the Québec Legislature are available on the Internet at the Assembly's Internet site: (http://www.assnat.qc.ca/eng/publications/Projets-loi/publics/index.htm). Once the bills are assented to, legislation is available in print or electronic form for a charge. As of October 21, 1997 the Québec Status of Bills is available in electronic form only at http://www.asnat.qc.ca/fra/Publications/Projets-loi/Etat-001.htm, in French only but updated daily.

3. Coming into force of legislation

The most commonly used mechanism governing the entry into force of statutes is the proclamation. These are published in the *Gazette officielle du Québec: Part 2, Laws and Regulations* and can be found under the heading "proclamations" in the most recent quarterly index of the Gazette; these are in turn supplemented by individual issues of the Gazette. There is no cumulative index for more than one year.

Caveat: the list of legislative provisions brought into force by proclamation [to date] that appears in the annual volumes of the statutes is incomplete and therefore unreliable.

If there is no mention regarding the coming into force of a given statute, it comes into force 30 days after the assent, following the *Interpretation Act,* R.S.Q. 1977, chap. 1-16, s. 5 [re-en. 1982, c. 62, s. 152]. This is very seldom the case.

4. Further references

Other aspects of Québec legislation are discussed below:

(a) the Civil Code (section C)
(b) annotated statutes/Statute citators (section E)
(c) Statutes in computerized version (section J).
(d) Compilations of statutes. Compilations draw together statutes and regulations dealing with specific legal topics. Both SOQUIJ and various private publishers have produced a number of compilations.

C. THE CIVIL CODES

Civil Codes are legislation and, as such, they could be discussed under the topic of statutes. Because of the special place they hold in civil law systems, it is appropriate and usual to study them in a separate chapter.

Historically, the main difference between Québec and the Common Law jurisdictions has related to codification (a systematic unified body of law). In Québec, most of the private law is in the *Civil Code*; however, there is a growing number of laws enacted outside the *Civil Code*.

For a good presentation of the present situation including Codes in the civilian legal tradition, civilian legal concepts and their evolution in Québec, see *Québec Civil Law: An Introduction to Québec Private Law* by J.E.C. Brierley and R.A. Macdonald, eds. (Toronto: Emond Montgomery Publications Ltd., 1993). The first 200 pages of this book offer a well-written and thoroughly documented introduction to the actual operation of the Québec Civil Law System, while explaining the foundations and broader concepts of civil law as a whole. The relevant portion of Part One (Nature, Scope, and Techniques of the Civil Law) are: "I Beginnings of Canadian Civil Law... II The Place of the Civil Law and the Civil Code in the Legal Order... III The Course of the Civil Law Since 1866... IV The Civil Code and the Sources of Civil Law... V Basic Jural Conceptions of Québec Civil Law".

1. Definition and scope of the Civil Code

The *Civil Code* is the general legislation of Québec in matters of private law. The Code applies as the general law of Québec, whenever there is no other, more explicit, legislative pronouncement. The *Civil Code* is always to be looked at in matters of private law, case law being only complementary.

The relation between statute law and the Code is twofold; there is similarity in that the Code is legislated just like statute law. On the other hand, there is an important difference: statute law in Common Law jurisdictions is to be interpreted strictly; this cannot apply to the Code because it is the common law in private law matters.

Evidence of this is drawn from the Preliminary Provision of the *Civil Code of Québec* which provides:

> The Civil Code of Québec, in harmony with the *Charter of Rights and Freedoms* and the general principles of law, governs persons, relations between persons and property. The Civil Code comprises a body of rules, which, in all matters within the letter, spirit or object of its provisions, lays down the jus commune, expressly or by implication. In these matters, the Code is the foundation of all other laws, although other laws may complement the Code or make exceptions to it.

2. The present Code

The basic Code is the *Civil Code of Québec,* entered into force January 1, 1994. Adopted in December 1991 as Bill 125, it became c. 64 of the 1991 Québec statutes. It is a major piece of legislation covering 3,168 articles (sections) divided into ten books as follows: Book One: Persons; Book Two: The Family; Book Three: Successions; Book Four; Property; Book Five: Obligations; Book Six: Prior Claims and Hypothecs; Book Seven: Evidence; Book Eight: Prescription; Book Nine: Publication of Rights, and Book Ten: Private International Law.

The new Code replaced the *Civil Code of Lower Canada* and many more recent statutes that have been adopted to modernize the Code in the 1970s and 1980s. There is separate legislation respecting the implementation of the Civil Code reform that deals with transitional measures, acquired rights and the application of the old law. See *An Act Respecting the Implementation of the Reform of the Civil Code*, S.Q. 1992, c. 57. The effect of the new Code on existing law and the extent to which it applies to current or recent situations is entirely governed by this Act. The basic rule is that while the new legislation has no retroactive effect (s. 2), it nonetheless immediately applies to existing situations (s. 3). Most of the statute sets forth special rules for each Book of the Code (ss. 11 to 170), modifies the Code of Civil Procedure (ss. 171 to 422), and finally, deals with the provisions relating to other Acts (ss. 423 to 718).

To obtain an overview of the code in chart form, one may use D. Le May, *Le Code civil du Québec en tableaux synoptiques* (Montréal: Wilson et Lafleur, 1992), where the Code is presented in a tabular fashion aimed at showing graphically the logic of the Code.

3. The Code, the Revised Statutes, and private editions

The Code has never been included in revisions. The new Code is part of the 1991 Statute book (Chapter 64). There are several private looseleaf and bound editions of the Code available from private publishers in French or bilingual versions.

Electronic sources: Since the Code is not revised, (*i.e.*, not included in the R.S.Q.), the Code will not be found in the corresponding online database. The Code is not a separate online database on either SOQUIJ or QUICKLAW.

Many publishers offer an electronic version on CD-ROM or on the Internet with annotations and complementary texts (SOQUIJ, CCH/FM, Editions Yvon Blais, *etc.*). Carswell offers an Internet subscription at http://www.dacfo.ca/ to *Droit Civil en direct* (text of the Code and commentaries in French only). The only free Internet access to the Code is to the French version only at: (http://www.droit.umontreal.ca/doc/ccq/cgi-bin/ccfTDM).

4. Updating the Code

A list of amendments brought to the Codes in one year can be found in the *Répertoire législatif de l'Assemblée nationale* (see section B above). These are not carried in the table of amendments of the annual volumes.

5. Interpretation of the Code

One of the most useful immediate tools to interpret the Code is the official commentaries of the Department of Justice published in French only (Commentaires du Ministre de la justice: le Code Civil du Québec: une mouvement de société : Québec: Gouvernement du Québec, 1993, three volumes).

Electronic sources: The Commentaries are always available in the commercial electronic versions. In them is found a reference to the corresponding article in the former code (The *Civil Code of Lower Canada*), and a cite to the relevant part of the *1978 Report on the Civil Code* published by the Civil Code Revision Office (under the title *Draft Civil Code and Commentaries*). This Report, tabled in the National Assembly on June 20, 1978, remains an invaluable source for the simple reason that many of its provisions were adopted, finally, in 1991. The explanations and annotations are thus readily usable.

Bar course materials offer useful commentaries for the continuing education of practitioners. There is an English translation of these materials. The structure of the five volume English edition differs somewhat from the French edition since the English edition more closely follows the actual structure of the bar courses:

v. 1: Persons. v. 1-B: The family. v. 2-A: Property. v. 2-B: Obligations I, II. v. 2-C: Obligations III, IV, V, VI. v. 3-A: Obligations VII, VIII. v. 3-B: Sale. v. 4-A: Marine insurance, Carriage by water, Affreightment. v. 4-B: Successions. v. 5-A: Prior Claims and Hypethecs Reform of Security Publication of Rights. v. 5-B: Evidence Prescription Transitional law. Private International Law.

See: *Reform of the Civil Code*/Texts written for the Barreau and the Chambre des notaires du Québec. - Montréal: [s.n.] 1993.

The Bar course materials are also available on video tapes in French only (10 cassettes), from the Québec Bar (1-800-361-8495; service in English is also available).

6. Finding cases under the Code

The general tools outlined below (digests, citators, and encyclopedias) are all relevant for retrieving cases decided under the Code. You will find it faster and more convenient, however, to use the various specialized tools available. All the electronic editions noted above are in fact annotated codes, and as such, carry many references to case law. Additionally, annotated codes in print form (bound or looseleaf) will give the most references to cases: *Kelada Code civil du Québec: texte annoté*, available in both looseleaf and bound editions by Carswell. From Wilson and Lafleur publishers: the master *Code civil du Québec annoté* by Baudouin and Renaud is available. It features 10 bound volumes and is updated by a looseleaf publication (each volume may be purchased and can be updated individually). Carswell also publishes a multi-volume looseleaf edition titled *Droit civil québécois*. Also, SOQUIJ is offering on its internet site, a glance at citations of relevant cases under the new Code, since January 1, 1994. You may freely browse at the Internet site: (http://www.soquij.qc.ca/prod/infojuri/listeccq.htm).

You can search by article, by date, or by court docket number. New cases are added weekly. For each case, you will get the court docket number, the citation to the publication (if it is published), cite to the summary in the weekly *Jurisprudence Express* and the number of pages. You may order the case through E-mail.

7. Four basic questions about the Code

One is likely to encounter these four main difficulties when working with the Code:

(i) How to find the relevant article or chapter? Use the index and keep in mind that many of the matters in common law jurisdiction will have counterparts in the Code. Also, do not forget to "translate" the concept from common law to civil law. For example, "mortgage" = "hypothec".

(ii) Is it new law? The best tools to answer this question are the government commentaries, the bar course materials, and ordinary doctrinal writings.

(iii) To what extent is existing case law still valid? Up to 70 per cent of the new Code continues from former law. The annotated Codes usually carry old but relevant cases.

(iv) Does this apply immediately? Yes, as per the application statute and its provisions, which must be read in conjunction with substantive provisions (see section 2 of this chapter: The Present Code).

D. SUBORDINATE LEGISLATION

Regulations in Québec are very similar to Regulations in other jurisdictions so that the introductory remarks of Chapter 5, Subordinate Legislation, are valid for Québec as well.

A multitude of different terms are in use to designate regulations (*e.g.*, Treasury Board Decisions, Letters patent, Tariff, *etc.*). The most common one, for regulations adopted by the government, is Order in Council (o.c. or in French; Décret, abbreviated D.). The general statute on regulations, providing definition, publication requirements or exemptions is the *Regulations Act,* R.S.Q. c. R-18.1.

1. Revised Regulations of Québec 1981 (the current regulations revision)

(a) The main volumes: volumes 1 through 10 contain the full texts of regulations in force on December 31, 1981. Regulations appear in separate French and English editions. They are arranged in alphanumerical sequence according to the enabling statutes following their French denomination. Under each statute, regulations are numbered in sequence.

(b) Index volume: volume 11 is the index. As noted earlier, it is similar to that of other provinces containing a list of keywords that appear in titles and a list of regulations by enabling statutes.

(c) Supplements: Two volumes of supplements have been published to bring the whole set up to date as of August 1, 1982.

Electronic sources: Most of the general remarks regarding electronic legislation sources to applicable for subordinate legislation. In many instances, the tools are the same, and in other instances, the process is similar.

The Revised Regulations are available as a SOQUIJ online database (=REGU). This online database updates the 1981 Regulations with about a two-week lag time after publication of the texts in the *Gazette officielle.*

The Revised Regulations are also on the CD-ROM titled "Lois et règlements du Québec", but with a major shortcoming: the regulations are not available bilingually (however, the statutes are). Recent texts are published in the *Gazette officielle du Québec Part II.*

Electronic sources: This tool is also available for retrieving texts from the Publications de Québec's electronic bookstore.

2. Updating

Contrary to the situation with statutes, there are no provisions for keeping the revision up to date; therefore no looseleaf edition is available. Current regulations appear in the *Gazette officielle du Québec: Part 2, Laws and Regulations.* The quarterly cumulative index is used as a finding tool for regulations issued during the year.

Electronic sources are, of course, updated.

3. Research tool

The main tool to use to find a regulation in force in any given year is the *Tableau des modifications et index sommaire des Règlements refondus du Québec,* published twice a year by l'Editeur officiel du Québec (in French only). It does not carry regulations repealed or replaced. Complete the search with the *Gazette officielle.*

Electronic sources: If you do not subscribe to the *Tableau des modifications*, you can determine whether there is a regulation relating to your topic by browsing the Publications du Québec's Internet site: (http://www.lois.gouv.qc.ca/rechreglement.html). You may easily obtain the text if you are an electronic subscriber (an easier task than if you are dealing in print form). Note that you cannot transfer research from this point to the *Gazette officielle* in either electronic or print form format because you have no cite to the regulation.

4. Unpublished regulations

Most regulations are published. Orders in Council whose purpose is other than adopting a regulation may be published only in the form of a notice in some cases. (O.C. 1884-84, 16 August 1984 Orders in Council (Exemption from complete publication) Regulation, (1984) II O.G. 3315). Access to the full texts may of course remain possible through the *Act respecting access to documents held by public bodies and the protection of personal information,* R.S.Q., c. A-2.1 by a request to the regulating body. This applies as well to any unpublished regulation, should there be one.

5. Availability of texts

It is possible to buy separate up to date texts of regulations directly from the Official Printer. Write to Les Publications du Québec, C.P. 1005, Québec (Québec) G1K 7B5.

Electronic sources: As is true for the legislation, the regulations are available commercially at the electronic bookstore of the government's Publications du Québec. You can search by statute (*e.g.*, B-1) or by topic (broadly defined) to find the relevant texts and download them for a fee, within minutes of having obtained the password. The Internet site for the search is: (http://www.lois.gouv.qc.ca/rechreglements.html).

If you wish to retrieve all the relevant regulations under a statute, the easiest method is to search by the alphanumeric code of the statute followed by "r." (*e.g.*, T-3,r.). While you are at the Internet site and without cost, you can get an idea of which regulations are relevant to your topic and an idea of how large the file is (in terms of bytes). However, you will not get the cite that will allow you to find the text in the *Gazette officielle*.

6. Court rules

The extent of court rules is somewhat reduced in Québec since most of the rules are codified in the *Code of civil procedure,* R.S.Q. c. C-25. Other rules are usually published as an appendix to commercially available Codes of Civil Procedure, the best of which is a looseleaf edition of the Code, statutes pertaining to civil procedure (both federal and Québec) and court rules with texts in French and English: *Code de procédure civile annoté du Québec (Code of civil procedure)* by H. Reid (Montréal: Wilson et Lafleur, looseleaf).

Research can be completed by referring to annotations, mostly in French, contained in *Code de procedure civile: complément jurisprudence et doctrine* by H. Reid. (Montréal: Wilson et Lafleur, annual editions).

Both are available from Wilson et Lafleur, 40 rue Notre-Dame est, Montreal (Québec) H2Y 1B9. Phone (514) 875-6326, fax (514) 875-8356.

Rules are issued as regulations published under the *Code of civil procedure,* R.S.Q. c. C-25 and as such, are published in the *Gazette officielle du Québec: Part 2, Laws and Regulations;* they can also be purchased like regulations (see Section 5 above).

Electronic sources: SOQUIJ is a CD-ROM product titled, "Code de procedure civile interactif, 1997-", which is both annotated and hypertually linked. The produce contains the text in bilingual format and the related statutes and regulations in French, summaries of cases, and forms.

E. DIGESTS AND INDEXES FOR LAW REPORTS

1. Introduction

Historically, Québec case law has been in general less extensive and important than in Common Law jurisdictions. The multiplicity of specialized tribunals and the improvement of reporting processes has increased, however the relevancy and use of case law in Québec. Even back in 1953, Professor Friedmann stated that "In its total practical effect, the Québec doctrine and practice of precedent is remarkably close to that of the common law" (Friedmann, "Stare Decisis at Common Law and under the Civil Code of Québec" (1953), 31 *Can. Bar Rev.* 723, at 746).

Although we are mainly concerned here with cases that bear on Québec's legal peculiarities, it must be remembered that many decisions handed down by Québec courts are of interest at a more general level (*i.e.*, they can be decisions in matters of federal legislative competence or matters of public law/common law).

2. Format of law reports in Québec

Most of the law reporting in Québec is done through SOQUIJ, the legal information Society *(Société québécoise d'information juridique).* SOQUIJ publishes reports of the Superior Court and of the Court of Appeal of Québec and a whole series of topical administrative decisions from a variety of tribunals. Contact SOQUIJ to receive the catalogue of its publications: 10 rue Saint-Jacques, bureau 101, Montréal (Québec) H2Y 1L3. Phone (514) 842-8745 or 1-800-363-6718, fax (514) 842-5357.

Electronic sources: The catalogue is also on the Internet at (http://www.soquij.qc.ca/prod/produits/index.htm). The catalogue, both in print form and electronically, is in French only. There are a few pamphlets in English on specific products.

Some series are published by private publishers.

3. Current finding tools

(a) New cases in Québec are digested and summarized in the weekly *Jurisprudence express* published by SOQUIJ since the end of 1977. More than 2,000 cases a year are digested shortly after they are handed down by the different courts.

There are also two specialized Expresses: one in Labour Law, the other one in Taxation. It is possible to acquire from SOQUIJ a copy of any case mentioned in the *Express* no matter whether it will be published or not. Also available is a microfiche subscription service to the full texts of all cases.

Electronic sources: As of 1997, the microfiche service has been replaced by a CD-ROM titled *Jurisprudence Plus,* which combines the features of *Jurisprudence Express* by providing the summaries of all judgments published in the SOQUIJ series *Recueils de jurisprudence du Québec* (R.J.Q.), *Recueil en droit immobilier* (R.D.I.), *Recueil en responsibilité et assurance* (R.R.A), and *Recueil de droit de la famille* (R.D.F.), plus the full text of all those judgments whether or not they are to be published in print form. Hypertext links are established between summaries and full texts. For every case summarized it is possible to find out the docket number, the name of the judge, the price of a copy, whether or not the case will be heard in appeal and whether it will be published in the reports.

Three times a year, a cumulative list of Codes and Statutes cited and an index are published.

Electronic sources: The online database version of *Express* provides case summaries only (unlike the CD-ROM), but covers a broader base. Everything covered in the CD-ROM is on the database *Express* (plus Federal Court, Fiscal, *Revue de droit judiciaire*, and other Wilson et Lafleur reports which are covered in *L'Annuaire de jurisprudence*). Currently, SOQUIJ also adds about 1500 micro-summaries of unpublished judgments. These micro-summaries are not published in either *Jurisprudence Express* or *L'Annuaire de jurisprudence*. Text may be purchased from SOQUIJ thereafter.

(b) Recent case law is available from the following publishers and vendors: Les editions Yvon Blais (phone: 1-800-363-3047; fax: (514)263-9256; E-mail commandes a: @editionsyvonblais.qc.ca). Since 1993, *La Presse juridique* provides case summaries and analysis every two weeks and covers over 1,200 decisions annually. You may buy texts from the publisher at phone (514)842-3937 or fax (514)842-7144. At year's end, the summaries are gathered in a bound volume which includes an index.

Electronic sources: QUICKLAW users will find two online *La Presse juridique* databases: LPJR for summaries and LPJA for the articles and commentaries on certain cases. Yvon Blais is offering a new CD-ROM, "Repertoire Electronique de jurisprudence du Barreau" (REJB), in collaboration with the Québec bar. This CD-ROM is a major product providing more than 3,000 case summaries per year and the full text of all judgments summarized. This CD-ROM will be updated through an Internet account. There will be a weekly newsletter providing the summaries. For more information, contact les éditions Yvon Blais at 1-800-267-2524.

(c) In mid-1997, QUICKLAW offered a new online database, "Jurisprudence en ligne" (access code JEL), which covers recent selected Québec cases. The advantages of the database are the hyperlink function which allows you to obtain the full text of a case and the updating function which links to other publications in print form by providing parallel cites through QL's "QUICKCITE".

4. Annual digest

Every year, most of the summaries are published in one volume called the *Annuaire de jurisprudence et de doctrine du Québec.* The *Annuaire* is the most useful and used finding tool for case law in Québec. It cumulates all the summaries published in *Jurisprudence express* (so that it is possible to discard *Jurisprudence express* for the corresponding year). Additionally, there are numerous other entries and summaries of other series not covered by *Jurisprudence express.* The main disadvantage of the *Annuaire* is the lack of consolidation since 1955; there are a great number of annual volumes to be consulted.

Since 1993, one may also use *Recueil de jurisprudence de La Presse juridique*, which is the annual cumulation of case summaries published by Yvon Blais in *La Presse juridique*. The coverage of the general series of law reports by the *Canadian Abridgment Revised (2d) edition* and *Canadian Current Law* is not as in-depth as Québec-produced publications.

5. Former digests

Prior to 1955, there have been consolidations that allow a search to extend as far back as 1770. All in French, these consolidations are the only tool in existence that allow such exhaustive coverage. They are *Répertoire général de jurisprudence canadienne* by Beauchamp (4 vols.) (1770-1913); Supplement by Saint-Cyr (2 vols) (1913-1925);

Supplement by Tellier (2 vols.) (1926-1935); and
Supplement by Lévêque (2 vols.) (1935-1955).

Note that the *Canadian Abridgment* and its electronic counterpart have insufficient coverage of old Québec materials (except at the Supreme Court level).

6. Relationship between Annuaire and Jurisprudence express

(a) continuity: *Jurisprudence express* is the best way to find cases until the *Annuaire* is published. When the *Annuaire* is published, it is no longer necessary to keep *Jurisprudence express.*

(b) differences: *Jurisprudence express* contains only the summaries for the cases that are published by SOQUIJ while the *Annuaire* also gives summaries of series published by other publishers. The *Annuaire* also covers some legal periodicals and some administrative decisions.

The same applies to the relationship between *La Presse juridique* and its annual cumulation, the *Recueil de jurisprudence.* However, one should not discard the weekly issues because the articles are only summarized in the annual cumulation. Non-subscribers to the weekly issue could obtain the articles from QL's online database LPJA.

As with other publishers in other provinces, there is not complete duplication between the weekly case summaries published by SOQUIJ or Yvon Blais. Parallel cites for cases are not always given. However, QUICKLAW provides all known parallel cites to the cases in its new QL online database "Jurisprudence en ligne" (access code JEL).

7. Administrative board decisions

The finding tool for these cases when published as a series is the index to the publication itself rather than the *Annuaire,* since it mentions but a few.

Electronic sources: More of these decisions are becoming available as online databases or CD-ROM products through SOQUIJ or Les Publications du Québec.

F. STATUTE AND CASE CITATORS

There are no complete fully annotated citators either for statutes or for cases in Québec.

1. Common features

Most of the citators used in Québec are simple lists of citations with no annotations whatsoever as to whether a case has been followed, discussed, varied, etc. Unfortunately the same method is used for all cases, leaving the researcher with no other alternative than to actually go to the cited cases to check if they are relevant to the issue.

Statute citators are, likewise, of minimal use as they never give notice of the amendments brought to a section nor to proclamation dates (these two elements of information are, however, fully retrievable through the statute finding tools (e.g., see Section B). They also do not give an excerpt of the text of the decisions cited.

Most of the publications mentioned here are available from SOQUIJ.

2. Statute citators

Different publications may be used, each with severe shortcomings:

(a) *Table de la législation citée* (Montréal: SOQUIJ): This covers cases decided from the time of the 1964 revision of the Statutes until the new one in 1977; it also covers the *Civil Code* for the period 1956-1977. A second volume was published in 1989 and covers the years 1978-1987. A third volume covers the years 1988-1993. Until a new consolidation is published, this is completed by the annual table published in the *Annuaire de jurisprudence et de doctrine du Québec* ("Tables des codes et lois cités") and after that, it is cumulated every four months in the weekly *Jurisprudence express.*
There was a *Québec Statute and case citator* for the R.S.Q. 1925 up to 1937.

(b) *Canadian Statute Citations* covers provincial legislation including Québec. On the positive side, the coverage goes back in time much farther than the Québec tools and also the volumes are readily available in most Common Law law libraries. On the negative side, one must be aware that the coverage of Québec cases in the past has been so selective that the use of this volume in private law matters in Québec is almost useless, and is limited for public law purposes. This volume is completed of course by *Canadian Citations.*

(c) Since about 1980 there is a much better and comprehensive coverage of citations by the Canadian Abridgment system, its different parts and products, due to cooperation with SOQUIJ. Contrary to the situation described above for the digests, the use of Abridgment facilities is productive and probably sufficient.

3. Case citators

Here again, there are two different ways to ascertain whether a case has been cited or not.

(a) We suggest, first, the use of the *Table de la jurisprudence citée* (Montréal: SOQUIJ). It covers from 1965 to 1979 and 1980 to 1987 in a second volume. A third volume covers the years 1988-1993. Further consolidation by the annual tables (bearing the same title) in the *Annuaire de jurisprudence et de doctrine du Québec* is pending, and from there by *Canadian Citations* which covers citations of cases from Québec in a full, satisfactory manner.

(b) For previous years, it is possible to use the *Index Gagnon.* It has now ceased publication, but used to be the only tool in Québec serving this purpose from 1920 to 1978.

(c) *Canadian Case Citations* may be used with the caution about the shortcomings as to the limited coverage of Québec cases as stated in Section F.2(b) and (c) above.

4. Annotated legislation

There are more and more fully annotated statutes published by various publishers. SOQUIJ, Wilson et Lafleur, and Editions Yvon Blais publish annotated legislation in a variety of formats: annual, looseleaf, irregulars, *etc.* Wilson et Lafleur is a major publisher and a very large bookstore with an Internet catalogue at http://www.typolitho.com/site-now/irst-fr-lib-cat.html. Note that the catalogue is not restricted to WL's titles but covers the whole field of Québec titles (and many more).

G. LEGAL ENCYCLOPEDIAS

There is no Legal Encyclopedia as such in existence in Québec. However, the following are of interest and may be very useful.

1. Doctrinal writings

Filling the function of an encyclopedia, there are many doctrinal writings including high-quality texts which cover many topics of law. For an overview of the most useful basic references in about 100 fields of legal research in Québec, you may use *Les références essentielles en droit québécois*, D. LeMay and J. Mercier (Montreal: Wilson et LaFleur, 1996).

2. Dictionaries

Dictionnaire de droit privé et comparé du Québec, published by Les Editions Yvon Blais, is a dictionary of technical vocabulary applicable to and used in Québec law, with either provincial or federal sources. An English language edition is also available: *Private Law Dictionary and Bilingual Lexicons.*

3. Suitability of the C.E.D.

It may be useful to remember here the possible applicability of existing encyclopedias such as the *Canadian Encyclopedic Digest* for a great many legal situations dealt with in Québec. The following are clear instances:

(i) matters of federal legislative competence such as banking and copyright;
(ii) matters of public law (constitutional, administrative, etc.) where much of the law is common law;
(iii) statutory matters where it is known that Québec provisions are similar if not identical to much of the provincial legislation across Canada.

4. French encyclopedias

French legal encyclopedias, usually very well conceived and up to date, are useful in civil law areas where deeper research is needed or when there is no case law in Québec and the provisions are similar to the French legislation. These encyclopedias are always available in Québec in universities and (some) bar libraries and in many university libraries in Canada. They can be purchased in Montréal along with most French materials from France and Belgium at Les Editions Arts, Lettres et Techniques Inc., 901 Boul. Ste-Croix, Montréal (Québec), H4L 3Y5. Phone (514) 747-4784.

H. LEGAL PERIODICALS AND LEGAL PERIODICAL INDEXES

Québec' s legal periodical literature is usually well covered by existing Canadian indexes (see Chapter 8, Legal Periodicals and Legal Periodical Indexes).

The same is not true, however, of the American indexes which do not as a rule include material in French.

Some periodicals are covered in the *Annuaire de jurisprudence et de doctrine du Québec,* but since it is always published late, its use is limited for that purpose.

As an additional research device, if further reading is needed on civil law matters, French and Belgian periodical articles can be retrieved through *Index to Foreign Legal Periodicals.*

I. OTHER SECONDARY LITERATURE RESEARCH SOURCES

1. New legal publications

New legal publications are covered by the *Index to Canadian Legal Literature* and its electronic counterpart (on QL:ICLL).

2. Looseleaf services

Many new services are now offered in French by CCH or Carswell directly, or through a subsidiary. Examples:

(a) *Fiscalité québécoise* (tax)
(b) *Droit corporatif québecois* (corporations)
(c) *Cités et villes* (Cities and Towns)
(d) *Droit familial québecois* (families)
(e) *Code du Travail* (labour)
(f) *Santé et sécurité au Travail* (occupational health)

3. Forms and precedents sets

There are two major sets covering commercial law: *Formulaire de droit de commercial* (Wilson et LaFleur), and *Recueil des conventions commerciales: contrats types au Québec* (Jewel Publications).

Other civil and commercial contracts in French can be adapted from French or Belgian forms sets when they exist.

For precedents of civil procedure, use *Formulaire de procédure civile* by H. Kelada and F. Payette (Montreal: Wilson & Lafleur, looseleaf).

4. Words and phrases

For words and phrases judicially defined see under "interpretation" in the *Annuaire de jurisprudence et de doctrine du Québec.* No cumulation is available. Up to 250 judicial definitions of civil law terms have been collected in the following: R. Boult, "Recueil de définitions judiciaires" (1974-1975) 77 *Revue du Notariat,* 182, 258, 332, 389, 448; full index at page 594.

J. CONCLUSION

The foremost conclusion of this chapter is that even though much of the legal background of Québec is different, the general pattern of research and many features are alike. There is no doubt, therefore, that the master legal research checklist, provided for Chapter 11 is, save for a few minor exceptions, fully relevant and directly applicable. The authors of this textbook and the author of this chapter will be glad if the information outlined throughout has contributed to further reduce legal separatism in Canada (see J. Deschênes, "On Legal Separatism in Canada" (1978) XII L.S.U.C. Gaz. 1).

Chapter 13

Researching English Law

Canadian common law is rooted in English law, as evidenced by ultimate appeal from the Supreme Court of Canada to the Judicial Committee of the Privy Council in England throughout the first half of the twentieth century, and by the retention of English statute law (if applicable) and English case law by Canada upon each province entering Confederation. Many of the landmark cases cited by Canadian courts today are older English cases. The Canadian researcher should be familiar with older and current English statute and case law sources.

English secondary authority literature plays a basic role in Canadian legal research. The English textbooks were heavily relied upon until recent decades when publication of many Canadian textbooks filled in gaps in Canadian legal literature. *Halsbury's Laws of England* (3rd ed.) with Canadian Converters has been a much-used encyclopedia source. *The Digest* (formerly *English and Empire Digest)* provides access to Commonwealth cases as well as English case law.

This chapter covers English law (England and Wales), with some of the publications providing access to law of Great Britain (England, Wales, and Scotland) and of the United Kingdom (Great Britain plus Northern Ireland).

The computer is becoming increasingly important in English legal research with the introduction of such systems as LEXIS-NEXIS.

For more detailed information about English legal research, see *Butterworths Legal Research Guide* by Guy Holborn, 1993.

A. LEGISLATIVE AND JUDICIAL STRUCTURES

1. Legislative structure

When bills pass through Parliament (House of Commons and House of Lords), they come into force as statutes upon Royal Assent by the Queen. Parliament is the supreme lawmaking body. The more than 3,000 statutes passed by Parliament over the centuries remain in force until repeal by Parliament. Courts may interpret legislation, but may not declare any acts *ultra vires*.

England is a unitary jurisdiction, and therefore does not have subdivisions with legislatures at the provincial level. Scotland, Wales, and Northern Ireland are each represented in Parliament in London.

Prior to 1962, English statutes were cited by regnal year and chapter number. A parliamentary session might extend from one regnal year to another, so the cite might be 12 & 13 Geo. 5, c. 10 (parliamentary session extending from the

12th year of the reign of George V to the 13th year). A parliamentary session may have included the reigns of two monarchs, and the abbreviations for both would be used in the citation to statutes passed during the session. Abbreviations for the monarchs' names are:

Ann.	Anne	M. (Ma.)	Mary
Chas. (Car.)	Charles	Ph. & M.	Phillip and Mary
Edw. (Ed.)	Edward	Rich. (Ric.)	Richard
Eliz.	Elizabeth	Vict. (Vic.)	Victoria
Geo.	George	Wm. (Will.)	William
Hen.	Henry	Wm. & M.	William and Mary
Jas. (Jac.)	James		

After 1962, the citation of the act need only include the year - *e.g., Courts Act 1971.*

2. Judicial structure

Law reports covering the English court structure extend back to the thirteenth century. There are several categories of law reports covering the early years. The most recent major change in court structure affecting an understanding of the case law reporting system occurred in the 1870s.

The *Supreme Court of Judicature Act 1873* (in force in 1875) eliminated the then-existing superior courts, except for the House of Lords, and instituted a High Court of Justice and a Court of Appeal. With this consolidation of courts, the number of law reports series was reduced. The High Court of Justice had five divisions, each of which had its own law reports series.

In the 1880s there was a further reduction to three divisions and a corresponding reduction in the number of law reports covering these courts. See the chart in Section B, 2, (a) below, for this consolidation of courts and the corresponding reduction in the number of law reports.

The present judicial structure consists of:

(a) House of Lords as the ultimate court of appeal.
(b) Supreme Court of Judicature
  (i) Court of Appeal, which receives appeals from the High Court.
  (ii) High Court of Justice, which now has three divisions:
    (A) Queen's Bench Division, including the Admiralty Court;
    (B) Chancery Division;
    (C) Family Division.
  (iii) Crown Court became the criminal court by the *Courts Act 1971,* and exercises original and appellate jurisdiction.
  (iv) The lower tier of courts are county, local, or special courts, such as Magistrates' Court and Industrial Relations Court.

B. LAW REPORTS

1. Pre-1865 law reports

(a) Summary of pre-1865 reports

Year	*English Reports, Full Reprint*	*The Year Books*	*Nominate Reports*	*All England Law Reports Reprint*	*Revised Reports*
1220	XX				
	XX				
1272	XX	XX			
	XX	XX			
1535	XX	XX	XX		
	XX		XX		
1558	XX		XX	XX	
	XX		XX	XX	
1785	XX		XX	XX	XX
	XX		XX	XX	XX
1865	XX		XX	XX	XX
				XX	
1935				XX	

(i) The *Year Books* contain the early reporting which evolved from mere notes to reports more resembling present-day law reports. These reports were written in "Law French" but there are some translations, such as the *Translation and Reprint Series* currently being published by the Selden Society of London. These reports are primarily of interest to legal history scholars rather than practising lawyers.

(ii) The *Nominate Reports are* published under the authority of private reporters for whom the more than 100 such law report series are named. A case may be reported in more than one nominate report series, and accuracy varies between sets. The reprint series mentioned below have selected the more reliable of the *Nominate Reports.*

(iii) The *English Reports, Full Reprint* is a selection of early cases and cases from the *Nominate Reports.* This reprint consists of 176 volumes plus two index volumes.

(iv) The *Revised Reports* reprints cases from the *Nominate Reports* in 149 volumes.

(v) The *All England Law Reports Reprint* publishes selected earlier cases.

(b) Locating cases in older reports

If only the citation to a case reported in the *Nominate Reports* is known and the location of the case in the *English Reports* or *Revised Reports* is needed, Appendix A: "Table of Reports and Digests Abbreviations" cross-references from the nominate abbreviation to volume numbers in E.R. or R.R.

Some nominate reports are not reprinted. The *English Reports* and *Revised Reports* contain tables of cases so that a specific case from a nominate may be located in these reprints. The *English Reports* and *Revised Reports* indicate the pagination of the original reports so that if only a case citation without a style of cause is known, the case may be located with ease.

2. The Law Reports

(a) Summary of the Law Reports (1865 to date)

See accompanying chart.

In 1865, the Incorporated Council of Law Reporting commenced publication of individual series of law reports, each with the designation of the court covered. The *Nominate Reports* ceased publication. Changes in titles for the various series of the *Law Reports* usually reflect changes in court structure over the years. The chart summarizes the title changes since 1865.

(b) Citation and index access to the Law Reports

These reports are semi-official, and when a case has been reported in the *Law Reports* and in another series of reports, citation to both series should be made. The method of citing cases in the *Law Reports* has changed in the following manner:

(i) From 1865 to the court change in 1875, citation included the abbreviation for the *Law Reports. Queen's Bench* cases were cited, for example, as L.R. 7 Q.B.

(ii) From 1875 to 1890, individual volume numbers were used as well as the abbreviation for division. *Queen's Bench Division* cases were cited, for example, as 7 Q.B.D.

(iii) After 1890 the sequence of volume numbering did not carry over from year to year, but rather each volume had the year and volume within the year. *Queen's Bench Division* cases are now cited, for example, as [1890] 1 Q.B.

Index access is provided through the cumulative consolidated indexes published every ten years with updating by cumulative "red" indexes published annually and quarterly cumulative indexes (pink in colour) which cumulate from the last cumulative "red" index. The index includes a "Subject Matter Index", "Table of Cases", "Table of Statutes Judicially Considered", and "Table of Cases Judicially Considered" (listing cases in the *Law Reports* that cite earlier cases from reported source).

The Law Reports (1865 to date)

1865	1875	1880	1901	1952	1970	1972
Chancery Appeal Cases *Equity Cases*	*Chancery Division*				(some Probate matters included)	
Queen's Bench Cases *Common Pleas Cases* *Exchequer Cases* *Crown Cases Reserved*	*Queen's Bench Division* *Common Pleas Division* *Exchequer Division*	*Queen's Bench Division*	*King's Bench Division*	*Queen's Bench Division*	(includes Admiralty)	
Probate & Divorce Cases *Admiralty & Ecclesiastical Cases*	*Probate, Divorce & Admiralty Division*				*Probate/Family Division*	
Privy Council Appeals *English & Irish Appeals* *Scottish & Divorce Appeals*	*Appeal Cases*					

3. Other general law reports (1800s to date)

(a) Summary of other reports (1800s to date)

See accompanying chart.

In addition to the *Law Reports,* other general law reports series appeared in the 1800s. Some have continued with others merging into other titles or ceasing publication. The chart summarizes the time span covered by these reports.

(b) Arrangement of and index access to other reports

(i) *All England Law Reports Reprint* in 36 volumes selectively reports older cases, while *All England Law Reports* covers current cases. The *All England Law Reports Reprint Extension* is discussed in the Chapter 15 section on Australian law reports. The *All England Law Reports* is a selective reporting service; some reported cases are not included.

Index access to *All England Law Reports* is through the "Consolidated Tables and Index" which cover 1936 to a recent year with supplementation by the annual "Tables and Index". Further supplementation is included in the quarterly "Cumulative Current Tables and Index" (year to date). These indexes include subject matter index, tables of cases, statutes judicially considered sections and cases judicially considered sections (citing cases in the All E.R.'s that treat earlier cases from any law report). Included in subscriptions is the noter-up service which supplies perforated sheets listing subsequent citing cases. The sheets can be applied to the All E.R. page containing the cited case (a cases judicially considered service). The separate "Canadian Annotations to the Consolidated Tables and Index" is a listing of cases reported in the All E.R.'s, which have been considered in cases reported in various series of Canadian law reports.

In 1982, the *All E.R. Annual Review* service commenced in order to provide an annual collection of articles offering case comments on the cases reported in that year's All E.R. reports volumes plus other series.

All E.R.'s are available on CD-ROM from Butterworths.

(ii) *Law Journal Reports* included nine volumes in the Old Series and 118 volumes in the new series. In 1949, the case reports featured in this publication merged with the *All England Law Reports.*

Locating cases in this series can be confusing because cases were grouped according to court, and page numbering for the various courts were kept separate. A single numbered volume may contain cases from several courts, and each court division of the book commences with page 1 (*e.g.*, more than one page 25 within the volume). If cases for a reporting period could not be included in one volume, the divisions for the various courts were spread among several books, each of which had the same volume number (*e.g.*, three books labeled volume 107).

(iii) *Law Times Reports* were published in 177 volumes, superseded the *Law Times Old Series* in 1860, and merged with the *All England Law Reports* in 1948.

Other Reports (1800s to date)

1558	1823	1831	1843	1860	1865	1884	1936	1948	1952
All England Law Reports Reprint							*All England Law Reports*		
	Law Journal Reports (old series)	*Law Journal Reports* (new series)						(merge with All E.R)	
			Law Times (old series)	*Law Times Reports*				(merge with All E.R)	
						Times Law Reports			
					Weekly Notes				*Weekly Law Reports*

(iv) *Times Law Reports,* in 68 volumes (1884-1952), derived its title from the publisher, *The Times* of London. *The Times* newspaper continued to publish law reports in newspaper format, and in 1982, the law reports series resumed. The law report is printed by Professional Books Ltd. in a looseleaf binder with monthly releases and indexes on an issue, quarterly, and annual consolidated basis.

(v) *Weekly Notes,* published in 87 volumes from 1866 to 1952, included many cases later reported in the *Law Reports.*

(vi) *Weekly Law Reports,* 1953 to date, is published by the Incorporated Council of Law Reporting which is responsible for the *Law Reports.* Weekly loose parts are cumulated into three bound volumes per year, with volume 1 containing cases not published in the *Law Reports* and volumes 2 and 3 containing cases that later were reported in the *Law Reports.* "JUSTIS Weekly Law" CD-ROM available from Micromedia Ltd. (Toronto) includes *Weekly Law Reports* from 1971.

4. Subject reports (1800s to date)

(a) Criminal law subject reports

(i) *Cox's Criminal Cases,* 1843 to 1941, in 31 volumes.
(ii) *Criminal Appeal Reports,* 1908 to date.
(iii) *Criminal Appeal Reports (Sentencing),* 1979 to date.
(iv) *Criminal Law Review,* 1954 to date, is a journal containing some digests of cases that remain unreported.
(v) *Justice of the Peace Reports* have undergone a number of title changes since they first appeared in 1837. The publication continues as a review entitled *Justice of the Peace* with its supplement, the *Justice of the Peace Weekly Law Digest.*

(b) Business law

Business law is covered in a variety of special reports including *Lloyd's Law Reports,* 1919 to date; and *Tax Cases,* 1975 to date, which includes some Canadian cases. *Butterworth Company Law Cases* and *Simon's Taxes* receive comments in the *All E.R. Annual Review.*

C. DIGESTS AND INDEXES

1. The Digest (formerly the English and Empire Digest)

(a) Format

The most complete digest of English case law is *The Digest,* which gives coverage back into the *Nominate Reports* and includes digests of Scottish, Irish, and Commonwealth cases. The former title, *English and Empire Digest,* was changed in 1981 to *The Digest: Annotated British, Commonwealth, and European Cases* to reflect the impact on English Law of England's participation in the European Economic Community. The case digests are arranged under topic and subtopic, with each case digest having its own paragraph number. The function of a case citator is fulfilled by the annotations that follow the case digest paragraphs and list later cases citing the digested case. Under each subsection, the English cases are grouped before the Scottish, Irish, and Commonwealth cases, with each grouping having its own sequence of digest paragraph numbers. There are cross-references from the sections and subsections to narrative discussion in the encyclopedia, *Halsbury's Laws of England.*

(b) Instructions for use

The methods of research in *The Digest* are the "legal topic" approach of examining the listing of sections and subsections, the "table of cases" method ("Consolidated Table of Cases" published in three volumes in 1996), and the "key word search" approach in general index ("Index" published in two volumes in 1996).

The method of updating research in the main volumes as accessed by the Index is to check the index in the annual Cumulative Supplement. The annual Cumulative Supplement listing arranged by digest paragraph number will indicate whether there are later cases which have judicially considered the case from the main-volume paragraph. It will also indicate whether there are new cases on the point of law that may be found in the annual Cumulative Supplement. Cases from the annual Cumulative Supplement will eventually be placed into either continuation volumes or in reissues of the main volumes. Update by consulting individual issues of *The Digest Quarterly Survey* which records cases appearing after publication of the annual Cumulative Supplement. The *Quarterly Survey*'s format is similar to the annual Cumulative Supplement.

Reissue of volumes is a continuing process. Until the early 1990s, old volumes with blue-band spine labels were being replaced by green-band reissue volumes. All of the volumes now have green-bands, but some of the original reissue volumes are now being replaced by second reissue volumes. A case digest may have had the number 2984 in an older reissue volume, but when the case appears in a newer second reissue volume, it likely will have a new number. Cross-references from the older, original reissue volumes will still cite to digest 2984. Each second reissue volume has a Reference Adapter table listing a case's number (*e.g.*, 2984) in the older reissue volume with a cross-cite to the digest's new number in the new second reissue volume.

2. Indexes to the Law Reports and All England Law Reports

(a) Law Reports indexes

(i) *Law Reports: Digests* provides subject arrangement of digests of cases from 1865 to 1949.

(ii) *Consolidated Index* has volumes covering increments of ten years. These indexes contain a "Subject Matter Index", "Cases Judicially Considered", and "Statutes Judicially Considered". The coverage now extends to special subject law reports and the *All England Law Reports* in addition to the *Law Reports.*
(iii) The red index annually cumulates from the last *Consolidated Index.*
(iv) The pink quarterly index updates from the red index.
(v) For further update of cases, the index of each recent issue of *Weekly Law Reports* should be researched.
(vi) Check with Micromedia Ltd (Toronto) about the JUSTIS Weekly Law CD-ROM which includes the *Law Reports* Index from 1981.

(b) All England Law Reports indexes

(i) *All England Law Reports Reprint: Index and Tables of Cases, 1558-1935.*
(ii) *All England Law Reports: Consolidated Tables and Index*, 1936- (a recent year):
 (A) Vol. 1: "Cases Reported and Considered", "Practice Directions & Notes", "Statutes Considered", and "Words and Phrases Considered".
 (B) Vols. 2 and 3: "Subject Index".
(iii) *All England Law Reports: Canadian Annotations to the Consolidated Tables and Index, 1936-1976. Canadian Annotations, 1977- (a recent year)*
(iv) *Cumulative Current Tables and Index.*

3. Current Law

(a) Format

This detailed indexing and digesting publication covers the period from the 1940s to date, and includes case digests, cases judicially considered, and statutes judicially considered. *Current Law* appears as a monthly issue with the annual cumulations being titled *Current Law Year Book.* After an increment of several years, the year books are cumulated into the *Current Law Consolidation.*

The "Cases Judically Considered" and "Statutes Judicially Considered" sections of *Current Law are* cumulated into separate titles.

(b) Research approaches

Subject access is through the *Cumulative Index* (for year to date) in the latest *Current Law* monthly issue followed by search in the "Cumulative Index" of the latest *Year Book* (1947 to past year). The indexes cite to the digest of the case, and the digests in the *Year Books* have citations to the cases. The current cumulations of the various elements of the *Current Law* series are:

(i) *Current Law* monthly issue to update the various elements which have been cumulated into separate bound volumes listed below.
(ii) *Current Law Year Book* which has a cumulative index covering the period since 1947. The digests of cases may be located in recent individual *Year Books* or in *Current Law Consolidations* which separately cover increments for five years (1951, 1956, 1961 ...).
(iii) *Current Law Legislation Citator:* (1947-1971), (1972-1988), (1989-1995), (1996-); This subtitle has always contained the element "Statute Citator" and in 1993 added the element "Statutory Instrument Citator".
(iv) *Current Law Case Citator* (1947-1976), (1977-1988), (1989-1995), (1996-).

Check with Carswell about Sweet and Maxwell's CD-ROM collection which includes *Current Law Year Books,* 1981-; *Current Law Case Citator*, 1989-, and *Current Law Legislation Citator*, 1989-.

4. Mew's Digest of English Case Law

This publication digested selected cases. Updating supplements ceased in 1970.

5. Electronic sources for English case law

The LEXIS-NEXIS online databases are grouped into libraries, each of which has one or more files (databases). The English General Library, ENGGEN, has the CASES files which include reported cases from the All E.R.'s and about 50 other titles (1936 to-date generally, but tax cases from 1875), and unreported cases from 1980 to-date. In the library, UK, the ENGGEN cases are duplicated in the file ENGCAS, and additionally, there are Scottish cases (SCOCAS file) and cases from Northern Ireland (NIRCAS file). In the U.K. Library, the ALLCAS file searches the combined file of all United Kingdom cases.

House of Lords judgments since November 14, 1996, are available through the Internet:

(www.parliament.the-stationery-office.co.uk/pa/ld1996.97/ldjudgmt/ldjudgmt.htm).

QL System Ltd.'s QUICKLAW offers the following English case law: House of Lords judgments (1986-); Judicial Committee (Privy Council) judgments (1987-); New Law Online Reports (1995-); English Newspaper Law Reports (*e.g.*, Times Newspaper Law Reports) (1991-). QL also offers Scotland Judgments, 1995-.

Check the Sweet & Maxwell Publishers Internet site for Internet delivery of House of Lords, Court of Appeals, and High Court (Q.B. Division) decisions:

(www.smlawpub.co.uk).

D. STATUTES AND STATUTORY INSTRUMENTS

1. Summary of statutes

English statutes extend back to the 13th century. Various publications of English statutes are outlined on the time line below:

Year	*Statutes at Large*	*Statutes of the Realm (official)*	*Acts and Ordinances of the Interregnum*	*Statutes Revised*
1215	XX			
	XX			
1235	XX	XX		
	XX	XX		
	XX	XX		
	XX	XX		
1642	XX	XX	XX	
	XX	XX	XX	
1660	XX	XX	XX	
	XX	XX		
1713	XX	XX		
	XX			
	XX	*Public General*		
	XX	*Acts &*		
	XX	*Measures*		
	XX	*(official)*		
1831	XX	XX		
	XX	XX		
1865	XX	XX		
		XX		
	Law Reports	XX		
	-Statutes	XX		
1870	XX	XX		
	XX	XX		
1878	XX	XX		XX
	XX	XX		1st ed. (Acts
	XX	XX		from 1235-1878)
1920	XX	XX		XX
	XX	XX		2nd. ed.
	XX	XX		(1235-1920)
1950	XX	XX		XX
		XX		3rd. ed.
		XX		(1235-1950)
Statutes		XX	*Halsbury's*	*Statutes in*
Currently		XX	*Statutes of*	*Force: Official*
in Force		XX	*England*	*Revised Edition*
are:		*to date*	*4th edition*	*(looseleaf)*

2. Older statutes

(a) *Statutes of the Realm: 1235-1713.* By the *Interpretation Act* of 1889, this collection of statutes is considered official, and subsequent legislation cites earlier statutes in this series. Ten volumes contain all of the statutes passed during this time period, and there is a subject index volume and a chronological listings volume. This set does not include Acts or Ordinances from the Interregnum.

(b) *Acts and Ordinances of the Interregnum (1642-1660).* These statutes are reproduced in two volumes, with the third volume being a chronological listing of statutes, subject index, and index of names-places-things (about which legislation was passed).

(c) *Statutes at Large.* With the official *Statutes of the Realm* ending in 1713, *Statutes at Large* were published in several series by private publishers until 1801, when official printing was commenced by His Majesty's Stationery Office. Private publications included several editions of *Ruffhead's Statutes at Large* and *Pickering's Statutes at Large.*

3. Modern statutes

(a) The *Statutes Revised* (three editions) and *Statutes in Force: Official Revised Edition.* Statutes in force as of fixed dates were the basis of publication of three editions of the *Statutes Revised* for the years 1878, 1920, and 1950. Because the printings included only those statutes in force, repealed Acts and repealed sections were excluded. There is no cumulative index for this set, but Her Majesty's Stationery Office publishes annual reference works entitled *Index to the Statutes in Force* and the *Chronological Table of Statutes* (from 1235 to date).

- *Statutes in Force: Official Revised Edition* is published in 90 looseleaf binders. The looseleaf format allows it to be kept current, showing only those statutes in force. Each subject is updated by an *Annual Cumulative Supplement* listing amendments or repeal of Acts within the group. This supplement includes Acts in other subject groupings which amend the Acts in the particular subject grouping being researched. If there are substantial amendments, the Act will be reissued.

(b) *Halsbury's Statutes of England and Wales* (4th ed.)
Butterworths' 50 volume hardbound set arranges current statutes in a subject title scheme similar to the arrangement of *Halsbury's Laws of England* encyclopedia. Notes accompanying the statute wording include judicial interpretation and cross-references to other statutes.

Access is through the annual cumulative "Tables of Statutes and General Index" volume. Each volume contains both an alphabetical and a chronological list of statutes, as well as tables of cases, tables of statutory instruments, and an index.

Updating includes:

(i) Reissue volumes. The 50 volume set was reissued during the 1990s.
(ii) Current statutes service (looseleaf). These binders contain new Acts which are awaiting reprinting as part of the "reissue" hardbound main volumes.
(iii) Cumulative Supplement (annual volume). This updates the 50 main volumes and the current statutes service binders by reporting new Acts, subordinate legislation, and case notes.
(iv) "Is It in Force?" This is a guide to the commencement of statutes passed over the last 25 years.
(v) Noter-up Service (looseleaf). This is a quarterly update to the above-mentioned materials.

(c) Law Reports-Statutes
Features similar to indexes for Public General Acts and Measures — see (d) below.
(d) Public General Acts and Measures
These annual volumes include alphabetic listings of and an index to the statutes passed during the year. They also have tables tracing the derivations of the Consolidation Acts for the year and the destinations of the enactments consolidated and tables showing the effect of the year's legislation in repealing or amending prior legislation. There is no cumulative index.
(e) Current Law Statutes Annotated
As new statutes are enacted throughout the year, releases containing the statutes and annotations are published for the looseleaf binder service. Bound volumes are issued at the year end.

4. Chronological Table of the Statutes

These two volumes are published annually by Her Majesty's Stationery Office. They provide a chronological listing of all public general Acts made since 1235, with citation to amendments and repeals.

5. Statutory instruments

Statutory instruments, a term encompassing subordinate legislation, may be accessed by government and unofficial publications.

(a) Government publication sources, in reverse chronological order, are:

(i) *Daily List of Government Publications.*
(ii) *List of Statutory Instruments* issued monthly and annually.
(iii) *Statutory Instruments* bound volumes' indexes.

(iv) *Index to Government Orders* which has a "Table of Statutes" cross-referencing from the enabling statute titles to subject headings.
(v) *Statutory Rules and Orders and Statutory Instruments* (Revised 3rd ed.) Published in 1949.

(b) Private publishers' sources include:
(i) *Halsbury's Statutory Instruments*
Butterworths' 22 volume hardbound set arranges statutory instruments for England and Wales in a subject title scheme similar to the arrangement of *Halsbury's Laws of England* encyclopedia. This is a companion set to the *Halsbury's Statutes of England and Wales,* 4th edition. The 13,500 statutory instruments are covered by full text, by summary, or by notation.

Access is through the "Annual Consolidated Index" which includes an alphabetical list of instruments. Each volume has an index, and each "Monthly Survey" includes an index.

Updating includes:

(a) Reissue Volumes
(b) "Annual Cumulative Supplement" volume updates the main volumes.
(c) Main Service Binder: chronological list of instruments and volumes in which they are printed; table of enabling statutes; list of commencement and Appointed Day Orders.
(d) Additional Texts Binder: selected, recent statutory instruments in full text.
(e) The Monthly Survey: summaries of new instruments and updating index.

(ii) Other current updating sources are *Current Law* and the "Monthly Reviews" in *Halsbury's Laws of England* (4th ed.).
(iii) Electronic sources: Check with Micromedia Ltd. (Toronto) about "SI-CD", statutory instruments on CD-ROM.

6. Court rules

The latest edition of the *Supreme Court Practice,* known as the "White Book", publishes court rules and cases considering the rules. The case citator function is an important source of persuasive authority for Canadian researchers when Canadian court rules are derived from the wording of the English rules. "Supreme Court Practice Digital Edition" CD-ROM is available through Carswell.

7. Electronic sources for English legislation

The LEXIS-NEXIS library, ENGGEN, has the file STAT (current Public and General Acts of England and Wales, which include all Acts covered by *Halsburys Statutes of England and Wales,* 1267 to date), the file SI (Statutory Instruments, 1861 to date), and the file STATIS (combination of STAT and SI files).

E. CITATORS

1. Case citators

(a) *The Digest* performs the function of a case citator through its annotations listed under case digests in the main work. Later cases may be found by tracing the digested case's paragraph number to the latest cumulative supplement.

(b) The *All England Law Reports: Consolidated Tables and Index* 1936 - (a recent year) contains a listing of cases judicially considered, and updating indexes include the same tables.

(c) *Current Law Case Citator 1947-1976. Current Law Citator 19—: Cases in 1977—, Statutes in 1972— is* paperbound and is updated in the individual issues of *Current Law.*

2. Statute citators

(a) *Halsbury's Statutes of England* performs a statute citator function by the citing of cases considering the statutes. The publication's "Table of Cases" indicates location of digests of those citing cases in *The Digest* (formerly *English and Empire Digest).*

(b) *All England Law Reports: Consolidated Tables and Index 1936-19—* has a "Statutes Judicially Considered" table. This is updated in subsequent indexes for All E.R.

(c) *Current Law Statute Citator 1947-1971. Current Law Citator 19—: Cases In 1977—, Statutes in 1972—* is paperbound and is updated in the individual issues of *Current Law.* Cited statutes date back to 1235, but citing cases are from 1947 to date.

F. LEGAL ENCYCLOPEDIAS

Halsbury's Laws of England is the English legal encyclopedia, and Butterworths now has completed the process of publishing its fourth edition. Because earlier English law formed such a foundation for Canadian law, the third edition and even the second edition are read by Canadian researchers for a general narrative description of legal topics. The third edition had volumes cross-referencing to Canadian case law, but the fourth edition does not have this feature.

Butterworths' *Laws of Scotland* has been published in 25 volumes and has looseleaf updating services.

1. Halsbury's Laws of England (3rd Edition)

This edition has volumes entitled *Canadian Converters* for each five volumes of the main work. The *Converters* serve to footnote the main text with Canadian law. Since the *Converters* were reissued a number of times, the researcher should note the date of the *Converters* accompanying the set being researched.

Access is by a two-volume *General Index,* with each main volume containing a more detailed subject index.

2. Halsbury's Laws of England (4th Edition)

Butterworths' 58 volume hardbound set narrates the law of England and Wales derived from current statutes, statutory instruments, case law, codes of practice, conventions, and command papers. The set is divided into a subject title scheme which is similar to the schemes now used in *Halsbury's Statutes of England* (4th) and *Halsbury's Statutory Instruments.* There is extensive footnoting and cross-referencing within the set. Volumes 51 and 52 cover the law and institutions of the European Communities. Other volumes consist of a Consolidated Table of Statutes and Statutory Instruments, a Consolidated Table of Cases, and a two-volume Consolidated Index.

In addition to the Consolidated Index volumes, access is through:

(a) Reissue volumes
(b) "Cumulative Supplement" (annual plus the monthly "Cumulative Noter-Up" to the narrative text)
(c) "Current Service" (two looseleaf binders) which features the paper-bound "Monthly Review": case law summaries from over 70 law report series (U.K., European Communities, and the Commonwealth), summaries of new statutes, Progress of Bills, summaries of statutory instruments, Practice Directions, and reference to journal articles.
(d) "Annual Abridgment" volume is a consolidation of the twelve "Monthly Reviews". It is separate from but cross-referenced to the main volumes and "Cumulative Supplement".

The "Monthly Review" is the basis for the LEXIS-NEXIS online "United Kingdom Current Awareness Law Library" (UKCURR).

G. LEGAL PERIODICALS

A variety of legal periodicals are published in England including law school reviews (*e.g., Cambridge Law Journal),* bar association and law society periodicals (*e.g., Law Society Gazette),* and special journals (*e.g., Criminal Law Review).*

Current Law includes a listing of periodical articles under each subject heading in its monthly issues. The *Current Law Year Books* contain a listing of periodical articles for the year in a separate section. The "Annual Abridgment" for *Halsbury's 4th edition* lists periodical articles by subject for the year. The *Index to Legal Periodicals* and *Current Law Index* cover a large selection of English legal periodicals. Commencing in 1986, the *Legal Journals Index* covers over 250 journals from Great Britain.

Electronic sources include LEXIS-NEXIS online "United Kingdom Law Journal Library" (UKJNL), which has about five journals from the 1980s to date.

H. TEXTBOOKS AND REFERENCE MATERIAL

1. Textbooks

English textbooks were considered a basic part of even a small Canadian law library until recent years, when subject-area gaps in Canadian textbook publishing began to close. While English texts are still important comprehensive sources some Canadian law libraries do not purchase each new edition of English texts for several reasons: Canadian texts cite landmark English cases; the recent and rapid increase in the Canadian cost of English texts; and some new editions of text have been updated to cover recent English legislation.

The largest English textbook publishers have Canadian sales agents to distribute advertising literature - *e.g.*, Butterworths Canada for Butterworths U.K., and Carswell for Sweet & Maxwell. The addresses of other English law publishers may be obtained from a law librarian, or a law firm may peruse the recent acquisitions list of titles acquired by the nearest court house or law school library.

2. Forms and precedents sets

The *Encyclopedia of Forms and Precedents* (4th ed.), in approximately 42 volumes, provides a comprehensive set of forms that can be adapted to the Canadian scene. It is kept current by a looseleaf binder service and has a general index volume. The multi-volume *Atkin's Encyclopedia of Court Forms in Civil Proceedings* and *Archbold's Pleading, Evidence, and Practice in Criminal Cases* contain precedents that may be adapted to Canadian use.

3. Dictionaries, directories, and words and phrases

English dictionaries and words and phrases publications should be treated together as noted below:

(a) *Jowitt's Dictionary of English Law* is a two-volume legal dictionary which issues bound supplements.

(b) *Stroud's Judicial Dictionary of Words and Phrases,* in six volumes, is comprehensive enough to be considered a words and phrases publication. It has bound supplements. There are selected Canadian entries.
(c) *Words and Phrases Legally Defined* (3d ed.), in five volumes, has bound supplements. Digest of English cases defining the words are listed first, but selected digests from other jurisdictions including Canada are listed by country.
(d) The "General Indexes" to *Halsbury's Laws of England* (3rd and 4th editions) have a "Word and phrases" listing citing the main volumes.

Directories listing English barristers and solicitors include the *Martindale-Hubbell Law Directory, Kime's International Law Directory,* and Waterlow's *The Solicitors' & Barristers' Directory and Diary.*

I. ONLINE DATABASES

LEXIS-NEXIS databases (files) are often grouped into libraries to yield a broader search from a query. United Kingdom case law is duplicated in four large libraries: "English General Library" (ENGGEN); the "United Kingdom Library" (UK); "International Law Library" (INTLAW); and "Commonwealth Cases Library" (COMCAS). INTLAW covers United Kingdom case law, cases from other Commonwealth countries including Canada, country analysis reports (non-case information), treaties, and publications. COMCAS is a library within the larger grouping in the "United Kingdom & Commonwealth Legal Libraries" made available by Butterworths (Telepublishing) Ltd.

COMCAS includes files from: England, Scotland, Northern Ireland (discussed below); Ireland, Australia and New Zealand (discussed in Chapter 15). The COMCAS library includes the following files:

1. ENGCAS (England)

(a) Reported cases (1936 to date) from more than 50 law report series (*e.g., All E.R., Lloyd's Law Reports, Butterworths Company Law Cases, Weekly Law Reports.*
(b) Unreported cases (1985 to date) from more than 50 sources which are different than the reported cases sources (*e.g., Current Law, Financial Times, Lloyd's Maritime Law Newsletter, The Times).*

2. SCOCAS (Scotland)

(a) Reported cases from 1950 in three law reports (*e.g., Scots Law Times).*
(b) Unreported cases from 1982 in several sources.

3. NIRCAS (Northern Ireland)

Northern Ireland Law Reports from 1945 and unreported cases from 1984.

UKTAX is the United Kingdom tax library, and EURCOM is the European Communities Library. Above sections of this chapter have noted the contents of the ENGGEN Library legislative files (STAT and SI); the "United Kingdom Current Law Library" (UKCURR, based upon *Halsburys Laws of England*'s "Monthly Review"); and the "United Kingdom Law Journal Library" (UKJNL).

QL System Ltd.'s QUICKLAW offers the following English case law: House of Lords judgments (1986-); Judicial Committee (Privy Council) judgments (1987-); New Law Online Reports (1995-); English Newspaper Law Reports (*e.g.*, Times Newspaper Law Reports)(1991-). QL also offers Scotland Judgments (1995-).

Chapter 14

Researching American Law

As is the case with Canadian common law, American law is largely rooted in English law. One of the most divergent areas between Canadian and American law had been constitutional law. Because of the passage of the *Canadian Charter of Rights and Freedoms,* which has some similarities in phrasing to the American *Bill of Rights,* the body of American case law interpreting the American *Bill of Rights* may be examined in Canada to see whether it offers persuasive authority. This research was of most importance in the mid-1980s when the body of Canadian case law on the Charter was first building.

The large volume of reported American cases has always been a basis for research in narrow areas of law or in unusual fact situations that have not been previously litigated in Canada. Such narrow areas, as well as *Bill of Rights* interpretations, are conducive to computerized research, and American legal computer databases are available in Canada.

A. LEGISLATIVE AND JUDICIAL STRUCTURES

1. Federal and state legislative structures

Congress (the federal legislature) consists of the House of Representatives and the Senate. The President of the United States is not an elected member of Congress, and the heads of federal departments are political appointees rather than elected members of Congress. Congress has authority to enact legislation as directed by the *Constitution* of the United States. It is a written constitution, consisting of the basic document and more than 20 amendments, the first 10 of which are known as the *Bill of Rights.*

The division of powers between the federal government and the states results in a division of responsibilities different from that in Canada. State legislatures are authorized to enact legislation according to individual, written state constitutions. All states but one have bicameral legislatures, and the governor of each state is an elected official but not an elected member of the legislature. Powers not specifically granted to the federal government under the United States *Constitution* fall within the jurisdiction of the states.

2. Federal and state court structures

The two types of courts, federal courts and state courts, are more separate structures than are the federal and provincial court systems in Canada. Both court systems have trial and appellate levels.

Each state has trial courts for both the federal structure and the state structure.

State trial courts usually have general jurisdiction at the county level and are often referred to as Superior Courts. One-third of the states have an intermediate tier of courts with such a court designated Court of Appeals. In all states but New York, the highest court is the state Supreme Court. Some matters may be appealed from a state Supreme Court to the United States Supreme Court, but a state matter such as the interpretation of that state's constitution would be decided by the highest state court.

The federal trial court, known as the District Court, has special jurisdiction in accordance with the *United States Code,* the American statute revision. An example of the special jurisdiction of the District Court would be a matter involving more than a certain dollar amount in a dispute between residents of different states. The District Court might apply federal law or state law to a situation. The intermediate appellate level federal court is the Federal Court of Appeals, the popular name being Circuit Court. The Federal Court of Appeals is divided into 11 separate circuits, and if a matter has not reached the United States Supreme Court, different circuits may hold differently on the same subject matter. The ultimate appeal is to the United States Supreme Court.

B. LAW REPORTS

1. Law reports covering federal courts

(a) Supreme Court

United States Supreme Court cases are reported in three sources: the official government publication entitled *United States Reports* (abbreviated U.S.), plus two privately published reports titled *Supreme Court Reporter* (abbreviated S. Ct.), and *United States Supreme Court Reports (Lawyers' Edition)* (abbreviated L. Ed.).

(i) *United States Reports* publishes the full text of all cases from the time of the beginning of the court. The first 90 volumes are often cited by the name of the reporter, *e.g.*, Dallas (abbreviated Dall.).

(ii) *United States Supreme Court Reports (Lawyers' Edition)* covers all cases back to the time of the beginning of the court in two series of reports. Counsels' factums are summarized, and articles often appear as annotations to the reports.

(iii) *Supreme Court Reporter* commences reporting cases at volume 106 of the official *United States Reports.* This law report forms part of West Publishing Company's National Reporter System, and therefore can be accessed through the digests to the National Reporter System.

(iv) Rapid reporting services for the United States Supreme Court are in the two weekly publications entitled *United States Law Week* and *CCH U.S. Supreme Court Bulletin.*

(b) Federal Court of Appeals

The judgments of the Federal Court of Appeals, the intermediate appellate level, are published in the *Federal Reporter* 2d, which is part of the National Reporter System. This is the only current reporter for federal appellate cases. It commenced in 1879 and included District Court judgments until 1932. Selected federal trial court cases (District Court) are reported in the *Federal Supplement* which is also part of the National Reporter System. This is the only current reporter of federal trial court cases, and it commenced in 1932. *Federal Cases* reprinted all available United States Circuit and District Court decisions from 1789 to 1879. This reprint arranges cases alphabetically by style of cause.

2. Law reports covering state courts

(a) Generally

State courts' judgments are reported in official state reports series and in the unofficial National Reporter System published by West Publishing Company. Official government report titles are usually composed of the name of the state followed by the term "reports", *e.g.*, *South Dakota Reports.* The only index access to these reports is by the individual index included with each reports series. More than one-third of the states abandoned publication of official reports to rely upon the coverage of the National Reporter System.

(b) The National Reporter System

The National Reporter System covers all 50 states in series of reports which have titles based upon geographical area. The National Reporter System began in the late 1800s, and the titles of the report series reflect the volume of cases from the various geographic regions in the late 1800s. The reports' names and geographic coverage are:

Title & Abbreviation	*Coverage* (State abbreviations)
Atlantic Reporter (A.) 1885-	Me., N.H., Vt., R.I., Ct., N.J., Pa., Md., De., and Washington D.C.
Pacific Reporter (P.) 1883-	Ak., Az., Ca., Co., Hi., Id., Ks., Mt., Nv., N.M., Ok., Or., Ut., Wa., and Wy.
North Eastern Reporter (N.E.) 1885-	N.Y., Ma, Oh., In., and Il.
North Western Reporter (N.W.) 1879-	Mi., Mn., Wi., N.D., S.D., Ne., and Ia.
South Eastern Reporter (S.E.) 1887-	Va., W.V., N.C., S.C., and Ga.

South Western Reporter (S.W.) 1886-	Tx., Ar., Tn., Mo., and Ky.
Southern Reporter (S.) 1887-	Fl., Al., Ms., and La.

In addition to the geographical reporters, three of the most populous states have their own reporters: *California Reporter, Illinois Decisions,* and *New York Supplement.*

3. American Law Reports (A.L.R.)

American Law Reports (abbreviated A.L.R.), is infrequently used as a source of full text judgments because of the very few cases that it reports in full. The value of this several-hundred-volume series is the often-lengthy annotations, which footnote many additional cases. The reported case serves as an illustration of the main theme of the annotation. The purpose is to treat narrow topics in article form, since these narrow topics are not generally the subject of law review articles or encyclopedia articles. A.L.R. has been published in several series (5th series starting in 1992), and since the appearance of A.L.R. Federal, A.L.R. now primarily covers state case law.

Access to the A.L.R. system is provided by the six-volume A.L.R. Index which covers A.L.R. 2d to 5th series, A.L.R. Federal and the annotations in *U.S. Supreme Court Reports (Lawyers' Edition, 2d series).* An upating index is the annually issued A.L.R. Quick Index. Updates with more case digests relating to the annotation articles are located in the paper pocket parts issued annually and slipped inside the back cover of each A.L.R. volume. Transferring research to other sources is facilitated by a paperback volume titled: *Electronic Search Queries and West Digest Key Numbers for Annotations in ALR 4th.*

An electronic source for the A.L.R. series is the LEXIS-NEXIS "American Law Reports Library" (access code ALR). A.L.R. Federal is available on CD-ROM from Carswell.

4. Special subject reports

Special subject reports accessed by digests to the National Reporter System include: *Federal Rules Decisions* (1940-) covering judgments of the District Courts; and West's *Bankruptcy Reporter* (1979-) covering bankruptcy decisions from United States Bankruptcy Courts and other federal courts. There are far more special subject law reports titles in Canada than in the U.S.

5. Electronic sources for law reports

The LEXIS-NEXIS MEGA Library is a one-stop search of all available federal and state case law, and the query may be restricted to searches from 1944 to date, within the past year, or by geographic subdivisions. The WESTLAW system includes the following database collection identifiers for federal and state cases: ALLCASES, 1945 to date; ALLCASES-OLD, 1789-1944; and various geographic subdivisions.

C. DIGESTS

1. American Digest System's similarity to Maritime Law Book's System

The digest system that provides access to almost all case law appearing in American law reports is West Publishing Company's American Digest System, which provides access to the National Reporter System. The indexing and digesting scheme of Maritime Law Book's "Key Word Index" and "Topical Index" Number System is modeled after West's "Key Number" scheme, used in the American Digest System. The chart below shows the terminology used for elements of the digesting scheme of the two publishers:

Maritime Law Book's Indexing and Digest Scheme	West Publishing's Keynumber System
— Key Word Index to topics	— Descriptive word index
— Topical Index with topic numbers	— General Digest, Decennial Digest, or Centennial Digest with keynumbers
— Index to Cases Reported and Case Comments	
— Index to Cases Noticed	— Table of Cases
— Index to Statutes Noticed	— These four functions are fulfilled by other American legal reference publications
— Words and Phrases Noticed	
— Authors and Works Noticed	

2. Instructions for use: American Digest System

The American Digest System covers all of the cases reported in the various reports comprised in the National Reporter System, but the American Digest System is subdivided into three series: *Centennial Digest* (digest of reported American cases to 1896), *Decennial Digest* (individual series covering increments of ten or five years beginning with 1896-1906; 1906-1916; ..., 1966-1976; 1976-1981; 1981-1986; 1986-1991; 1991-1996), and the *General Digest* (9th series, 1996-), which serves as an update for the last time increment covered by the *Decennial Digest.*

(a) Key word search approach

The key word search approach to research may be initiated by turning to the "Descriptive Word Indexes" of the American Digest System.

(i) The first step is to search for a narrow key word in the two-volume "Descriptive Word Index" to the latest *Decennial Digest.* The key words can be very narrow in scope, and search for broader terms may be employed only if necessary. When an appropriate key word has been found, the digest topic and key number appear in the same manner as the topic and topic number appear in Maritime's Key Word Index to Topics — *e.g.*, the entry in Maritime's digest may be "family law, custody, considerations, capacity of parents — FAMILY LAW 1889", while the West System entry may be "parent and child, custody and control of child, competency ... of parent — PARENT AND CHILD 2.(3.3)".

(ii) The next step is to turn to the many volumes of the *Decennial Digest* and locate the volume containing the topic. There are more than 400 major topics, and the key numbers identify the subtopics. When the subtopic of key number is located under a major topic, there may be several pages of digests listed. The digests are arranged alphabetically by jurisdiction, and each one must be read until the digest, which fits the briefer description given in the "Descriptive Word Index", is found. This is the same method of search employed in the Maritime Law Book scheme; however, the great volume of cases can make this a time consuming task.

(iii) The citation to the case appears with the digest (*e.g.*, 245 P.2d 1), and the researcher may read the full judgment as it is reported in one of the law report series of the National Reporter System.

(iv) To find additional cases, the researcher may either take key words or topics with key numbers found in the latest *Decennial Digest* to the *General Digest* to update the search. The key word entries in the cumulative "Descriptive Word Indexes" for increments of approximately ten volumes of the *General Digest* will again refer to a topic and key number.

These "Descriptive Word Index" volumes do not inform as to which *General Digest* volume contains the case digest, so that the researcher must read through the digests under each topic and key number in each *General Digest* volume until the appropriate case digest is located. Again, this is a time-consuming task which cannot be avoided unless a computer search is made.

(v) The search may continue back through the *Decennial Digests* to the *Centennial Digest.*

(b) Legal topic approach

In the Maritime Law Book scheme, the knowledgeable researcher may bypass the "Key Word Index" section and search directly in the "Topical Index" section. Similarly, the legal topic approach may be used in the American Digest System by first examining the topic and key number digests without searching the "Descriptive Word Index".

(c) Digests for the regional reporters, individual states, and specific courts

Because of the large number of cases reported and digested in the National Reporter System, the task of researching in the American Digest System is very time-consuming. When researching for a specific geographical region, a particular court level, or a special court, research may be made in one of the many digests containing only a portion of the information housed in the all-inclusive American Digest System. Not all of the regional units of the National Reporter System have their own digests, but the current ones are *Atlantic Digest, Northwestern Digest, Pacific Digest, Southeastern Digest,* and *Southern Digest.* Case digests are extracted from the regional digest publications to create many digest publications devoted to individual states (*e.g.*, California, New York, Washington, *etc.*).

West Publishing Company produces digests for almost all states, and some states have their own digests from other publishers in addition to the West digest. The *Federal Practice Digest* 4th contains digests for federal court opinions. There are also specialty digests such as West's *Bankruptcy Digest.* The United State Supreme Court has two digests:

(i) *United States Supreme Court Digest,* produced by West Publishing Company using the Key Number system.
(ii) *United States Supreme Court Reports Digest,* produced by Lawyers' Cooperative Publishing Company with its own topic classification system (*not* West's Key Number system) to access the *United States Supreme Court Reports (Lawyers' Edition).*

Note regarding electronic sources: The WESTLAW online system includes headnotes using West Publishing's "Topics with Key Numbers" found in its American Digest System.

D. STATUTES AND REGULATIONS

1. Federal statute revisions and annotations to the Constitution

Most bills become statutes after being passed by both houses of Congress and being signed by the President. The new statutes are first available from the government publisher as "slip laws", in *U.S. Code Congressional and Administrative News Service* (West Publishing Company), in advance sheets to *United States Code Service, Lawyers' Edition* (Lawyers' Cooperative Publishing Company), or in *U.S. Law Week.*

Members of Congress are elected every two years, and at the end of each two-year congressional session, all slip laws are published in numerical sequence in the *United States Statutes at Large.* The publication analogous to the *Revised Statutes of Canada* is the *United States Code.* The *United States Code* is divided into titles, each of which contains statutes on a particular subject. Only some of the titles have been re-enacted into law. For titles not re-enacted, wording in the

Statutes at Large would take precedence if there was a conflict with the wording in the *United States Code.*

There is a time lag in publishing the official government edition of the *United States Code.* It is republished as a consolidation of American federal statutes every six years, with cumulative supplements being issued between new publication dates. The two privately published editions of the Code, *United States Code Annotated* (U.S.C.A.) published by West Publishing Company, and *United States Code Service, Lawyers' Edition* (U.S.C.S.) published by Lawyers' Cooperative Publishing Company, are both annotated with cases considering the Code sections. Both privately published annotated Codes are updated by annual pocket parts, monthly pamphlet supplements, and by reissue of volumes if necessary. The *United States Code Annotated* contains annotations referring to cases in the National Reporter System and other publications. The *United States Code Service, Lawyers' Edition,* refers to cases and to annotations contained in A.L.R. Federal or in the *United States Supreme Court Reports, Lawyers' Edition.*

The annotated Codes have tables listing federal Acts by their popular names.

The general index to the annotated Codes may be an initial entry point for research, but more detailed index coverage is provided in the individual title indexes. While the *United States Code* is published every six years, the two annotated Code services provide continuing coverage of the Code.

The *Constitution* of the United States is published in separate volumes of the two annotated Code services, and these volumes can act as statute citators to the federal *Constitution* including the *Bill of Rights.* Another approach to finding cases considering the *Constitution* is to examine the topic digests under the "Constitution" heading within the American Digest System.

The meaning of statutes may be obtained not only through cases judicially considering statutes, but also through researching the history of the passage of a bill. The meaning of particular phrases may be ascertained by studying Congressional committee reports, committee hearings, and debates within Congress. Such pre-passage material may be relevant and accepted by a court as providing an interpretation of wording. The most comprehensive current source of legislative histories is *CIS,* published by Congressional Informational Service Incorporated.

2. State statutes

State legislatures pass laws in a manner similar to Congress. At the end of state legislative sessions, laws are published in session laws, which are analogous to the *U.S. Statutes at Large.* State laws are codified in publications with titles varying from state to state. Codification titles contain such terms as "revised", "compiled", "consolidated", and "code". Most states have annotated Code services, and some looseleaf publications cover law from all states for certain areas.

In Canada, the most widely available digest of state law is the "Law Digests" volumes of the *Martindale-Hubbell Law Directory.* These volumes contains digests of law from many jurisdictions throughout the world, including each American state.

3. Federal regulations

Publication of federal regulations is made in the *Federal Register,* which is analogous to the *Canada Gazette Part II.* The codification of the *Federal Register* is produced in the *Code of Federal Regulations* (C.F.R.) which is analogous to the *Consolidated Regulations of Canada* (C.R.C.). Each calendar quarter, a portion of the C.F.R. is revised so that each title of the C.F.R. is revised annually.

The *Federal Register* is published daily except on the weekends or days following official holidays, and therefore the *Code of Federal Regulations* may have information that is obsolete. To update search in the C.F.R., the researcher must check the monthly pamphlet titled *L.S.A.: List of C.F.R. Sections Affected* and check the daily *Federal Register* section titled "C.F.R. Parts Affected During [current month]". To find new regulations, research may be made in the monthly, quarterly, or annual indexes to the *Federal Register.*

Regulations are also published in the *United States Code Congressional and Administrative News Service* and in the advance pamphlets to the *United States Code Service.*

4. Electronic sources for legislation

The LEXIS-NEXIS online system includes the "Codes Library" (CODES) which includes annotated revised statutes of the federal government and the 50 states. The files include revised Codes through to Bill tracking services. USCODE is the file for the federal statute revision, and USNAME is the file of federal legislation by popular name. The federal regulations are covered in the LEXIS-NEXIS libraries for the *Code of Federal Regulations* (CFR) and the *Federal Register* (FEDREG). The WESTLAW counterparts include the following database identifiers: USC for the *U.S. Code*, CFR for the *Code of Federal Regulations*, and ST-ANN-ALL for the annotated state statutes. Check with Micromedia Ltd. (Toronto) about the "Federal Register" CD-ROM or "The Federal Register Internet Library" (updated daily). Carswell offers the CD-ROM, "CFR on LawDesk".

E. CITATORS

Citators for American statutes and cases are provided by a series of publications entitled *Shepard's Citations.* For cases, *Shepard's Citations* are published for the following: all states, various regional reporters of the National Reporter System, *Federal Reporter, Federal Supplement,* and the United States Supreme Court.

Shepard's United States Citations is organized in a series of subtitles and covers cases citing United States Supreme Court cases, federal statutes, the United States *Constitution,* court rules of the United States Supreme Court, and decisions of selected federal administrative agencies. *Shepard's Federal Citations* provides cases citing earlier cases from the *Federal Reporter, Federal Supplement,* and *Federal Rules Decisions.*

To search for cases considering cited cases and statutes is to "Shepardize" a cited case. The earlier cited cases are listed by citation only (volume, law report abbreviation, and page number) with later citing cases listed below. Parallel citations of the cited cases are usually given when the case has been reported in more than one law report. The citing cases are divided into appellate consideration of the case (history of a case) and comment on a case by subsequent judicial opinion (treatment of case).

The state units of *Shepard's Citations* list in-state law review articles citing the case and selected leading law journals from across the country.

Shepard's Citations covering statutes include citations of cases considering the United States *Constitution* and state constitutions, the *United States Code,* codifications of state legislation, and municipal bylaws (called ordinances). The statute citators list amendments and new sections to statutes as well as cases considering the statutes.

Some units of *Shepard's Citations* provide citations to the *Code of Federal Regulations,* law reviews that have been cited by cases, cases that have cited the American Bar Association's *Code of Professional Responsibility,* and cases citing the *Restatements of the Law.* Other separate units cover subject areas such as labour, tax, and bankruptcy.

Electronic sources for citators include the LEXIS-NEXIS "Citations Library" (CITES) which includes the following files: Auto-Cite Service (AC), Shepard's Citations (SHEP), and LEXCITE. The WESTLAW citations databases includes Shepard's.

F. LEGAL ENCYCLOPEDIAS

The two legal encyclopedias that are national in scope are *Corpus Juris Secundum* (C.J.S.), published by West Publishing Company and *American Jurisprudence* 2d (Am. Jur. 2d) published jointly by Lawyers' Cooperative Publishing Company and Bancroft-Whitney Company. The publishers of the two national encyclopedias also publish state encyclopedias for the more populous states.

1. Corpus Juris Secundum

The text of *Corpus Juris Secundum* supersedes the text of *Corpus Juris,* but there are footnote references from C.J.S. to some earlier cases in C.J. The encyclopedia covers federal and state statutory and case law by an arrangement of topics throughout approximately 150 volumes. It attempts to comprehensively cite all relevant reported cases in footnotes and provides cross-references to West's Topics and Key Numbers for entry into the American Digest System.

Access to C.J.S. is through the newly revised, paperbound, three-volume *General Index.* Older main volumes of C.J.S. have their own indexes (not updated), and newer re-issue volumes do not have such indexes (i.e., reliance on the revised *General Index).*

An electronic source for the insurance and tax portions of C.J.S. is the WESTLAW system's identifiers CJS-INS and CJS-FTX.

2. American Jurisprudence 2d

American Jurisprudence 2d has a topic arrangement in more than 80 volumes. It does not attempt to cite all reported cases, but rather cites selected decisions and A.L.R. annotations. Further reported cases may be located by reference to the A.L.R. annotations. This encyclopedia gives broad treatment to law, while A.L.R. is a more narrow in-depth treatment of many selected topics. Access to Am. Jur. 2d is through multi-volume, paperbound indexes with supplements. Supplementation is through pocket parts and a looseleaf binder, Am. Jur. 2d New Topic Service. The volumes on federal taxation are reissued annually, and there is an Am. Jur. 2d Desk Book containing miscellaneous information similar to that included in Carswell's *The Legal Desk Book.*

An electronic source for Am. Jur. 2d is the LEXIS-NEXIS file AMJUR in the 2NDARY library. It is also available on CD-ROM from Carswell.

G. LEGAL PERIODICALS

The United States publishes numerous law school reviews, bar association journals, and special subject periodicals. The most comprehensive periodical indexes also cover Canadian periodical literature, and are discussed more fully in Chapter 8.

The leading current periodical indexes are *Index to Legal Periodicals,* and *Current Law Index* with its related publication, *Legal Resources Index.* There are several special subject journal indexes such as *Index to Federal Tax Articles* (Warren, Gorham, and Lamont Company), *CCH Federal Tax Articles, Criminal Justice Periodical Index* (University Microfilms International), and *Kindex* (National Centre for Juvenile Justice). There are separately published periodical digests such as *Law Review Digest, Monthly Digest of Legal Articles,* and *Monthly Digest of Tax Articles.*

Shepard's Law Review Citations covers more than 180 legal periodicals. This service provides cases that have cited a law review article as well as subsequent law review articles in which the earlier article is cited. *Shepard's Federal Law Citations in Selected Law Reviews* lists federal court cases, the United States *Constitution,* and the United States *Code* after the law has been cited in any of approximately twenty leading American law reviews.

An electronic source for law journals is the LEXIS-NEXIS "Law Review's Library", (LAWREV, covering more than 200 law journals). WESTLAW's legal journals database identifier is JLR. Both LEXIS-NEXIS (library LEXREF, file ILP) and WESTLAW (identifier ILP) include the *Index to Legal Periodicals*.

H. TEXTBOOKS AND REFERENCE MATERIAL

1. Textbooks

The great number and variety of American legal textbooks can give useful persuasive authority material to the Canadian researcher by supplying multi-volume depth to a subject or by treating a very narrow subject. The textbooks of some publishers, including Matthew Bender and Bancroft-Whitney, are directed toward the practising lawyer with such multi-volume works as *Attorney's Dictionary of Medicine* (15 volumes) and *Couch on Insurance* (24 volumes). There are many American titles on trial practice technique and law office management, which can be used as valuable idea books for Canadian lawyers. While only the larger private law firm libraries will have a substantial collection of American textbooks, larger court house libraries usually have a selection of American texts. Some multi-volume textbooks sets such as *Wigmore on Evidence* cite some Canadian and Commonwealth cases.

2. Restatements of the Law

The *Restatements of the Law* are publications of the American Law Institute, which has attempted to provide concise and clear general statements of the law in broad areas such as agency, conflict of laws, contracts, restitution, torts, landlord and tenant, trusts, *etc*. The *Restatements* are highly respected secondary legal literature, and they are often cited by courts as being a suitable summation of the law on a particular point. The value of the *Restatements* may be ascertained by reference to the two citators: *Restatements in the Courts* or *Shepard's Citations: Restatements of the Law.*

3. Looseleaf services

There are many American looseleaf services embracing a diverse number of topics. The largest publishers of looseleaf services are Commerce Clearing House (CCH), Prentice Hall (which uses a looseleaf page filing format similar to the CCH method familiar to Canadian researchers), and the Bureau of National Affairs which issues update pamphlets to be placed in binders rather than individual pages to be inserted. Most of the multi-volume texts by Matthew Bender Inc. are in looseleaf format.

4. Forms and precedents sets

American forms and precedents multi-volume sets may be used by Canadian lawyers as models to be adapted. Widely used general form sets from the United States include:

(a) Warren, *Forms of Agreement.* This multi-volume set contains specialized forms involving commercial transactions. The full set is four volumes but there is a one-volume abridged version.
(b) Rabkin and Johnson, *Current Legal Forms with Tax Analysis.* This loose-leaf edition of 33 volumes has separate tax analysis so that many of the forms, excepting tax discussions, can be adapted to Canadian use.
(c) *Wests' Legal Forms,* 2d ed. is recently completed in 29 volumes. There is a General Index plus unit indexes (*e.g.*, index for "Commercial Transactions", volumes 12-15).
(d) *American Jurisprudence, Legal Forms* 2d. This collection of approximately 50 volumes is supplemented by pocket parts and has cross-references to other publications in the Am. Jur. series.
(e) Nichols, *Cyclopedia of Legal Forms, Annotated.* This set has 38 volumes and is supplemented with pocket parts.
(f) *American Jurisprudence Pleading and Practice Forms, Annotated.* These volumes are supplemented by pocket parts and relate to trial preparation.

5. Am. Jur. Proof of Facts and Am. Jur. Trials

The multi-volume reference sets, *American Jurisprudence Proof of Facts,* in three series with more than 120 volumes (Am. Jur. Proof of Facts), and *American Jurisprudence Trials* in more than 65 volumes (Am. Jur. Trials), are aids to preparation for trials. These sets do not serve as a locator for American statute or case law, but rather are intended to assist lawyers in practical matters of interviewing clients, interviewing witnesses, taking depositions, preparing facta, witness examination, etc. They present elements essential in presenting or defending a *prima facie* case. Narrative discussion under each topic is often followed by sample questions and answers from court room situations. The first six volumes of Am. Jur. Trials cover general areas of practice, strategy, and control in considerable depth as indicated by the approximately 100-page article on client interviews. The remaining volumes in Am. Jur. Trials are collectively known as "Model Trials" and treat trials litigating specific topics. Am. Jur. Proof of Facts is available on CD-ROM from Carswell.

6. Dictionaries, directories, and word and phrases

Two widely used American legal dictionaries are *Black's Law Dictionary,* 6th ed. (West Publishing Company, 1990) and *Ballentine's Law Dictionary with*

Pronunciations (Lawyers' Cooperative Publishing Company). These dictionaries are used throughout Canada, but it should be noted that the application of some legal terminology in the United States is different from its application in Canada.

The primary words and phrases publication is West Publishing Company's *Words and Phrases,* published in approximately 50 volumes and supplemented by pocket parts.

An American legal directory often used in Canada is the *Martindale-Hubbell Law Directory,* which includes listing for Canadian and foreign lawyers and law firms as well as American listings. Law firms are listed by geographical location from throughout the world, and areas of practice that law firms consider to be their specialties are listed with each firm. The *Law Digest* volumes digest law from common law as well as other legal systems around the world, including each Canadian province and American state.

7. Electronic sources for secondary material

The LEXIS-NEXIS "Secondary Source Library" (2NDARY) includes the *Restatements of the Law,* A.L.R. annotations, many textbooks, and the *Martindale-Hubbell Law Directory.* The LEXIS-NEXIS "Bureau of National Affairs Library" (BNA) covers that publisher's texts and looseleaf services. The "Legal Reference Library" (LEXREF) includes the file Forensic Services Directory (EXPERT).

I. LEXIS-NEXIS AND WESTLAW COMPUTER DATABASE SYSTEMS

LEXIS-NEXIS (the 1997 directory is 492 pages) and WESTLAW (the 1997 directory is 417 pages) are massive online database systems. LEXIS-NEXIS is available through Butterworths Canada Ltd. and covers American law, Canadian law, other English language jurisdictions, other French language jurisdictions, and many general sources such as "News Library" (news, which has full text of 2,300 newspapers in many languages). WESTLAW is available through QL Systems Ltd. and focuses on American law. Brief mention of some of the online databases from both systems covering various American legal publications have been cited throughout this chapter.

Chapter 15

Researching Law of Australia, New Zealand, and Other Jurisdictions

A. AUSTRALIAN LEGISLATIVE AND JUDICIAL STRUCTURES

1. Federal and state legislative structures

Parliament (the federal legislature) consists of the House of Representatives and the Senate. Bills that have passed Parliament are given Royal Assent by the Governor General. The *Commonwealth of Australia Constitution Act, 1990* (U.K.) divides legislative authority between the federal government and the states. Unless the subject matter is exclusively federal, state parliaments may legislate on the matter. State legislation is given Royal Assent by Governors. For the reception of English law in Australia, see Alex C. Castles, "The Reception and Status of English Law in Australia" (1963), 2 *Adelaide Law Review* 1-32.

2. Federal and state court structures

The two types of courts, federal courts and state courts, do have overlapping jurisdiction in federal and state matters. At the top of the hierarchy of federal courts is the High Court of Australia, which exercises both original and appellate jurisdiction. By the *Privy Council Limitation of Appeals Act, 1968,* and by the *Privy Council (Appeals from the High Court) Act, 1975,* appeals are no longer taken from the High Court to the Judicial Committee of the Privy Council in England.

The *Federal Court Act, 1976* established the Federal Court, which has an Industrial Division and a General Division. The Federal Court has both original and appellate jurisdiction, and appeals may be made to it from state courts exercising federal jurisdiction (unless the appeal be from a "full state Supreme Court" which goes to the High Court).

There is a separate Family Court of Australia, exercising original and appellate jurisdiction. Appeal from this court lies directly to the High Court. Family Law matters may also be dealt with by state courts.

The lowest level of state courts vary in designation from state to state and are called Magistrates' Courts, Petty Sessions, Courts of Summary Jurisdiction, or Local Courts. The intermediate level of state courts are called District or County Courts. The highest court for each state is the state Supreme Court. In some instances, state courts may exercise federal jurisdiction, and from these decisions appeal may go to the High Court if there is special leave to appeal, or to the Federal Court.

B. AUSTRALIAN LAW REPORTS

An older series of English law reports relevant to Australia is the *All England Law Reports Reprint Extension* containing cases to 1935 not found in the *All England Law Reports Reprint.* The English cases have been considered by Australian courts and citations of the citing Australian cases are given. An electronic source for case law is the LEXIS-NEXIS Australian library (AUST), which has collections of files dealing with case law: "Case Law" (*e.g.*, AUSMAX file, combined unreported and reported cases); "Federal Courts" (*e.g.*, IRTDEC file, with Immigration Reviews Tribunal from 1990); "State Courts" (1980s-). Another electronic source for case law is the QUICKLAW collection of online databases, "Australian Court and Tribunal Decisions, global" (access code AUS). The CD-ROM titled, "Complete Legal Research System on CD-ROM" (available from Carswell) includes the component, "Federal Cases".

Australian law reports include:

1. Law reports covering federal courts

High Court of Australia cases are reported in a variety of reports, which include appeals to the Privy Council:

(a) *Commonwealth Law Reports* (C.L.R.), 1903 to date.

(b) *Australian Argus Law Reports* (A.L.R.), 1895-1972. This series has the pre-1960 title *Argus Law Reports,* and is superseded by the *Australian Law Reports.*

(c) *Australian Law Reports* (A.L.R.), 1973 to date. These federal court reports also include judgments of the State Supreme Courts exercising federal jurisdiction. In the back of each volume are the *Australian Capital Territory Reports* and the *Northern Territory Reports.* This grouping of reports is a LEXIS-NEXIS computer system database.

(d) *Australian Law Journal Reports* (A.L.J.R.), 1958 to date. This separate portion of the *Australian Law Journal* has separate page numbering so that the reports may be bound into annual law report volumes.

(e) Rapid digesting services for High Court judgments are Butterworths' *Australian Current Law* and the *Australian Legal Monthly Digest.*

(f) *Federal Law Reports* (F.L.R.), 1956 to date, predate the establishment of the Federal Court, and include judgments of various special federal courts and state supreme courts which exercise federal jurisdiction.

2. Law reports covering state courts and territorial courts

Judgments from the different state court levels have been reported in a variety of law reports series over the years. Listed below are some major law report series that have offered reporting over a long term. Title changes are noted.

(a) New South Wales:
New South Wales Reports: (N.S.W.R.), 1960-1970.
New South Wales Law Reports: (N.S.W.L.R.), 1971 to date.

(b) Victoria:
The Early Reprint, 1846-1928 (a collection of sources).
Victorian Law Reports (V.L.R.), 1861 - 1956.
Victorian Reports (V.R.), 1957 to date. Index covers 1861 to date.

(c) Queensland:
State Reports, Queensland (St. R.Q.), 1902-1957.
Queensland Reports (Qd. R.), 1958 to date.

(d) South Australia:
South Australian State Reports (S.A.S.R.), 1921 to date.

(e) Western Australia:
Western Australian Law Reports (W.A.L.R.), 1898-1959.
Western Australian Reports (W.A.R.), 1960 to date.
Index covers 1898-1988

(f) Tasmania:
Tasmanian Law Reports (Tas. L.R.), 1904-1940.
Tasmanian State Reports (Tas. S.R.), 1941 to date.

3. Subject reports

There is a variety of subject reports covering both Australia generally and particular state jurisdictions. Examples include:

(a) Local government cases:
Local Government Reports of Australia, 1956 to date.
Victorian Planning Appeal Decisions, 1969 to date.

(b) Tax cases:
Australasian Tax Reports, 1969 to date.
Australian Tax Cases, 1969 to date.

(c) Family law cases:
Australian Family Law Cases, 1976 to date.
Family Law Reports, 1976 to date.

C. AUSTRALIAN DIGESTS

Unless a researcher's library has digests published specifically for Australia, digest access to Australian case law will be found through *The Digest* (formerly the *English and Empire Digest).* The two major digests concentrating on Australian law are:

1. Australian Current Law

This Butterworths publication has two main parts ("The Reporter" and "Legislation") which form an advance service for *Halsbury's Laws of Australia.*

(a) "The Reporter" is a looseleaf service, which every two weeks produces a paperbound booklet digesting very recent cases. Tables include: Table of Cases, Cases and Statutes Judicially Considered. Notes of recent books and articles are given under subject headings. Many of the sentencing and quantum of damages digests will never be fully reported.

(b) "Legislation" is a looseleaf service detailing legislative amendments to Acts and regulations (federal, state, and territorial). The information is arranged by subject/jurisdiction and cumulates in the monthly booklets. Tables include: statutes amended, amending statutes, progress of bills, and proclamations.

(c) "Yearbooks": "The Reporter" and "Legislation" are consolidated annually and published separately as "Yearbooks".

2. Australian Digest (2d) and Australian Legal Monthly Digest

(a) Steps in using the *Australian Digest* (2d)
   (i) Locate digests under appropriate classifications in the main volumes of the second edition, which is almost complete (reference to some volumes in first edition is still necessary).
   (ii) Turn to the same classification number in the "Interim Supplement" to second edition, which has later case digests. This volume forms one of the three annual volumes collectively known as the *Annual Digest.* See "Master Volume" below for updating the first edition.
   (iii) Digests in the "Interim Supplement" are in skeleton form and a reference is given to the full digest of the case in the annual "Digest of Cases" volume, which is another volume in the three-volume *Annual Digest* and which arranges full digests in accordance with the classification scheme.
   (iv) The "Master Volume", another volume of the *Annual Digest,* includes a "Cumulative Table of Cases Digested, Key to Cases 1934-", which provides a later case service for volumes in the first edition not yet superseded, a "Cumulative List of Words and Phrases", a

"Cumulative Table of Cases Judicially Noticed", and a "Cumulative Index of Subject Matter".

(b) Updating from the *Annual Digest* is made in the *Australian Legal Monthly Digest* issues, which have cumulative tables under each classification heading showing where relevant cases may be found. The "Advance Information" section rapidly digests unreported cases.

(c) CD-ROM versions of these two publications are available from Carswell.

D. AUSTRALIAN STATUTES AND REGULATIONS

The 12-volume *Acts of the Australian Parliament 1901-1973* is a consolidation of statutes enacted during that period. Sessional volumes are published.

Subject access to Acts may be made in the "Index" to the *Acts of the Australian Parliament 1901-1973* and in *Subject Index to the Acts and Regulations of the Commonwealth of Australia.*

Updating the 1901-1973 consolidation may be made in two privately published works:

1. Butterworths' *Federal Legislation Annotations.* This publication does not print full text of amendments, but is an update service and case citator for Acts and regulations. A hardbound volume updates from 1973 and softbound cumulative supplements are issued semi-annually. Other annotations series include: *New South Wales Statutes Annotations, Queensland Statutes Annotations,* and *Victorian Statutes Annotations.*
2. *Acts of the Australian Parliament 1901-1973 Cumulative Supplement,* which is published annually. This lists all Acts with a full text of amendments, and is a statute citator with case law annotations to the statute sections.

To bring legislative research up to the most recent date, the researcher should check *Australian Current Law* or *Australian Legal Monthly Digest* (discussed in Section C).

Regulations are published in the *Commonwealth of Australia Gazette.*

Electronic sources include the LEXIS-NEXIS Australian library (AUST), with the "Legislation" collection of files (*e.g.*, COMACT, all Commonwealth of Australia Acts).

E. AUSTRALIAN CITATORS

Case citators include *Australian Current Law* and the *Australian Digest,* discussed in Section C. *Australian Case Citator,* a comprehensive case citator, is available in print-form and on CD-ROM from Carswell. Statute citators include Butterworths' *Federal Legislation Annotations,* the state annotation services, and *Acts of the Australian Parliament Cumulative Supplement,* discussed in Section D. Butterworths also publishes the *Australian and New Zealand Citator to*

U.K. Reports 1558-, which lists Australian cases considering English cases (1558-1972 main volume plus cumulative supplement 1973- (a recent year)).

F. AUSTRALIAN LEGAL ENCYCLOPEDIAS

Halsbury's Laws of England, 3rd ed., had a separately published *Australian Pilot (1955-1964),* which is analogous to the *Canadian Converters* for this encyclopedia. The new fourth edition of *Halsbury's Law of England* is publishing an *Australian Commentary* in looseleaf form to serve the same purpose as the *Australian Pilot.*

There are two encyclopedias published specifically for Australia:

1. *Halsbury's Laws of Australia.* Butterworths is publishing this 30-volume looseleaf work between 1991 and 1996. There will be 90 titles with extensive footnoting and cross-referencing. The work is structurally tied to *Australian Current Law* which acts as an updater (see Section D). Electronic source: LEXIS-NEXIS library (AUST), in files HALSAU (selected titles) or HALSTOC (table of contents).
2. *The Laws of Australia.* The Law Book Company (Carswell as Canadian agent) is publishing this 35-volume looseleaf work. There will be 135 titles with extensive footnoting and cross-referencing. There are tables of cases and statutes plus a comprehensive index. Bi-monthly update bulletins are filed directly into the binders. Updates include summary of recent unreported and reported cases. A CD-ROM version is available from Carswell.

G. AUSTRALIAN LEGAL PERIODICALS

Australian legal periodicals include law school reviews (*e.g., Adelaide Law Review),* commercially published general reviews (*e.g., Australian Law Journal,* which includes the *Australian Law Journal Reports),* bar association or law society journals (*e.g.,* Australian Bar Association's *Australian Bar Gazette,* and *Victorian Bar News),* and subject journals (*e.g., Australian Business Law Review).*

Index access to Australian periodical literature may be made in *Index to Legal Periodicals, Current Law lndex,* and *Index to Commonwealth Legal Periodicals.* The specialized *Current Australian and New Zealand Legal Literature Index* (1973 to date) has had a rather large time lag. It does index legal articles, case comments, book reviews, collections of essays, and some legal contents of general periodicals.

The *Australian Current Law* and the *Australian Digest* (2d) publications also list journal articles.

Electronic sources: LEXIS-NEXIS library (AUST), in the "Butterworths Journals" collection of files (*e.g.,* ABAR file, Australian Bar Review, 1994-) or "Journals" collection of files (*e.g.,* ALLI file, Australian Legal Literature Index, 1985-).

H. AUSTRALIAN TEXTBOOKS AND OTHER SECONDARY LITERATURE SOURCES

Australian textbooks that might fill a gap in Canadian textbook subject coverage or might be of supplementary interest to Canadian researchers are advertised by major Canadian law publishers and distributors (*e.g.*, Butterworths and Carswell), which have distribution agreements with the major Australian publishers.

The major publishers of looseleaf services are Butterworths, CCH Australia, and the Law Book Company. Butterworths' *Australian Income Tax Law and Practice* and CCH Australia's *Australian Federal Tax Reporter* are full tax reporting services. Butterworths' *Family Law Service* provides coverage of the federal *Family Law Act, 1975* including a case reports section entitled *Family Law Reports.* CCH Australia's *Australian Family Law and Practice* gives similar treatment, including judgments, in the section entitled *Family Law Cases.*

Butterworths' *Australian Encyclopedia of Forms and Precedents* is analogous to Butterworths' English publication of the same name.

There is no separately published Australian legal dictionary. The English publication by Butterworths, entitled *Words and Phrases Legally Defined,* 3rd ed., includes separate listings for Australian cases under each word or phrase defined by Australian courts.

There is an Australian section in the *Martindale-Hubbell Law Directory,* and Australian coverage in several other international legal directories.

I. LEXIS-NEXIS COMPUTER DATABASES

The Australian library (AUST), includes the following collection of files: "Case Law", "Federal Courts", "State Courts", "Halsburys", "Legislation", "Reported Judgments", "Unreported Judgments", "Journals", and "Butterworths Journals".

J. RESEARCHING NEW ZEALAND LAW

1. Legislative and judicial structures

The New Zealand Parliament has one chamber, the House of Representatives. The court system consists of the Court of Appeal, the Supreme Court, Magistrates' Courts, plus some courts with specialized functions.

2. Law reports

New Zealand Law Reports, 1883 to date (LEXIS-NEXIS: NZ library, NZLR file, 1958-).

3. Digests

(a) *Abridgment of New Zealand Law Cases* covers 1861 to present *(Gazette Law Reports* through *New Zealand Law Reports):* 18 volumes plus Annual Cumulative Supplements.

(b) Butterworths' *Current Law:* A looseleaf volume with 24 pamphlet parts per year. Digests very recent court cases and has legislative amendments. Analogous to Butterworths' *Australian Current Law.* LEXIS-NEXIS: NZ library, NZCL file.

(c) *The Digest* includes New Zealand case law.

4. Statutes and regulations

(a) *New Zealand Statutes* may be updated with Butterworths' *Current Law* or Butterworths' *Annotations to the New Zealand Statutes* (analogous to Butterworths' various annotation services for Australia).

(b) Regulations are published in the *New Zealand Gazette* and updated with the publications updating statutes.

5. Citators

(a) Case citator: *Australian and New Zealand Citator to U.K. Reports 1558-* (New Zealand cases citing U.K. cases). *Abridgment of New Zealand Law Cases* has a citator volume plus updates.

(b) Statute citator: *Annotations to the New Zealand Statutes.*

6. Legal encyclopedias

(a) Butterworths' *The Laws of New Zealand* is published in 142 subject booklets in 20 looseleaf volumes. References are made to *Halsbury's Laws of England* (4th) and *Halsbury's Laws of Australia. The Laws of New Zealand* is supplemented and updated by Butterworths' *Current Law.* LEXIS-NEXIS: NZ library, LONZ and LONTOC files.

(b) There was a *New Zealand Pilot* to older editions of *Halsbury's Laws of England.*

7. Legal periodicals

Periodicals such as the *New Zealand Law Journal are* indexed in sources mentioned in Section G of this chapter.

8. Other sources

Canadian publishers' representatives can provide information about such publications as Butterworths' *Taxation Library* and Butterworths' New *Zealand Family Law Service. Words and Phrases Legally Defined,* 3rd edition (by Butterworths U.K.) includes definitions derived from New Zealand sources.

9. LEXIS-NEXIS computer databases

The library NZ includes the following collections of files: "Law Reports" (*e.g.*, NZCAS, reported New Zealand cases), "Unreported Cases" (NZCLD, *Butterworths Current Law Digest),* "Recent Developments" (NZCL, *Butterworths Current Law*), "Legal Encyclopedia" (LONZ, *Laws of New Zealand*), and "Legislation and Commentary" (tax, corporate, and securities law).

K. RESEARCHING LAW OF OTHER JURISDICTIONS

For unusual fact situations requiring case law research, there may be a need to examine the law of jurisdictions not discussed elsewhere in this text. For English language material, the *Current Law Index* indexes more than 700 law journals in English from around the world. Butterworths' *The Digest* (formerly *English and Empire Digest)* covers case law of more than 15 jurisdictions including Scotland, India, South Africa, West Indies region, and Fiji. In recent years, many jurisdictions have become newly independent, and it is difficult to locate case law for these areas. Since 1985, *Law Reports of the Commonwealth* (three volumes annually by Butterworths) reports important cases from "all Commonwealth jurisdictions" (50 jurisdictions from Antigua and Barbuda to Zimbabwe). Butterworths also publishes *West Indies Reports* (1959-) covering 16 regional jurisdictions and the *Irish Reports* (1838-). The LEXIS-NEXIS library, COMCAS, includes case law from Singapore, Malaysia, South Africa, and Hong Kong. QUICKLAW offers the database, "South African Judgments" (SAJ) (1995-). The LEXIS-NEXIS library, PHLIPP, covers Philippine Supreme Court cases from 1901.

For French language material from other jurisdictions, French law forms part of LEXIS-NEXIS computer databases. The French law libraries on LEXIS-NEXIS include: REVUES (case interpretation), INTNAT (international), PRIVE (private cases), and PUBLIC (public cases). For bibliographic awareness of other materials, see Germain "Current Research Sources in French Law", 75 *Law Library Journal* 34-51 (1981).

The Irish coverage by LEXIS-NEXIS includes the IRELND library: *Irish Reports* (1950-), *Irish Law Reports Monthly* (1980-), *Irish Law Times* (1950-1980), judgments of the Court of Criminal Appeal (Frewen) (1950-1983), and selected unreported cases (1985-).

For European and International materials relevant to the *Canadian Charter of Rights and Freedoms,* check Canada Law Book Inc.'s *Canadian Charter of*

Rights Annotated. For English and French language material relating to Canada and International law (1755-1981) see Wiktor, *Canadian Bibliography of International Law* (Toronto: University of Toronto Press, 1984. 799 pp.). Treaties are discussed in Chapter 4.

It is not easy to research the law of other jurisdictions since even most medium to large law library centres have financial difficulty keeping pace with the explosion of Canadian published legal literature. Electronic sources such as LEXIS-NEXIS are a major asset in overcoming this problem.

Chapter 16

Law Firm Libraries

The largest law firms employ professional librarians or library technicians on a full or part-time basis, but law librarianship in the vast majority of firms consists of methods established in-house by lawyers, articling students, and legal support staff. Section A elaborates upon an outline of library functions that should be taking place in a law firm in the absence of a professional librarian or library technician. Section B discusses the advantages of employing a professional librarian or library technician. A professional librarian is a graduate of a university program with a B.A. or Master's degree in librarianship. A library technician has graduated from a vocational or technical institute having a one- or two-year course in library work.

A. LIBRARY FUNCTIONS REQUIRED IN ALL LAW FIRMS

The following subsections assume that there is no professional librarian or library technician employed, and describes functions that must be maintained by other staff.

1. Ordering new books

(a) Selecting new books

The law firm may have one or more lawyers who are primarily responsible for selecting new books for the library. One lawyer may be responsible for talking to book publishers' representatives or for screening advertising from the major law publishers. When ordering books by mail, one of the clerical staff should check to ensure that duplicate copies are not ordered. If a lawyer orders books when a sales representative visits the law firm, he or she should be supplied with a file of new books received and new books still on order from the publisher.

The person selecting new books for the law firm's collection should consider regular review of the following sources:

(i) Law publishers' advertising brochures, received by mail or from a sales representative. One book title may be advertised in several different brochure formats, and the order file should be checked to avoid duplicate orders.

(ii) Law firms should be certain that they are on their own province's mailing list for continuing legal education announcements of publications and seminar binders. The firm may also be placed on the mailing list for similar materials from other provinces and from the Canadian Bar Association.
(iii) Law firms may be on the mailing list of Supply and Services Canada and the provincial Queen's Printer to receive notification of new government publications and government documents.
(iv) Legal journals often contain book reviews, but the reviews appear long after the book is available.
(v) The foregoing sources contain brief descriptions that may assist in the selection process, but there are other sources which are mere listings of the title and essential bibliographic information about the book. The law firm should acquire the recent "acquisitions lists" published by the local law school or law society library to be aware of the many titles for which no advertising is received.

(b) On-order file for titles ordered but not yet received

A member of the firm's support staff should be charged with maintaining a record of book titles that have been ordered but not yet received. To avoid duplicate orders, a staff member should check through the file whenever a book title is suggested for ordering. If someone has requested a book for an area in which he or she specializes, the requester's name may be noted on the order file, so that when the book is received and matched against the on-order file, the book may be first routed to the person requesting it.

The information that should be kept on file includes the title of the book, author, publisher, company acting as sales agent (if different than publisher), edition, year, list price and number of books ordered. The brochure describing the publication may be kept, since it will provide a description of the book that may be helpful at a subsequent review of the on-order file. These elements of information are necessary to check against the invoice and book itself when they arrive, to ensure that the proper publication has been received.

The on-order file prevents duplicate orders, and also aids in other areas of budget control. Some titles do not appear for many months after they are advertised, and the dollar amount of funds committed to new purchases as shown by the on-order file may be substantial by the end of the fiscal year.

If the library budget is somewhat restricted, a separate desiderata file should be established. This file should contain brochures advertising books that may be purchased in subsequent months if current advertising yields many titles ordered, but future advertising offers fewer titles of interest.

(c) Selecting used books

Through amalgamation of law practices or retirement, major sets of law books frequently are available on the used market at prices considerably below the new cost from the publisher. Canada's used law book dealer who advertises nationally and internationally is J.L.Heath Used Law Books Ltd.: 166 Bullock Drive, Unit #8, Markam, Ont. L3P 1W2 (Tel: 905-472-0219; fax: 905-472-5578; B.C. telephone: 604-946-5333).

A number of publications contain ads for sale of used law books, and local law librarians and book publishers' representatives may know of local book collections for sale. There are several used law book dealers in the U.S. and their addresses may be obtained from local law librarians.

(d) Basic law firm book collection

Most new law firms are close to a law society or law school library, or can take advantage of rapid reference and mail loan service from the law society. The listing below presents a basic collection for firms with outside assistance available.

(i) The province's own law reports (see Chapters 2 & 11): For example, *Manitoba Reports* (2d).
(ii) The province's digest (see Chapters 3 & 11): *e.g.*, *Alberta Decisions* or *Alberta Weekly Law Digest.*
(iii) The province's statutes: Looseleaf edition, if careful looseleaf filing is assured (see Chapter 4). A statute citator; *e.g.*, *B.C. Statute Citator* or *Statutes of B.C. Judicially Considered* (see Chapter 6).
(iv) Butterworths' *Canadian Forms & Precedents* or *O'Brien's Encyclopedia of Forms and Precedents* (see Chapter 9).
(v) A basic collection of textbooks (hardbound or looseleaf service) and C.L.E. material, including bar admission course material (see Chapter 11).
(vi) A national digest such as *Lawyers Weekly, Canadian Current Law Case Digests,* or *All-Canada Weekly Summaries/Weekly Criminal Bulletin* (see Chapter 3).
(vii) The local law journal or law review; *e.g.*, *Saskatchewan Law Review* (see Chapters 8 & 11).

Costs in building a library can cumulate rapidly. To start, the most recent series of a provincial law report or only some divisions of a forms & precedents set might be purchased. The next step could be a legal encyclopedia (Chapter 7: C.E.D. Western or C.E.D. Ontario) which is a large set to purchase initially and then maintain. The major cost consideration with any law book purchase is cost of upkeep more than initial price. Savings may be realized on the purchase price through acquisition of older volumes of a set on the used market (subsection (c) above). See below subsection 5 ("Law firm library budgeting...") for further considerations such as your office's proximity to a law society library and the use of computer assisted legal research.

2. Receiving, cataloguing, classifying, and indexing new books

(a) Receiving

Receiving new books is accomplished by support staff, who match the book with the invoice and on-order file to be certain that the book received is the one ordered. While invoice records and total library expenses may be kept by the accounts staff, the person charged with maintaining the library may keep an orders-received file, which may be analyzed in detail for library expenditures.

(b) Cataloguing

Cataloguing books consists of creating records that contain essential bibliographic information about the book for future research purposes. Information similar to that placed on the on-order file is recorded and listings are produced, so that access may be made by title, author, or subject area. Cataloguing information may be contained on cards housed in card trays (which is the traditional way of storing information about books in libraries), or by keeping the listings on computer so that the author, title, and subject heading printouts may be made. Firms wishing to obtain cataloguing data for their books may check with local law society or law school library. The new acquisition lists, obtained from law societies or law schools and used for selection of new books, may also be retained for very basic cataloguing data.

(c) Classifying

Classifying books is the assigning of a unique call number to each book. The call number is placed on the spine of the book, and the purpose is to group books on the same topic at the same bookshelf location.

Many large libraries assign call numbers only to textbooks. Call numbers are probably not necessary for a very small collection of textbooks, which may be arranged on the shelf alphabetically by author or by very rough subject area.

If the texts are catalogued but not classified by call number, texts arranged on the shelves by author may be accessed by subject by examining the subject listing in either the card trays or computer printout, while texts arranged in rough subject order on the shelves would need a separate entry in the cataloguing data to indicate rough subject grouping assigned.

The general arrangement of most law firm libraries as well as larger law libraries is to make separate groupings of textbooks, reports, statutory material, government documents, and a reference section containing digests, encyclopedias, law journals, law journal indexes, *etc.*

Once cataloguing of texts has been established, access to the textbooks by the computer listings or catalogue card records should be thought of in the overall context of index access to a research law library. In addition to reviewing the textbook listing, search the reference section with its digests, legal periodical indexes, *etc.*

An access point to research in a law firm library not found in a law society or law school library is the law firm's index of memoranda. In-house indexing of legal memoranda may be prepared on cards or stored on the law firm's computer. Cataloguing of memoranda is a function similar to cataloguing texts, but the subject areas' terms should be supplied by the lawyer preparing the memorandum.

3. Receiving continuing book and looseleaf subscriptions

(a) Receipt by support staff

Most of the expenses of any law library lies in the upkeep of continuing subscription services, whether they are for law report series, digests with reissue volumes, or a variety of looseleaf textbooks and looseleaf reporter services. In addition to any invoicing records kept concerning these continuing expenses, a recording system for the new volumes or release numbers for looseleaf updates should be maintained. Receipt of this continuing material is not recorded in the card catalog, which would only list the title of a particular report series or looseleaf service, rather than each volume or release received. A separate record should be kept on the firm's computer or on a card system noting the number of each volume or looseleaf page release received. This record will not only provide a permanent inventory of the library's continuation material but will also act as a method for ensuring that subscriptions have not lapsed accidentally.

An important part of receiving continuing subscriptions is ensuring that looseleaf releases are filed promptly. Looseleaf releases can easily accumulate in a law office, so priorities should be established for the support staff doing the filing. The staff member should be certain to first file looseleaf statute additions, then looseleaf reporter services, and finally, looseleaf textbook inserts.

(b) Circulation to lawyers

For medium-size and larger law firms, lawyers may register the subscription materials they would like to review upon receipt. The material may include the "new matters" flyers accompanying looseleaf service releases, journal issues, reports looseparts, or photocopies of tables of contents.

4. Library book circulation within a law firm

In a medium-size or larger law firm, inconveniences may develop when it is not certain which lawyer has borrowed a book from the library. Law firms may overcome this inconvenience by keeping track of book circulation through the following means.

(a) The best system

A borrower's card system of the kind used in law school or law society libraries may be established. Support staff place a card pocket inside each book cover so that a borrower's card (containing identifying information about the book) may be slipped into the card pocket. When a lawyer removes a book from the library, he or she simply removes the card containing the identifying information from the book, signs the card, and deposits the card in a collection box. If a book is not located in the library, the collection box can be searched to see who has the book.

(b) Alternatives

An option is simply to leave large blank cards in the library, with the lawyer filling in both the book title and his own name. The lawyer places the card at the book's shelf location to indicate who has the book. Such cards can easily become misshelved or misplaced.

A sign-out book may be established in a looseleaf binder. The lawyer records the title of the book and his or her name. This is not as convenient as simply placing initials or a signature on a borrower's card from a book pocket.

The person reshelving returned books should ensure that the borrower's name is crossed out whether it is on the borrower's card, on a large card placed on a bookshelf, or on a sign-out book.

5. Law firm library budgeting and the battle against inflation

For the size of market, Canada has more choices (and duplication) in legal publications than other common law countries of the world. In recent years, some established legal publications have ceased and some new titles have been terminated after a short existence. Law firm library budgeting is difficult in Canada.

Following is a list of factors to be considered when attempting to cope with rising law book costs:

(a) How often is the firm likely to use this publication? Is it located at the nearby courthouse or law school library, or available by mail loan from the central law society library?
(b) Is there a co-operative acquisition programme with another law firm or firms, whereby one firm purchases in one subject area while the other purchases in another area?
(c) Is the publication available either in its entirety or in summary form as a computer database? Because a digest is only a case finder, the firm may want to eliminate printed versions of digests that may be searched on a computer.
(d) For the relative size of the market, Canada has many competing law publishers. There is a degree of duplication in services offered, and the lawyer must understand the function of each reference work to decide whether only one title per type of publication is retained.
(e) A law firm may wish to establish an exchange programme of reports' loose parts with other law firms or law society libraries. Loose parts are often discarded, but they can easily be bound and stored in permanent form at a fraction of the cost of the bound volume service.

(f) Consider purchasing sets of used law books as discussed in Section A.1.(c) above.

6. New technology, space problems, and bookbinding and preservation

Physical space limitations always become a problem for law libraries. The greatest potential for reducing needed shelf space is the increased availability of materials on CD-ROM. For example, *Dominion Law Reports*, 3rd and 4th series (1956 to date) are available on CD-ROM, which replaces about 300 bound volumes. Weeding out old books may mean that earlier editions of digests are discarded, while the older statute editions may be moved to the basement. Some older legal materials are now produced in microcopy to save shelf space, and shelving manufacturers make mechanical shelving units on tracks which can compact to save space and open at one point for retrieval of a book.

Services of bookbinders may be used to transform paper issues of journals, government publications, or law reports into bound volumes. To ensure that contents are bound properly with the possibility of saving on costs, the law firm may correlate the material by removing covers and staples and placing the index in the proper place before sending the parts to the binder. The law firm should keep a record of the type and colour of buckram binding (coloured binding cloth stiffened with starch filler) used to ensure that sets will have matched binding. The binder may keep a supply of the particular buckram used to be certain that the set will continue to have matched binding.

Older books which have substantially deteriorated may require rebinding, and many older books were originally bound in leather. The value of older sets may be retained by maintaining the set in leather binding which involves handcraft work and higher materials costs than buckram. Quality leather binding includes such elements as different grades of leather, tar board covers which are more durable than chip board covers, cleat sewing or oversewing to enable pages to lie flatter than when fan glued, proper skivering to blend the leather with buckram when the book is half-bound or quarter-bound rather than full-bound in leather, and inclusion of hubs on the spines to protect leather labels.

When maintenance of a valuable set is not a factor, a law firm may bind its own material in inexpensive covers by using a "Unibind" or similar machine. The loose pages or loose parts are placed inside the manufacturer's glue-lined vinyl cover and the glue is set by lowering the material and cover into the machine's heating element.

B. HIRING A LIBRARIAN

Smaller law firm libraries may be managed by articling students, paralegals, or clerical staff. A clerical staff member may manage a library that grows over the years as the firm expands, and the person may be capable of managing the routine affairs of the larger library. A growing library directed by the turnover of articling students will manifest the need for trained library assistance more quickly than a library directed by one person over time. There is more need for management of the large firm library by a person trained in librarianship, with monitoring by a lawyer, than there is need for management by a lawyer trying to find time to devote to the library.

A large law library needs to be controlled by a single person with library training, to ensure the smooth flow of book ordering, cataloguing, classifying, book awareness to lawyers, library budget control, assistance with locating research material within the library, and co-ordination with other libraries. When lawyers are not aware of publications or able to conduct research as conveniently or as efficiently as would seem possible, there is an indication that the library functions described above need more control.

Trained library personnel may be hired full-time or part-time. Some librarians divide their time among several law firms. The choice is between hiring a professional librarian or a library technician. For many library administrative duties such as book ordering, processing books received, and book circulation, the quality of work performed depends more upon the individual than the educational qualifications. For library duties involving book selection, reference assistance, and legal research, a librarian will probably be more qualified.

A person with a graduate degree in library science may have four or five more years of formal education than a library technician and will probably be able to grasp legal issues more readily. The librarian may become the in-house expert on computer searching or other levels of research. The professional librarian should be able to anticipate needs of the book collection and ensure the best books to facilitate legal research by lawyers. The librarian should be able to quickly answer more in-depth reference questions and create a more satisfactory current-awareness service for the firm's lawyers.

Advice about hiring in the local area may be obtained from the local law society librarian, law school librarian, or the local association of law libraries.

Chapter 17

Legal Citation

Legal citation form has one main objective — to provide the researcher with sufficient information to locate references easily. For example (1975), 23 C.C.C. (2d) 257 (B.C.S.C.) directs the researcher to a case reproduced beginning on page 257 of the 23rd volume of *Canadian Criminal Cases,* 2nd series. Citation form can also give the researcher an indication of a case's relative value. In the above example, the year, 1975, indicates the relative precedential value of the case with regard to the time factor, while B.C.S.C. indicates the jurisdiction and court.

The first edition of this textbook included a chapter on legal citation because at the time, there was no current Canadian text with such guidance. Following the first edition, Chin-Shih Tang authored *Guide to Legal Citation,* and in the second edition of my text I stated "the purpose is to complement other writings rather than conflict with [full-book treatments of the subject]". In the second edition, I reversed some statements to be consistent with Professor Tang. There is now published Tang, *Guide to Legal Citation and Sources of Citation Aid — A Canadian Perspective,* 2d ed. (Scarborough: Carswell, 1988). Subsequent to my second edition, the *McGill Law Journal* staff prepared *Canadian Guide to Uniform Legal Citation,* 3d ed., (Carswell, 1992). Ten law reviews/journals have officially adopted *Canadian Guide to Uniform Legal Citation,* and for this fourth edition of our textbook, we have endeavoured to make our text consistent with the more complete (165 pages) McGill effort. If we believed that our example was not clearly in conflict with the McGill text, we have retained our example. It is our belief that citation is an art more than a science, with so many situations and variations possible that no text can be expected to contain rules covering every possibility.

A. CASE CITATION

1. Style of cause (name of the case)

The name of a case is the style of cause, and it should appear in the citation before the other basic information. It is always correct to give the style of cause in full, and this may be necessary to enable a reader to know which of several similarly titled cases is being referenced. However, it is usually sufficient in citing a case to shorten the style of cause by omitting unnecessary words and abbreviating words for which widely known abbreviations exist. The style of cause is italicized, however the "*v.*", standing for "versus", need not be italicized.

Use may be made of the abbreviated form appearing as a heading at the top of the page (the running head) on each page of the case in the law report series. This approach may be helpful when dealing with cases on appeal which raise issues of reversal of names on appeal. Plaintiff is listed on the left side of the "v.", and if defendant becomes the appellant, it may be difficult to determine which party was originally the plaintiff. Before its demise, the Canadian Law Information Council developed the "CLIC Standards for Case Identification" which call for retaining the plaintiff's name first on appeal. This is accomplished by stating "Indexed as ..." This standard has been adopted by law publishers in attempt to have each case identified in one manner. If the terms, appellant and respondent, appear in the full style of cause, they may be retained when shortening the case name.

Acceptable shortenings of the case name are best explained through examples given below. The many possible shortenings illustrate the problems encountered and special techniques required when computer searching for cases considered.

(a) Abbreviations
Commonly used abbreviations may be made for designations and entities. Examples are:

Association = Ass'n	Incorporated = Inc.
Attorney General = A.G.	Limited = Ltd.
Brothers = Bros.	Minister of National Revenue = M.N.R.
Company = Co.	United Auto Workers = U.A.W.

(b) Multiple parties, corporations., and partnerships
June S. Smith and T.L. Jones Company Limited v. David Brown may be abbreviated to many acceptable forms:

Smith v. Brown which simply retains the surnames of the first parties listed

June Smith v. David Brown or *J.S. Smith v. D. Brown* which retains the first names or initials of very common surnames

J.S. Smith et al v. D. Brown although words such as "et al", indicating additional parties, are not commonly used

J.S. Smith and T.L. Jones Co. v. D. Brown which retains the first name or initials of a corporation but drops the "Ltd." or "Inc.", if other identifiers such as "Company", "Brothers", or "Association" appear in the name of the corporation (Also illustration of common abbreviations)

All partners' names should be included such as *Duns, Evans, & Smith v. Halle*

(c) Cases involving the Crown
In both criminal and civil cases, use "R." for "The Queen", "The King", "Regina", or "Rex" unless the Crown is the defendant or respondent. If so, use "The Queen" or "The King".

R. v. D.J. Smith (also illustration of initials with common surname)

D.J. Smith v. The Queen

(d) Special status of litigants

It is unnecessary to refer to the special status of one of the litigants:

Helen Richards, suing by her Guardian ad litem, Norma Richards and the said Norma Richards v. The Insurance Corporation of British Columbia

may be abbreviated:

Helen Richards v. I.C.B.C. (also illustration of abbreviating of commonly known entity)

(e) Procedural phrases

(1) Where procedural phrases are used, only the surname of the first party to whom the phrase refers is used.

Ex parte Davis rather than *Ex parte Norman Davis*

(2) Procedural terms need not be used when adversary parties are named.

Ferguson v. Ferguson rather than *Re Ferguson v. Ferguson*

R. v. Clark; ex parte Murchie may retain the procedural phrase to identify a case with respect to which an application is brought by one Murchie. Retention of the procedural phrase rather than citing *R. v. Clark* avoids confusion with a case merely of that name.

(f) "The"

The article "The" is omitted except:

(1) in reference to "The Queen" or "The King"

(2) when the thing referred to is an object proceeded against in rem. For example, *The Arantzazu Mendi,* where, a ship was proceeded against in rem.

(3) as part of the popular name of a case, or

(4) when the style of cause has only two words, "The" being one of them.

(g) Consolidation of actions

When two actions are consolidated, the word "same" is frequently used rather than repeating the name of one party.

June Smith v. Harold Black; June Smith v. The Walter Corporation may be rendered June Smith v. Harold Black; same v. Walter

(h) Geographical phrases

Geographical phrases such as "Province of", "City of", "Town of", and "Village of" may be shortened, using parentheses, unless this leads to confusion:

Regina (City) v. H. Black

(i) Preliminary motions or motions after judgment

The same proceeding may be reported both at trial and also on preliminary motions, or on motions after judgment (the reported decisions in this case will deal with a practice point). If this is done, the different reports will frequently be distinguished by number:

C.P.R. v. Bennett; C.P.R. v. Bennett (No. 2)
In such circumstances, the number, although not part of the case's style of cause, should be included to minimize the reader's confusion.

The key points are that different abbreviations are acceptable, and that transcribing the style of cause exactly as it appears in the decision or reports series is always correct even if it departs from suggested principles.

2. Year and volume number

The year of the decision or the year of the law report forms an essential part of every correct citation. When the year of the case is essential to locating it, it appears in brackets and is the year of the report's volume. When the year is not essential to locating the case, it appears in parentheses and is the year of the decision.

(a) *Rastad Const. Ltd. v. Port Coquitlam* (1979), 18 B.C.L.R. 97
This illustrates the year as an aid to evaluating the currency and probable authority of the case rather than a necessary aid to locating the case. The comma is used to close off the first part of the citation, as it is not absolutely essential to finding the report since this law report series has consecutively numbered volumes spanning a number of years.

(b) *R. v. G.E. Lemay,* [1980] C.T.C. 202
This illustrates the year as an essential reference to finding the case, and because it is essential, the year is after the comma allowing it to be an integral part of the volume — abbreviation — page number portion of the cite. The year is placed in brackets and precedes the report's abbreviation. The year is that of the volume rather than the case since 1979 cases could be printed in the 1979 or 1980 volume or even later.

(c) *R. v. D.J. Smith,* [1986] 2 W.W.R. 124
This illustrates a work which was issued in multiple volumes during the year but for which the year is essential to locating a case — *i.e.*, a volume number 2 appearing for each year. The date is placed in brackets and is followed immediately by the volume number.

3. Name of the work and series

Standard abbreviations for the names of the reports are used, and the approved abbreviation is usually given on the title page of the work.

The series designation is important because a particular law report series may have a volume number 25 appearing in each of its series which may run to fourth series or more. The series abbreviation appears in parentheses after the report's abbreviation. Common series abbreviations are: (2d), (3d), (4th), and (N.S.) for "new series". For example:

Oakfield Builders Ltd. v. Murrant (1977), 33 N.S.R. (2d) 449

Cites should be directed to the reader, and if it is known that the reader may not be familiar with Canadian citation, more complete abbreviations could be used. For example, C.C.C. might be changed to Can. Crim. Cas.

4. Page number

The page number at which the case begins is always included, without the abbreviation "p". Specific pages within a case are shown either with a comma and then the specific page, or by using "at", and then the page number.

Paquette v. Cruji (1979), 26 O.R. (2d) 294, at 296.

Note that some looseleaf services assign index numbers rather than a page number. For example, a case appearing in CCH's *Canadian Insurance Law Reporter* could be cited:

Findlay v. Madill, [1980] ILR. 1-1181

5. Court and jurisdiction

If the court cannot be identified from the report abbreviation, then the jurisdiction and court are placed at the end of the citation in parentheses.

MacDonald Const. Co. v. Ross (1980), 91 A.P.R. 450 (P.E.I.S.C.)

By including the court, readers can determine if the decision is binding on their jurisdictions or to what extent the decision might be persuasive.

If the report abbreviation includes a single jurisdiction, then only the court abbreviation need be used.

Shen Investments Ltd. v. Mosca, [1986] 2 0.R. 162 (H.C.)

6. Judges

Quoting a particular passage from a judgment requires giving the name of the judge unless his or her name appears elsewhere in the text. Proper abbreviations from judges' titles include:

C.J.C. = Chief Justice of Canada
C.J.O. = Chief Justice of Ontario
C.J.Q.B. = Chief Justice of Queen's Bench
J. = For most justices or judges other than the Chief Justice or Chief Judge.
J.A. = Court of Appeal Justice other than the Chief Justice.

JJ. and JJ.A. are plurals. Quoting a judge who was quoting another judge may be "... 340 at 342 per Ritchie, J. quoting the learned trial judge, Ruttan J."

7. Parallel citations

Including more than one report citation is helpful to those who may not have access to all law report series.

(a) Same case reported by several law reports

The style of cause is stated once and the year appears once preceding the report citations unless the first citation has a year parentheses which is the judgment's year. The citations are separated by commas, while the jurisdiction and court follow the last citation. The suggested order for citation in more than one law report series is:

> Official report (*e.g.*, S.C.R. or F.C.R.), semi-official report (*i.e.*, commercial report printed under authority of a provincial Law Society such as O.R.), and unofficial reports.

Within unofficial reports, the following order is suggested:

> Geographic reports in decreasing order of coverage — *i.e.*, national then regional and then provincial (*e.g.*, D.L.R., W.W.R., Sask. R.), specialty subject reports in alphabetical order (*e.g.*, C.C.C., C.R., M.V.R.), digesting or other services (*e.g.*, CCH's service titled *Dominion Tax Cases,* D.T.C.).

For example:

> *Neon Products Ltd. v. Children's Holdings Ltd.* (1979), 27 O.R. (2d) 126, 14 C.P.C. 232 (H.C.)
>
> *Burlingham v. Morrell* (1983), [1984] 1 W.W.R. 564, 29 Sask. R. 290 (C.A.) (illustrates use of parenthesized year and bracketed year).

(b) Cases appealed

If a case is appealed, whether the judgment was reversed, varied, or affirmed, the groupings of citations for each court level should be separated by semi-colons. The style of cause need not be listed again unless there is a significant change of name causing difficulty in locating the several reports. For example, *Gallie v. Lee* became *Saunders v. Anglia* on appeal, and the term *sub nom.* (under the name of) may be used to indicate earlier versions of the style of cause. The groupings of citations proceed from latest (highest court level) to earliest (lowest court level).

An example of citing a case appealed and reported at various levels would be:

> *R. v. Johnson,* [1978] 2 S.C.R. 391, 19 N.R. 476, [1978] 2 W.W.R. 478, 39 C.C.C. (2d) 479, 4 C.R. (3d) 269; affirming [1977] 2 W.W.R. 613, 34 C.C.C. (2d) 325, 37 C.R.N.S. 234 (N.W.T.C.A.); affirming [1976] 6 W.W.R. 747, 32 C.C.C. (2d) 177, 37 C.R.N.S. 236 (N.W.T.S.C.).

8. Unreported decisions

In citing an unreported decision, the style of cause may have to be given in more detail. The date of decision should always be given in full. The name of the judge and the registry action number should be included. Any unreported digesting service citation should be included as with a law report series. Fuller information is required to facilitate acquisition of the judgment by the reader (possibly from the court), but many publishers of digesting services provide a quick response full text judgments mailing, fax, or courier service for cases digested.

> *Datatech Systems Ltd. v. Commonwealth Insurance* (April 21, 1982) an unreported decision of Mr. Justice Berger (B.C.S.C., Vancouver Registry C814723), [1982] B.C. Decisions Civ. 1985-01.

9. Newspapers and periodicals

Newspaper citations should include newspaper name, issue date, and page number, column number at which the article starts:

> *Robert Smith v. Herbert Jones, The Globe and Mail,* March 20, 1981, at 32, col. 4 (Ont. H.C.)

Periodicals should follow the format suggested for citing periodical articles but adapting for a case citation:

> *R. v. Forst* (1980), 23 Crim. L.Q. 37 (Ont. C.A.)

10. Computer databases

If a case exists on computer database but not in a print-form publication, it may be cited as follows:

(a) For a case on Quicklaw, *R. v. Butler,* [1992] S.C.J. No. 15 (QL). In this example, the database is S.C.J. on QL.

(b) For a case on LEXIS-NEXIS, *Arnot v. Smith*, 1997 Can. Sup. Ct. Lexis 42. In this example, the file is CANSCT in CANADA library.

11. Administrative decisions

The name of the Board chairperson is normally cited together with the abbreviated name for the tribunal:

> *Re Four Star Applicators (Calgary)* and *Glaziers-Architectural Metal Mechanics and Glassworkers* (1982), 1 C.L.R.B.R. (N.S.) 1 (B.C.L.R.B., Germaine, Vice Chairman).

12. English case citation

Generally, English case citation follows the same form as Canadian citation. When referring to cases from the *English Reports,* cite the old nominate reference first, and then the *English Reports* reference.

Knight v. Marjoribanks (1849), 2 Mac. & G. 10, 42 E.R. 4

The order of preference for English parallel citations is as follows:

(a) Nominate reports — *English Reports* (as above)
(b) *Law Reports*
(c) *All England Law Reports*
(d) Other reports, such as *Weekly Law Reports*

13. American case citation

In American citation, the name of the court and the year follow the volume and series information. There are no parentheses around the series designation.

Toth v. Coming Glass Works, 411 F.2d 912 (6th Cir. 1969)

B. STATUTE CITATION

A correct citation consists of the title of the statute, an abbreviation of the jurisdiction, the year of the statute, and the chapter or number of the statute.

1. The title

For the title, use the short title as given in the statute itself. Where no official short title is given in the statute, use the short title found in the official volume where the statute appears. If no short title is to be found, use the full title. Use "The" only when the word is part of the title. A date may be part of the title. For example:

The Family Law Reform Act, 1978, S.O. 1978, c. 2
Canada Evidence Act, S.C. 1970, c. E-10
An Act to incorporate The Army and Navy Veterans in Canada, S.C. 1917, c. 70

2. Jurisdiction and statutory reference

Citation to a statute should, unless deliberate reference is made to an earlier edition of the Act, be to the latest revision of the statute and should include in abbreviated form a reference to the jurisdiction. In a citation, reference is first made to the statutes or revised statutes (abbreviated either Rev. Stat. and Stat. or R.S. and S.) before the jurisdictional abbreviation. Jurisdictional abbreviations are:

Canada	C.
Newfoundland	N.
Nova Scotia	N.S.
Prince Edward Island	P.E.I.
New Brunswick	N.B.
Québec	Q.
Ontario	O.
Manitoba	M.
Saskatchewan	S.
Alberta	A.
British Columbia	B.C.

For provinces using a different numbering scheme for the looseleaf version of the statutes, citation to the looseleaf edition should be given in parentheses following the bound volume version.

3. The year

Statutes must be cited by year. Though the regnal year reference may be given in the volume, it is not used in the citation. If a legislative session extends over more than one year, all years of the session should be included: S.C. 1980-81-82-83.

If an Act first appears in a sessional volume, and appears subsequently in a statutory revision, reference is made to the revision. *Canada Pension Plan Act,* R.S.C. 1985, c. C-8.

If a year has more than one legislative session, then reference to the session must be included since reference to only the year would be insufficient. Thus:

S.M. 1959 (lst Session), c. 3
S.M. 1959 (2nd Session), c. 3

It is the practice of the Dominion and several provincial governments to publish a supplement the year the statutes are revised. Because the revised statutes replace (although not necessarily repeal) most of the important public statutes, the statutes passed that year are made part of the revision and called a "supplement". The statutes may appear before the revision is published; if so, they are cited in the usual fashion. Once the revision is issued, however, they should be shown as a supplement to the revision: R.S.C. 1985 (2nd Supp.), c. 10.

4. Chapter number

The chapter number is designated by "c." followed by the number or alphanumber. Plural chapters are designated "cc." Sections are designated "s." (plural being "ss."), while subsections may be "s." or "s-s." (plural being "s-ss.").

The Medical Profession Act, 1981, S.S. 1980-81, c. M-10.1

"Cap." is sometimes used for chapter (plural being "Cap.") and "sec." for section (plural being "sec."). Note that Newfoundland formerly did not use chapters but used numbers (singular and plural, "No.").

5. Amendments to statutes

Amendments are given only if they affect the statute as a whole or the particular section referred to. Use "am." and the citation of the amending Act.

Innkeepers Act, R.S.A. 1980, c. I-4, as am. by S.A. 1981, c. 18

If an Act or a section of it had been repealed, use "rep."; if repealed and substituted (re-enacted), use "re-en.". If new material is enacted, use "en.". If the amendment changes the name of the Act, use the new name. Note that amendments may be shown after a complete citation in square brackets and that inclusion of the jurisdiction in the citation of the amendments is optional.

Innkeepers Act, R.S.A. 1980, c. I-4 [am. 1981, c. 18]

Specific references may be made to section numbers.

The Mineral Taxation Act, R.S.A. 1955, c. 203, s. 9(2), as am. by S.A. 1966, c. 56, s. 3 (a)

6. Effective date of legislation

It may be useful to note the date on which a statute becomes effective. This is normally done by referring to the effective date and the instrument bringing the provision into force in parentheses after the citation of the Act. The abbreviations "eft." or "C.I.F." (effective, and coming into force) are frequently used.

7. Québec statutes

The Québec *Civil Code* is cited by reference to the Code, the article number and paragraph number.

Code civil, art. 351, al. 2

Other Québec codes (*e.g., Code municipal)* are cited in similar fashion.

8. English statute citation

The notations "(Imp.)" or "(U.K.)" are used after the titles of all English statutes or at the end of the citation. English statutes are cited differently before and after 1962:

(a) Up to and including 1962, the regnal year (year of the reign) and the chapter number cited.

Supreme Court of Judicature (Consolidation) Act, 1925 (U.K.), 15 & 16 Geo. 5, c. 49, s. 226

That is the 15th and 16th years of the reign of George V (written as "Geo. 5"). George V's reign began in 1910, so the date of the statute is 1925.

(b) After 1962, the regnal year is no longer cited.
Town and Country Planning Act 1971, 1971, c. 78, s. 1 (U.K.)
Amendments to the statutes use the same format as Canadian statutes.

9. Canadian Charter of Rights and Freedoms

Canadian Guide to Uniform Legal Citation, 3d ed. (Toronto: Carswell, 1992) at 10 suggests: *Canadian Charter of Rights and Freedoms,* Part I of the *Constitution Act, 1982,* being Schedule B to the *Canada Act 1982* (U.K.), 1982, c. 11.

C. REGULATION CITATION

Regulations should be cited as far as possible in a form similar to that used for statutes. Different citations are used depending on whether the regulation has been assigned an identifying number (in which case it is cited by that number) or not (in which case it is cited by the page number where it appears in the gazette).

1. Citing by page

When citing a regulation by its page number, give the name of the regulation (if one is assigned; if not, use a descriptive title), the name of the volume in which the regulation appears (in abbreviated form), and the page number of the regulation. For example:

New Brunswick Fishery Regulations, (1966) 100 *Canada Gazette Part II* 1025, August 24, 1966

This is page 1025 of volume 100 of the *Canadian Gazette Part II* which was published in 1966. The final date is the date on which that portion of volume 100 appeared.

2. Citing by number

When citing a regulation by its regulation number, give the name of the regulation (if one is assigned, if not, use a descriptive title), the abbreviation of the jurisdiction and the regulation number. For example:

Private Aeroplanes Passenger Transportation Order, SOR/82-278

The number refers to the federal Statutory Order and Regulation number 278 of the year 1982.

Some jurisdictions revise their regulations periodically. Citation should be to the most recent revision unless there is reason to cite to the older instrument. The most recent federal consolidation is the *Consolidated Regulations of Canada,*

1978, which is divided into chapters and sections (*e.g.*, C.R.C. 1978, c. 1017).
An amended regulation would be cited in this format:
C.R.C. 1978, c. 1361, s, 3(2)(b), as am. by SOR 80/214

3. Unpublished regulations

Canada Gazette Part II, Table III lists regulations exempt from publication. Unpublished regulations should be cited in detail, allowing the reader to know the source as well as the name or a description of the regulation.

4. Legislative authority

It will periodically be necessary to refer the reader to the statute empowering the making of regulations. This may be done by noting that it is "issued under the authority of" or is "made pursuant to" the relevant statute.

5. Guide to citing regulations by jurisdiction

The following table gives examples of the form of the numbered portion of the citation. If there is a lower listing, the reference is to the jurisdiction's looseleaf, revised, or consolidated version of regulations.

Yukon	O.I.C. 1982/339
Northwest Territories	N.W.T. Reg. 099-92 R.R.N.W.T. 1990, c. A-5 (revised regulations)
British Columbia	B.C. Reg. 3126/93 Consolidation cited in same manner
Alberta	Alta. Reg. 104/92 Revised regulation cited in same manner
Saskatchewan	Sask. Reg. 240/79 R.R.S., c. C-19.1 Reg. 1
Manitoba	Man. Reg. 140/83 Man. Reg. 25/91 R. for re-enacted regulations
Ontario	O. Reg. 10/91 R.R.O. 1990, Reg. 101
Québec	R.R.Q. 198l, c. A-1 r. 1 O.C. 1194-83

New Brunswick	N.B. Reg. 92-34 Looseleaf regulations are not official revision
Prince Edward Island	EC 506/83 Looseleaf regulations are not official revision
Nova Scotia	N.S. Reg. 15/93
Newfoundland	Nfld. Reg. 16/93
Canada	S.O.R./93 - 121 C.R.C. 1978, c. 1017, s. 5

D. PARLIAMENTARY DOCUMENTS

Citation of documents recording the work of Parliament or a Legislative Assembly or of documents laid before the House should be in accordance with the general principles of citation already enunciated.

The following form of citation is recommended:

1. Debates

Identify the jurisdiction (if necessary), the legislative assembly, the year, and the page or column number. Unless the debates are not numbered consecutively, it is not necessary to give the exact date of the document. Examples:

Commons Debates (1982) 17170
Ontario Debates (1964) 1664
Senate Debates (1959) 153

2. Votes and Proceedings

Votes and Proceedings should be cited according to the exact date and page number, to prevent confusion with similarly paged copies from a different session. The jurisdiction may be indicated in parentheses at the end of the reference:

(June 9th, 1983) Votes and Proceedings 189 (Ont.)
(July 15th, 1983) Votes and Proceedings 3 (B.C.)

3. Bills

The citation of Bills should note the Bill number, short title, legislative session, jurisdiction, the year, and the date on which it received first, second, or third reading as the case may be:

Bill C-208, An Act to amend the Department of Agriculture Act, 3d Sess. 34th Parl., 1991 (lst reading 27 May 1991)

4. Papers laid before Parliament

Several sorts of documents are laid before Parliament and they receive descriptive titles, a date, and often an identifying number. If they are the result of an inquiry or a commission, it is good practice to include the name of the chairperson. Examples:

(a) Report of the Royal Commission of Inquiry into Civil Rights (McRuer Report), Report 2, 1968

(b) Commons — Special Committee on Human Rights and Fundamental Freedoms, Minutes of Proceedings and Evidence (1960) Canada

E. SECONDARY AUTHORITY LITERATURE CITATION

Citation of textbooks and other secondary authority materials should follow principles of legal citation rather than guidance offered by general style manuals.

1. Periodical articles

A full citation includes the author's name, title of the article (in quotation marks), date of publication, volume number, name of the journal, and page. If the name of the periodical is cited in full, it should appear in italics; if it is abbreviated, it appears in Roman type.

> Kim E. Johnson, "Estate Planning for Farmers" (1981-82), 46 *Saskatchewan Law Review* (or Sask. Law. Rev.) 123 at 124

2. Textbooks

A textbook citation consists of the volume number (if any), the author's surname (and first initial or initials if a common surname), an abbreviated form (omit subtitle) of the title as it appears on the title page (may differ from title on cover or spine of the book), the edition (if 2d or more), the year, and page number. Subsequent references take the same form unless the titles of the work may conveniently be shortened. The citation of non-legal materials in legal writing normally takes the legal form. If there are more than three authors, cite the name of the first author, followed by "et al.". If the date of publication is unknown, use "n.d.".

After many editions of a work, there may be a new author who has substantially updated or rewritten the work, but the book may be still commonly known by the original author's name. If the original author's name appears as part of the title on the title page, both the original and new authors are included:

> F. Rhodes, *Williams' The Canadian Law of Landlord and Tenant,* 4th ed., 3rd Supp. (Toronto: Carswell, 1981), at 37

3. Digests, encyclopedias, and dictionaries

Legal dictionaries are cited as ordinary legal texts:

Black's Law Dictionary (6th ed. 1990)

Digests and encyclopedias may be cited by volume number, the title, edition if second or higher, and page number. Paragraph or section numbers may be more specific and appropriate than a page number.

A digest cite may be 25 Can. Abr. Rev. (2nd) 120. An encyclopedia article may also include the name of the article: "Evidence" 12 C.E.D. (Western 3rd. ed.) 58-278.

4. Electronic sources

At present, computer online databases store information also available in print form which should be used for citation purposes. If it is desired to make reference to a particular search, however, the following form is recommended: Transcribe the search query exactly as it is used, identify the computer service used, the databases searched, the date and time of the search. For example, "Negligen* & dentist", QUICKLAW (D.R.S., A.C.W.S., W.L.P.), April 13, 1993, 1:30 p.m.

The recent proliferation of CD-ROM titles raises a citation issue not even addressed by citation books of the early 1990s. We have chosen to place CD-ROM titles in quotation marks rather than in italics or underlining because a CD-ROM collection more resembles a series of individual titles, each of which is italicized or underlined, than a new publication. When law publishers advertise a grouping of individual titles in a collected series, the name of the series is often placed in quotes because the series title does not represent a publication that is different from the individual titles collected. For example, Canada Law Book advertises seven separate books (*e.g.*, *A Practical Guide to the Ontario Human Rights Code*) as its "The Practical Guide Series". For example, we have placed in quotations Carswell's "Family Law Partner" CD-ROM, which contains law reports, case digests, statutes and regulations, and several individual textbooks. If future Canadian books devoted to legal citation offer a different approach or format, it is not the intention of this textbook to create differences in citing CD-ROMs.

5. Footnotes, repeated references, and introductory signals

(a) Legal writing for academic publication may include footnote references. Footnotes are less frequently used in other legal writing. If footnotes are not used, the authority cited is included as part of the text, in parentheses, or set off by a comma or a colon.

(b) Repeated references involve footnotes and antecedent and subsequent references in the text of a writing. Repeated statutory references usually repeat the citation. For other material, if the repeated reference does not fit into one of the following categories, then the citation should be repeated in full. But if the repeated reference does fit one of these categories, then the term listed in the rule may be used in place of the full citation:

(1) *"Ibid."* (abbreviation of *Ibidem)* is used when the subsequent footnote follows the prior one closely (not more than a few pages away), when there are no intervening footnotes, and when the two footnotes are the same including the page number. For example:
14. B. Smith, *Introduction to the Canadian Law of Trusts* (1979) 23
15. *Ibid.*

(2) *"Id." (ldem)* is used when the subsequent footnote follows the prior one closely, when there are no intervening footnotes, but when a qualification is necessary. For example:
14. B. Smith, *Introduction to the Canadian Law of Trusts* (1979) 23
15. *Id.*, at 24

(3) *"Supra"* and *"Infra" are* used to refer to portions of the writing or footnotes which appear before or after the present footnote, respectively. If the present footnote number 14 is at page 262 and refers to the text on page 272, write:
14. *Infra,* at 272
If the present footnote number 14 is at page 262 and refers to the text on page 125, write:
14. *Supra,* at 125

(c) Introductory signals:
Signals introducing citations in footnotes indicate the degree of support given by the cited material to the present statement being footnoted. If the material cited in the footnote is the source of the present statement or simply supports the statement, the footnote is written without an introductory signal. For clarity of illustration of signals, the present document being written is Document X, and the writer's preparation has included review of documents A, B, C, *etc*. Commonly used introductory signals include (footnote 14 or Document X used as an example):

(1) E.g.
"14. E.g., citation to document A". Document A is but one example of several documents which support the proposition in document X footnoted by footnote 14. Citation is not given to the other documents.

(2) See
"14. See document B". Document B directly supports the proposition in X; the support is not explicit but rather follows from it.

(3) Cf.
"14. Cf. document C". Document C supports the proposition in X, but the statement in C is directed to a different point. Cf. means "compare".

(4) See also
"14 See also documents D and E". Document X has discussed the

proposition by mentioning several sources in the main text of X, but this footnote points to additional supporting material.

(5) See generally
"14. See generally document F". Document F provides background information helpful in understanding the proposition in document X.

(6) Contra
"14. Contra document G". Document G contradicts the proposition in document X.

(7) But Cf.
"15. But Cf. document H". Document H supports a proposition analogous to the proposition stated in (for the sake of example) document G which contradicts X's proposition.

(8) "14. But see document K". Document K strongly supports a proposition contrary to the proposition in X.

Chapter 18

Business, Social Science, Science, and Government Publications Research

Research in the social sciences, in the sciences, and in federal, provincial, and municipal government publications can be of critical value to litigation preparation. Competition litigation may employ business and economics research, while criminal law cases may involve criminology, psychology, and psychiatry. Family law draws support from many disciplines such as sociology, economics and statistics, government publications and social services, and psychiatry. Personal injury cases may require medical sciences knowledge and economics. Cases centring on broad social issues such as abortion, discrimination and hate literature are dependent on many interdisciplinary aspects of the sciences and social sciences.

For the legal profession which is faced with the rapidly increasing number of publications in the relatively narrow legal field, the prospects of researching in all the fields of knowledge can seem a formidable task. The DIALOG system of databases challenges the researcher of social science and science literature by holding more than 100,000,000 references and documents. Just as there are separate law school libraries, large universities maintain separate libraries for many of the science and social science disciplines. University libraries have separate government publications departments.

The purpose of this chapter is to provide the legal researcher with an overview of research in other fields. Such research may include direct library research which is becoming more difficult with even the largest libraries having only selected holdings in most fields, but the more likely prospect is the legal researcher consulting other types of researchers such as librarians and other information brokers. For larger or specialized law firms, the firm librarian searching the "legal support" databases of QUICKLAW, LEXIS-NEXIS, or DIALOG may be standard procedure. The firm librarian can obtain hard copies of material retrieved in a computer search.

Research may concentrate on locating expert witnesses to testify about a very narrow business, scientific, or social science issue or on locating particular research institutes. There are several directories of specialists such as the Canadian Bar Association's *Book of Experts,* and the LEXIS-NEXIS and DIALOG computer systems have listings of experts in all fields.

A. BUSINESS, SOCIAL SCIENCE, AND SCIENCE RESEARCH

In the interest of time, the legal researcher will probably rely heavily upon the assistance of librarians and/or computer research. If either of these two options is exercised, the legal researcher should understand the basics of research in other fields to facilitate communication with librarians and to possess general knowledge about the publications comprised in the computer database. This chapter subsection gives general background on the library's card catalogue and periodical indexes, reference sources, and abstract services.

Initial access to a general library collection may be through the library's card catalogue (the traditional cards in cabinet trays), through a microfiche catalogue, or through an online computer catalogue. The call number scheme (classification scheme) may be the Dewey Decimal System or the Library of Congress Classification System which has categories running for A to Z (*e.g.*, K is law, H is social sciences, R is medicine, *etc.*). Many law libraries use a Canadian modified KF scheme as a Canadian adaptation of the law portion of this comprehensive scheme developed by the Library of Congress in the U.S. The main catalogue probably contains bibliographic information about all titles held by the university's library system whether the material is in the main library or in a satellite library. Because the catalogue lists only titles (*e.g.*, *Canadian Tax Journal),* it is estimated that only five per cent of a library's documents and articles may be directly accessed through the catalogue. The researcher must remember that access to individual articles in journals is provided by periodical indexes (*e.g.*, all articles in the title, *Canadian Journal of Political Science,* may be accessed through the title, *Canadian Periodical Index).*

If general background reading for a subject is necessary, the library's reference section may be a logical starting point. Similar to background reading provided by a legal encyclopedia, a specialized work such as the *International Encyclopedia of the Social Sciences* or *The Canadian Encyclopedia* may be a launching point with its footnotes and cites. Guides such as Winchell's *Guide to Reference Books,* Brown's *Canadian Business and Economics: A Guide to Sources of Information* (published by Canadian Library Association), and Ryder's *Canadian Reference Sources* (published by the Canadian Library Association) indicate the most respected sources in the reference section. One of the Canadian reference sources listed in Ryder's book is the listing of dissertations, *Canadian Theses,* compiled by the National Library. Canadian theses also appear in the international listing, *Dissertation Abstracts International,* which may contain summaries of theses written about Canada but written at foreign universities. There are many bibliographies on all scientific and social science topics and subtopics and even comprehensive bibliographies of bibliographies. The title, *Canadiana,* produced on a monthly basis by the National Library of Canada, is a bibliographic listing of books about Canada, written by Canadians, or published in Canada. Directories include the multi-volume *Encyclopedia of Associations* and directories of experts. Every discipline has its dictionaries similar to legal dictionaries which are valuable for researchers needing definitions of jargon as they read the literature of a new field. Statistics Canada can be a valuable source for statistical data.

Periodical Indexes and abstracting services in other fields are similar in function to the *Index to Canadian Legal Periodical Literature* and *Index to Canadian Legal Literature* in coping with an overwhelming volume of published literature. Legal researchers are familiar with a handful of journals and indexes, but it is estimated that there are more than 1,000 indexing/abstracting services allowing subject access to more than 50,000 English and foreign language social science and science journals. For most disciplines, index services list references under alphabetically arranged key words and/or phrases, while an abstracting service goes a step further. An abstract is a terse presentation of all points made in the document which may be a book, a research report, a journal or newspaper article, a speech, conference proceedings, an interview, government publication, *etc*. The abstract should cover the methodology, arguments, essential results, and conclusions of the document being summarized. The abstract is usually in the author's own words unlike the legal digesting services where commercial editors digest judges' opinions. A representative title is *Sociological Abstracts.*

Similar to legal publications such as the *Canadian Abridgment Revised 2nd edition,* an abstracting service may have a classification scheme as indicated by the table of contents showing the topics and subtopics, a subject index, a listing of titles indexed and abstracted, and cumulations. Titles of indexes and abstract publications may suggest a narrow focus, but coverage may be considerably broader than would be indicated by such key title words as "art" or "education". Related fields are often considered, and anyone doing a subject analysis in depth should consult indexes which take in fringe area topics.

Several Canadian publishers of business information in print form also are active in offering computer database systems to subscribers. These database systems often provide computer access to many print publications in legal and non-legal areas. A law firm's most ready access to print publications is through the firm's computer link to these database systems rather than time consuming trips to large libraries.

General researchers may classify computer databases by the standard divisions of business, social science, science, and government publications. Legal researchers may seek all types of material within a special subject, for example, scientific proofs but sociological factors in a criminal case; child psychology and economics in a divorce case; scientific data and business statistics in an environmental action; medical evidence and economic projections in a personal injury case. For a practitioner specializing in corporate law, there is a wealth of business-related information available through the database systems. Computer search techniques for business, social science, and science databases are similar to techniques described in Chapter 10, Computer-Assisted Legal Research. Some of the products are offered in CD-ROM format.

Prior editions of this textbook have provided some detail about non-legal online databases, but the growth of both legal and non-legal print and electronic material precludes continuing such detailed coverage of non-legal online databases. A suggested approach would be to check the non-legal online database listings in your LEXIS-NEXIS catalogue from Butterworths and your news and science and technology sections of QL's "Complete Database List". Note that QL acts as a gateway to Info Globe Online. *The Globe and Mail*'s division Globe Information Services has an online service called Info Globe, which includes more than 140 Canadian sources and more than 250 international publications. Micromedia Ltd. of Toronto offers many electronic products, and some of its legal products have been cited in this textbook. DIALOG has changed Canadian agents and you may check with your local librarian or the DIALOG Internet address: www.dialog.com.

B. RESEARCH IN GOVERNMENT PUBLICATIONS

1. Federal government publications overview

Government publications can be of vital importance to the legal researcher whether they are primary authority material in the form of statutes and regulations or whether they are government departmental papers giving background information for litigation preparation. Government publications may be federal, provincial, or municipal, but only federal publications are within the scope of this chapter.

Federal government publications may be Parliamentary papers, production of which is required by Parliament, or non-Parliamentary reports produced by government departments for use by non-government and government entities. Parliamentary papers include Parliamentary publications such as *Votes and Proceedings* and reports for presentation to Parliament such as annual reports of departments. Parliament consists of the Sovereign represented by the Governor General, the appointed Senate, and the elected House of Commons. A Parliament may last up to five years before being dissolved, and it is divided into sessions which end by prorogation. The Governor General, who executes duties on the advice from the Privy Council (Prime Minister and the Cabinet), signs state documents including giving royal assent to bills passed by the House and Senate.

The publications of Parliament include:

(a) Records of proceedings

(1) The House of Commons' daily agenda is published as *Order Papers and Notices* (no index). A record of what transpired during daily sitting is published in the *Votes and Proceedings*. The *Votes and Proceedings* include introduction of bills, referral of questions to committees, resolutions, record of votes, proclamations, notice of committee meetings, and reports tabled in the House. At the end of the session, they are cumulated and bound into the *Journal of the House of Commons* which has

an index.

(2) The *Minutes of the Proceedings* of the Senate which serves a function similar to the Commons' *Votes and Proceedings* plus *Order Papers Notices*. It is cumulated into the *Journal of the Senate* which has an index.

(b) Verbatim records of speeches and debates (Hansards)

The *Debates of the House of Commons* and the *Debates of the Senate* are issued daily and are cumulated into bound volumes at the sessions' end. They have indexes and are accessed through QUICKLAW computer search. The popular title, Hansard, is derived from the *English Parliamentary Debates* which were originally published by the Hansard family.

(c) Sessional papers

Sessional papers are those tabled in Parliament, and they are listed in the index of the *Journal of the House of Commons* with the designation of whether they have been printed for dissemination or not. Sessional papers include departmental annual reports, the Estimates, the Public Accounts, and Reports of Royal Commissions.

(d) Proceedings of committees

Committees of the House and Senate are designated Standing, Select, or Special. A committee with members from both Chambers is a Joint Committee, and a chamber may meet as a Committee of the Whole. The committees may order that Minutes of Proceedings be published, and they are indexed in the *Government of Canada Publications: Quarterly Catalogue.*

(e) Canada Gazette

Part I of the *Canada Gazette* (weekly) contains government notices, proclamations, and certain Orders-in-Council. Part II (issued every two weeks) contains regulations and other statutory instruments. Part III (issued irregularly) contains new statutes which have just received royal assent. The steps to the transformation of a bill into a statute are three readings. Bills are printed after First Reading. After Second Reading, the appropriate Committee reviews the wording of the bill and may propose amendments. After Third Reading, bills as passed are printed. When *Statutes of Canada* chapter numbers are assigned, groups of new statutes are printed in the *Canada Gazette Part III.* Research in statutes and regulations are treated in detail in Chapter 4: "Statutes", and Chapter 5: "Subordinate Legislation".

(f) Royal commissions and task forces

Royal Commissions (frequently known as Commissions of Inquiry), are appointed to obtain information in anticipation of legislative enactments, to sample public opinion, to investigate government administrative functions, *etc*. Commissions are appointed by Order-in-Council appearing in the *Canada Gazette Part I* and exist outside of Parliament (*i.e.*, do not cease at prorogation of a session). When a Commission's report is tabled in Parliament, it receives a Sessional paper number. Micromedia Ltd. has issued a microfiche collection of all Commission reports with a guide as an update to Henderson's *Federal Royal Commissions in Canada 1867-1966: a Checklist.*

A task force is assigned to gather information, but there is no requirement to publish their reports.

While the annual reports of administrative tribunals, councils, and many departments are required to be tabled in Parliament, there are many publications of these entities which are non-Parliamentary in nature. Access to these publications is often in the general research sources for government publications described in the section below.

2. Research access to government publications

In a large library, government publications may be housed in a separate department with a catalogue listing of documents held. They may be accessed by subject which may be a "key-word in title" listing. Documents may have seemingly complex number assignments, while call number schemes for such publications are usually different than the general classification scheme used by the library. A Parliamentary Committee report may be assigned a number XC12-304/103 by the Government Publishing Centre (X = House, C = Committee, 1 = Standing, 2 = Committee #, 30 = 30th Parliament, 4 = 4th session, 1 = type of report, and 3 = third report), while a document may be assigned a call number from a scheme which is different in format; *e.g.*, CA1SG13 80S57 ENG(BK-G) where CA1 = Canada, Federal level, SG13 = Department of Solicitor General — Research Branch, 80 = 1980, S57 = title number, ENG = English language, BK = "book" (more than 100 pages), and G = location in government publication section.

The researcher must realize that many library departments only collect selective documents, but comprehensive listings are available.

(a) *Weekly Checklist of Canadian Government Publications* has two parts: parliamentary publications and departmental publications. The cumulation of this government publication is *Government of Canada Publications: Quarterly Catalogue* which has the two parts of the weekly list plus an index.

(b) *Canadiana* is a monthly government publication listing books about Canada, written by Canadians, or published in Canada. This has a subject index and includes federal, provincial, and municipal publications.

(c) *Microlog Index* by Micromedia Ltd. is a monthly reference guide to federal, provincial, and local government publications as well as institutional report literature (research institutes, universities, laboratories, societies, corporations, and associations). Single publications and reports are included as well as report series. The indexes are by author, title, and subject. Among the entities indexed is the Law Reform Commission of Canada whose reports and studies are important sources of information especially for newly enacted legislation resulting from these studies. This service is available on the CAN/OLE computer system and as "Microlog on CD" disk.
Micromedia Ltd. produces a number of microfiche series and guides for government publications including parliamentary papers, Department of External Affairs: Treaty Series, Documents from Federal-Provincial Conferences of First Ministers, and the Law Reform Commission.

(d) Indexing of Canadian government documents has been carried on computer databases, but for the current status of computer access to government publications, the researcher should check with a local law librarian or government publications librarian. The CODOC database of government publication references is on the National Research Council's CAN/OLE system. Another government system is the National Library of Canada's DOBIS system with over 3,500,000 bibliographic references.

(e) "British Official Publication (HMSO)" is a database on DIALOG with coverage from 1976.

(f) Internet addresses: Government and university library websites can provide bibliographic and/or text access to government publications.
An example of a library catalogue website is York University's URL: www.library.yorku.ca
Parliament's address: www.parl.gc.ca/
Revenue Canada's address: www.rc.gc.ca

Chapter 19

Improving Legal Writing

Virtually every law school now incorporates instruction on legal writing in the first year legal research course. "Legal writing" is difficult to teach and is difficult to define. It is more than just writing about the law and more than simply what lawyers and judges write. The term implies that the writing is in a style appropriate for the type and purpose of the writing. Different types of legal writing (trial brief, legal memorandum, opinion letter, *etc.*) are taught in depth at law schools and many books are devoted to the subject. The scope of this chapter permits an overview of these different types. "Legal writing" implies a weaving together of legal analysis and good, clear, expository English or French. Weaving legal analysis into a clear, expository style is what distinguishes lawyers from other craftspersons, and is a skill which requires continual care and honing. There are many articles on sharpening legal writing skills, and this chapter gives the legal writer some checklists of points against which his or her own writing may be easily compared.

An expanded discussion of legal writing is found in Chapter 10, "Legal Writing" in Fitzgerald's *Legal Problem Solving: Reason, Research, & Writing* (Markham: Butterworths, 1996). Another expanded discussion of legal writing is found in Chapter 3, subsections B through D in Yogis, Christie, and Iosipescu's *Legal Writing and Research Manual, 4th edition*, (Markham: Butterworths, 1994).

A. TYPES AND PURPOSES OF LEGAL WRITING

The general types of legal writing are law school exams, letters, pleadings and instruments such as contracts or wills, memoranda and briefs, legislative drafting, and judgment writing. Each type of writing requires clarity and logic, but techniques employed for each type must fit the purpose of each.

1. Law school examinations

For essay examination questions, the law student must analyze the problem and pay particular attention to the question asked. Issues should be framed using fact words from the problem and legal jargon words from the student's review of course concepts (more discussion of issue framing in Chapter 1). Only after analyzing the problem and developing the issues raised does the student start writing or typing the answer.

A very basic format often used for the answer is the IRAC method which presents a logical flow from Issue to Rule to Application to Conclusion. The Rule or statement of applicable law should include the rationale behind the law. The Application of the law to the facts of the problem should show how each element of the law can be tied to particular facets of the problem's facts. The Application should flow into a Conclusion which is supported by the preceding analysis.

A very simplified examination answer would be:

Is the defendant, who was a grocery store owner notified of a banana peel hazard in the store's aisle but who took no action, negligent and therefore liable to customer plaintiff who slipped on the peel?

By the *X v. Y* case where the plaintiff fell into unmarked hole in the floor of the defendant's department store and collected damages, an occupier is negligent and therefore liable if there is awareness of an in-store hazard such as an unexpected, unmarked hole and a customer is injured.

In the present problem, the defendant was notified of the banana peel hazard which is analogous to an unexpected hole in the floor since customers do not expect to find slippery material on store floors.

Because the defendant was notified of the banana peel hazard which was unexpected to a customer, the defendant is a negligent store owner and is liable to plaintiff.

The imaginative law student may argue that the *X v. Y* case was wrong because customers should expect to find something like a banana peel in a grocery store aisle and should be prepared to exercise caution. The determining factor may be whether the peel was in a garden produce aisle or the housewares aisle. The key point about the writing of law school examination is that the evidence of analysis is more important than statements of conclusions and rules which might not be tied together with analysis.

2. Letters

Letters may advise a client, or may be addressed to the opposing party. Other forms of legal writing follow rigid structure, but letters are more flexible. Assuming that legal analysis of the problem has been made, the writer must concentrate on factors such as the audience (a lay client or another lawyer). There is the challenge of writing clearly so that a complex legal issue can be incorporated into an answer to a lay person.

In a letter to a client, the lawyer is not being an advocate but is more in the position of writing a judgment — *i.e.*, a statement of the law and a conclusion. The client's question should be answered, but the client should understand that it is an opinion. The client's position should be stated clearly with a recitation of the facts relied upon, and a favourable conclusion may be stated initially with supporting material following. Where there is a doubtful or negative conclusion, the lawyer may want to lead up to the conclusion and suggest a range of alternative actions. The material supporting the conclusion should be tailored for the sophistication of the client or audience.

The key point is that letters to other lawyers may resemble the flow of other types of legal writing, but a letter to a lay person must be appropriate to the audience. Fitting the wording to the audience may involve using rules of general conciseness and clarity in legal writing.

In Weihofen's *Legal Writing Style* (St. Paul: West Publishing Co., 1961) at page 129, he illustrates a client letter which is inappropriate:

> I am of the opinion that there can be but little doubt that if Mr. Connor were to bring this transaction into litigation, the plaintiff's case would predicate liability on your part on a theory of agency. In the event of such litigation, however, the probabilities are adverse to such a claim's succeeding. My reasons for this conclusion lie in these facts which tend to destroy the assumption that Mr. Sirkin acted in a representative capacity on your behalf and in the fact that the burden of proof would devolve upon the plaintiff to establish the existence of such alleged agency.

A more direct letter would tell the client:

> If Mr. Connor were to sue you, he would probably assert that Mr. Sirkin was acting as your agent when he authorized Mr. Connor to do the work. Mr. Connor would have to establish that Mr. Sirkin was your agent, but the facts do not tend to support the proposition that he was your agent. Therefore, it is probable that Mr. Connor's claim would fail.

3. Pleadings and instruments

Pleadings and instruments require a high degree of preciseness, but the drafter is assisted by such form sets as *Williston and Rolls' Court Forms,* Butterworths' *Canadian Forms & Precedents,* and O'Brien's *Encyclopedia of Forms and Precedents.*

The key point is that a standard form may not fit all of the requirements of a client's problem. Adaptation of a form to the problem at hand or complete originality may be necessary. A complete discussion of the principles of drafting is presented by Dick's *Legal Drafting in Plain Language,* 3rd edition (Toronto: Carswell, 1995).

4. Memoranda and briefs

A legal memorandum is a law firm's internal analysis of the essential facts and relevant law relating to a client's problem. It uses the analytical techniques required in answering law school examinations, and may be the step preliminary to an opinion letter to a client, the drafting of court pleadings or drafting a legal instrument, or to preparation of a brief given to a court. The memorandum analyzes both sides of an issue, while a brief may be more persuasive in asserting the client's claim. Preparations of legal memoranda are standard requirements for beginning law students in preparation for moot court appearances.

Formats for memoranda vary from law firm to law firm, but legal memoranda usually contain the following elements. An outline format may assist the reader in mentally breaking down elements of the presentation.

(a) Identifying data such as client's name, principal requesting the research and memorandum, *etc*.

(b) Questions presented. This may be a statement of the issue or issues. The facts should be sufficient to enable the reader to understand the problem. The statement of law should be sufficient for an indexer to assign terms for adding the memorandum to the law firm's computer database of internal memoranda summaries. If there are many issues involved, the statement of facts may be presented first. Narrow issues should be identified rather than trying to sum up the problem with one ultimate question.

(c) Brief answer. Specific answers should be given to each question so that the principal will immediately know the answer. This will facilitate his or her reading of the discussion which progresses logically to the answer.

(d) Statement of facts. Only the essential facts should be summarized, but caution must be taken to include all facts which might have legal ramifications. Facts can be grouped into units which raise separate issues.

(e) Applicable statutes. If the problem is controlled by a statute, relevant sections and clauses may be quoted before a full discussion is given.

(f) Discussion. This section contains analysis of relevant statutory, regulatory, and case law. There should be counter-analysis to show what positions might be advanced by the opposing side. The memorandum must be balanced to allow the principal to decide whether the conclusion or answer (be it favourable or unfavourable to the client) is supportable. Unknown elements and areas of uncertainty should be explicitly stated. A general introduction to the area of law may be given if the principal might not be completely familiar with the subject.

    The discussion must be completed by explaining the conclusion. The discussion must be concise by avoiding lengthy quotations through use of the writer's own paraphrasing and by avoiding string citations through citing the strongest and most recent cases. The key point is that carefully selected and summarized law related to the facts of the problem is more important than long listings of case summaries which the writer only cursorily ties to the facts.

(g) Conclusion. The conclusion may be omitted if it closely resembles the brief answer. However, the conclusion may expand on which steps should be taken in clarifying unknowns or uncertainties. The conclusion may elaborate on suggestions for pursuing the client's claim to settlement or litigation.

The analysis in a legal memorandum may ease the preparation of trial and appellate briefs. A trial brief should be complete enough for a barrister to conduct the trial when that barrister was not the writer of the brief.

The appellate brief, which accompanies the pleadings, exhibits, transcript of testimony, and judgment, may contain the following elements:

(a) Jurisdictional statement explaining how the case has come before the appellate court.
(b) Questions presented and statement of facts.
(c) The argument and conclusion. The advocate's writing in these sections is more persuasive than the balanced analyses of the memorandum. The advocate should not overstate or exaggerate, but should present the argument in terms most favourable to the client's position.

5. Legislative drafting

This type of drafting may incorporate many of the general principles of pleadings and instrument drafting such as preciseness and avoidance of ambiguity. Most practitioners deal with legislation when considering application of a statute or regulation to a client's problem rather than drafting legislation. It is perhaps easier to pick apart legislative legal writing than to draft it. But knowing that a statute may be picked apart word by word or clause by clause may assist the legislative drafter in exercising cautions to examine each clause for potential ambiguity.

A regulation which states that: "persons engaged in the apiary business must make their premises freely accessible for inspection by departmental health inspectors" may seem clear until questions arise about the meanings of elements of the regulation:

(a) Does "business" mean an operation for profit or a hobbyist beekeeper who sells an occasional jar of honey?
(b) Does "premises" mean that the health inspector can inspect more than the beehive?
(c) Does "freely accessible" mean that the hobbyist and sometimes absent beekeeper must leave the pasture gate unlocked or should the beekeeper expect notice of inspection and simply assist the inspector with access at that time?

6. Judgment writing

Judgment writing contains many of the elements of the above types of legal writing and is covered in detail in Komar's *Reasons for Judgment* (Toronto: Butterworths, 1980). This text is no longer in print.

B. LEGAL WRITING IMPROVEMENT CHECKLIST

An exhaustive effort to improve one's legal writing involves reading the philosophies and suggestions of many writers on the subject including law faculty, judges, and practitioners. In the limited scope of this chapter, the most efficient approach is to present points which can be rapidly scanned by the legal writer.

The legal writer hopefully will detect some areas for improvement since every writer probably needs to improve some aspects of his or her writing and probably slips, at times, into usages of the language which are not the best. Checklist items are usually found in articles on grammar and usage for business, technical, and professional writers including lawyers. Law schools publish style guides which sometimes include grammar sections. A comprenhensive treatment of plain language writing for lawyers is found in Dick's *Legal Drafting in Plain Language*, 3rd ed. (Toronto: Carswell, 1995).

An overview of effective writing is given in Brusaw's *The Business Writer's Handbook* (New York: St. Martin's Press, 1976) at page xiii. Five steps to successful writing outlined in the book with some of the author's points included are:

(1) Preparation: establish an objective, identify the audience, establish a scope.
(2) Research: manual, computerized, interviews.
(3) Organization: outlining is essential.
(4) Writing the draft: opening, body with topic sentences and paragraphs, and conclusion.
(5) Revision: check the draft for completeness, accuracy, clarity and ambiguity. Check for style, conciseness, transactions, logical progression, grammar, mechanics, and format.

A text used by this author in teaching at the University of Regina was Wydick's *Plain English for Lawyers,* 2nd ed. (Durham, N.C.: Carolina Academic Press, 1985, 128 pages) which has an abridged version in 66 *California Law Review* 727. Because the primary content of this text expands as Canadian legal literature grows, the summary of Wydick's basic points below are condensed from prior editions of this text.

1. Omit surplus words

(a) Avoid poor construction by using fewer glue words. The sentence, "A trial by jury was requested by the defendant", has four working words (trial, jury, requested, and defendant) but five glue words. The improved sentence, "The defendant requested a jury trial", has only two glue words.
(b) Avoid compound prepositions such as "at that point in time" and "in connection with" which can be replaced by "then" and "concerning".
(c) Eliminate verbose word clusters such as "the fact that", which can simply be dropped from clauses such as "because of the fact that". "He was aware of the fact that" should be "he knew that". "In many cases you will find" is better changed to "often you will find".
(d) Shorten clauses and phrases. Opportunities for shortening are presented by which, who, that, it is, and there are. "Witness, who had been convicted of a crime," could be "witness, a convicted criminal".

(e) Avoid redundant legal phrases which arose historically from English lawyers having two languages to choose from (Celtic and Anglo-Saxon, English and Latin, and later English and French) and taking a word from each ("free and clear" coming from old English's "free" and old French's "cler"). Such roots are deep in tradition and it is difficult to steer away from ancient usage thought to have established meanings at law.

2. Use familiar, concrete words

(a) Concrete words should be used unless vagueness is necessary such as in drafting statutes where not every fact situation can be foreseen. Why cannot the overly abstract phrase "In our present circumstances, the budgetary aspect is a factor which must be taken into consideration to a greater degree" be shortened to "Today, we must think more about finances and budgeting"?

(b) Use words familiar to the audience. Words in a submission may use legal jargon, but an explanation to a client may use words more familiar to the lay public.

(c) Do not use lawyerisms such as words like "aforementioned" or "hereinafter" which carry little or no legal substance.

3. Use short sentences

Long sentences which interject qualifiers between spread out subjects, verbs, and objects are difficult for another to read. Reading flows better if there is a break in long, multi-thought sentences with shorter, single-thought sentences.

A complicated clause may be clarified by tabulating information in the same class. Tabulating is placing points in numbered, indented outline form.

4. Use base verbs and the active voice

Derivative nouns and adjectives should not be overused in place of base verbs because they attract surplus words. When the base verb, "object", in the following clause is changed to a derivative noun, the number of surplus words grows. "Please state why you object to the question" is preferable to "Please make a statement of why you are interposing an objection to the question."

The active voice has an advantage over the passive voice because it takes fewer words and conveys to the reader who is doing what to whom. "The trial judge ruled that..." is more concise than "The ruling was made by the trial judge that ...". The passive voice is proper when the thing done is important, not the person doing it. For example, "the papers were served on Saturday."

5. Careful word arrangement

The normal word order of subject-verb-object should be maintained unless inversion is used for emphasis. For example, "basic to our liberties is fair procedure".

Subject and verb should be close, and verb and object should be close. Modifying words should be close to what they modify. Do not state: "my client has discussed your proposal to fill the drainage ditch with his partners."

6. Avoid language distractions

Avoid variations if they create doubts about whether the variations are intended to have the same meaning. In the example, "The use fee shall be one per cent of the franchise's gross revenue, and franchise payments shall be made on or before...", are "use fee" and "franchise payments" the same?

Retaining sexism in legal writing serves no purpose other than to distract persons attuned to modern usages. "Each judge has his own ideals" should be replaced by "all judges have their own ideals".

Appendix A

Table of Report and Digest Abbrevations

The purpose of this Appendix is to provide Canadian researchers with an abbreviations table integrating a comprehensive listing of Canadian reports from the earliest times to 1997, a list of recently appearing Canadian digests providing access to unreported cases, a cross-reference from old English nominate reports to their locations in the English Reports or Revised Reports, and a selective list of current English, Australian, American, and New Zealand reports.

The basic listing is from the table in The Digest entitled "Reports Included in this Work and Their Abbreviations", and that source was used when there was a difference in the abbreviation used between it and other sources. For multiple name nominate reports abbreviations not immediately found in this table, check the single letter combinations and match the year if known. For example, the citation might be "Cromp. & Jer." (for Crompton & Jervis), while this table has entries under both "Cr. & J." and "C. & J."

A.	*Atlantic Reporter*	U.S.
A.C. (preceded by date)	*Law Reports, Appeal Cases, House of Lords,* since 1890 (*e.g.*, [1891] AC)	Eng.
A.C.W.S.	*All-Canada Weekly Summaries,* 1977-1979	Can.
A.C.W.S. (2d)	*All-Canada Weekly Summaries (Second Series),* 1981 - 1986	Can.
A.C.W.S. (3d)	*All-Canada Weekly Summaries (Third Series),* 1986-(current)	*Can.*
A.C.W.S. (Ont.)	*All-Canada Weekly Summaries (Ontario Edition),* 1981 - 1986	*Can.*
A.L.J.	*Australian Law Journal,* 1927-(current)	Aus.
A.L.R.	*American Law Reports*	U.S.
A.L.R.	*Australian Law Reports,* 1973-(current)	Aus.
A.L.R. Fed.	*American Law Reports, Federal*	U.S.
A., N.W.T. & Y Tax R.	*Alberta, N.W.T. & Yukon Tax Reports*	Can.
A.P.R.	*Atlantic Provinces Reports,* 1974-(current)	Can.
A.R.	*Alberta Reports,* 1976-(current)	Can.
A.W.L.D.	*Alberta Weekly Law Digest*	Can.

Act.	*Acton's Reports, Prize Causes,* 2 vols., 1809-1811	12 E.R.
Ad. & El.	*Adolphus and Ellis's Reports, King's Bench and Queen's Bench,* 12 vols. 1834-1842	110-113 E.R.
Add.	*Addam's Ecclesiastical Reports,* 3 vols., 1822-1826	162 E.R.
Admin. L.R.	*Administrative Law Reports,* 1983-(current)	Can.
Aleyn	*Aleyn's Reports, King's Bench,* fol., 1 vol., 1646-1649	82 E.R.
All.	*New Brunswick Reports (Allen),* 1848-1866	Can.
All E.R. (preceded by date)	*All England Law Reports,* 1936-(current)	Eng.
All E.R. Rep.	*All England Law Reports Reprint,* 1558-1935	Eng.
All E.R. Rep. Ext.	*All England Law Reports Reprint Extension,* 1861-1935	Eng.
Alta D.	*Alberta Decisions*	Can.
Alia L.R.	*Alberta Law Reports,* 1908-1932	Can.
Alta. L.R. (2d)	*Alberta Law Reports (Second Series),* 1976-1992	Can.
Alta. L.R. (3d)	*Alberta Law Reports (Third Series),* 1992-(current)	Can.
Amb.	*Ambler's Reports, Chancery,* 1 vol., 1716-1783	27 E.R.
And.	*Anderson's Reports, Common Pleas,* fol., 2 parts in 1 vol., 1535-1605	123 E.R.
Andr.	*Andrews' Reports, King's Bench,* fol., 1 vol., 1737-1740	95 E.R.
Anst.	*Anstruther's Reports, Exchequer,* 3 vols., 1792-1797	145 E.R.
App. Cas.	*Law Reports, Appeal Cases, House of Lords,* 15 vols., 1875-1890	Eng.
Armour	*Manitoba Reports temp Wood (ed Armour),* 1875-1883 (see also temp Wood)	Can.
Am. & H.	*Arnold and Hodges' Reports, Queen's Bench,* 1 vol., 1840-1841	Eng.
Atk.	*Atkyn's Reports, Chancery,* 3 vols., 1736-1754	26 E.R.
B.	*Beavan's Reports, Rolls Court,* 36 vols., 1838-1866	48-55 E.R.

B. & Ad.	*Barnewall and Adolphus' Reports, King's Bench,* 5 vols., 1830-1834	109-110 E.R.
B. & Ald.	*Barnewall and Alderson's Reports, King's Bench,* 5 vols., 1817-1822	106 E.R.
B. & B.	*Broderip and Bingham's Reports, Common Pleas,* 3 vols., 1819-1822	129 E.R.
B. & C.	*Barnewall and Cresswell's Reports, King's Bench,* 10 vols., 1822-1830	107-109 E.R.
B. & G.	*Brownlow and Goldesborough's Reports, Common Pleas,* 2 parts, 1569-1624	123 E.R.
B. & L.	*Browning and Lushington's Reports, Admiralty,* 1 vol., 1863-1866	167 E.R.
B. & P.	*Bosanquet and Puller's Reports, Common Pleas,* 3 vols., 1796-1804	126-127 E.R.
B. & S.	*Best and Smith's Reports, Queen's Bench,* 10 vols., 1861-1870	121-122 E.R.
B.C.A.C.	*British Columbia Appeal Cases,* 1991-(current)	*Can.*
B.C. Corps L.G.	*British Columbia Corporations Law* Guide	Can.
B.C.D.	*British Columbia Decisions,* 1972-(current)	Can.
B.C.L.A.	*British Columbia Labour Arbitration*	Can.
B.C.L.R.	*British Columbia Law Reports,* 1976-(current)	Can.
B.C.L.R.B.D.	*British Columbia Labour Relations* Board Decisions	Can.
B.C.R.	*British Columbia Reports,* 1867-1947	Can.
B.C.T.C.	*British Columbia Trial Cases,* 1997- current Note: Electronic format only	Can.
B.C.T.R.	*British Columbia Tax Reports*	Can.
B.C.W.L.D.	*British Columbia Weekly Law Digest*	Can.
B.L.R.	*Business Law Reports,* 1977-1991	Can.
B.L.R. (2d)	*Business Law Reports (Second Series),* 1991 -(current)	Can.
B.N.C.	*Sir R. Brooke's New Cases,* 1 vol., 1515-1558	73 E.R.
B.O.D.	*Butterworths' Ontario Digest,* 1901-1989	Can.
B.R.	*Rapports judiciares de Québec, Cour du* Banc du Roi/Quebec Official Reports, *Queen's (or King's) Bench,* 1892-1966	Can.
Ball & B.	*Ball and Beatty's Reports, Chancery (Ireland),* 2 vols., 1807-1814	12 R.R.

Barn. Ch.	*Barnardiston's Reports, Chancery,* fol., 1 vol., 1740-1741	27 E.R.
Barn. K.B.	*Barnardiston's Reports, King's Bench,* fol., 2 vols., 1726-1734	94 E.R.
Barnes	*Barnes' Notes of Cases of Practice, Common Pleas,* 1 vol., 1732-1760	94 E.R.
Beav.	*Beavan's Reports, Rolls Court,* 36 vols., 1838-1866	48-55 E.R.
Bell C.C.	*T. Bell's Crown Cases Reserved,* 1 vol., 1858-1860	169 E.R.
Bellewe	*Bellewe's Cases temp. Richard H, King's Bench,* 1 vol., 1378-1400	72 E.R.
Belt's Supp.	*Belt's Supplement to Vesey Sen., Chancery,* 1 vol., 1746-1756	28 E.R.
Ben. & D.	*Benloe and Dalison,* 1 vol., 1486-1580	123 E.R.
Benl.	*Benloe's (or Bendloe's) Reports, King's Bench,* fol., 1 vol., 1530-1627	73 E.R.
Ber.	*New Brunswick Reports (Berton),* 1835-1839	Can.
Bing.	*Bingham's Reports, Common Pleas,* 10 vols., 1822-1834	130-131 E.R.
Bing. N.C.	*Bingham's New Cases, Common Pleas,* 6 vols., 1834-1840	131-133 E.R.
Bl. Com.	*Blackstone's Commentaries*	Eng.
Bl. H.	*Blackstone, H.,* 1-2, 1788-1796	126 E.R.
Bl. W.	*Blackstone, W.,* 1-2, 1746-1780	96 E.R.
Bli.	*Bligh's Report's, House of Lords,* 4 vols., 1819-1821	4 E.R.
Bli. N.S.	*Bligh's Reports, House of Lords, New Series,* 11 vols., 1827-1837	4-6 E.R.
Bos. & P.	*Bosanquet and Puller's Reports, Common Pleas,* 3 vols., 1796-1804	126-127 E.R.
Bos. & P.N.R.	*Bosanquet and Puller's New Reports, Common Pleas,* 2 vols., 1804-1807	127 E.R.
Bridg. J.	*Bridgman, Sir J.,* 1613-1621	123 E.R.
Bridg. O.	*Bridgman, Sir 0.,* 1660-1667	124 E.R.
Bro. C.C.	*W. Brown's Chancery Reports,* 4 vols., 1778-1794	28-29 E.R.
C. & F.	*Clark and Finnelly's Reports, House of Lords,* 12 vols., 1831-1846	6-8 E.R.
C. & J.	*Crompton and Jervis's Reports, Exchequer,* 2 vols., 1830-1832	148-149 E.R.
C. & K.	*Carrington and Kirwan' s Reports, Nisi Prius,* 3 vols., 1843-1853	174-175 E.R.

C. & M.	*Carrington and Marshman's Reports, Nisi Prius,* 1 vol., 1841-1842	174 E.R.
C. & M.	*Crompton and Meeson's Reports, Exchequer,* 2 vols., 1832-1834	149 E.R.
C. & P.	*Carrington and Payne's Reports, Nisi Prius,* 9 vols., 1823-1841	171-173 E.R.
C. & P.	*Craig and Phillips' Reports, Chancery,* 1 vol., 1840-1841	41 E.R.
C.A. (preceded by date)	*Recueils de jurisprudence du Québec: cour d'appel,* 1970-(current)	Can.
C.A.S.	*Commission Des Affaires Sociales*	Can.
C.B.	*Common Bench Reports,* 18 vols., 1845-1856	135-139 E.R.
C.B .N.S.	*Common Bench Reports, New Series* 20 vols., 1856-1865	140-144 E.R.
C.B.R.	*Canadian Bankruptcy Reports,* 1920-1960	Can.
C.B.R.	*Copyright Board Reports*, 1990- (current)	Can.
C.B.R. (N.S.)	*Canadian Bankruptcy Reports (New Series),* 1960-1990	Can.
C.B.R. (3d)	*Canadian Bankruptcy Reports (Third Series),* 1991 -(current)	Can.
C.C.C.	*Canadian Criminal Cases,* 1893-1962	Can.
C.C.C. (preceded by date)	*Canadian Criminal Cases,* 1963-1970	Can.
C.C.C.	*Choyce Cases in Chancery,* 1557-1606	21 E.R.
C.C.C. (2d)	*Canadian Criminal Cases (Second Series),* 1971-1983	Can.
C.C.C. (3d)	*Canadian Criminal Cases (Third Series),* 1983-(current)	Can.
C.C.E.L.	*Canadian Cases on Employment Law,* 1983-(current)	Can.
C.C.L.	*Canadian Current Law,* 1948-(current)	Can.
C.C.L.I.	*Canadian Cases on the Law of Insurance,* 1983-1991	Can.
C.C.L.I. (2d)	*Canadian Cases on the Law of Insurance (Second Series),* 1991-current	Can.
C.C.L.T.	*Canadian Cases on the Law of Torts,* 1976-1990	Can.
C.C.L.T. (2d)	*Canadian Cases on the Law of Torts (Second Series),* 1990-(current)	Can.
C.C.L.S.	*Canadian Cases on Law of Securities,* 1992-(current)	Can.
C.C.P.B.	*Canadian Cases on Pensions and Benefits,* 1994-(current)	Can.

C.E.B. & P.G.R.	*Canadian Employment Benefits & Pension Guide Reports*	Can.
C.E.L.R.	*Canadian Environmental Law Reports,* 1972-1986	Can.
C.E.L.R. (N.S.)	*Canadian Environmental Law Reports (New Series),* 1987-(current)	Can.
C.E.P.A.R.	*Canadian Estate Planning and* Administration Reporter	*Can.*
C.E.R.	*Customs and Excise Reports,* 1980-1989	Can.
C.E.S.H.G.	*Canadian Employment, Safety and Health Guide*	Can.
C.F.	*Recueil des arrets de la cour federale du Canada (Canada Federal Court Reports)*	Can.
C.H.R.R.	*Canadian Human Rights Reporter,* 1980-(current)	Can.
C.I.L.R.	*Canadian Insurance Law Reporter,* 1934-(current)	Can.
C.I.P.R.	*Canadian Intellectual Property Reports,* 1984-1990	Can.
C.L.A.S.	*Canadian Labour Arbitration Summaries,* 1991-(current)	Can.
C.L.J.N.S.	*Canada Law Journal, New Series,* 58 vols., 1865-1922	Can.
C.L.J.O.S.	*Canada Law Journal, Old Series,* 10 vols., 1855-1864	Can.
C.L.L.C.	*Canadian Labour Law Cases,* 1944-(current)	Can.
C.L.R.	*Construction Law Reports,* 1983-(current)	Can.
C.L.R.	*Commonwealth Law Reports*	Aus.
C.L.R.B.R.	*Canadian Labour Relations Board Reports,* 1974-1982	Can.
C.L.R.B.R. (N.S.)	*Canadian Labour Relations Board Reports (New Series),* 1983-1989	Can.
C.L.R.B.R. (2d)	*Canadian Labour Relations Board Reports (Second Series),* 1989-(current)	Can.
C.L.S.	*Canada Labour Service,* 1976-(current)	Can.
C.L.T.	*Canadian Law Times*	Can.
C.L.T. Occ. N.	*Canadian Law Times, Occasional Notes*	Can.
C.M. & R.	*Crompton, Meeson, and Roscoe's Reports, Exchequer,* 2 vols., 1834-1835	149-150 E.R.
C.M.A.R.	*Canada Court Martial Appeal Reports,* 1957-1977	Can.
C.M.L.R. (preceded by date)	*Common Market Law Reports,* 1962-current	Eng.

C.N.L.C.	*Canadian Native Law Cases*	Can.
C.N.L.R.	*Canadian Native Law Reporters,* 1977-(current)	Can.
C.O.H.S.C.	*Canadian Occupational Health & Safety Cases,* 1988-1995	*Can.*
C.P.	*Upper Canada Common Pleas,* 1850-1882	Can.
C.P. (preceded by date)	*Recueils de jurisprudence du Québec: Cour provinciale,* 1975-(current)	Can.
C.P.C.	*Carswell's Practice Cases,* 1976-1985	Can.
C.P.C. (2d)	*Carswell's Practice Cases (Second Series),* 1985-1992	*Can.*
C.P.C. (3d)	*Carswell's Practice Cases (Third Series),* 1992-(current)	Can.
C.P.C.	*C.P. Cooper's Reports, Chancery Practice,* 1 vol., 1837-1838	47 E.R.
C.P.D.	*Law Reports, Common Pleas Division,* 5 vols., 1875-1880	Eng.
C.P.R.	*Canadian Patent Reporter,* 1942-1971	Can.
C.P.R. (2d)	*Canadian Patent Reporter (Second Series),* 1972-1984	Can.
C.P.R. (3d)	*Canadian Patent Reporter (Third Series),* 1985-(current)	Can.
C.R.	*Criminal Reports,* 1946-1967	Can.
C.R. (N.S.)	*Criminal Reports (New Series),* 1967-1978	Can.
C.R. (3d)	*Criminal Reports (Third Series),* 1978-1991	Can.
C.R. (4th)	*Criminal Reports (Fourth Series),* 1991-(current)	Can.
C.R. [Vol. or date] A.C.	*Canadian Reports, Appeal Cases,* e.g., C.R. [1911] A.C. 137, 1828-1913	Can.
C.R.D.	*Charter of Rights Decisions,* 1982-(current)	Can.
C.R.R.	*Canadian Regulatory Reporter,* 1981-1987	*Can.*
C.R.R.	*Canadian Rights Reporter,* 1982-1991	Can.
C.R.R. (2d)	*Canadian Rights Reporter (Second Series),* 1992-(current)	Can.
C.R.T.C.	*Canadian Railway and Transport Cases,* 1939-1966	*Can.*
C. Rob.	*C. Robinson,* 1-6, 1798-1808	165 E.R.
C.S.	*Rapports judiciares de Québec, Cour* supérieure/Quebec Official Reports, *Superior Court,* 1892-1941	Can.

C.S. (preceded by date)	*Rapports judiciares de Québec, Cour supérieure,* 1942-1966	Can.
C.S. (preceded by date)	*Recueils de jurisprudence du Québec : Cour supérieure,* 1967-(current)	Can.
C.S.P. (preceded by date)	*Recueils de jurisprudence du Québec : Cour des sessions* de la paix	Can.
C.S.S.T.	*Jurisprudence en Santé et sécurité du travail*	Can.
C.T.C. (preceded by date)	*Canada Tax Cases,* 1917-(current)	Can.
C.T.C. (preceded by date)	*Canada Transport Cases,* 1966-1967	Can.
C.T. & C.T.C.	*Canadian Trade & Commodity Tax Cases,* 1990-(current)	Can.
C.W.L.R.B.D.	*Canadian Wartime Labour Relations Board Decisions,* 1944-1948	Can.
C.W.L.S.	*Canadian Weekly Law Sheet,* 1959-(current)	Can.
Cal. Rptr.	*California Reporter*	U.S.
Calth.	*Calthrop's City of London Cases, King's Bench,* 1 vol., 1609-1618	80 E.R.
Cam.	*Cameron's Privy Council Decisions*	Can.
Cam. Cas.	*Cameron's Supreme Court Cases*	Can.
Cam. Prac.	*Cameron's Supreme Court Practice*	Can.
Camp.	*Campbell's Reports, Nisi Prius,* 4 vols., 1807-1816	170-171 E.R.
Can. Abr.	*Canadian Abridgment*	Can.
Can. Abr. Rev. (2nd)	*Canadian Abridgment (Second Edition)* (current)	Can.
Can. C.L.G.	*Canadian Commercial Law Guide*	Can.
Can. Com. R.	*Commercial Law Reports of Canada,* 4 vols., 1901-1905	Can.
Can. Envtl. L.	*Canadian Environmental Law*	Can.
Can. F.L.G.	*Canadian Family Law Guide*	Can.
Can. Gaz.	*The Canadian Gazette*	Can.
Can. L.R.B.R. (preceded by date)	*Canadian Labour Relations Boards Reports,* 1974-(current)	Can.
Can. P.S.G.	*Canadian Product Safety Guide*	Can.
Can. Ry. Cas.	*Canadian Railway Cases,* 1902-1966	Can.
Can. S.L.R.	*Canadian Securities Law Reports*	Can.
Can. S.T.R.	*Canadian Sales Tax Reports*	Can.
Car. & Kir.	*Carrington and Kirwan's Reports, Nisi Prius,* 3 vols., 1843-1853	174-175 E.R.
Car. & M.	*Carrington and Marshman's Reports, Nisi Prius,* 1 vol., 1841-1842	174 E.R.

Car. & P.	*Carrington & Payne,* 1-9, 1823-1841	171-173 E.R.
Car. C.L.	*Carrington's Treatise on Criminal Law*	Can.
Carey's M.R.	*Carey's Manitoba Reports*	Can.
Carl.	*New Brunswick Reports (Carleton),* 1895 - 1902	Can.
Cart.	*Carter's Reports, Common Pleas,* fol., 1 vol., 1664-1675	124 E.R.
Cart.	*Cases on the British North America Act (Cartwright),* 1868-1896	*Can.*
Carth.	*Carthew's Reports, King's Bench,* fol., 1 vol., 1687-1700	90 E.R.
Cary	*Cary's Reports, Chancery,* 1 vol.	21 E.R.
Cas. temp Finch	*Cases temp Finch, Chancery,* fol., 1673-1680	23 E.R.
Cas. temp Hard.	*T. Lee's Cases temp Hardwicke, King's Bench,* 1 vol., 1733-1738	95 E.R.
Cas. temp Talb.	*Cases in Equity temp Talbot,* fol., 1 vol., 1730-1737	25 E.R.
Cass. Prac. Cas.	*Cassels' Practice Cases*	Can.
Cass. S.C.	*Cassels' Supreme Court Decisions*	Can.
Ch. (preceded by date)	*Law Reports, Chancery Division,* since 1890 (*e.g.*, [1891] 1 Ch.)	Eng.
Ch. App.	*Law Reports, Chancery Appeals,* 10 vols., 1865-1875	Eng.
Ch. Ca.	*Cases in Chancery,* 1-3, 1660-1698	22 E.R.
Ch. Cas. in Ch.	*Choyce Cases in Chancery,* 1557-1606	21 E.R.
Ch. Ch.	*Upper Canada Chancery Chambers Reports,* 1857-1872	Can.
Ch. D.	*Law Reports, Chancery Division,* 45 vols., 1875-1890	Eng.
Ch. Rob.	*Christopher Robinson's Reports, Admiralty,* 6 vols., 1798-1808	165 E.R.
Chip.	*New Brunswick Reports (Chipman),* 1825-1835	Can.
Chit.	*Chitty's Practice Reports, King's Bench,* 2 vols., 1770-1822	22-23 R.R.
Chitty' s Abr.	*Chitty' s Abridgment*	Can.
Chitty's L.J.	*Chitty's Law Journal,* 1948-(current)	Can.
Cl. & Fin.	*Clark and Finnelly's Reports, House of Lords,* 12 vols., 1831-1846	6-8 E.R.
Cl. & Sc. Dr. Cas.	*Clark and Scully's Drainage Cases,* 1898-1903	Can.
Co. A.	*Cook's Lower Canada Admiralty Court Cases,* 1873-1884	Can.
Co. Rep.	*Coke's Reports,* 13 parts, 1572-1616	76-77 E.R.

Coch.	*Nova Scotia Reports (Cochran),* 1859	Can.
Coll.	*Collyer's Reports, Chancery,* 2 vols., 1844-1846	63 E.R.
Colles	*Colles,* 1697-1713	1 E.R.
Com.	*Comyns' Reports, King's Bench, Common Pleas, and Exchequer,* fol., 2 vols., 1695-1740	92 E.R.
Comb.	*Comberbach's Reports, King's Bench,* fol., 1 vol., 1685-1698	90 E.R.
Cong. Dig.	*Congdon's Digest*	Can.
Cook V. Adm.	*Cook's Vice Admiralty Reports,* 1873-1884	Can.
Cooke, Pr. Cas.	*Cooke's Practice Reports, Common Pleas,* 1 vol., 1706-1747	125 E.R.
Coop. Pr. Cas.	*C.P. Cooper's Reports, Chancery Practice,* 1 vol., 1837-1838	47 E.R.
Coop. Temp Brough.	*C.P. Cooper's Cases temp Brougham, Chancery,* 1 vol., 1833-1834	47 E.R.
Coop. Temp Cott.	*C.P. Cooper's Cases temp Cottenham, Chancery,* 2 vols., 1846-1848 (and miscellaneous earlier cases)	47 E.R.
Cout.	*Coutlee's Unreported Cases,* 1875-1907	Can.
Cout. Dig.	*Coutlees' Digest*	Can.
Cowp.	*Cowper's Reports, King's Bench,* 2 vols., 1774-1778	98 E.R.
Cox, C.C.	*E.W. Cox's Criminal Law Cases,* 1843-1945	Eng.
Cox, Eq. Cas.	*S.C. Cox's Equity Cases,* 2 vols., 1745-1797	29-30 E.R.
Cr. App. R.	*Criminal Appeal Reports*	Eng.
Cr. App. R. (S.)	*Criminal Appeal Reports (Sentencing)*	Eng.
Cr. & J.	*Crompton and Jervis's Reports, Exchequer,* 2 vols., 1830-1832	148-149 E.R.
Cr. & M.	*Crompton and Meeson's Reports, Exchequer,* 2 vols., 1832-1834	149 E.R.
Cr. & Ph.	*Craig and Phillips' Reports, Chancery,* 1 vol., 1840-1841	41 E.R.
Cr. M. & R.	*Crompton, Meeson, and Roscoe's Reports, Exchequer,* 2 vols., 1834-1835	149-150 E.R.
Crim. L.R.	*Criminal Law Reports*	Eng.

Cro. Car.	*Croke's Reports temp Charles I, King's Bench and Common Pleas,* 1 vol., 1625-1641	79 E.R.
D.	*Denison's Crown Cases Reserved,* 2 vols., 1844-1852	169 E.R.
D.	*Dyer's Reports, King's Bench,* 3 vols., 1513-1581	73 E.R.
D. & B.	*Dearsly and Bell's Crown Cases Reserved,* 1 vol., 1856-1858	169 E.R.
D. & C.	*Dow and Clark's Reports, House of Lords,* 2 vols., 1827-1832	6 E.R.
D & J.	*De Gex and Jones's Reports, Chancery,* 4 vols., 1857-1859	44-45 E.R.
D. & L.	*Dowling and Lowndes' Practice Reports,* 7 vols., 1843-1849	67-82 R.R.
D. & Mer.	*Davison and Merivale's Reports, Queen's Bench,* 1 vol., 1843-1844	64 R.R.
D. & R.	*Dowling and Ryland's Reports, King's Bench,* 9 vols., 1822-1827	24-30 R.R.
D. & R.N.P.	*Dowling and Ryland's Reports, Nisi Prius,* 1 part, 1822-1823	171 E.R.
D. & S.	*Drewry and Smale's Reports, Chancery,* 2 vols., 1859-1865	62 E.R.
D & Sm.	*De Gex, Jones and Smith's Reports, Chancery,* 4 vols., 1862-1865	46 E.R.
D.C.A.	*Dorion's Queen's Bench Reports,* 1880-1884	Can.
D.D.C.P.	*Décisions Disciplinaires Concernant les Corporations Professionelles*	Can.
D.F. & J.	*De Gex, Fisher and Jones's Reports, Chancery,* 4 vols., 1859-1862	45 E.R.
D.F.Q.E.	*Droit fiscal québecois Express*	Can.
D.J. & Sm.	*De Gex, Jones and Smith's Reports, Chancery,* 4 vols., 1862-1865	46 E.R.
D.L.R.	*Dominion Law Reports,* 1912-1922	Can.
D.L.R. (preceded by date)	*Dominion Law Reports,* 1923-1955	Can.
D.L.R. (2d)	*Dominion Law Reports (Second Series),* 1956-1968	Can.
D.L.R. (3d)	*Dominion Law Reports (Third Series),* 1969-1984	Can.
D.L.R. (4th)	*Dominion Law Reports (Fourth Series),* 1984-(current)	Can.
D.M. & G.	*De Gex, Macnaghten and Gordon's, Reports, Chancery,* 8 vols., 1851-1857	42-44 E.R.

D.R.L.	*Decisions de la Régie du Logement*	Can.
D.R.S.	*Dominion Report Service,* 1968-(current)	Can.
D.T.C.	*Dominion Tax Cases,* 1920-(current)	Can.
Dan.	*Daniell's Reports, Exchequer in Equity,* 1 vol., 1817-1823	159 E.R.
Dan. & Ll.	*Danson and Lloyd's Mercantile Cases,* 1 vol., 1828-1829	34 R.R.
Day. & Mer.	*Davison and Merivale's Reports Queen's Bench,* 1 vol., 1843-1844	64 R.R.
Day. Ir.	*Davys' (or Davis or Davy's) Reports (Ireland),* 1 vol., 1604-1612	80 E.R.
Dea. & Sw.	*Deane and Swabey's Ecclesiastical Reports,* 1 vol., 1855-1857	164 E.R.
Dears.	*Dearsly,* 1852-1856	169 E.R.
Dears. & B.	*Dearsly and Bell's Crown Cases Reserved,* 1 vol., 1856-1858	169 E.R.
Dears. C.C.	*Dearsly's Crown Cases Reserved,* 1 vol., 1852-1856	169 E.R.
De G. & J.	*De Gex and Jones's Reports, Chancery,* 4 vols., 1857-1859	44-45 E.R.
De G. & Sm.	*De Gex and Smale's Reports, Chancery,* 5 vols., 1846-1852	63-64 E.R.
De G.F. & J.	*De Gex, Fisher and Jones' s Reports, Chancery,* 4 vols., 1859-1862	45 E.R.
De G.J. & Sm.	*De Gex, Jones and Smith's Reports, Chancery,* 4 vols., 1862-1865	46 E.R.
De. G.M. & G.	*De Gex, Macnaghten and Gordon's Reports, Chancery,* 8 vols., 1851-1857	42-44 E.R.
Den.	*Denison's Crown Cases Reserved,* 2 vols., 1844-1852	169 E.R.
Di	*Canada Labour Relations Board Decisions/Information,* 1974-(current)	Can.
Dick.	*Dickens' Reports, Chancery,* 2 vols., 1559-1797	21 E.R.
Dods.	*Dodson's Reports, Admiralty,* 2 vols., 1811-1822	165 E.R.
Donnelly	*Donnelly's Reports, Chancery,* 1 vol., 1836-1837	47 E.R.
Doug. K.B.	*Douglas Reports, King's Bench,* 4 vols., 1778-1785	99 E.R.
Dow	*Dow's Reports, House of Lords,* 6 vols., 1812-1818	3 E.R.
Dow & Cl.	*Dow and Clark's Reports, House of Lords,* 2 vols., 1827-1832	6 E.R.

Dow. & L.	*Dowling and Lowndes' Practice Reports,* 7 vols., 1843-1849	67-82 R.R.
Dow. & Ry. K.B.	*Dowling and Ryland's Reports, King's Bench,* 9 Vols., 1822-1827	24-30 R.R.
Dow. & Ry. N.P.	*Dowling and Ryland's Reports, Nisi Prius,* 1 part, 1822-1823	171 E.R.
Dowl.	*Dowling's Practice Reports,* 9 vols., 1830-1841	36-61 R.R.
Dowl. N.S.	*Dowling's Practice Reports, New Series,* 2 vols., 1841-1843	63-65 R.R.
Dra.	*Draper's King's Bench Reports,* 1828-1831	Can.
Drew.	*Drewry,* 1-4, 1852-1859	61-62 E.R.
Drew. & Sm.	*Drewry and Smale's Reports, Chancery,* 2 vols., 1859-1865	62 E.R.
Drinkwater	*Drinkwater's Reporters, Common Pleas,* 1 vol., 1840-1841	60 R.R.
Dyer	*Dyer's Reports, King's Bench,* 3 vols., 1513-1581	73 E.R.
E.	*East's Reports, King's Bench,* 16 vols., 1800-1812	102-104 E.R. 28 E.R.
E. & A.	*Spinks (Ecclesiastical & Admiralty Reports),* 1-2, 1853-1855	164 E.R.
E. & A.	*Upper Canada Error and Appeal Reports,* 1846-1866	Can.
E. & B.	*Ellis and Blackburn's Reports, Queen's Bench,* 8 vols., 1852-1858	118 - 120 E.R.
E. & E.	*Ellis and Ellis's Reports, Queen's Bench,* 3 vols., 1858-1860	120-121 E.R.
E.B. & E.	*Ellis, Blackburn, and Ellis's Reports, Queen's Bench,* 1 vol., 1858-1860	120 E.R.
E.L.R.	*Eastern Law Reporter,* 1906-1914	Can. E.R.
(or Eng. Rep.)	*English Reports*	1-176 E.R.
E.R.	*Ontario Election Reports,* 1884-1900	Can.
E.T.R.	*Estates and Trusts Reports,* 1977-(current)	Can.
East	*East's Reports, King's Bench,* 16 vols., 1800-1812	102-104 E.R.
Eden	*Eden's Reports, Chancery,* 2 vols., 1757-1766	28 E.R.
Edw.	*Edwards' Reports, Admiralty,* 1 vol., 1808-1812	165 E.R.
Eq. Ca. Abr.	*Equity Cases Abridged,* 1-2, 1667-1744	21-22 E.R.

Esp.	*Espinasse's Reports, Nisi Prius,* 6 vols., 1793-1810	170 E.R.
Ex. C.R. (preceded by date)	*Exchequer Court Reports,* 1923-1971	Can.
Ex. D.	*Law Reports, Exchequer Division,* 5 vols., 1875-1880	Eng.
Exch.	*Exchequer Reports (Welsby, Hurlstone and Gordon),* 11 vols., 1847-1856	154-156 E.R.
Exch. C.R.	*Exchequer Court Reports,* 21 vols., 1881-1922	Can.
F.	*Federal Reporter*	U.S.
F. & F.	*Foster and Finlason's Reports, Nisi Prius,* 4 vols., 1856-1867	175-176 E.R.
F.C. (preceded by date)	*Canada Federal Court Reports,* 1971-(current)	Can.
F.C.A.D.	*Federal Court of Appeal Decisions*	Can.
F.L.J. (Can.)	*Canada Fortnightly Law Journal*	Can.
F.L.R.	*Federal Law Reports,* 1959-(current)	Aus.
F.L.R.A.C.	*Family Law Reform Act Cases,* 1981-1985	Can.
F.L.R.R.	*Family Law Reform Reporter*	Can.
F. Supp.	*Federal Supplement*	U.S.
F.T.R.	*Federal Trial Reports,* 1986-(current)	Can.
Fam. (preceded by date)	*Family Division,* 1972-(current)	Eng.
Fam. L. Rev.	*Family Law Review*	Can.
Fitz.-G.	*Fitz-Gibbons's Reports, King's Bench,* fol., 1 vol., 1727-1731	94 E.R.
For.	*Forrest's Reports, Exchequer,* 1 vol., 1800-1801	145 E.R.
Fortes. Rep.	*Fortesque's Reports,* fol., 1 vol., 1692-1736	92 E.R.
Fost.	*Foster's Crown Cases,* 1 vol., 1708-1760	168 E.R.
Fox Pat. C.	*Fox's Patent Trade Mark, Design and Copyright Cases,* 1940-1971	Can.
Freem. Ch.	*Freeman's Reports, Chancery,* 1 vol., 1660-1706	22 E.R.
Freem. K.B.	*Freeman's Reports, King's Bench and Common Pleas,* 1 vol., 1670-1704	89 E.R.
G. & D.	*Gale and Davison's Reports, Queen's Bench,* 3 vols., 1841-1843	55-62 R.R.
G. & O.	*Nova Scotia Reports (Geldert & Oxley),* 1807-1874	Can.

G. & R.	*Nova Scotia Reports (Geldert & Russell),* 1895-1929	Can.
G. Coop.	*Cooper,* G., 1815	35 E.R.
G.I. Dig.	*General Index Digest*	Can.
Gal. & Day.	*Gale and Davison's Reports, Queen's Bench,* 3 vols., 1841-1843	55-62 R.R.
Geld. Dig.	*Geldert's Digest*	*Can.*
Giff.	*Giffard's Reports, Chancery,* 5 vols., 1857-1865	65-66 E.R.
Gilb.	*Gilbert's Cases in Law and Equity,* 1 vol., 1713-1714	93 E.R.
Gilb. Ch.	*Gilbert's Reports, Chancery and Exchequer,* fol., 1 vol., 1706-1726	25 E.R.
Godb.	*Godbolt's Reports, King's Bench, Common Pleas, and Exchequer,* 1 vol., 1574-1637	78 E.R.
Godson	*Mining Commissioner's Cases (Ont.),* 1911-1917	Can.
Gouldsb.	*Gouldsborough's Reports, Queen's Bench and King's Bench,* 1 vol., 1586-1601	75 E.R.
Gow	*Gow's Reports, Nisi Prius,* 1 vol., 1818-1820	171 E.R.
Gr.	*Upper Canada Chancery (Grant),* 1849-1882	Can.
H. & C.	*Hurlstone and Coltman's Reports, Exchequer,* 4 vols., 1862-1866	158-159 E.R.
H. & H.	*Horn and Hurlston's Reports, Exchequer,* 2 vols., 1838-1839	51 R.R.
H. & M.	*Hay & Marriott's Decisions, Admiralty,* 1 vol., 1776-1779	165 E.R.
H. & M.	*Hemming and Miller's Reports, Chancery,* 2 vols., 1862-1865	71 E.R.
H. & N.	*Hurlstone and Norman's Reports, Exchequer,* 7 vols., 1856-1862	156-158 E.R.
H. & Tw.	*Hall and Twells' Reports, Chancery,* 2 vols., 1846-1850	47 E.R.
H. & W.	*Harrison and Wollaston's Reports, King's Bench and Bail Court,* 2 vols., 1835-1836	47 R.R.
H. & W.	*Hurlstone and Walmsley's Reports, Exchequer,* 1 vol., 1840-1841	58 R.R.
H.E.C.	*Hodgin's Election Reports,* 1871-1879	Can.
H.L.C.	*House of Lords Cases,* 1-11, 1847-1866	9-11 E.R.
Hag. Adm.	*Haggard's Reports, Admiralty,* 3 vols., 1822-1838	166 E.R.

Hag. Con.	*Haggard's Consistorial Reports,* 2 vols., 1789-1821	161 E.R.
Hag. Ecc.	*Haggard's Ecclesiastical Reports,* 4 vols., 1827-1833	162 E.R.
Han.	*New Brunswick Reports (Hannay),* 1867-1871	Can.
Har. & W.	*Harrison and Wollaston's Reports, King's Bench and Bail Court,* 2 vols., 1835-1836	47 R.R.
Hard.	*Hardres' Reports, Exchequer,* fol., 1 vol., 1655-1669	145 E.R.
Hare	*Hare's Reports, Chancery,* 11 vols., 1841-1853	66-68 E.R.
Harr. & Hodg.	*Harrison & Hodgins' Municipal Reports,* 1845-1851	Can.
Hay & Marr.	*Hay & Marriott's Decisions, Admiralty,* 1 vol., 1776-1779	165 E.R.
Hem. & M.	*Hemming and Miller's Reports, Chancery,* 2 vols., 1862-1865	71 E.R.
Het.	*Hetley's Reports, Common Pleas,* fol., 1 vol., 1627-1631	124 E.R.
Hob.	*Hobart's Reports, Common Pleas,* fol., 1 vol., 1613-1625	80 E.R.
Hodg.	*Hodges' Reports, Common Pleas,* 3 vols., 1835-1837	42-43 R.R.
Hodg.	*Hodgin's Election Petitions,* 1871-1879	Can.
Holt Eq.	*W. Holt's Equity Reports,* 2 vols., 1845	71 E.R.
Holt K.B.	*Sir John Holt's Reports, King's Bench,* fol., 1 vol., 1688-1710	90 E.R.
Holt N.P.	*F. Holt's Reports, Nisi Prius,* 1 vol., 1815-1817	171 E.R.
Horan	*Mining Commissioner's Cases,* 1918-1960	Can.
Horn & H.	*Horn and Hurlston's Reports, Exchequer,* 2 vols., 1838-1839	51 R.R.
Hov. Supp.	*Hovenden's Supplement to Vesey Jun's Reports, Chancery,* 2 vols., 1753-1817	34 E.R.
Hunt.	*Hunter's Torrens Cases,* 1865-1893	Can.
Hut.	*Hutton's Reports, Common Pleas,* fol., 1 vol., 1617-1638	123 E.R.
Hy. Bl.	*Henry Blackstone's Reports, Common Pleas,* 2 vols., 1788-1796	126 E.R.
I.A.C.	*Immigration Appeals Cases,* 1969-1977	Can.
I.C.L.D.	*Insurance Case Law Digest,* 1985-(current)	Can.

I.L.R. (preceded by date)	*Insurance Law Reports* (see *Canadian Insurance Law Reporter)*	Can.
Imm. L.R. (2d)	*Immigration Law Reporter (Second Series),* 1987-(current)	Can.
J. Bridg.	*Sir John Bridgman's Reports, Common Pleas,* fol., 1 vol., 1613-1621	123 E.R.
J. & H.	*Johnson and Hemming's Reports, Chancery,* 2 vols., 1859-1862	70 E.R.
J. & W.	*Jacob and Walker's Reports Chancery,* 2 vols., 1819-1821	37 E.R.
J.E.	*Jurisprudence Express,* 1977-(current)	Can.
J. Kel.	*Sir John Kelynge's Reports, Crown Cases,* fol., 1 vol., 1662-1707	84 E.R.
J.L.	*Jurisprudence logement*	Can.
J.P.	*Justice of the Peace,* 1837-(current)	Eng.
J.P. Sm.	*J.P. Smith's Reports, King's Bench,* 3 vols., 1803-1806	7-8 R.R.
Jac.	*Jacob's Reports, Chancery,* 1 vol., 1821-1823	37 E.R.
Jac. & W.	*Jacob and Walker's Reports, Chancery,* 2 vols., 1819-1821	37 E.R.
James	*Nova Scotia Reports (James),* 1853-1855	Can.
Jenk.	*Jenkin's Reports,* 1 vol., 1220-1623	145 E.R.
John.	*Johnson's Reports, Chancery,* 1 vol., 1858-1860	70 E.R.
John. & H.	*Johnson and Hemming's Reports, Chancery,* 2 vols., 1859-1862	70 E.R.
Jones, T.	*Jones, T.,* 1667-1685	84 E.R.
Jones, W.	*Jones, W.,* 1620-1641	82 E.R.
K. & J.	*Kay and Johnson's Reports, Chancery,* 4 vols., 1853-1858	69-70 E.R.
K.B. (preceded by date)	*Law Reports, King's Bench Division,* 1900-1952 (*e.g.*, [1901] 2 K.B.)	Eng.
Kay	*Kay's Reports, Chancery,* 1 vol., 1853-1854	69 E.R.
Keb.	*Keble's Reports,* fol., 3 vols., 1661-1677	83-84 E.R.
Keen	*Keen's Reports, Rolls Court,* 2 vols., 1836-1838	48 E.R.
Keil.	*Keilwey's Reports, King's Bench,* fol., 1 vol., 1327-1578	72 E.R.
Kel.	*Sir John Kelynge's Reports, Crown Cases,* fol., 1 vol., 1662-1707	84 E.R.

Kel. W.	*W. Kelyng's Reports*, fol., 1 vol., *Chancery*, 1730-1732; *King's Bench*, fol., 1731-1734	25 E.R.
Keny.	*Kenyon's Notes of Cases, King's Bench*, 2 vols., 1753-1759	96 E.R.
Kerr	*New Brunswick Reports (Kerr)*, 1840-1848	Can.
Knapp	*Knapp's Reports, Privy Council*, 3 vols., 1829-1836	12 E.R.
L. & C.	*Lefroy's & Cassels' Practice Cases*, 1881-1883	Can.
L.A.C.	*Labour Arbitration Cases*, 1948-1972	Can.
L.A.C. (2d)	*Labour Arbitration Cases (Second Series)*, 1972-1982	Can.
L.A.C. (3d)	*Labour Arbitration Cases (Third Series)*, 1982-1988	Can.
L.A.C. (4th)	*Labour Arbitration Cases (Fourth Series)*, 1989-(current)	Can.
L.C. & M.	*Local Courts and Municipal Gazette*, 1865-1872	Can.
L.C.J.	*Lower Canada Jurist*, 1848-1891	Can.
L.C.L.J.	*Lower Canada Law Journal*	Can.
L.C.R.	*Land Compensation Reports*, 1970-(current)	Can.
L.C.R.	*Lower Canada Reports*, 1851-1867	Can.
L. Ed.	*United States Supreme Court Reports (Lawyers' Edition)*	U.S.
L.J. Adm.	*Law Journal, Admiralty*, 1865-1875	Eng.
L.J. Bcy.	*Law Journal, Bankruptcy*, 1832-1880	Eng.
L,J.C.C.R.	*Law Journal (County Courts Reporter)*, 1912-1947	Eng.
L.J.C.P.	*Law Journal, Common Pleas*, 1831-1875	Eng.
L.J. Ch.	*Law Journal, Chancery*, 1831-1946	Eng.
L.J. Eccl.	*Law Journal, Ecclesiastical Cases*, 1866-1875	Eng.
L.J. Ex.	*Law Journal, Exchequer*, 1831-1875	Eng.
L.J. Ex. Eq.	*Law Journal, Exchequer in Equity*, 1835-1841	Eng.
L.J.K.B. or Q.B.	*Law Journal King's Bench or Queen's Bench*, 1831-1946	Eng.
L.J.M.C.	*Law Journal Magistrates' Cases*, 1831-1896	Eng.
L.J.N.C.	*Law Journal Notes of Cases*, 1866-1892 (from 1893, see *Law Journal*)	Eng.

L.J.O.S.	*Law Journal Old Series,* 10 vols., 1822-1831	Eng.
L.J.P.	*Law Journal Probate, Divorce and Admiralty,* 1875-1946	Eng.
L.J.P. & M.	*Law Journal Probate and Matrimonial Cases,* 1858-1859, 1866-1875	Eng.
L.J.P.C.	*Law Journal, Privy Council,* 1865-1946	Eng.
L.J.P.M. & A.	*Law Journal, Probate, Matrimonial and Admiralty,* 1860-1865	Eng.
L.J.R. (preceded by date)	*Law Journal Reports,* 1947-1949 (e.g., [1947] L.J.R.)	Eng.
L. Med. Q.	*Legal Medical Quarterly*	*Can.*
L.N.	*Legal News*	Can.
L.R.C.C.R.	*Law Reports, Crown Cases Reserved,* 2 vols., 1865-1875	Eng.
L.R.C.P.	*Law Reports, Common Pleas,* 10 vols., 1865-1875	Eng.
L.R. Eq.	*Law Reports, Equity Cases,* 20 vols., 1865-1875	Eng.
L.R. Exch.	*Law Reports, Exchequer,* 10 vols., 1865-1875	Eng.
L.R.H.L.	*Law Reports, English and Irish Appeals and Peerage Claims, House of Lords,* 7 vols., 1866-1875	Eng.
L.R. Ir.	*Law Reports (Ireland), Chancery and Common Law,* 32 vols., 1877-1893	Ir.
L.R.P. & D.	*Law Reports, Probate and Divorce,* 3 vols., 1865-1875	Eng.
L.R.P.C.	*Law Reports, Privy Council,* 6 vols., 1865-1875	Eng.
L.R.Q.B.	*Law Reports, Queen's Bench,* 10 vols., 1865-1875	Eng.
L.R.Q.B.	*Quebec Reports, Queen's Bench*	Can.
L.R. (Vol.) R.P.	*Law Reports Restrictive Practices,* 1957-1973	Eng.
L.R. Sc. & Div.	*Law Reports, Scotch and Divorce Appeals, House of Lords,* 2 vols., 1866-1875	Eng.
L.T.	*Law Times Reports,* 1859-1947	Eng.
L.T.O.S.	*Law Times Reports, Old Series,* 34 vols., 1843-1860	Eng.
L.W.C.D.	*Lawyer's Weekly Consolidated Digest,* 1983-(current)	Can.
Lane	*Lane's Reports, Exchequer,* fol., 1 vol., 1605-1611	145 E.R.

Lat.	*Latch's Reports, King's Bench,* fol., 1 vol., 1625-1628	82 E.R.
Law Rep.	*The Law Reporter (Ramsay & Morin),* 1853-1854	*Can.*
Ld. Raym.	*Lord Raymond's Reports, King's Bench and Common Pleas,* 3 vols., 1694-1732	91-92 E.R.
Leach	*Leach's Crown Cases,* 2 vols., 1730-1814	168 E.R.
Le. & Ca.	*Leigh and Cave's Crown Cases Reserved,* 1 vol., 1861-1865	169 E.R.
Lee	*Sir G. Lee's Ecclesiastical Judgments,* 2 vols., 1752-1758	161 E.R.
Leon.	*Leonard's Reports, King's Bench, Common Pleas and Exchequer,* fol., 4 parts, 1552-1615	74 E.R.
Lev.	*Levinz's Reports, King's Bench and Common Pleas,* fol., 3 vols., 1660-1696	83 E.R.
Lew. C.C.	*Lewin's Crown Cases on the Northern Circuit,* 2 vols., 1822-1838	168 E.R.
Ley	*Ley's Reports, King's Bench,* fol., 1 vol., 1608-1629	80 E.R.
Lilly	*Lilly's Reports and Pleadings of Cases in Assize,* fol., 1 vol.,	170 E.R.
Litt.	*Littleton's Reports, Common Pleas,* fol., 1 vol., 1627-1631	124 E.R.
Lloyd's Rep.	*Lloyd's List Law Reports,* 84 vols., 1919-1950	Eng.
Lloyd' s Rep. (preceded by date)	*Lloyd' s List Law Reports,* 1951-1967	Eng.
Lloyd's Rep. (preceded by date)	*Lloyd's Law Reports,* 1968-(current)	Eng.
Lofft	*Lofft's Reports, King's Bench,* fol., 1 vol., 1772-1774	98 E.R.
Lush.	*Lushington's Reports, Admiralty,* 1 vol., 1859-1862	167 E.R.
Lut.	*Sir E. Lutwyche's Entries and Reports, Common Pleas,* 2 vols., 1682-1704	125 E.R.
M. & C.	*Mylne and Craig's Reports, Chancery,* 5 vols., 1835-1841	40-41 E.R.
M. & G.	*Macnaghten and Gordon's Reports, Chancery,* 3 vols., 1849-1852	41-42 E.R.
M. & G.	*Maddock and Geldart's Reports, Chancery,* 1 vol., 1819-1822 (Vol. VI of *Madd)*	56 E.R.
M. & G.	*Manning and Granger's Reports, Common Pleas,* 7 vols., 1840-1845	133-135 E.R.

M. & H.	*Murphy and Hurlstone's Reports, Exchequer,* 1 vol., 1837	51 R.R.
M. & K.	*Mylne and Keen's Reports, Chancery,* 3 vols., 1832-1835	39-40 E.R.
M. & M.	*Moody and Malkin's Reports, Nisi Prius,* 1 vol., 1826-1830	173 E.R.
M. & P.	*Moore and Payne's Reports, Common Pleas,* 5 vols., 1827-1831	29-33 R.R.
M. & R.	*Maclean and Robinson's Scotch Appeals (House of Lords),* 1 vol., 1839	9 E.R.
M. & R.	*Manning and Ryland's Reports, King's Bench,* 5 vols., 1827-1830	31-34 R.R.
M. & R.	*Moody and Robinson's Reports, Nisi Prius,* 2 vols., 1830-1844	174 E.R.
M. & S.	*Maule and Selwyn's Reports, King's Bench,* 6 vols., 1813-1817	105 E.R.
M. & W.	*Meeson and Welsby's Reports, Exchequer,* 16 vols., 1836-1847	150-153 E.R.
M.C.C.	*Mining Commissioner's Cases*	Can.
M.C.R.	*Montreal Condensed Reports,* 1853-1854	Can.
M.L. Dig. & R.	*Monthly Law Digest & Reporter,* 1892-1893	Can.
M.L.R. (Vol.) K.B. or Q.B.	*Montreal Law Reports, King's Bench or Queen's Bench*	Can.
M.L.R. (Vol.) S.C.	*Montreal Law Reports, Superior Court*	Can.
M.M. Cas.	*Martin's Reports of Mining Cases,*Can. 1853-1908	
M.P.L.R.	*Municipal and Planning Law Reports,* 1976-1990	Can.
M.P.L.R. (2d)	*Municipal and Planning Law Reports (Second Series),* 1991-(current)	Can.
M.P.R.	*Maritime Provinces Reports,* 53 vols., 1930-1968	Can.
M.T.R.	*Maritimes Tax Reports*	Can.
M.V.R.	*Motor Vehicle Reports,* 1979-(current)	Can.
M.V.R. (2d)	*Motor Vehicle Reports (Second Series),* 1988-(current)	Can.
Mac. & G.	*Macnaghten and Gordon's Reports, Chancery,* 3 vols., 1849-1852	41-42 E.R.
M'Cle.	*M'Cleland's Reports, Exchequer,* 1 vol., 1824	148 E.R.
M'Cle. & Yo.	*M'Cleland and Younge's Reports, Exchequer,* 1 vol., 1824-1825	148 E.R.

McFarland	*Mining Commissioner's Cases,* 1853-1908	Can.
Macl. & Rob.	*Maclean and Robinson's Scotch Appeals (House of Lords),* 1 vol., 1839	9 E.R.
Madd. & G.	*Maddock and Geldart's Reports, Chancery,* 1 vol., 1819-1822 (Vol. VI of *Madd)*	56 E.R.
Man. & G.	*Manning and Granger's Reports, Common Pleas,* 7 vols., 1840-1845	133-135 E.R.
Man. & Ry. K.B.	*Manning and Ryland's Reports, King's Bench,* 5 vols., 1827-1830	31-34 R.R.
Man. D.	*Manitoba Decisions*	Can.
Man. L.J.	*Manitoba Law Journal*	Can.
Man. L.R.	*Manitoba Law Reports* (to volume 29), 1884-1962	Can.
Man. R.	*Manitoba Reports* (from volume 30)	Can.
Man. R. (2d)	*Manitoba Reports (Second Series),* 1979-(current)	*Can.*
Man. R. temp Wood	*Manitoba Reports temp Wood (ed. Armour),* 1875-1885 (see also *Armour* and *Temp Wood)*	Can.
Man. & Sask. Tax R.	*Manitoba & Saskatchewan Tax Reporter*	Can
March	*March's Reports, King's Bench and Common Pleas,* 1 vol., 1639-1642	82 E.R.
Marr.	*Hay & Marriot's Decisions, Admiralty,* 1 vol., 1776-1779	165 E.R.
Marsh.	*Marshall's Reports, Common Pleas,* 2 vols., 1813-1816	15, 17 R.R.
Mer.	*Merivale's Reports, Chancery,* 3 vols., 1815-1817	35-36 E.R.
Mod. Rep.	*Modern Reports,* 12 vols., 1669-1755	86-88 E.R.
Moo. & P.	*Moore and Payne's Reports, Common Pleas,* 5 vols., 1827-1831	29-33 R.R.
Moo. & S.	*Moore and Scott's Reports, Common Pleas,* 4 vols., 1831-1834	34-38 R.R.
Moo. Ind. App.	*Moore's Indian Appeal Cases, Privy Council,* 14 vols., 1836-1872	18-20 E.R.
Moo. P.C.C.	*Moore's Privy Council Cases,* 15 vols., 1836-1863	12-15 E.R.
Moo. P.C.C.N.S.	*Moore's Privy Council Cases, New Series,* 9 vols., 1862-1873	15-17 E.R.
Mood. & M.	*Moody and Malkin's Reports, Nisi Prius,* 1 vol., 1826-1830	173 E.R.

Mood. & R.	*Moody and Robinson's Reports, Nisi Prius,* 2 vols., 1830-1844	174 E.R.
Mood. C.C.	*Moody's Crown Cases Reserved,* 2 vols., 1824-1844	168-169 E.R.
Moore C.P.	*J.B. Moore's Reports, Common Pleas,* 12 vols., 1817-1827	19-29 R.R.
Moore K.B.	*Sir F. Moore's Reports, King's Bench,* fol., 1 vol., 1485-1620	72 E.R.
Mos.	*Moseley's Reports, Chancery,* fol., 1 vol., 1726-1730	25 E.R.
Mun. Rep.	*Municipal Reports,* 1845 - 1851	Can.
Murd. Epit.	*Murdoch's Epitome*	Can.
Murp. & H.	*Murphy and Hurlstone's Reports, Exchequer,* 1 vol., 1837	51 R.R.
My. & Cr.	*Mylne and Craig's Reports, Chancery,* 5 vols., 1835-1841	40-41 E.R.
My. & K.	*Mylne and Keen's Reports, Chancery,* 3 vols., 1832-1835	39-40 E.R.
N. & M.	*Nevile and Manning's Reports, King's Bench,* 6 vols., 1832-1836	38-43 R.R.
N. & P.	*Nevile and Perry's Reports, King's Bench* 3 vols., 1836-1838	44-45 R.R.
N.B. Dig.	*New Brunswick Digest (Stevens)*	Can.
N.B. Eq. Rep.	*New Brunswick Equity Reports,* 1894-1911	Can.
N.B.R.	*New Brunswick Reports,* 1825-1929	Can.
N.B.R. (All.)	*New Brunswick Reports (Allen),* 1848-1866	Can.
N.B.R. (Ber.)	*New Brunswick Reports (Berton),* 1835-1839	Can.
N.B.R. (Carl.)	*New Brunswick Reports (Carleton),*Can. 1895-1902	
N.B.R. (Chip.)	*New Brunswick Reports (Chipman),* 1825-1835	Can.
N.B.R. (Han.)	*New Brunswick Reports (Hannay),* 1867-1871	Can.
N.B.R. (Kerr)	*New Brunswick Reports (Kerr),* 1840-1848	Can.
N.B.R. (P. & B.)	*New Brunswick Reports (Pugsley and Burbidge),* 1878-1882	Can.
N.B.R. (P. & T.)	*New Brunswick Reports (Pugsley and Trueman),* 1882-1883	Can.
N.B.R. (Pug.)	*New Brunswick Reports (Pugsley),* 1872-1877	Can.

N.B.R. (Tru.)	*New Brunswick Reports (Trueman),* 1894-1912	Can.
N.B.R. (2d)	*New Brunswick Reports (Second Series),* 1968-(current)	Can.
N.E.	*North Eastern Reporter*	U.S.
N.R.	*National Reporter,* 1973-(current)	Can.
N.S.L.N.	*Nova Scotia Law News,* 1974-(current)	Can.
N.S.R.	*Nova Scotia Reports,* 1834-1929	Can.
N.S.R. (Coch.)	*Nova Scotia Reports (Cochran),* 1859	Can.
N.S.R. (G. & O.)	*Nova Scotia Reports (Geldert and Oxley),* 1867-1874	Can.
N.S.R. (G. & R.)	*Nova Scotia Reports (Geldert and Russell),* 1894-1929	Can.
N.S.R. (James)	*Nova Scotia Reports (James),* 1853-1855	Can.
N.S.R. (Old.)	*Nova Scotia Reports (Oldrights),* 1860-1867	Can.
N.S.R. (R. & C.)	*Nova Scotia Reports (Russell and Chesley),* 1875-1879	Can.
N.S.R. (R. & G.)	*Nova Scotia Reports (Russell and Geldert),* 1879-1894	Can.
N.S.R. (Thom.)	*Nova Scotia Reports (Thomson),* 1834-1852	Can.
N.S.R. (Wall.)	*Nova Scotia Reports (Wallace),* 1884-1907	Can.
N.S.R. [1965-1969]	*Nova Scotia Reports*, 1965-1969, 5 vols.	Can.
N.S.R. (2d)	*Nova Scotia Reports (Second Series),* 1969-(current)	Can.
N.S.W.L.R.	*New South Wales Law Reports*	Aus.
N.W.	*North Western Reporter*	U.S.
N.W.T.R.	*North-West Territories Reports,* 1887-1898	Can.
N.W.T.R. (preceded by date)	*Northwest Territories Reports,* 1983-(current)	Can.
N.Y. Supp.	*New York Supplement*	U.S.
N.Z.L.R. (preceded by date)	*New Zealand Law Reports,* 1883-(current)	N.Z.
Nels.	*Nelson's Reports, Chancery,* 1 vol., 1625-1693	21 E.R.
Nev. & M.K.B.	*Nevile and Manning's Reports, King's Bench,* 6 vols., 1832-1836	38-43 R.R.
Nev. & P.K.B.	*Nevile and Perry's Reports, King's Bench,* 3 vols., 1836-1838	44-45 R.R.
Nfld. & P.E.I.R.	*Newfoundland and Prince Edward Island Reports,* 1970-(current)	Can.
Nfld. R.	*Newfoundland Reports,* 1817-1949	Nfld.

Nfld. Sel. Cas	*Newfoundland Select Cases (Tucker),* 1817-1828	Nfld.
Notes Imm.	*Notes of Recent Judgments rendered by the Immigration Appeal Board*	Can.
Noy	*Noy's Reports, King's Bench,* fol., 1 vol., 1558-1649	74 E.R.
O.A.C.	*Ontario Appeal Cases,* 1984-(current)	Can.
O.A.R.	*Ontario Appeal Reports,* 1876-1900	Can.
O. Bridg.	*Sir Orlando Bridgman's Reports, Common Pleas,* 1 vol., 1660-1666	160 E.R.
O.L.R.	*Ontario Law Reports,* 1901-1930	Can.
O.L.R.B. Rep. (preceded by year)	*Ontario Labour Relations Board Reports*	Can.
O.L.W.	*Ontario Lawyers Weekly,* 1983-1987	Can.
O.M.B.R.	*Ontario Municipal Board Reports*	Can.
O.R.	*Ontario Reports,* 1882-1900	Can.
O.R. (preceded by date)	*Ontario Reports,* 1931-1973	Can.
O.R. (2d)	*Ontario Reports (Second Series),* 1973-1991	Can.
O.R. (3d)	*Ontario Reports (Third Series),* 1991-(current)	Can.
O.S.	*Upper Canada Queen's Bench, Old Series,* 1831-1844	Can.
O.T.R.	*Ontario Trial Cases,* 1996-(current)	Can.
O.W.N.	*Ontario Weekly Notes,* 1909-1932	Can.
O.W.N. (preceded by date)	*Ontario Weekly Notes,* 1933-1962	Can.
O.W.R.	*Ontario Weekly Reporter,* 1902-1916	Can.
Old.	*Nova Scotia Reports (Oldrights),* 1860-1867	Can.
Ont. Corps. L.G.	*Ontario Corporations Law Guide*	Can.
Ont. D.	*Ontario Decisions*	Can.
Ont. Dig.	*Digest of Ontario Case Law,* 4 vols., 1823-1900	Can.
Ont. Elec.	*Ontario Election Cases,* 1884-1900	Can.
Ont. R.E.L.G.	*Ontario Real Estate Law Guide*	Can.
Ont. Tax R.	*Ontario Tax Reporter*	Can.
Owen	*Owen's Reports, King's Bench and Common Pleas,* fol., 1 vol., 1557-1614	74 E.R.
P.	*Pacific Reporter*	U.S.
P. (preceded by date)	*Law Reports, Probate, Divorce and Admiralty Division,* 1891-1971	Eng.
P. & B.	*New Brunswick Reports (Pugsley and* Burbidge)	Can.

P. & T.	*New Brunswick Law Reports (Pugsley and Trueman)*	Can.
P.D.	*Law Reports, Probate. Divorce, and Admiralty Division,* 15 vols., 1876-1890	Eng.
P.E.I.	*Prince Edward Island Reports (Peters),* 1850-1872	Can.
P.E.I.	*Prince Edward Island Reports (Haszard and Warburton),* 1850-1882	Can.
P.P.S.A.C.	*Personal Property Security Act Cases,* 1977-(current)	Can.
P.R.	*Ontario Practice,* 1848-1900	Can.
P. Wms.	*Peere Williams' Reports, Chancery and King's Bench,* 3 vols., 1695-1735	24 E.R.
Palm.	*Palmer's Reports, King's Bench,* fol., 1 vol., 1619-1629	81 E.R.
Park.	*Parker's Reports, Exchequer,* fol., 1 vol., 1743-1767; App. 1678-1717	145 E.R.
Patr. Elec. Cas.	*Patrick's Election Cases,* 1824-1849	Can.
Peake	*Peake's Reports, Nisi Prius,* 1 vol., 1790-1794	170 E.R.
Peake, Add. Cas.	*Peake's Additional Cases, Nisi Prius,* 1 vol., 1795-1812	170 E.R.
Per. & Dav.	*Perry and Davison's Reports, Queen's Bench,* 4 vols., 1838-1841	48-54 R.R.
Per. C.S.	*Perrault's Counseil Supérieur,* 1827-1859	Can.
Per. P.	*Perrault's Prévoste de Québec,* 1726-1756	Can.
Peters	*Peters' Reports,* 1850-1872	Can.
Ph.	*Phillips' Reports, Chancery,* 2 vols., 1841-1849	41 E.R.
Phillim.	*J. Phillimore's Ecclesiastical Reports,* 3 vols., 1809-1821	161 E.R.
Plowd.	*Plowden's Reports,* fol., 2 vols., 1550-1580 and *Plowden's Quaeries,* 1 vol.	75 E.R.
Poll.	*Pollexfen's Reports, King's Bench,* fol., 1 vol., 1670-1682	86 E.R.
Poph.	*Popham's Reports, King's Bench,* fol., 1 vol., 1591-1627	79 E.R.
Prec. Ch.	*Precedents in Chancery,* fol., 1 vol., 1689-1722	24 E.R.
Price	*Price's Reports, Exchequer,* 13 vols., 1814-1824	145-147 E.R.
Price	*Price's Mining Commissioners' Cases,* 1906-1910	Can.

Pug.	*New Brunswick Reports (Pugsley),* 1872-1877	Can.
Py. R.	*Pykes' Lower Canada Reports,* 1809-1810	Can.
Q.A.C.	*Quebec Appeal Cases,* 1987-(current)	Can.
Q.B.	*Queen's Bench Reports (Adolphus and Ellis, New Series),* 18 vols., 1841-1852	113-118 E.R.
Q.B. (preceded by date)	*Law Reports, Queen's Bench Division,* 1891-1901 and 1952-(current) (*e.g.*, [1891] 1 Q.B.)	Eng.
Q.B.D.	*Law Reports, Queen's Bench Division,* 25 vols., 1875-1890	Eng.
Qd. R.	*Queensland Reports*	Aus.
Q.L.R.	*Quebec Law Reports,* 1875-1891	Can.
Q.P.R.	*Quebec Practice Reports,* 1898-(current)	Can.
Q.R. (Vol.) K.B. or Q.B.	*Rapports Judicaires de Québec, Cour du Banc du Roi,* 1892-1966	Can.
Q.R. (Vol.) Sc.	*Rapports Judicaires de Québec, Cour Superieure,* 1892-(current)	Can.
Que. C.A. (preceded by date)	*Recueils de Jurisprudence de Québec, Cour d'Appel,* 1892-(current)	Can.
Que. Tax R.	*Quebec Tax Reporter*	Can.
R. & C.	*Nova Scotia Reports (Russell and* Chesley)	Can.
R. & G.	*Nova Scotia Reports (Russell and Geldert)*	Can.
R. & M.	*Russell and Mylne's Reports, Chancery,* 2 vols., 1829-1833	39 E.R.
R. & M.	*Ryan and Moody's Reports, Nisi Prius,* 1 vol., 1823-1826	171 E.R.
R. & R.	*Russell and Ryan's Crown Cases Reserved,* 1 vol., 1800-1823	168 E.R.
R.A.C.	*Ramsay, Appeal Cases,* 1873-1886	Can.
R.C.	*La Revue Critique de Legislation et de* Jurisprudence de Canada	Can.
R.C.S.	*Recueil des arrêts de la Cour suprême du* Canada (Canada Supreme Court Reports)	Can.
R.D.F.Q. (preceded by date)	*Recueil de Droit Fiscal Quebécois,* 1977-	Can.
R.D.J.	*Revue de droit judiciaire*	Can.
R.D.T. (preceded by date)	*Revue de Droit du Travail,* 1963-	Can.
R. de J.	*Revue de Jurisprudence,* 1895-1942	Can.
R. de L.	*Revue de Legislation et de Jurisprudence,* 3 vols., 1845-1848	Can.

R.E.D.	*Ritchie's Equity Decisions (Russell),* 1873-1882	Can.
R.F.L.	*Reports of Family Law,* 1971-1978	Can.
R.F.L. (2d)	*Reports of Family Law (Second Series),* 1978-1986	Can.
R.F.L. (3d)	*Reports of Family Law (Third Series),* 1986-(current)	Can.
R.F.L. Rep.	*Reports of Family Law, Reprint Series,* 5 vols.	*Can.*
R.J.R.Q.	*Quebec Revised Reports,* 1726-1891	Can.
R.L.	*Revue Legale,* 1943-(current)	Can.
R.L.N.S.	*Revue Legale, New Series,* 1895-1942	Can.
R.L.O.S.	*Revue Legale, OM Series,* 21 vols., 1869-1892	Can.
R.N.-B.	*Recueil des arrêts du Nouveau-* Brunswick (New Brunswick Reports)	Can.
R.P. (preceded by date)	*Rapports de Pratique du Québec*	Can.
R.P.R.	*Real Property Reports,* 1977-1989	Can.
R.P.R. (2d)	*Real Property Reports (Second Series),* 1989-(current)	*Can.*
R.R.	*Revised Reports*	Eng.
Raym. Ld.	*Raymond, Lord,* 1-3, 1694-1732	91-92 E.R.
Raym, T.	*Raymond, Sir T.,* 1660-1684	83 E.R.
Rep. Ch.	*Reports in Chancery,* fol., 3 vols., 1615-1710	21 E.R.
Rep. t. Finch	*Reports, temp. Finch,* 1673-1681	23 E.R.
Ridg. temp H.	*Ridgeway's Reports temp Hardwicke,* 1 vol., *King's Bench,* 1733-1736; *Chancery,* 1744-1746	27 E.R.
Ritch. Eq. Rep.	*Ritchie's Equity Reports,* 1873-1882	Can.
Rob. Eccl.	*Robertson' s Ecclesiastical Reports,* 2 vols., 1844-1853	163 E.R.
Roll. Rep.	*Rolle's Reports, King's Bench,* fol., 2 vols., 1614-1625	81 E.R.
Rus. E.R.	*Russell's Election Reports,* 1874	Can.
Russ.	*Russell's Reports, Chancery,* 5 vols., 1824-1829	38 E.R.
Russ. & M.	*Russell and Mylne's Reports, Chancery* 2 vols., 1829-1833	39 E.R.
Russ. & Ry.	*Russell and Ryan's Crown Cases Reserved,* 1 vol., 1800-1823	168 E.R.
Ry. & M.	*Ryan and Moody's Reports, Nisi Prius,* 1 vol., 1823-1826	171 E.R.

Ryde, Rat. App.	*Ryde's Rating Appeals,* 3 vols., 1871-1893	Eng.
S.	*Southern Reporter*	U.S.
S. & G.	*Smale and Giffard's Reports, Chancery,* 3 vols., 1852-1857	65 E.R.
S. & S.	*Simons and Stuart's Reports, Chancery,* 2 vols., 1822-1826	57 E.R.
S. & T.	*Swabey and Tristram's Reports, Probate and Divorce,* 4 vols., 1858-1865	164 E.R.
S.A.G.	*Sentences arbitrales de griefs,* 1970-	Can.
S.A.S.R.	*South Australian State Reports*	Aus.
S.C.C.D.	*Supreme Court of Canada Decisions*	Can.
S.C.C.R.S.	*Supreme Court of Canada Reports Service*	Can.
S.C.R.	*Canada Supreme Court Reports,* 64 vols., 1876-1922	Can.
S.C.R. (preceded by date)	*Canada Law Reports (Supreme Court),* 1923-(current); Canada Supreme Court Reports, 1970-	Can.
S. Ct.	*Supreme Court Reporter*	U.S.
S.E.	*South Eastern Reporter*	U.S.
S.R.C.	*Stuart's Lower Canada Reports,* 1810-1835	Can.
S.V.A.R.	*Stuart's Vice-Admiralty Reports,* 1836-1874	Can.
S.W.	*South Western Reporter*	U.S.
Salk.	*Salkeld's Reports, King's Bench,* 3 vols., 1689-1712	91 E.R.
Sask. D.	*Saskatchewan Decisions*	Can.
Sask. L.R.	*Saskatchewan Law Reports,* 1908-1932	Can.
Sask. R.	*Saskatchewan Reports,* 1979-(current)	Can.
Saund.	*Williams' Notes to Saunders' Reports, King's Bench,* 2 vols., 1666-1673	85 E.R.
Saund. & C.	*Saunders and Cole's Reports, Bail Court,* 2 vols., 1846-1848	82 R.R.
Say.	*Savile's Reports, Common Pleas,* fol., 1 vol., 1580-1591	123 E.R.
Say.	*Sayer's Reports, King's Bench,* fol., 1 vol., 1751-1756	96 E.R.
Sc. R.R.	*Scots Revised Reports*	41-54 R.R. 56-66 E.R.
Seign.	*Seigniorial Reports*	Can.
Sel. Cas. Ch.	*Select Cases in Chancery, temp King,* 1724-1733	23 E.R.

Sess. Cas. K.B.	*Sessions Settlement Cases, King's Bench,* 2 vols., 1710-1747	93 E.R.
Show.	*Shower's Reports, King's Bench,* 2 vols., 1678-1695	89 E.R.
Show. Parl. Cas.	*Shower's Cases in Parliament,* fol., 1 vol., 1694-1699	1 E.R.
Sid.	*Siderfin's Reports, King's Bench, Common Pleas and Exchequer,* fol., 2 vols., 1657-1670	82 E.R.
Sire.	*Simon's Reports, Chancery,* 17 vols., 1826-1852	57-60 E.R.
Sire. & St.	*Simons and Stuart's Reports, Chancery,* 2 vols., 1822-1826	57 E.R.
Sim. N.S.	*Simons' Reports, Chancery, New Series,* 2 vols., 1850-1852	61 E.R.
Skin.	*Skinner's Reports, King's Bench,* fol., 1 vol., 1681-1697	90 E.R.
Sm. & G.	*Smale and Giffard's Reports, Chancery,* 3 vols., 1852-1857	65 E.R.
Sin. & S.	*Smith & Sager's Drainage Cases,* 1904-1917	Can.
Smith K.B.	*J.P. Smith's Reports, King's Bench,* 3 vols., 1803-1806	7-8 R.R.
Sp. Ecc. & Ad.	*Spinks (Ecclesiastical & Admiralty Reports),* 1-2, 1853-1855	164 E.R.
Spinks	*Spinks' Prize Court Cases,* 2 parts, 1854-1856	164 E.R.
Stark.	*Starkie's Reports, Nisi Prius,* 3 vols., 1814-1823	171 E.R.
Stewart	*Stewart's Nova Scotia Admiralty Reports,* 1803-1813	Can.
Stockton	*Stockton's Vice-Admiralty Report and Digest,* 1879-1891	Can.
Stra.	*Strange's Reports,* 2 vols., 1716-1747	93 E.R.
Stuart	*Stuart's Vice Admiralty Reports,* 1836-1874	Can.
Stuart Adm.	*Stuart's Vice-Admiralty (Lower Canada) Cases,* 1836-1856	Can.
Stuart Adm. N.S.	*Stuart's Vice-Admiralty (Lower Canada) Cases, Second Series,* 1859-1874	Can
Stuart K.B.	*Stuart's Reports of Cases in King's Bench, etc. (Lower Canada),* 1810-1835	Can.
Sty.	*Style's Reports, King's Bench,* fol., 1 vol., 1646-1655	82 E.R.

Sw.	*Swabey's Reports, Admiralty,* 1 vol., 1855-1859	166 E.R.
Sw. & Tr.	*Swabey and Tristram's Reports, Probate and Divorce,* 4 vols., 1858-1865	164 E.R.
Swan.	*Swanston's Reports, Chancery,* 3 vols., 1818-1821	36 E.R.
T.A.	*Décisions du Tribunal d'arbitrage*	Can.
T.B.R.	*Tariff Board Reports/Rapports de la Commission du Tarif,* 1936-1989	Can.
T.E.	*Tribunal de l'Expropriation*	Can.
T. & M.	*Temple and Mew's Criminal Appeal Cases,* 1 vol., 1848-1851	169 E.R.
T. & R.	*Turner and Russell's Reports, Chancery,* 1 vol., 1822-1825	37 E.R.
T.J. (preceded by date)	*Recueils de jurisprudence du Québec; Tribunal de la jeunesse*	Can.
T. Jo.	*Sir T. Jone's Reports, King's Bench and Common Pleas,* fol., 1 vol., 1667-1685	84 E.R.
T.L.R.	*The Times Law Reports,* 1884-1950	Eng.
T.L.R. (preceded by date)	*The Times Law Reports,* 1951 & 1952 (*e.g.*, [1951] 1 T.L.R.)	Eng.
T.R.	*Term Reports (Durnford and East),* fol., 8 vols., 1785-1800	99-101 E.R.
T. Raym.	*Sir T. Raymond's Reports, King's Bench,* fol., 1 vol., 1660-1683	83 E.R.
T.T.	*Jurisprudence de droit du travail,* 1970-	Can.
T.T.R.	*Trade and Tariff Reports,* 1990-(current)	Can.
T.W.L.	*This Week's Law,* 1982-(current)	Can.
Taml.	*Tamlyn's Reports, Rolls Court,* 1 vol., 1829-1830	48 E.R.
Tas. S.R.	*Tasmanian State Reports*	Aus.
Taunt.	*Taunton's Reports, Common Pleas,* 8 vols., 1807-1819	127-129 E.R.
Tax A.B.C.	*Tax Appeal Board Cases,* 1949-1971	Can.
Tay.	*Taylor's King's Bench Reports,* 1823-1827	Can.
temp Wood	*Manitoba Reports temp Wood (ed. Armour),* 1875-1883 (see also *Armour* and Man. R. temp Wood)	Can.
Term Rep.	*Term Reports (Durnford and East),* fol., 8 vols., 1785-1800	99-101 E.R.
Terr. L.R.	*Territories Law Reports,* 1885-1907	Can.
Thom.	*Nova Scotia Reports (Thomson),* 1834-1859	Can.
Toth.	*Tothill's Transactions in Chancery,* 1 vol., 1559-1646	21 E.R.

Tru.	*New Brunswick Reports (Trueman),* 1876-1893	Can.
Turn. & R.	*Turner and Russell's Reports, Chancery,* 1 vol., 1822-1825	37 E.R.
Tyr.	*Tyrwhitt's Reports, Exchequer,* 5 vols., 1830-1835	35-40 R.R.
Tyr. & Gr.	*Tyrwhitt and Granger's Reports, Exchequer,* 1 vol., 1835-1836	46 E.R.
U.C. Cham.	*Upper Canada Chambers Reports,* 1846-1852	Can.
U.C.C.P.	*Upper Canada Common Pleas Reports,* 1850-1882	Can.
U.C.E. & A.	*Upper Canada Error & Appeal Reports,* 1846-1866	Can.
U.C. Jur.	*Upper Canada Jurist,* 1844-1848	Can.
U.C.K.B.	*Upper Canada King's Bench Reports,* 1831-1844	Can.
U.C.L.J.N.S.	*Upper Canada Law Journal, New Series,* 1865-	Can.
U.C.L.J.O.S.	*Upper Canada Law Journal, OM Series,* 10 vols., 1855-1864	Can.
U.C.Q.B.O.S,	*Upper Canada, Queen's Bench Reports,* 1823-1831	Can.
U.C.R.	*Upper Canada Reports, Queen's Bench,* 1844-1881	*Can.*
U.S.	*United States Supreme Court Reports*	U.S.
V. & B.	*Vesey and Beames's Reports, Chancery,* 3 vols., 1812-1814	35 E.R.
V.R. (preceded by date)	*Victorian Reports,* 1957-(current)	Aus.
Vaugh.	*Vaughan's Reports, Common Pleas,* fol., 1 vol., 1666-1673	124 E.R.
Vent.	*Ventris' Reports* (Vol. I, *King's Bench;* Vol. II, *Common Pleas),* fol., 2 vols,, 1668-1691	86 E.R.
Veto.	*Vernon's Reports, Chancery,* 2 vols., 1680-1719	23 E.R.
Ves.	*Vesey Jun's Reports, Chancery,* 19 vols., 1789-1817	30-34 E.R.
Ves. & B.	*Vesey and Beames's Reports, Chancery,* 3 vols., 1812-1814	35 E.R.
Ves. Sen.	*Vesey Sen's Reports,* 2 vols., 1747-1756	27-28 E.R.
W.A.C.	*Western Appeal Cases,* 1992-(current)	Can.
W.A.R.	*Western Australian Reports*	Aus.

W. Bl.	*William Blackstone's Reports, King's Bench and Common Pleas,* fol., 2 vols., 1746-1779	96 E.R.
W.C.A.T.R.	*Workers' Compensation Appeals Tribunal Reporter,* (current)	Can.
W.C.B.	*Weekly Criminal Bulletin,* 1976-1987	Can.
W.C.B. (2d)	*Weekly Criminal Bulletin (Second Series),* 1987-(current)	Can.
W.C.D.	*Western Charter Digest,* 1982-1984	Can.
W.D.C.P.	*Weekly Digest of Civil Procedure*	Can.
W.D.F.L.	*Weekly Digest of Family Law*	Can.
W. Jo.	*Sir W. Jones's Reports, King's Bench and Common Pleas,* fol., 1 vol., 1620-1640	82 E.R.
W.L.A.C.	*Western Labour Arbitration Cases,* 1966-1985	Can.
W.L.R. (preceded by date)	*Weekly Law Reports,* 1953-(current)	Eng.
W.L.R.	*Western Law Reporter,* 1905-1916	Can.
W.L.T.	*Western Law Times and Reports,* 1889-1896	Can.
W.N. (preceded by date)	*Law Reports, Weekly Notes,* 1866-1952	Eng.
W. Rob.	*W. Robinson,* 1-3, 1838-1850	166 E.R.
W.W. & D.	*Willmore, Wollaston, and Davison's Reports,* 1 vol., 1837	52 R.R.
W. W. & H.	*Willmore, Wollaston, and Hodges' Reports, Queen's Bench and Bail Court,* 2 vols., 1838-1839	52 R.R.
W.W.D.	*Western Weekly Digest,* 1975-1976	Can.
W.W.R.	*Western Weekly Reports,* 1912-1916; 1955-1970	Can.
W.W.R. (preceded by date)	*Western Weekly Reports,* 1917-1950; 1971-(current)	Can.
W.W.R. (N.S.)	*Western Weekly Reports (New Series),* 1951-1954 (Vols. 1-13)	Can.
West	*West's Reports, House of Lords,* 1 vol., 1839-1841	9 E.R.
West temp Hard.	*West's Reports temp Hardwicke, Chancery,* 1 vol., 1736-1740	25 E.R.
Wight.	*Wightwick's Reports, Exchequer,* 1 vol., 1810-1811	145 E.R.
Will. Woll. & Dav.	*Willmore, Wollaston, and Davison's Reports,* 1 vol., 1837	52 R.R.

Will. Woll. & H.	*Willmore, Wollaston, and Hodges' Reports, Queen's Bench and Bail Court,* 2 vols., 1838-1839	52 R.R.
Willes	*Willes' Reports, Common Pleas,* 1 vol., 1737-1758	125 E.R.
Wilm.	*Wilmot's Notes of Opinions and Judgments,* 1 vol., 1757-1770	97 E.R.
Wils.	*G. Wilson's Reports, King's Bench and Common Pleas,* fol., 3 vols., 1742-1774	95 E.R.
Wils. Ch.	*J. Wilson's Reports, Chancery,* 2 vols., 1818-1819	37 E.R.
Wils. Ex.	*J. Wilson's Reports, Exchequer in Equity,* 1 part, 1817	159 E.R.
Win.	*Winch's Reports, Common Pleas,* fol., 1 vol., 1621-1625	124 E.R.
W. Bl.	*William Blackstone's Reports, King's Bench and Common Pleas,* fol., 2 vols., 1746-1779	96 E.R.
Wm. Rob.	*William Robinson's Reports, Admiralty,* 3 vols., 1838-1850	166 E.R.
Wms. Saund.	*Williams' Notes to Saunders' Reports, King's Bench,* 2 vols., 1666-1673	85 E.R.
Y. & C. Ch. Cas.	*Younge and Collyer's Reports, Chancery Cases,* 2 vols., 1841-1843	62-63 E.R.
Y. & C. Ex.	*Younge and Collyer's Reports, Exchequer in Equity,* 4 vols., 1833-1841	160 E.R.
Y. & J.	*Younge and Jervis' Reports, Exchequer,* 3 vols., 1826-1830	148 E.R.
Y.A.D.	*Young's Vice-Admiralty Reports,* 1865-1880	Can.
Y.B.	*Year Books*	Eng.
Y.R.	*Yukon Reports,* 1987-1989	Can.
Yelv.	*Yelverton's Reports, King's Bench,* fol. 1 vol., 1602-1613	80 E.R.
You.	*Younge's Reports, Exchequer in Equity,* 1 vol., 1830-1832	159 E.R.

Appendix B

Electronic Sources for Canadian Law (English Language)

The fourth edition of this textbook highlights electronic sources for Canadian law (English and French language) and for English language law from around the world. Appendix B gathers electronic sources for Canadian law (English language) under three types of electronic format: online databases, CD-ROM, and the Internet. Check the following chapters for other electronic sources: Québec — Chapter 12; United Kingdom — Chapter 13; United States — Chapter 14; Australia and New Zealand and other Commonwealth and English speaking countries — Chapter 15.

A. ONLINE DATABASES

QL Systems Ltd.'s QUICKLAW with its origins at Queens University, concentrates on Canadian law, while LEXIS-NEXIS from Butterworths, encompasses a global perspective with a rapidly growing body of Canadian law. Following the chapter sequence of topics in this book, the tables below lists print-form and/or "online database only" titles with their LEXIS-NEXIS and QL access codes. This is not an exhaustive list of databases, but the scope and range of coverage is presented. There is a charge per time unit of use, and the rate may vary by whether you are in a law firm or law school setting as a student. Because it is a time charge, you should make your search as efficient as possible. The advantage of online services is the ability to access databases which are continuously updated by the provider.

Titles	**LEXIS-NEXIS Access Codes**

1. Law reports

(a) Federal and multi-provincial law reports and online databases

All Canadian Cases	CANCAS
Dominion Law Reports	DLR
Federal Court of Appeal Cases	CANFCS
Federal Court Trial Division Cases	CANFTC
Federal Trial Reports	FTREP

National Reporter	NATREP
Privy Council Cases	CANPRV
Supreme Court of Canada Cases	CANSCT
Tax Court of Canada Cases	CANTCT

(b) Provincial law reports and online databases

Alberta Reports	ALTAR
British Columbia Appeal Cases	BCAC
British Columbia Trial Cases	BCTC
Manitoba Reports	MANREP
New Brunswick Reports	NBREP
Newfoundland and P.E.I. Reports	N&PEIR
Nova Scotia Reports	NSREP
Ontario Court of Appeal Cases	ONTCA
Ontario Court of Justice Cases	ONTCJ
Ontario Appeal Cases	ONTAC
Ontario Provincial Court Cases	ONTCJP
Ontario Trial Cases	ONTTC
ONTCA & ONTCJ, Combined	ONTLAW
Saskatchewan Reports	SASKR

(c) Subject law reports

Canadian Criminal Cases	CCRIM
Canadian Labour Relations Boards Reports	CLRBR
Canadian Patent Reporter	CPR
Canadian Rights Reporter	CRR
Labour Arbitration Cases	LAC
Trade and Tariff Reports	CNTT

2. Digests

All-Canada Weekly Summaries	ACWS
All Canadian Digests	CANDIG
Canadian Labour Arbitration Summaries	CLAS
Ontario Family Reporter	OFLR
Weekly Criminal Bulletin	WCB

3. Statutes

Federal Statutes	CANSTA
Federal Statutes Table of Contents	CNSTTC
Ontario Statutes	ONTSTA
Ontario Statutes Table of Contents	ONTSTTC

4. Regulations

Federal Regulations	CANREG
Federal Regulations Table of Contents	CNRGTC

5. Law journals

All Canadian Journals	CANJNL
Canadian Current Tax	CCT
Canadian Journal of Insurance Law	CJIL
Commercial Insolvency Reporter	CCIR
Employment and Labour Law Reporter	CELLR
Health Law in Canada	CHL
McGill Law Journal	MCGILL
National Banking Review	CNBLR
National Creditor-Debtor Review	CNCDR
National Insolvency Review	CNIR

6. Other titles

Canadian Companies Information	CANCO
Canadian Publications	CANPUB
CANPUB & CANNWS, Combined	ALLNWS
Country Reports — Canada	CANREP
Free Trade Agreement Panel Review Decisions	USCFTA
Investment Banking Industry Reports, All	INVTXT
Library/File Descriptions	GUIDE
North America Free Trade Agreement	NAFTA
North America Free Trade Agreement Panel Decisions	NAFDEC
Stories about Canada	CANNWS
U.S.-Canada Free Trade Agreement Implementation Act	USCAN

Title	**QL Access Codes**

1. Law Reports

(a) Federal and multi-provincial law reports and online databases

Canadian Judgments, global	CJ
Dominion Law Reports (1955-)	DLR
Federal Court, global	FCC
Recent SCC Applications for Leave to Appeal	LNA
Recent SCC Judgments	LNET
Supreme Court of Canada, global	SCC

Western Appeal Cases (1991-)	WAC
Western Provinces Judgments, global	WPJ
Western Weekly Reports (1968-)	WWR

(b) Provincial law reports and online databases

Alberta Law Reports (1984-)	ALR
British Columbia Judgments, global	BCJ
British Columbia Law Reports (1984-)	BCLR
Manitoba Judgments (1986-)	MJ
New Brunswick Judgments (1986-)	NBJ
Newfoundland Judgments (1979-)	NJ
Northwest Territories Judgments (1986-)	NWTJ
Northwest Territories Reports (1987-)	NWTR
Nova Scotia Judgments (1986-)	NSJ
Ontario Reports Plus, global (1931-)	ORP
Ontario Trial Cases (1996-)	OTC
Prince Edward Island Judgments (1985-)	PEIJ
Québec Appeal Cases (1986-)	QAC
Québec Judgments (1987-)	QJ
Saskatchewan Judgments (1986-)	SJ
Saskatchewan Reports (1979-)	SASK
Yukon Judgments (1986-)	YJ
Yukon Reports (1986-1989)	YR

(c) Subject law reports

Administrative Law Reports (1983-)	ADM
Arbitration Decisions, global	ARB
Business Law Reports (1986-)	BLR
Canadian Bankruptcy Reports (1984-)	CBR
Canadian Cases on the Law of Torts (1983-)	CCLT
Canadian Native Law Reporter (1979-)	CNLR
Carswell's Practice Cases (1976-)	CPC
Construction Law Reports (1994-)	CR
CCH Canadian Tax Collection	various
Court Martial Appeal Judgments (1975-)	CMAJ
Court Martial Appeal Reports (1978-)	CMAR
Criminal Law, global	CRIM
Employment Law, global	EMPL
Environmental Law, global	ENV
Estates and Trusts Reports (1984-)	ETR
GST Global database	GSTG
Health Law Cases (1880-)	HLC
Human Rights Boards of Inquiry Decisions, global	HRBD
Immigration & Refugee Law, global	IMRE

Insurance Law, global	INS
Intellectual Property, global	IP
Labour Arbitration Cases	LAC
Labour Relations Board Decisions, global	LRBD
LAW/NET Civil Practice and Procedure (1990-)	LNPR
LAW/NET Family Law	LNFA
Municipal Law, global	MUN
Real Property Reports (1978-)	RPR
Reports of Family Law (1984-)	RFL
Securities Law, global	SEC
Taxation Court Decisions, global	TAX
Telecommunications Law, global	TC
Trade Law, global	TRAD

2. Digests

All Canada Weekly Summaries (1977-)	ACWS
Canadian Abridgment, Case Law Digests (1803-)	ABRD
Canadian Labour Arbitration Summaries	CLAS
Nova Scotia Law News	NSJ
Payne's Digests on Family Law, global	PDFL
Summaries of Judicial Decisions, global (1968-)	SJD
Note: Its components may be searched separately:	
Dominion Report Service & Lawyers Weekly Digests	
Weekly Criminal Bulletin (1976-)	WCB
Western Legal Publications, global (1979-)	WLP
Note: Its components may be searched separately:	
S.C.C. Decisions, F.C.A. Decisions, B.C. Decisions,	
Alta. Decisions, Sask. Decisions, Man. Decisions	

3. Statutes

Alberta Statutes	RSA
British Columbia Statutes and Bills	RSBC
Canada Bills	CB
Canada Status of Bills	CSB
Constitutional Acts of Canada (1763-1982)	CAC
House of Commons Hansard oral questions (1973-)	HOQ
House of Commons Hansard written questions (1973-)	HWQ
New Brunswick Statutes (R.S.N.B. 1973, amended to 1986)	SNB
Ontario Statutes and Bills	ONSB
R.S.C. 1985, Amended to current year	RSCC
Saskatchewan Statutes (R.S.S. 1978, amended to 1995)	SS
Yukon Statutes (R.S.Y. 1986, amended to 1989)	SYK

4. Regulations

Canada Regulations	SOR
Ontario Regulations, A to H (in mid-1997)	RO

5. Citators

Canadian Case Citations (Can. Abr. Rev. 2nd) (1867-)	ABRC
QUICKCITE Case Citator by QUICKLAW	QC

6. Law journals

Law Journal global	JOUR
Note: Its components may be searched separately:	
Alta. L. Rev., McGill L.J., Ottawa L. Rev.,	
Queen's L.J., Sask L. Rev.,	
Revue de droit — U. de Sherbrooke	
Index to Canadian Legal Literature (1987-)	ICLL

7. Other titles

Bench Notes (Computer News for Judges) by QUICKLAW	BN
Canada Taxation Publications, global	CTP
Canadian Law Symposia Index	CLSI
Canadian Lawyer's Internet Guide, 2nd ed.	CLIG
Health Law Articles (U. of Alberta) (1900-1995)	HLA
Human Rights Bibliography (U. of Ottawa) (1980-1991)	HRV
Law Societies Discipline Decisions (1991-)	LSDD
National Articling Database	NAD

Note: For many tribunal and board decisions, see Chapter 3, section B.12 "Chart L: Coverage of Board and Tribunal Decisions".

8. Carswell's "Canadian Tax Online"

database collection available from Carswell

B. CD-ROM TITLES AVAILABLE AT TIME OF WRITING

CD-ROM enables publishers to gather different types of print-form publications into a single disc. At time of writing, some publishers have produced many CD-ROM titles, while some publishers are just beginning. Therefore, the following list is arranged by publisher to enable you to know what is available from other publishers when you talk to a particular publisher's representative. CD-ROM subscriptions are periodically updated by replacement discs. While the subscriptions for many CD-ROM titles can cost more then $1,000 per year, the advantage of CD-ROM is the ability to have unlimited search time on your own discs for an annual cost.

1. Carswell

"The Abridgment: Canadian Case Digests on CD-ROM"
"Attorneys Medical Advantage" (U.S. publication)
"Bankruptcy Partner"
"The Canada Reporter Collection"
Note: The "National Courts" option is $1,800
Individual provinces are $1,450; Nfld. & P.E.I. are on one disc.
"Canadian Encyclopedic Digest on CD-ROM"
"Canadian Forms on Disc" (Taxation)
"Civil Practice Partner"(Alberta)
"Civil Practice Partner" (Ontario)
"Corporate Law Partner"
"Criminal Law Partner"
"Employment Law Partner"
"Environmental Law Partner"
"Family Law Partner"
"GST Partner"
"Immigration Law Partner"
"The Income Tax Act in transition"
"Income Tax References"
"Labour Law Partner"
"Personal Injury Damages Partner"
"Provincial TaxPartner — B.C."
"Securities Partner Plus"
"TaxPartner"
"TaxPartner Basic"
"TaxPartner — Ontario"

2. Butterworths

"British Columbia Civil Practice Library"
"Insurance Case Law Digest on CD-ROM"
"The Lawyers Weekly CD"
"Williston & Rolls Court Forms on CD-ROM"

3. Maritime Law Book

Note: The following law report print-form titles are available in three CD-ROM formats: full text of all reported cases, full text of cases chosen from seven areas of practice, or headnote service.

"Alberta Reports"
"Atlantic Provinces Reports"
"British Columbia Appeal Cases"
"British Columbia Trial Cases Unedited"
"Federal Trial Reports"
"Manitoba Reports 2d"
"National Reporter"
"New Brunswick Reports 2d"
"New Brunswick Reports 2d Supp."
"Newfoundland & Prince Edward Island Reports"
"Nova Scotia Reports 2d"
"Ontario Appeal Cases"
"Ontario Trial Cases"
"Saskatchewan Reports"
"Western Appeal Cases"

4. Canada Law Book

"The Canada Statute Service on CD-ROM with Consolidated Federal Statutes and Regulations"
"Canadian Criminal Law Library"
"Canadian Law List on CD-ROM"
"The Dominion Law Reports on CD-ROM" (1956-)
"Ontario Citator Service on CD-ROM with Consolidated Ontario Statutes and Regulations"
"Ontario Municipal and Planning Statutes and Regulations on CD-ROM"

5. Western Legal Publications

Note: WLP's DART (digital archive research tool) CD-ROM collection is available in a four-volume set covering from approximately 1980 to the present.

Volume 1 — Civil Decisions: digests collected from:
Alberta Decisions Manitoba Decisions
British Columbia Decisions Saskatchewan Decisions
Volume 2 — Criminal Decisions: digests collected from:
Alberta Decisions Saskatchewan Decisions
British Columbia Decisions

Manitoba Decisions
Ontario Decisions
Volume 3 — Labour and Employment Law: digests collected from:
B.C. Decisions, Labour Arbitration
B.C. Employment Standards Tribunal Decisions
B.C. Labour Relations Board/Industrial Relations Council Decisions
Volume 4 — Federal Decisions: digests collected from:
Charter of Rights Decisions
Federal Court of Appeal Decisions
Immigration Law Decisions
Supreme Court of Canada Decisions

6. CCH Canadian Ltd.

"Alberta, N.W.T. & Yukon Tax Reporter"
"British Columbia Tax Reporter"
"Canada Income Tax Guide"
"Canada Income Tax Guide with Canadian Income Tax Act, Regulations & Rulings"
"Canadian Goods and Services Tax Reports"
"Canadian Master Tax Guide"
"Canadian Securities Law"
"Canadian Tax Library"
"Canadian Tax Reporter"
"Dominion Tax Cases on CD-ROM"
"Income Tax Act and Regulations"
"Income Tax: Bulletins, Circulars and Rulings"
"Manitoba & Saskatchewan Tax Reporter"
"Maritimes Tax Reporter"
"Ontario Tax Reporter"
"Practitioner's Suite"
"Québec Tax Reporter"
"Window on Canadian Tax"
"Ontario Family Law"

7. Micromedia Ltd. (20 Victoria Street; Toronto, Ontario, M5C 2N8)

"Index to Canadian Legal Literature"
"Info CRTC"
"North America Free Trade Agreement (NAFTA) on CD-ROM"

C. INTERNET URLS

Additions to the Internet are made daily, and Internet users keep lists of useful URLs. This list was made in mid-1997 and will serve as a starting point for you.

There is a fee for some access to individual web sites, but free access to many sites is included in your monthly fee paid to your communications company. These monthly Internet connection fees are now quite low, which will promote growth of the Internet. Along with their URLs, below are listed print form titles, collections of titles, and collections of some material which appears only in electronic form. The University of Calgary Law Library maintains a current bibliography of legal materials available over the Internet in abstract or full-text form. This bibliography is accessed through the Internet address:
www.ucalgary.ca/~sanders/.

1. Law reports

Recent Supreme Court of Canada rulings are available at
www.droit.umontreal.ca/doc/csc-scc/index.html.
Federal Court of Canada rulings available at
www.fja-cmf.gc.ca/en/cf/index.html.
British Columbia Supreme Court and Court of Appeal rulings available at www.courts.gov.bc.ca.
All of Maritime Law Book Ltd.'s titles are available in CD-ROM and on the Internet (see list of titles above in subsection B) at www.mlb.nb.ca.

2. Digests

The Maritime Law Book headnotes with its topical index and key number scheme constitutes a digest service on the Internet.

3. Tribunal and board decisions

Alberta Labour Relations Board Decisions (Recent)
www.gov.ab.ca/~alrb/
Atomic Energy Control Board
http//ulysses.srv.gc.ca/aecb/docs/reporter/ecover.htm
B.C. Environmental Appeal Decisions
www.eab.gov.bc.ca
B.C. Environmental Protection Compendium Appeal Decisions
www.env.gov.bc.ca/epd/cpr/appeal.html
B.C. Information and Privacy Commissioner
http://oipcbc.org/
B.C. Securities Commission
www.bcse.gov.bc.ca/new_inside.htm
Canadian Artists and Producers Professional Relations Tribunal
homer.ic.gc.ca/capprt_e.html
Canadian International Trade Tribunal
www.citt.gc.ca/menu_e.htm

Competition Tribunal
www.ct-tc.gc.ca/
CRTC
www.crtc.gc.ca/eng/english.htm
Environmental Assessment Board of Ontario
gopher://govonca.gov.on.ca/11/env/decision
Indian Claims Commission
www.indianclaims.ca/english/pub/pub.htm

4. Statutes and regulations

Federal Statutes: http://canada.justice.gc.ca/
Federal Regulations: http://canada.justice.gc.ca/Loireg/index_en.html
Alberta Statutes: www.gov.ab.ca/qp/acts.html
Alberta Regulations: www.gov.ab.ca.qp.regs.html
British Columbia Statutes: www.qp.gov.bc.ca/stat_reg/statutes/
New Brunswick Statutes: www.gov.nb.ca/justice/asrlste.htm
Nova Scotia Statutes: www.gov.ns.ca/legi/legc/legislat.htm
Nova Scotia Regulations: www.gov.ns.ca/just/publish/registry/index.htm
Newfoundland Statutes: www.gov.nf.ca/just/jus_regHTM
Ontario Statutes: legis.acjnet.org/Ontario/en/Laws/Search.html
Ontario Regulations: http://legis.acjnet.org/Ontario/en/index.html
Saskatchewan Statutes: www.qp.justice.gov.sk.ca
Saskatchewan Regulations: www.qp.justice.gov.sk.ca
Northwest Territories Statutes: legis.acjnet.org/ACJNet/TNO/1988_en.html

5. Other titles and services

Law journals, bibliography of electronic formats: www.law-lib.utoronto.ca/
Library holdings of Osgoode Hall Law School: www.library.yorku.ca

6. Publishers' home page URLs

Butterworths: www.butterworths.ca
Canada Law Book: www.canadalawbook.ca
Carswell: www.carswell.com
CCH Canadian Ltd.: www.ca.cch.com
Emond Montgomery: www.io.org/~emplaw
Micromedia Ltd.: www.micromedia.on.ca
QL Systems Ltd.: http://www.quicklaw.com
Western Legal Publications: http://www.westernlegal.com
Wilson & Lafleur (publisher and large legal bookstore):
http://www.wilsonlafleur.com/cat

See also the Alphabetical List of Canadian Publishers:
www.harbour.sfu.ca/ccsp/citation/prov/all.htm.

Appendix C

Glossary of Legal Research Terms and Concepts

The following are offered as brief aids to understanding the text rather than being formal dictionary type definitions. The listing generally excludes terms of substantive law and political science. The explanations are intended to permit the reader to read through material without becoming mired down in jargon.

ACT:	May be used interchangeably with the term "statute".
ANNOTATED:	Articles or notes following the law (*e.g.*, notes following a statute in an annotated legislation publication, or an article following a case in a law report).
APPELLANT:	One who appeals a case to a higher court.
AUTHORITY:	The respect commanded by legal writing and materials in a court. Primary authority refers to law itself (statutes, regulations, case law), and may be mandatory (binding on the court) or persuasive. Secondary authority refers to materials written about the law and is only persuasive (see Chapter 1).
BILL:	Proposed legislation before Parliament or legislative assembly. When passed, it is known as an Act (statute).
CASE LAW:	The body of law arising from judges' opinions (decisions, judgments) in court cases.
CASEBOOK:	A book primarily intended for law students where cases or portions of cases are reproduced followed by explanatory notes and questions to evoke insightful responses.
CASES JUDICIALLY CONSIDERED/ NOTICED:	The concept of updating research to find subsequent citing cases which have commented upon earlier cited cases.
CATALOGUED:	Indicated that descriptive bibliographic information has been recorded about a law library's books. The information is stored in a card catalogue, in microform, or in book catalogue form.
CD-ROM:	"Compact Discs Read-Only Memory". In legal publishing CD-ROMs are similar to the music discs which replaced phonograph records, but in law, their function is to provide legal literature data rather than music.

CHARTER OF RIGHTS: The *Canadian Charter of Rights and Freedoms* stating fundamental freedoms. Part of the *Constitution Act, 1982,* which is part of the *Canada Act, 1982* (U.K.).

CITATION: An abbreviated statement indicating the book location of a statute, regulation, case or other type of legal literature (see Chapter 17).

CITATOR: A book or book portion which lists statutes, regulations, cases or other literature, and then immediately under each entry, lists subsequent cases which have commented upon them (see Chapter 6).

CITED CASE: A case commented upon by a subsequent case.

CITING CASE: A later case commenting upon a earlier case.

CIVIL LAW: (1) Cases which do not deal with criminal law.
(2) The Civil Law system upon which Québec law is founded (differs from English Common Law traditions).

CLASSIFIED Indicates that books in a law library have been assigned call numbers for placement on book shelves in subject arrangement.

COMMON LAW: (1) The legal system rooted in the tradition of England's legal history. (2) The body of case law based on the evolution of general legal concepts through cases as opposed to cases applying and interpreting statutes.

CONSTITUTION: The fundamental law of a nation which may be written in a single instrument, written in several instruments, and/or may be part of unwritten tradition.

DATABASE: A segment or portion of computer's stored information which may be searched and retrieved.

DEFENDANT: The party defending in litigation or in a criminal action.

DIGEST: A summary or abstract of a case.

E-MAIL: Electronic mail service offered through the Internet.

GAZETTE: The official publication of a government providing notification of legal matters such as regulations.

FORM BOOK: A guide book for lawyers supplying sample documents which may be used in drafting legal instruments through simply filling in blanks or, more usually, adapting the suggested forms.

FULL TEXT: The entire document is stored, searched and retrieved from the computer database.

HANSARD: The Debates of Parliament or a legislative assembly.

HEADNOTES: The publisher's summaries or digests of cases printed immediately before the text of the judges' opinions in law reports.

INTERNET: The worldwide system of *inter*connected computer *net*works, provides such services as the "worldwide web" of

	information/entertainment networks of databases/files and E-Mail.
ISSUE:	Statement of the law and essential facts of a legal problem.
JURISDICTION:	(1) The power of a legislature or court to enact legislation or render a decision on a point. A body without jurisdiction on a matter cannot consider it. (2) A geographic entity possessing its own law.
LAW REPORTS:	Publications containing case law.
LEXIS-NEXIS:	Available through Butterworths, this is a collection of computer online databases relating largely to the legal field. The system is worldwide in scope, and encompasses legal, government, business, other social science, and science information fields.
LOOSELEAF:	A publishing format in which updating pages are mailed to subscribers for insertion in the binder after removing replaced, outdated pages.
NATIONAL REPORTER SYSTEM:	(1) Maritime Law Book Ltd.'s grouping of databases on LEXIS-NEXIS. (2) The collection of American law reports published by West Publishing Co.
ONLINE:	Online searching is the accessing of an organization's databases through telecommunications. It is one of the electronic sources of law along with CD-ROM and the Internet. Examples of online information systems are QUICKLAW, LEXIS-NEXIS, and WESTLAW.
PERIODICAL:	A law journal, law review, magazine or other such legal publication issued on a subscription or regular basis.
PLAINTIFF:	The party who brings the action in litigation (opposite of defendant).
PRECEDENT:	(1) The value of an earlier case in deciding a present manner. (2) A form which may be adapted or used directly in drafting legal instruments.
PROCLAMATION:	A statute may come into force on a future date to be proclaimed (proclamation date), which allows the administrative machinery to be set in place.
QUERY:	A question asked to a computer database.
QUICKLAW:	QL Systems Ltd.'s collection of computer online databases relating largely to the legal field. A Canadian database system with its origins at Queen's University in the late 1960s and early 1970s.
REGNAL YEAR:	A year in the reign of a monarch. The year may be used in citing a statute (see p. 279-80).
REPORTED:	The full text of the case appears in a law report series or other type of publication.

RESPONDENT:	The party against whom an appeal to a higher court is made.
REGULATIONS:	Subordinate legislation promulgated by government departments pursuant to a statute in order to supply detail not found in the statute.
REVISED STATUTES:	Periodic consolidation and re-enactment of a jurisdiction's statutes as of a certain date. For example, *Revised Statutes of Canada,* R.S.C. 1985 (see Chapter 4).
ROYAL ASSENT:	The act of approving legislation by the Governor General (federal) or a Lieutenant Governor (provincial). The effective date of legislation unless the legislation specified a different date.
RULES OF COURT:	Rules of procedure to be used in court.
SLIP OPINION:	The typed copy of a court's judgment (judge's decision, opinion) released by a court as the first publically available form of the judgment before its appearance in law reports or as a digested case.
SOFTWARE:	The stored instructions on a computer directing it to perform programmed functions such as word processing, accounting, indexing, *etc.*
STARE DECISIS:	A Latin phrase meaning that in the common law tradition a court tends to stand by matters decided in earlier cases. The theory is based on stability of the law and resulting norms and expectations. Society changes and *stare decisis* is not always a concept that should be practised (see Chapter 1).
STATUTE:	May be used interchangeably with the term "Act".
STATUTE JUDICIALLY CONSIDERED/ NOTICED:	The concept of updating statutory research to find citing cases which have applied or interpreted the statutes listed in the table or book of statutes considered.
STYLE OF CAUSE:	The names of the parties in a court case.
SUBORDINATE LEGISLATION:	Legislation subordinate to statutes. Examples include regulations and municipal by-laws. It is made pursuant to an authorizing or enabling statute.
TABLE OF CASES:	A listing of cases contained in or commented upon by the book.
TABLE OF PUBLIC STATUTES:	A listing of statutes with the original citation and subsequent amendments to each section.
TABLE OF STATUTES:	A listing of statutes commented upon by the book.
TREATISE:	A textbook.
TRIBUNAL:	An administrative body which may perform a quasi-judicial function by hearing cases relating to the administered statute and by rendering decisions.

UNREPORTED: A case which appears commercially only in digested or abstracted form and/or a case which is not yet reported in full text in a law report series.

URL: *Uniform Resource Locator* designation used as an address for a world wide web file/database (website). The following is an example of the URL format, which is typed on the computer keyboard when connected to the Internet: www.butterworths.ca.

WWW: The *worldwide web* service on the Internet which allows you to view the many database/files (websites) made available by commercial organizations (*e.g.*, law publishers' catalogues and products), governments (*e.g.*, legislation and decisions), and universities (*e.g.*, research publications). Currently, there are more than 25 million web pages.

Index

B

C

Y